THE
World of Wolves

ENERGY, ECOLOGY, AND THE ENVIRONMENT SERIES

ISSN 1919-7144

This new series will explore how we live and work with each other on the planet, how we use its resources, and the issues and events that shape our thinking on energy, ecology and the environment. The Alberta experience in a global arena will be showcased.

THE
World of Wolves

NEW PERSPECTIVES ON
ECOLOGY, BEHAVIOUR AND MANAGEMENT

Edited by

MARCO MUSIANI,
LUIGI BOITANI,
AND PAUL C. PAQUET

UNIVERSITY OF
CALGARY
PRESS

ENERGY, ECOLOGY, AND THE ENVIRONMENT SERIES
ISSN 1919-7144

University of Calgary Press
2500 University Drive NW
Calgary, Alberta
Canada T2N 1N4
www.uofcpress.com

LIBRARY AND ARCHIVES CANADA CATALOGUING IN PUBLICATION

The world of wolves : new perspectives on ecology, behaviour, and management / edited by Marco Musiani, Luigi Boitani, and Paul C. Paquet.

(Energy, ecology, and the environment series, ISSN 1919-7144 ; no. 3)
Includes bibliographical references and index.
ISBN 978-1-55238-269-1

1. Wolves—Ecology—Case studies. 2. Wolves—Behavior—Case studies. 3. Wolves—Conservation—Case studies. 4. Wildlife management—Case studies. I. Musiani, Marco, 1970- II. Boitani, Luigi III. Paquet, Paul C. (Paul Charles), 1948- IV. Series: Energy, ecology, and the environment series; no. 3

QL737.C22W67 2010   599.773   C2010-902399-4

The University of Calgary Press acknowledges the support of the Alberta Foundation for the Arts for our publications. We acknowledge the financial support of the Government of Canada through the Book Publishing Industry Development Program (BPIDP) for our publishing activities.

We acknowledge the financial support of the Canada Council for the Arts for our publishing program. This book has been published with the support of Education 4 Conservation, the UK Wolf Conservation Trust, the Wilburforce Foundation, and the Department of Environment and Natural Resources of the Government of the Northwest Territories.

Cover design by Melina Cusano
Page design and typesetting by Melina Cusano

CONTENTS

Section II – Wolves' Role in Wildlife Management Planning:
Human Impacts in Protected Wolf Populations,
Hunting and Removal of Wolves

LIST OF TABLES

Baltic states, Belarus Republic and Poland; data for 2005–2007. [a] Census conducted by scientists, forestry and national park services; [b] Data from official hunting statistics; [c] Only wolves frequently causing damage to domestic animals are culled.

level. Data recalculated from: southern Poland – Nowak et al. (2005), eastern Poland – Jędrzejewski et al. (2002b), north-eastern Belarus – Sidorovich et al. (2003), south-western Estonia – M. Kübarsepp (unpublished data), and central Estonia – Kübarsepp and Valdmann (2003). 229

LIST OF FIGURES

However, a cluster exclusive to North American is defined by haplotype lu33 and historic haplotypes lu47, lu50 andlu51 (the southern clade). Haplotypes lu33 and lu47 are found only in samples of current and historic Mexican wolves whereas haplotypes lu50 and lu51 are found in historic samples of gray wolves from Utah to Nebraska and are intermixed with haplotypes common in northern gray wolves. The wide distribution of the southern clade suggests that gene flow was extensive across the recognized limit of the Mexican subspecies providing a wider mandate for reintroduction. Further, the large diversity of historical haplotypes reflects the greater diversity in the American Ice Age refugial population (see text).

competition (P1 and P2). Commensalism (+ and 0) is not shown. Finally, the dashed line between C1 and P1 illustrates an indirect effect of carnivores on plant density. Note for simplicity only some direct and one indirect effect is shown, but the number of indirect effects are far greater than direct effects.   74 unpublished data), mule deer (T. Lemke, unpublished data), pronghorn antelope (P. J. White, unpublished data), bighorn sheep (P. J. White, unpublished data), wolf (Smith 2005), coyote (Gese et al. 1996, S. Grothe, unpublished data, A. Switalski, unpublished data), cougar (Ruth 2004), grizzly bear (Schwartz et al. 2006), beavers (Smith 2005), and songbirds (unpublished data, USGS Patuxent Wildlife Research Center 2006).   94

radio-collared caribou cows tracked by satellite (Gunn et al., 2001). Radio-collared wolves from the Bathurst caribou range also moved into the overlap area, which included Rennie Lake.

MARCO MUSIANI

LUIGI BOITANI

PAUL C. PAQUET

Biographies for Editors, Contact Authors, and Artists

(drawings and photos of wild wolves only)

BOOK EDITORS

MARCO MUSIANI, Faculty of Environmental Design, University of Calgary, Calgary, Alberta, T2N 1N4, Canada.

Marco Musiani, Ph.D., is an associate professor with the University of Calgary, and a faculty affiliate with the University of Montana. He is currently analyzing ecological data on wolves and their prey, which was gathered throughout northern and western Canada. He has published papers on various applied ecology journals, which also include articles on wolf management in Poland, Italy, Canada, and the United States. In 2003, Dr. Musiani organized the World Wolf Congress in Banff, Canada. He serves as reviewer for research and management projects such as the Wolf Reintroduction Programs in the northwestern and the south-western United States, and acts as a consultant for the Food and Agriculture Organisation of the United Nations (to protect livestock from wolves).

LUIGI BOITANI, Department of Animal and Human Biology, University of Rome "La Sapienza", Viale Università 32, 00185-Roma, Italy.

Professor Boitani is Head of the Department of Animal and Human Biology, University of Rome. He is President Elect of the Society for Conservation Biology. He has been associated with the Species Survival Commission (SSC) of IUCN-World Conservation Union (Gland, Switzerland) since 1973 and has been member of the Steering Committee for the past 15 years. Professor Boitani has been in charge of an extended series of research and conservation projects on the wolf population in Italy. He has authored more than 200 peer-reviewed scientific publications, 75 technical reports, and 8 books. Prof. Boitani is a leading authority on wolves.

PAUL C. PAQUET, Box 150, Meacham, Saskatchewan, S0K 2V0, Canada.

Paul Paquet, Ph.D., is an adjunct professor of Biology and of Environmental Design at the University of Calgary. He is also an adjunct professor at the University of Saskatchewan, Brandon University, and the University of Manitoba; and a faculty associate at Guelph University and the University of New Brunswick. Dr. Paquet, who has studied wolves and coyotes for more than 35 years, is a recognized authority on mammalian carnivores, with research experience in several regions of the world. He has published more than 100 peer-reviewed reports and articles. Dr. Paquet was the founder and director of the Central Rockies Wolf Project, Canmore, Canada, and the Conservation Biology Institute, Corvallis, Oregon, U.S.

CHAPTER CONTACT AUTHORS

Since the book details wolf research cases that in many instances involve collaborative efforts, some chapters have more than one author. However, one or two corresponding author(s) served as contact for each research group.

H. DEAN CLUFF, Department of Environment and Natural Resources, Government of the Northwest Territories, Box 2668, Yellowknife, Northwest Territories, X1A 2P9, Canada.

Dean Cluff, M.Sc., is a regional biologist with the Government of the Northwest Territories, NWT, and has been involved in research and management of caribou, moose, bison, grizzly bears, black bears, and wolves. Mr. Cluff is the project leader for the NWT`s Central Arctic Wolf Project. Since 2001, he has been one of the two representatives for Canada on the Wolf Specialist Group of the IUCN-World Conservation Union. Mr.

Cluff has also accompanied Dr. David Mech to Ellesmere Island and other locations in the Arctic on several occasions to observe and study wolves there.

RAYMOND COPPINGER, School of Cognitive Science, Hampshire College, Amherst, Massachusetts, 01002, U.S.A.

Raymond Coppinger, Ph.D., is a professor of biology at Hampshire College. Dr. Coppinger is considered the leading world expert on dogs and their behaviour, as domesticated as well as wild animals. He has written extensively on this subject, having published over 50 papers and numerous books. Studies led by Dr. Coppinger unequivocally demonstrate substantial influence on the environment exerted by wolves, dogs and people. His latest book, co-authored with Lorna Coppinger, is called *DOGS: A Startling New Understanding of Canine Origin, Behaviour and Evolution.*

MARK HEBBLEWHITE, Wildlife Biology Program, College of Forestry and Conservation, University of Montana, Missoula, Montana, 59812, U.S.A.

Mark Hebblewhite, Ph.D., is an assistant professor with the University of Montana. His research interests broadly lie in understanding how ungulates balance the costs of predation from carnivores like wolves with the benefits of foraging, and also how humans influence this balance. Dr. Hebblewhite presently leads with Dr. Musiani a caribou research project in west-central Alberta and east-central British Columbia. Other projects study the effects of climate change on elk population dynamics, the growth of urban elk populations, and the recovery of threatened sierra Nevada bighorn sheep.

WŁODZIMIERZ JĘDRZEJEWSKI, Mammal Research Institute, Polish Academy of Sciences, 17-230 Białowieża, Poland.

Dr. Włodzimierz Jędrzejewski is the Scientific Deputy Director of the Mammal Research Institute of the Polish Academy of Sciences. Studies by Dr. Jędrzejewski are typically focused on animal ecology, forest ecology, and conservation biology. He is the author of three scientific books and over 120 papers published in peer-reviewed journals. Dr. Jędrzejewski has several years of experience in radio-telemetry projects on large carnivores (wolves, Eurasian lynx) and ungulates. In 1999, Dr. Jędrzejewski was given the Award of the Prime Minister of Poland "For an Outstanding Scientific Achievement."

OLOF LIBERG, Department of Conservation Biology, Grimsö Wildlife Research Station, S-730 91 Riddarhyttan, Sweden.

Olof Liberg, Ph.D., is affiliated with the Swedish University of Agricultural Sciences. His research projects are focused on lynx population dynamics and predator prey interactions, especially with roe deer; and on conservation and management of the Scandinavian wolf population. Dr. Liberg is the Coordinator of the Scandinavian Wolf Research Project, SKANDULV. His studies addressed ecological, genetic, and human-related aspects of wolf recovery in Scandinavia. Dr. Liberg has also finalized action plans and management recommendations as well as a wolf Population Viability Analyses for Scandinavia.

DOUGLAS W. SMITH, Yellowstone Center for Resources, PO Box 168, Yellowstone National Park, Wyoming, 82190, U.S.A.

Douglas W. Smith, Ph.D., is the Project Leader for the Yellowstone Wolf Project, and has been with the wolf program since its inception in 1994. Dr. Smith has also conducted beaver research in Wisconsin and Michigan and studied wolves in Minnesota with Dr. L.D. Mech. He has published a number of articles and book chapters on beavers and wolves and co-authored two popular books on wolves. He participated in documentaries about wolves for National Geographic and British Broadcasting Company (BBC) as well as for other media. His professional interests include wolf population dynamics, wolf-prey relationships, and the restoration of ecological processes.

JOHN A. VUCETICH, School of Forest Resources and Environmental Science, 186 Noblet Building, Michigan Technological University, Houghton, Michigan, 49931, U.S.A.

John A. Vucetich, Ph.D., is an assistant professor at the Michigan Technological University. Dr. Vucetich has studied the wolves and moose of Isle Royale since 1990, and since 2000 he has collaborated with Rolf Peterson on the wolf-moose project. Since 1998, Dr. Vucetich has worked on wolf recovery in Michigan. He has acted as scientific advisor for issues concerning wolves in Algonquin Provincial Park and Denali National Park. He has also worked for the Central Rockies Wolf Project (Canada) and the Mongolian Wolf Center, and for a IUCN project on wolf reintroduction in the southern Rockies of the United States.

ROBERT K. WAYNE, Department of Ecology and Evolutionary Biology, University of California, Los Angeles, California, 90095-1606, U.S.A.

Robert K. Wayne, Ph.D., is a professor with the University of California Los Angeles. He teaches courses on Conservation Biology and Evolutionary Biology, and is the world's leading authority on population and conservations genetics of canids. The majority of his work on canids has focused on wolf-like canids such as the gray wolf, coyote, red wolf, and Ethiopian wolf. Dr. Wayne authored more than 180 peer-reviewed publications and is also an editor of several books and book-chapters focused on current topics in molecular ecology and conservation genetics.

ARTISTS

PETER A. DETTLING, Terra Magica – Images of Peter A. Dettling, Award-winning nature photography & paintings, Canmore, Alberta, Canada, www.TerraMagica.ca

Peter A. Dettling, born in 1972 in Sedrun, Switzerland, is a multiple award-winning photographer and painter whose passion for the natural world has taken him all over the globe. The artist resides now near Banff National Park in Alberta, Canada. His images are regularly published in various magazines, calendars, and books, and they are featured in gallery shows, such as the world-renowned American Museum of Natural History in New York. Peter hopes his art will promote a better relationship between humans and nature, in particular large predators, such as wolves and bears. His wildlife images are of free roaming animals only.

DAVID C. OLSON, David C. Olson Photography, Rockford, Illinois, U.S.A. www.davidolsonphoto.com.

For David, photography is more than just taking a picture. It is about composition, light and colour all coming together at the same time to capture a moment that will never happen again. Holding a degree in photography from the Colorado Institute Of Art in Denver, and studies in environmental biology and animal behaviour allow David to capture these breathtaking visual images of wolves for this book, some of which were also rendered into drawings (see below). Whether David is photographing a newborn or a howling wolf in a blizzard, his unfaltering patience and sensitivity to his subjects show in his work. His images appear in publications, magazines, and books.

SUSAN SHIMELD, Nature in Fine Art, Larmer Tree Studio, Larmer Tree Gardens, Tollard Royal, Nr. Salisbury, Wiltshire SP5 5PY U.K.

We included drawings in this book because wolves have strong emotional values and drawings, being inevitably an interpretation of reality, are good at capturing and translating emotions. Su Shimeld, an accomplished wildlife artist (also see http://www.natureinart.com) produced one pencil drawing per chapter, included under the chapter's title. Su's love of nature is reflected in her artwork; her choice of subjects is varied and her paintings and fine art prints can be found in a number of private collections. For this book project, Su has studied wolf behaviour in a captive wolves' facility run by the U.K. Wolf Conservation Trust.

ROBERT J. WESELMANN, Raptor's Roost Photography, Northwood, Iowa, U.S.A.

Robert J. Weselmann has been photographing wolves since their re-introduction into the Northern Rocky Mountains of the U.S.A.. He is the co-author of Wild About Yellowstone, a book featuring wolves of Yellowstone National Park. He is also the photographer of Wolfs of Northern Yellowstone, a wolf identification chart for the packs living in the northern range of the park. You can find more of Bob's work at www.robertweselmann.com.

ACKNOWLEDGMENTS

Education 4 Conservation (www.education4conservation.org), the UK Wolf Conservation Trust (www.ukwolf.org) and its Director, Denise Taylor served to all intents and purposes as project managers. The Wilburforce Foundation and the Government of the Northwest Territories (Department of Environment and Natural Resources) also supported some aspects of this project logistically and financially.

Mimosa Arienzo inspired, motivated, and encouraged the book editors, even while fighting terminal cancer.

Tyler Muhly helped organizing information and writing several sections of the book. Special thanks also go to the other graduate students who contributed valued, passionate as well as eccentric ideas on wolf ecology: Allan Mcdevitt, Astrid Vik Stronen, Byron Weckworth, Carly Sponarski, Elisabetta Tosoni, Hugh Robinson, Isabelle Laporte, James Rogala, Jenny Coleshill, Joann Skilnick, Nick DeCesare, and Sk. Morshed Anwar.

Many collaborators who also became friends and a couple of friends who also became collaborators supported this book from its initial conception to completion, or some essential aspects of the book project: Mark Hebblewhite and Carolyn Callaghan in particular, as well as Carita Bergman, Charles Mamo, Elisabetta Visalberghi, Gary Sargent, Gordon Haber (who died this year conducting aerial telemetry of wolves), Jesse Whittington, Joel Berger, Layla Neufeld, Luigi Morgantini, Mark Bradley, Mark Sherrington, Nina Fascione, Piero Musiani, Roberta Mulders, Roger Creasey, Stefano Mariani, Tsa Palmer, Toni Shelbourne, the hunters of Alberta, the Northwest Territories, and Nunavut, the ranchers of Alberta, Idaho, Montana, and Wyoming, and the wildlife officers working with various Canadian Provinces and Territories, in particular Alberta, the Northwest Territories, and Nunavut.

The following organizations supported the editors and their wolf projects right through completion of this book: the Alberta Beef Producers, Alberta Conservation Association, Alberta Ecotrust, Alberta Fish and Wildlife Division, Alberta Sustainable Resource Development and Community Development, Bailey Wildlife Foundation Compensation Trust,

B.C. Ministry of Forests, Biodiversity Challenge Grants, Calgary Foundation, Calgary Zoological Society, Canadian Association of Petroleum Producers, Circumpolar/Boreal Alberta Research, Consiglio Nazionale delle Ricerche, Italy, Defenders of Wildlife, Department of Indian and Northern Affairs Canada, Humane Society United States, Izaak Walton Killam Memorial, Kendall Foundation, Mountain Equipment Coop, National Sciences and Engineering Research Council of Canada (NSERC), Northern Scientific Training Program Grant, Parks Canada, Shell, TD Canada Trust, TD Friends of the Environment, The National Science Foundation (USA), United States Department of Agriculture-Wildlife Services, United States Fish and Wildlife Service, University of Rome, West Kitikmeot/Slave Study Society, Weyerhaueser Company, and World Wildlife Fund Canada.

Two anonymous reviewers contributed comments, suggestions, and thorough critiques, which greatly improved the final version of all chapters.

Introduction –
The Key Role Played by Wolves in Community Ecology and Wildlife Management Planning

Marco Musiani, Luigi Boitani and Paul C. Paquet

INTRODUCTION

The gray wolf is perhaps one of the world's most polarizing and controversial species. As the epitome of charismatic megafauna, it has evoked the respect and adoration of many. However, in nearly all ecological and socio-political contexts, wolves have also stirred deep and often extreme sentiments of fear and hatred. These feelings in turn are derived from, and contribute to, conflicts with people, including the occasional threat to human life. The strong negative reactions to wolves have facilitated widespread programs of eradication across much of their historic range.

Academically, wolves have also received much attention, and are one of the most studied mammalian species in nature. The scientific literature on their ecology and behaviour approaches several thousand publications, with programs all over the world continuing to study wolf biology and management. The strength and persistence of this interest is a direct result of ongoing wolf/human relationships, wolves' ecological flexibility, and our increased understanding of their evolution and behaviour. Wolves' future will depend largely upon decisions made by people that in turn are based upon attitudes and emotions, in addition to ecological findings. Our mission with this book is to contribute to the examination of the human/

wolf interface. We wish to evaluate the biological issues with the intent of providing counsel on how to ease conflict and promote the coexistence of wolves and humans.

This book uses research sample cases from Eurasia and North America to explain the key role played by wolves in community ecology of natural ecosystems and of systems where domestic animals and people are also present. It also analyzes the pivotal role always played by wolves in wildlife management and conservation biology programs, due both to the species' ecological relevance and to passionate human attitudes and conflicts with wolves.

RESEARCH SAMPLE CASES FOR WOLF MANAGEMENT

The World of Wolves project arose from the idea of using representative case studies to illustrate current trends in wolf and wildlife management. This book provides insights into wolf behaviour and biology. Such insights act as effective "entry points" for delving into the broader aspects of ecology and evolution relating to a myriad of species, ecosystem processes, and functions. The organization of this approach unites several aspects of wildlife management, thereby contributing to an advanced understanding of contemporary conservation theory and practice.

Each chapter details a research project or a research area representative of a specific aspect of wolf management and conservation. We emphasize projects from distant and culturally diverse regions of the world to highlight their original, unexpected, or previously undocumented contributions. For example, Cluff et al. document a management strategy of wolves where the primary objective is to affect densities of prey, such as caribou, for the benefit of aboriginal hunters and at the potential expense of wolves. Additional chapters consider potential cascade-effects initiated by reintroduction of wolves in Idaho and Yellowstone and their effects on wildlife management in the United States. Still others document management of wolf populations that straddle the border between Western and Eastern Europe, where human culture and attitudes are clearly diversified.

WHAT IS A WOLF?

The first section of this book describes wolf ecology, genetics, and behaviour in ecosystems and conditions that are generally considered as 'natural.' However, humans have arguably had a major influence on wolves throughout the species range and throughout history. Wayne describes genetic variability in current, historic, and 'long past' wolf populations. He establishes a link between historical human-caused population declines, loss of genetic diversity, and trends in canid evolution. These findings confirm that contemporary population genetics as well as the evolution of wolves into the future will continue to depend upon human influences, a fact that should not be underestimated, even with wolf populations in many areas on the road to recovery (see Fabbri et al. 2007, vonHoldt et al. 2008).

Wayne also indicates that human influences on wolves and alterations of their habitat could contribute to hybridization between wolves and other canids. For example, in some areas of southeastern Canada, the resident wolf may be a genetically distinct species of North American wolf, *Canis lycaon*. In addition, individuals assigned to *lycaon* might belong to a remnant population segment of eastern North American wolves, also including the Red Wolf, *Canis rufus*. Thus, some authors maintain that the two species (i.e., *lycaon* and *rufus*) should be lumped. In the book, Wayne illustrates that both *lycaon* and *rufus* hybridize with coyotes, and *lycaon* also hybridizes with common wolves. The author argues that hybridization could be induced by reductions in wolf densities through both persecution by humans and habitat loss. With a lack of conclusive evidence on species' taxonomy, significant resources are spent each year for the conservation of these putative wolf species, in particular for *Canis rufus*, which is critically endangered and could not be viable without management intervention.

Finally, Coppinger et al. describe human influences (i.e., through artificial selection) on an important 'species' of wolf, the domestic dog.

Chapters by Coppinger et al. and by Wayne show that stray dogs and wolves may also live and interbreed in nature. According to Coppinger et al., interbreeding between dogs and wolves invalidates the biological species concept that would classify them into two separate species. Clearly, there is substantial gene flow between existing populations and species of wolf-like canids. Some canids are considered separate species of high conservation value, but have never been demonstrated to be separate species. Given these unknowns, Coppinger et al. suggest that conservation programs should encourage viable populations of the genus *Canis* in the habitats they wish to restore. Notwithstanding the 'genetic melting pot,' conservation of canids is warranted given the critical functions and ecological roles these carnivores exert across a variety of ecosystems.

KEY FUNCTIONS OF WOLVES IN THE ECOSYSTEM

Predation is an intensively studied phenomenon in ecology, and the body of knowledge on wolves and prey is significant. Wolf and ungulate ecology and behaviour provide an easily accessible gateway through which to understand predator-prey relationships. Accordingly, this book provides some responses to a fundamental and pragmatic question posed by Mark Boyce (2005). Specifically, what has this incredible catalogue of research on wolves done to enhance our understanding of the biology and ecology of predation? Hebblewhite and Smith examine the role of wolves in 'trophic cascades,' ecosystem effects in which the consumer-resource relationship (e.g., wolves vs. elk) alters the abundance, biomass or productivity of a population community or trophic level across more than one link in a food web (e.g., forage). The authors found evidence for direct effects as well as for trophic cascades triggered by wolves in Yellowstone and Banff National Parks. Direct effects in both systems included limitation or regulation of elk populations by wolves, behavioural avoidance of wolves by elk, and competition (both exploitative and interference) with other large carnivores. Evidence for trophic cascade effects in the elk/wolf system include its influence on willow and aspen growth, and subsequently on species that rely on these plants, including beavers and a number of riparian songbirds. Furthermore, a trophic cascade effect may also explain apparent competition between elk and alternate prey, such as bison, moose, and caribou, that are mediated by wolf predation.

A book is the ideal medium with which to provide results for long-term studies, in combination with summaries and syntheses of findings. Vucetich et al. (this volume) consider the relationship of wolves and moose in the world's most intensely studied wolf and prey system, Isle Royale. The chapter demonstrates how after 50 years of observation by academics, each five-year period of the wolf-moose chronology seems decisively different from every other five-year period. The significance of this chapter is that lessons from such a dynamic system are frequently presented in articles, and most ecology textbooks, as static dogmas, therefore informing management in ways that vary every five years. Vucetich et al. also show that journal articles have seem to have primarily focused on the relationships between wolf and prey, on modeling those relationships, and then predicting future trends. The authors provocatively conclude that, in fact, ecological explanations entailing predictive ability were not found. On the other hand, various studies provided ecological explanations entailing accurate, but non-predictive explanations of the past. Finally, by studying wolf and prey relationships, researchers have learned about new mechanisms regarding predation and its ecosystem effects. For example, unexpected mechanisms were reported linking wolves, moose, scavengers, and vegetation, and some fundamental effects of climate and disease on these mechanisms were also uncovered.

Although clearly avoiding scholarly discussions, this book is at the core of current enquiries concerning bottom-up and top-down effects on ecosystems. As an apex predator, the wolf is often defined at the top of ecological pyramids. Vucetich et al. underscore the intellectual effort that is being invested into assessing whether, and if so, how, wolves affect the densities of herbivores. As shown by Creel and Christianson (2008), it is necessary to consider that herbivore densities may be affected both by wolf predation and by difficult to detect and measure costs of anti-predator behaviour. In turn, Hebblewhite and Smith investigate how herbivores may affect densities of plants and other animal species. In theory, these relationships could also work in a bottom-up pattern, from nutrients to plants to herbivores to predators. In practice, recent studies and reviews (Terborgh 2005, Schmitz 2006; reviewed by Borer et al. 2006), also including this book's case studies on wolves, have found strong asymmetry and greater strength in top-down than in bottom-up forces. Thus, these findings support the notion that, by managing wolves, people manage or mismanage whole ecosystems.

CONSERVATION CHALLENGES: HUMAN IMPACTS IN REGIONS WHERE WOLVES ARE PROTECTED AND AT THEIR BOUNDARIES

All of Section 2 of this volume deals with wolves where their ecosystems are affected by human land use. Five chapters describe various scenarios for management intervention, ranging from none (which can be considered a management practice) to intense intervention. We recognize that, as the human population increases, fewer environments exist where wolves and wilderness do not interact with people. Consequently, we focus particularly on findings that are relevant to management where wolves overlap or conflict with people. We believe that focusing on wolf-human is more realistic in addressing future scenarios than focusing merely on remote wilderness areas that are quickly dwindling in the face of human pressure.

Wildlife managers are faced with several issues when working with wolves. Managing for the persistence of wolves in rural ranching communities presents one set of problems (see below), while managing wolves in protected areas involves another set of problems. In protected areas, wolf persistence depends on availability of good habitat and wild prey. However, the needs of wolves can conflict with transportation systems as protected areas may have significant traffic levels (e.g., automobiles). Conversely, wolves might adapt to human development and begin using human roads and trails to their advantage, such as in ways described by

Paquet et al. In winter, human-caused alterations of snow conditions on roads and trails may attract wolves, influencing their movements, and thus also indirectly influencing wolf and prey survival. Paquet et al. speculate that wolf speed and the rate at which wolves kill their prey may also be affected by human infrastructure, a crucial aspect of wolf-prey relationships. The typical long-term habitat modifications related to industrial activities such as forestry, mining, and residential development are known to affect wolves as well as other large carnivores (Noss et al. 1996), but the results from Paquet et al. indicate that short-term modifications of habitat may also impact wolves and their function in the ecosystem.

Wolves have only been recognized as valuable ecosystem components by ecologists and the general public in the last part of the twentieth century. Subsequently, governments and other interest groups have promoted initiatives to help wolf recovery and recolonization, or to reintroduce wolves in areas where they had been previously extirpated. Nevertheless, the long-term prospects for recovering wolf populations may still be uncertain due to enduring difficulties of coexistence with humans and, in particular, due to both real and perceived conflicts between wolf needs and human interests (Morell 2008).

Liberg et al. describe wolf recolonization in Scandinavia during the 1980s, and the challenges encountered in managing and conserving those wolves. The wolf population likely originated from a few individuals that migrated from Russia and recolonized Scandinavia through Finland. As for other recovering populations, lack of genetic variability and genetic isolation are major concerns. Wolves now occur in two countries: Norway and Sweden. The universal problems of mismatching wildlife units and jurisdictional units and the arising inconsistencies in management are here extreme. Wolf management policies have never been identical, but rather the differences have been extreme, with one country considering wolf control and the other advocating wolf protection, and vice versa.

In addition, wolves occur in multi-use areas, including those used for agriculture, livestock production, hunting and recreation and characterized by high human density. Conflicts between wolves and humans arise, in particular with hunters, shepherds, and ranchers. Such conflicts are largely due to the perceived effects of wolf predation on wild prey densities, and because of depredation on livestock and dogs. Although wolf numbers have increased in recent years, results collected by Liberg et al. show that the growth rate is decreasing, perhaps because of poaching and inbreeding depression. Therefore, conflicts with humans may still pose major challenges for the long-term viability of recovering populations of wolves.

Using Eastern European wolf populations as sample cases, Jedrzejewski et al. highlight the efforts invested into understanding, monitoring, and managing wolves. Similar efforts are devoted to monitoring livestock losses due to wolves in these populated rural regions, and significant difficulties are encountered in managing losses. The authors claim that, in order to manage wolves, it is essential to understand the specific ecology of wolves in any particular region. As an example, they highlight recently discovered unique characteristics of wolf populations in Eastern Europe. Wolf dispersal patterns in the region and sink and source areas appear to be influenced by differences in habitats and in wolf management practices. In light of this information, such practices could be adjusted, for instance with the objective to foster wolf conservation in countries now belonging to the European Union. Yet, in some countries, the status of wolf populations is largely unknown due to the lack of any monitoring program.

The age structure of the population in Eastern Europe was different from that documented for North America. Jedrzejewski et al. further speculate that in these heavily exploited wolf populations, wolves are also producing more daughters, perhaps as an adaptive strategy. In one final example, the authors describe wolf diet and its dependence on both wild and domestic ungulates. Some East European countries have introduced effective systems of financial compensation for wolf-caused losses of livestock. In general, the authors emphasize the importance of further implementation of livestock damage compensation programs, which are not in place in some jurisdictions. These examples all support the need for the integration and coordination of monitoring and research efforts with management initiatives, in order to effectively deal with wolves at the interface with people.

MANAGEMENT CHALLENGES: HUNTING AND REMOVAL OF WOLVES

Wolves are not only hunted as vermin and out of retaliation and fear, but also as trophies and for the value of their fur. In northern Canada, some communities of Aboriginal people still rely on hunting for their subsistence and some hunters specialize in wolves. Cluff et al. report on a case of extremely intense wolf harvesting, which serves as a paradigm for the countless relationships between wolves and humans that would be considered unusual by most western urban dwellers. A wolf hunt in the Northwest Territories became controversial in 1998 when 633 wolves killed in the Rennie Lake area by approximately 10 aboriginal hunters received national media attention. A major public concern was the use of snowmobiles to pursue wolves to exhaustion. Wolves in the area are killed each year for their fur and many are exported to international markets, from which there is significant demand. Although the number of wolves in the area is not precisely known, hunting rates are considered sustainable by the territorial governments. In addition, use of snowmobiles to hunt wolves is also considered legal. The Rennie Lake hunting area is located at the transition between the boreal forest and tundra ecoregions. Although not able to sustain such a high number of resident wolves, the area is subject to large influxes of barren-ground caribou (*Rangifer tarandus groenlandicus*) as they migrate there from the tundra in the winter. Wolves associated with these caribou follow the migratory herds as they move to the winter ranges in the fall and back in spring. Thus, the Rennie Lake becomes a remarkable sink area for wolves. This study describes the unique characteristics of local people and governments as well as wolves, in particular, their newly discovered migratory behaviour, which explain the extraordinary hunting quotas.

Considering at once the complexities of wolf behaviour and of wolf interactions with the environment and with people, it would appear that the fundamental question is: What can we do to foster coexistence between wolves and humans? The last chapter of this book provides a case sample of research toward this end, specifically applying to the local circumstances encountered in the ranchlands of Alberta, Canada. As described by Muhly et al., wolves in rural areas sometimes kill or harass livestock. In response, managers, ranchers, and farmers often kill wolves to reduce depredation. In such areas, managers may have to plan for wolf management objectives that appear to be contradictory to those of wolf conservation groups: the objective of preventing livestock depredation, while simultaneously maintaining a viable wolf population on the landscape. The contradiction has historic roots, where in the past higher levels of wolf control resulted in extirpation and local extinction of wolves.

Muhly et al. is the first study that uses livestock husbandry practices to model and predict wolf depredation at the landscape level. Their approach produces depredation probability maps indicating where depredation risk is higher, and therefore providing a focal point for management in the future. The added value of relying on husbandry factors is that these can be managed by people to prevent depredation, i.e., these are more malleable to human influences than biophysical factors of the environment. However, additional research is necessary to evaluate the best management practices throughout wolves' global distribution. As indicated above, specific factors might affect wolf depredation in certain areas, but not in others, as factors' relationship to depredation is likely affected by interaction with other aspects and the local biophysical, social, and economic environment. However, the general pattern of wolf attack on livestock seems predictable. In general, humans want to reduce wolf populations not only when they threaten domestic animals, but also when they are perceived to affect the abundance of wild ungulates. In order to evaluate the value of wolf control, managers and researchers are evaluating the efficacy and the long-term effects of all reduction programs (Hayes et al. 2003, Brainerd et al. 2008, Cluff et al. this volume).

We hope that this book demonstrates the broad range of ecological issues that can be addressed by examining the ecology and behaviour of wolves, a species of choice for conservation planning due to its charisma or conflict with people worldwide. Wolves may not be keystone species in the widely accepted sense of the term, but they are certainly a pivotal component influencing the dynamics of ecological systems. Although they have been extensively studied in all types of environments, research continues to gather a wealth of fresh, new, unexpected and exciting results. The exceptional ecological and behavioural flexibility of wolves has allowed for a historic range across the whole of North America and Eurasia. Their ecological plasticity now forces us to expand our research over a similar range of different conditions if we hope to base our management on adequate data and rigorous information. The examples and conclusions of this book are an attempt to highlight this global diversity and to provide a contribution toward understanding wolf ecology beyond local adaptations and into the difficult exercise of broadly applicable generalizations. This book illustrates a common pattern: that scientific information is concordant in highlighting a critical role played by wolves in various natural and human-dominated systems worldwide. Such knowledge, as well as (mis)perceptions on wolves held by the most important keystone species (*Homo sapiens*), are both being incorporated in management and conservation programs affecting wolves, as well as their prey (livestock included) and their ecosystems.

Rediscovering the Real Wolf
Role of Wolves in Natural and
Semi-natural Ecosystems

1.1 Recent Advances in the Population Genetics of Wolf-like Canids

Robert K. Wayne

INTRODUCTION

The last decade has witnessed dramatic technical and analytical advances in the characterization of vertebrate genomes. The beginning of the twenty-first century also has ushered in the genomics revolution, and the study of wolf genetics promises to benefit substantially through association with the dog genome project (Lindblad-Toh et al. 2005; Kohn et al. 2006). In fact, wolves were used in the design of a genotyping chip that can potentially type over 100,000 genetic loci in a single individual. Similarly, gene expression can now be directly studied (Gibson & Muse 2004). However, even long-standing approaches to characterizing variation in natural populations of wolves, such as those involving mitochondrial DNA sequencing or microsatellite typing, have evolved dramatically through the use of new analytical techniques to address questions of population history, substructure, and genetic distinction (Excoiffer & Heckel 2006). These new analytical approaches allow accurate assignment of individuals to populations and species and comparison of current migration rates to historic levels of gene flow. Further, landscape genetic approaches allow for integration of genetic and spatial data to determine population limits and connectivity and the ecological and topographic factors that influence genetic differentiation (Manel et al. 2003; Storfer et al. 2007).

New markers and improved molecular technology have led to expanded and comprehensive surveys of wild wolf populations, such as the Scandinavian wolf (see Liberg et al. this volume). Sex specific markers, such as Y-chromosome loci, have been used to study sex specific gene flow and the genetic composition of founders. Genes under selection, such as those of the major histocompatibility complex (MHC) have been typed in wild canid populations leading to inferences about natural selection and population history (e.g., Hedrick et al. 2002; Aguilar et al. 2004; Seddon & Ellegren 2004). The gray wolf was one of the first wild vertebrates to be typed for a new class of nuclear markers called single nucleotide polymorphisms (SNPs) (Seddon et al. 2005). Although the scope of this study was limited to only 22 SNPs, the availability of a SNP genotyping chips with over 100,000 markers promises to allow far greater resolution to long-standing questions about population variation and differentiation than any other current approach (Morin et al. 2004). Finally, techniques to use low copy or degraded DNA samples have become prominent and allowed non-invasive population monitoring and reconstruction of historical patterns of variation in recent and ancient populations of wolf-like canids (Kohn et al. 1999a; Adams et al. 2003a; Leonard et al. 2005; Prugh et al. 2005; Scandura et al. 2006; Stiller et al. 2006; Randall et al. 2007).

In this review, I first focus on new genetic markers, molecular techniques, and methods of analysis. I then discuss recent studies that address consequential questions in wolf biology such as population history and demography, population connectivity, the importance of ecology in influencing patterns of genetic variation, and hybridization between wolves and other wolf-like canids. A comprehensive analysis of more traditional approaches to wolf population genetics and evolution has been published elsewhere (Wayne & Vilà 2003). Finally, I discuss the future of molecular genetic studies in wolves.

NEW MARKERS

Early studies characterized protein polymorphisms in wolf populations (Ferrell et al. 1978; Wayne & O'Brien 1987; Kennedy et al. 1991; Wayne et al. 1991; Randi et al. 1993), but the bulk of recent genetic studies concern mitochondrial DNA (mtDNA) sequences and microsatellite loci (Wayne & Vilà 2003). Mitochondrial DNA resides in the mitochondria, an extranuclear organelle that contains multiple copies of a small circular DNA molecule, about 16,000 to 18,000 base pairs in length in mammals. This genome is maternally inherited without recombination and hence, barring any mutations, all offspring of a female contain her identical genome. Mitochondrial DNA sequences have a very high mutation rate, generally much higher than nuclear gene sequences, and hence provide higher resolution for population genetic questions. The first comprehensive studies of wolf populations analyzed mtDNA sequence variation indirectly by typing restriction fragment length polymorphisms (e.g., Lehman et al. 1991; Wayne et al. 1992), whereas more recent studies directly sequence hypervariable fragments of the mitochondrial genome, such as the control region (e.g., Vilà et al. 1999; Randi et al. 2000; Wilson et al. 2000; Leonard et al. 2005).

Microsatellite loci are composed of tandem repeats of short sequences 2–6 base pairs (bp) in length and are highly abundant in the nuclear genome of vertebrates (Bruford & Wayne 1993; Hancock 1999). Microsatellite loci evolve rapidly and are biparentally inherited. Therefore, they have been used for a wide variety of questions at the population level ranging from paternity to population differentiation (e.g., Roy et al. 1994; Forbes & Boyd 1997; Smith et al. 1997; Wilson et al. 2000; Flagstad et al. 2003; Grewal at al. 2004; Lucchini et al. 2004; Weckworth et al. 2005; Pilot et al. 2006). The use of linked microsatellites (i.e., microsatellites in close proximity on the same chromosome, and inherited together without recombination) has provided increased resolution to questions about dog/wolf hybridization (Randi & Lucchini 2002; Vilà et al. 2003b; Lucchini et al. 2004; Verardi et al. 2006). Further, studies of wolf populations have increasingly used large panels of unlinked microsatellites (i.e., microsatellites found within the genome at a distance, which allows for recombination during reproduction) in contrast to early studies that generally used 10 or fewer (e.g., Lucchini et al. 2004; Grewal et al. 2004; Andersen et al. 2006).

Most recently, microsatellite loci on the Y chromosome have been used to study sex-specific patterns of reproduction and movement in wild canid populations (See Grewal et al. 2004: Liberg et al. this volume). These results provided a paternal view on evolutionary patterns that complement studies on maternally inherited mtDNA and biparentally inherited nuclear genes (Jorde et al. 2000). In general, Y-chromosome studies represent an independent test for hypotheses based on mitochondrial sequences or microsatellite loci and permit estimation of sex-biased migration and dispersal (Favre et al. 1997; Seielstad et al. 1998; Prugnolle & de Meeus 2002). Finally, genes under selection are a critical missing element in population genetic studies and in conservation assessments (Crandall et al. 2000; Wayne & Morin 2004; Kohn et al. 2006). Genes from the major histocompatibility complex (MHC) are potentially under selection and have now been studied in gray wolves and other canids (Sundqvist et al. 2001; Hedrick et al. 2002; Seddon & Ellegren 2002; Seddon & Ellegren 2004; Berggen & Seddon 2005). The MHC is a 4-million base pair segment of DNA in vertebrates containing over 80 genes arranged in three functional classes (Edwards & Hedrick 1998) and has been completely sequenced in the dog (Linblad-Toh et al. 2005). Unlike other genetic markers, overdominance, frequency dependence and geographically varying directional selection influences variation at the MHC and may maintain high levels of polymorphism (Potts & Wakeland 1993; Edwards & Hedrick 1998) as a result of MHC parasite-mediated selection, sexual selection, and in some instances, maternal-foetal interactions. Finally, the most exciting research frontier in molecular population genetics attempts to characterize sequence variation of the nuclear genome directly and compares patterns of neutral, adaptive, and deleterious variation among populations (Kohn et al. 2006). Promising markers for probing the genome are single nucleotide polymorphisms, and even small panels of SNPs have proved useful in wolf populations (Seddon et al. 2005; Andersen et al. 2006). The >100,000

SNPs available on the dog genome chip will offer powerful tools for exploring nuclear variation in wild canids (Kohn et al. 2006), as will whole genome sequencing technology (Stiller et al. 2006).

A FEW WORDS ABOUT TECHNIQUES

Molecular techniques are now less expensive and require less effort than in the past. DNA sequencing can be done economically on a large scale and principally uses automated sequencers housed in a core facility. Genotyping of microsatellite loci involves similar automated facilities with the principal cost being marker development. However, given the completion of the dog genome sequence and associated resources (Lindblad-Toh et al. 2005), there is a huge reservoir of markers, new analytical approaches, and bioinformatics databases that can readily be applied to population genetic issues in wolves and other canids (Kohn et al. 2006; Stiller et al. 2006).

DNA can now be extracted and amplified from specimens having degraded or low copy DNA. An exciting new possibility for monitoring the demography of wolves, especially in areas where they are difficult to observe and capture, utilizes organic material that wolves leave behind. New molecular techniques allow for the extraction of DNA from animal and plant remains such as feces, feathers, hair, bone, and fish scales (Höss et al. 1992; Kohn & Wayne 1997; Wayne et al. 1999) and hence reveal a noninvasive genetic record of individuals. Characterization of these remains with genetic markers offers a means to count and identify individuals in a population, determine their sex and movement patterns, infer parentage or relatedness, and assess pathogens and diet (e.g., Kohn & Wayne 1997; Waits & Paetkau 2005).

The vast majority of population genetic studies use a current sample of individuals to reconstruct past events and historic patterns of variation (see above). However, this inference requires assumptions about the continuity of populations and the processes that generate divergence between them. A direct historical perspective can be potentially obtained from preserved remains, ranging from the vast holdings of museums to the remains preserved in natural deposits. For example, historic museum specimens less than 200 years old were used to address the origins and the relationships of the red wolf and historic gray wolf to the current population (see below).

NEW ANALYSES

Individual-based method

Most population genetic studies in wolves have used phylogenetic approaches and allele frequency variation to reconstruct population relationships and history. However, such approaches require that the population be defined a priori. Increasingly, individual-based approaches have been used in a Bayesian framework to determine natural population units and probabilistically assign individuals to these populations (e.g., Pritchard et al. 2000; Beaumont & Rannala 2004; Manel et al. 2005). Spatially explicit variations of this approach that use the exact location of individuals, such as embodied in the program Geneland, have also been developed (Guillot et al. 2005a, 2005b). Assignment tests, especially with linked loci (Falush et al. 2003), provide a powerful method for deducing the hybrid ancestry of individuals and, through comparison to frequency-based methods, allow estimation of recent and historic migration (e.g., see Manel et al. 2005; Riley et al. 2006; Verardi et al. 2006). Finally, landscape corridors that connect populations can be examined through a pathway analysis that evaluates that likelihood of individuals using different landscape pathways between populations (e.g., Coulon et al. 2004; Ray 2005). Similarly, individual-based landscape genetic approaches can quantitatively assess the variables that affect connectivity in complex landscapes (e.g., reviewed in Manel et al. 2003; Cushman 2006; Storfer et al. 2007). Consequently, these analyses can identify the most influential landscape obstacles to individual dispersal and be used to better manage wolf populations as well as to provide insights into their biology.

Demographic history and connectivity

Population history and connectivity also have been more accurately revealed by a suite of Bayesian coalescent statistical techniques using the inferred genealogical history of a population (Rosenberg & Nordborg 2002; Beaumont & Rannala 2004; Drummond et al. 2005). Through comparisons with frequency-based techniques, different time depths can be examined or through analyses such as skyline plots (Strimmer & Pybus 2001) effective population size during specific episodes of population history can be reconstructed (e.g., Drummond et al. 2005). On a shorter time scale, less than a few hundred generations, various frequency- and alleles-based approaches can be applied to estimate demographic factors such as effective population size and gene flow (e.g., Prugh et al. 2005; Goossens et al. 2006; see review in Pearse & Crandall 2004; Leberg 2005; Excoiffer & Heckel 2006). As a result, a combination of analytical approaches can be used that together allow a complete population history to be reconstructed.

Lastly, past studies on wolves generally invoke geographic barriers and distance as the cause between population differentiation. However, multivariate and autocorrelation approaches have suggested that in wolf-like canids, ecological factors are more important (e.g., Carmichael et al. 2001, 2007; Geffen et al. 2004; Sacks et al. 2004, 2005; Pilot et al. 2006). Application of new analytical techniques along with more detailed environmental and spatial data may allow identification of populations that are isolated and adaptively distinct. Moreover, such synthetic approaches provide a mechanism for collaboration between ecologists and geneticists and a fuller understanding of wolf biology.

NEW QUESTIONS

Pedigree construction

With the availability of hypervariable markers, such as microsatellite loci, constructing an exact pedigree for a large number of wolves in a single population has become feasible. Earlier studies of wolf-like canids assessed paternity and relatedness structure within and between social groups (e.g., Sillero-Zubiri et al. 1996; Girman et al. 1997; Smith et al. 1997; Liberg et al. 2005; Liberg et al. this volume; Jedrzejewski et al. 2005b), but a full pedigree of a population of wolves requires more loci and more extensive population sampling than used in these studies (e.g., Bensch et al. 2006; vonHoldt et al. 2008). A population pedigree would be extremely useful for determining levels of inbreeding, reproductive skew, and the influence kinship has on patterns of behaviour and dispersal. For example, Liberg et al. (2005; this volume), established a full pedigree for 24 of 28 breeding pairs that existed in the isolated Swedish population of wolves from the period 1983–2002 (Fig. 1.1.1). The authors used microsatellite data from 32 microsatellite loci and field information such as radiotelemetry and snow track information. The population was founded by only three individuals and was isolated thereafter. Consequently, inbreeding coefficients derived from analysis of the pedigree were high, with much of the population after 1997 having inbreeding coefficients greater than 0.25, a level corresponding to full sib mating. Such high levels of inbreeding suggest inbreeding depression (e.g., Laikre & Ryman 1991) and the authors found that the size of winter litters was highly correlated with the level of inbreeding ($R^2 = 0.39$, p< 0.0001). They then used a population growth model to show that this level of inbreeding was the equivalent of a reduction of 1.15 winter pups per litter for each increase of 0.1 in the inbreeding coefficient. Zero population growth would be reached when the average inbreeding coefficient was 0.48. The results do not bode well for small isolated wolf populations. However, despite severe inbreeding and loss of genetic variation, some small and isolated populations (e.g., Isle Royale in

Minnesota) can survive for more than 50 years given appropriate conditions (Peterson & Page 1988; Wayne et al. 1991). Recently, these results were extended to show that high heterozygous individuals were more fit, giving some hope that the population might survive (Bensch et al. 2006). Future studies, using larger pedigrees and a similar number of molecular markers may reveal much more about the affects of kinship on inbreeding depression as well as on co-operative and antagonistic behaviour in wolves (vonHoldt et al. 2008).

Current, historic and long past population size

Large-scale microsatellite surveys along with new analytical techniques have greatly increased the specificity of historical reconstructions. Demographic history can sometimes be inferred directly by reconstructing the founder genotypes and identifying sources of migration. For example, in the Swedish wolf population, genetic analysis of a large proportion of the population over a 17-year period showed that before 1990 the genotypes of all sampled wolves could be explained by descent from a single pair of wolves. Subsequently, a single migrant that genetic assignment tests suggested was from neighbouring populations to the east, reproduced and dramatically increased genetic variation. Following the immigration event there was an increase in inbreeding avoidance behaviour, rapid spread of new alleles, and exponential population growth. The single immigrant appears to have "genetically rescued" the formerly inbred population (Flagstad et al. 2003; see Liberg et al. this volume). Finally, both immigration and emigration may occur in Sweden as wolves from northern Sweden were found to be a mix of immigrants from Finland and wolves migrating from the southern Swedish breeding population (Seddon et al. 2006).

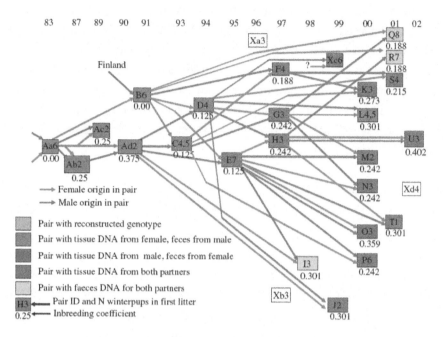

Figure 1.1.1. Pedigree of a Scandinavian wolf population based on analysis of microsatellite data and field information (Liberg et al. 2005, Liberg et al. this volume, page 183). Boxes indicate breeding pairs and arrows indicate the ancestry of male and female wolves in each pair. The source of material used to infer genotypes is indicated by the shades of grey of the boxes.

Methods that are more indirect infer historical population size changes from DNA sequence and allele frequency information. Very recent population changes can be estimated from the allele frequency change across generations. A certain allele frequency change due to drift is expected across generations as a function of effective population size. Consequently, the magnitude of allele frequency change across generations can be used to estimate changes in effective size (Waples 1989, 2005). For example, the Finnish population of wolves was sampled in three periods (1998–1998, 1999–2001, 2002–2004) and 118 individuals were genotyped with 10 microsatellite markers. Various methods to estimate population size from these data all provide estimates of about 40 individuals despite changes in census population size (Aspi et al. 2006). Very recent population declines also leave distinct signatures in the allele frequency spectrum that can readily be detected (Luikart & Cornuet 1998; Leberg 2005; Prugh et al. 2005; Goossens et al. 2006;). For example, the Italian wolf population shows evidence of a population bottleneck within the last few centuries, which likely reflects human control efforts and prey decline (Lucchini et al. 2004). Similarly, using a different analytical approach, a recent decline dating to the nineteenth century was identified in the Finnish population as well, showing that the current population is about 8% of that which existed historically (Aspi et al. 2006). However, in the Italian population, the genetic data suggest that in the past 2,000 to 10,000 years a 100- to 1000-fold population contraction occurred, a change that is superimposed on recent population changes. Finally, even very ancient population declines can be detected by changes in genetic variability. Vilà et al. (1999) showed that wolf populations across Europe were much larger in the mid-Pleistocene than in historic times. Therefore, genetic data allow current, historic, and evolutionary timescales to be assessed with respect to changes in effective population size. Establishing the contribution of historical trends is essential to evaluating the conservation significance of recent population changes and understanding the causes of population fluctuations.

Population structure

Wolves can disperse over large distances and across substantial geographic barriers. Hence, relatively high rates of gene flow are predicted among wolf populations and levels of population structure might be expected to be low. However, recent anthropogenic changes and glacially imposed barriers might also be predicted to leave a signal of differentiation. Initial mitochondrial surveys showed little geographic structure in the New World and identified only the Italian wolf population as being highly distinct in Europe (Wayne et al. 1992; Vilà et al. 1999; Randi et al. 2000). However, assignment-based methods, in combination with microsatellite and SNP surveys, showed greater resolution and could detect isolation over the past tens of thousands of years. For example, Finnish and Swedish populations appear genetically distinct with a high percentage of wolves correctly assigned to each population (Flagstad et al. 2003; Seddon et al. 2005; Aspi et al. 2006). The relatively high uniqueness of the Swedish population probably reflects the fact that it was likely founded by only two individuals and experienced only one subsequent migrant (see above). Similarly, the effective population size of the Finnish population was only about 40 individuals and drift in this population along with low rates of migration from elsewhere likely led to differentiation. In agreement with the mitochondrial DNA results, microsatellite analysis of Italian wolves found them to be genetically distinct, and coalescent analysis of the genetic data suggested Ice Age isolation as well as recent loss of habitat as the cause (Fig. 1.1.2; Lucchini et al. 2004; as above). Moreover, other populations of wolves in Europe showed some genetic differentiation (Fig. 1.1.2). Finally, previous microsatellite analysis revealed few genetic subdivisions in North America (Roy et al. 1994; Forbes & Boyd 1997). However, research that is more recent suggests water barriers and ecology are important barriers to dispersal leading to differentiation (Carmichael et al. 2001, Geffen et al. 2004). Consistent with the importance of water barriers to genetic isolation, an extensive microsatellite analysis using a variety of analytical approaches, including a Bayesian-clustering analysis (see above), established southeast Alaska wolves as an interbreeding population distinct from wolves elsewhere in Alaska (Weckworth et al. 2005). This has conservation implications since the southeast Alaska population is heavily exploited.

The use of Bayesian-clustering analysis and assignment tests provides a powerful means to assess the effects of recent isolation, but also can be used to directly identify immigrants (see Wilson & Rannala 2003). For example, Riley et al. (2006) contrasted historical levels of gene flow based on allele frequency differences with rates of migration over an eight-year period as indicated by assignment tests and radiotelemetry data between coyote populations on different sides of a large freeway. The assignment and radiotelemetry results suggested high levels of movement across the freeway, but the estimates of historic gene flow suggested little movement of genes over the long term (Fig. 1.1.3). These conflicting results can be explained if dispersers that cross the freeway rarely reproduce. The authors

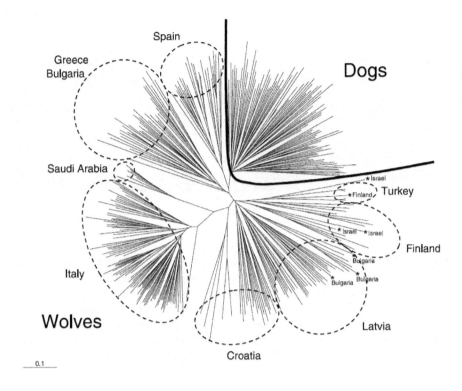

Figure 1.1.2. Unrooted genetic distance tree indicating the relationship between individual wolves from several European localities (Lucchini et al. 2004). The clusters in the tree suggest most European populations are distinct from each other and the domestic dog.

suggest that the freeway acts as a strong territorial boundary leading to a confluence of territories near the freeway (Fig. 1.1.3). This territory "pile up" causes an increased density of territorial coyotes near the freeway boundary. Thus, young coyotes that disperse across the freeway are unlikely to successfully establish a territory and reproduce. The freeway is a social barrier to gene flow rather than a physical one. Such contrasts between the actual number of migrants in a population based on assignment tests and that implied by levels of allele frequency differentiation allow for an assessment of the ecological and evolutionary constraints to migration.

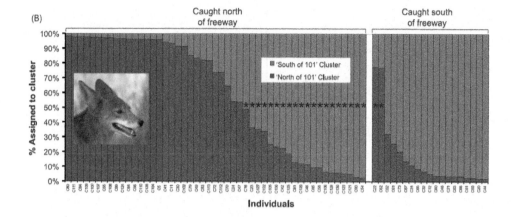

Figure 1.1.3. Identification of migrants using assignment tests in coyote populations sampled to the North and South of the 101 Freeway near Los Angeles, California. All starred individuals are classified to a population different from that in which they are found. For example, 20/49 (41%) of coyotes caught north of the freeway (starred in figure) may have migrated there from the south. The shade of grey indicates the proportion of the genotype of each coyote that derives from a specific population. For example, the predominance of light grey in misclassified individuals caught on the northern side of the freeway indicates that their genotypes derive from the southern population.

Ecological factors

The genetic differentiation that has been observed in gray wolves appears to show a weak pattern on isolation-by-distance such that adjoining populations are more closely related than distant ones (Forbes and Boyd 1997; Carmichael et al. 2001; Geffen et al. 2004). Such weak genetic patterns in the absence of topographic barriers to dispersal reflect a balance between drift and migration as predicted from theory (Slatkin 1993). However, dispersing individuals may actively choose specific habitats in which to establish territories, thus imposing an ecological influence on patterns of genetic differentiation. Past studies on vertebrates focused on demonstrating the degree of isolation-by-distance and the effect of specific historical topographic barriers on differentiation (Avise 1994). Recently, to develop more realistic models of differentiation, multivariate and hypotheses testing approaches have been used to assess the influence of habitat, climate, prey behaviour, and other variables on differentiation (Manel et al. 2003; Cushman 2006). The first such study on wolves, by Carmicheal et al. (2001), used partial Mantel's tests and showed that water barriers, such as the Mackenzie River in the Northwest Territories, Canada, impede gene flow and that island populations on Banks and Victoria Island are genetically similar to each other but distinct from mainland populations. Furthermore, the genetic data suggested that wolves that prey on and follow migratory caribou might be genetically distinct from those which hunt resident prey (Musiani et al. 2007). These data were later used in a specific Bayesian model to estimate migration rates over the past few generations (Wilson & Rannala 2003). The new analysis confirmed previous results and found high and often unidirectional migration between some populations. Revaluation of mitochondrial and microsatellite data on wolves from a variety of North American habitats likewise showed that climate and habitat variables explained a much larger proportion of genetic variation among populations than geographic distance alone (Geffen et al. 2004). The explicit multivariate framework used in this study, along with extensive geographic data on environmental differences, clearly identified the relative importance of different factors to genetic differentiation. For example, vegetation differences explained over 70% of the genetic variation among populations (Table 1.1.1). The authors suggested that because wolves learn prey skills as adolescents in specific habitats, when they disperse as adults they may travel long distances and across diverse habitats until they find an area that is similar to their natal environment. Consequently, distance between habitats explains a smaller fraction of the variation (31%) than habitat or climate (>70%, Table 1.1.1). Similar results were recently presented for Polish wolves (Pilot et al. 2006) and for California coyotes (Sacks et al. 2004, 2005). Extensive recent analysis of high Arctic wolves suggests multiple ecotypes exist there each corresponding to a distinct habitat type and varying in migratory behaviour (Carmichael et al. 2007; Musiani et al. 2007). Such "landscape genetic" approaches will become increasingly common given the availability of new statistical tools and more extensive microsatellite typing of wolf populations. However, results obtained thus far for wolves indicate that these animals may be considered as habitat or

Table 1.1.1. Statistical significance and the proportion of genetic variation explained by predictor geographic and environmental variables (Geffen et al. 2004). P-values less than 0.10 are highlighted in bold. The column headed "%var" indicates the percentage of the multivariate genetic variation explained by the particular set of predictor variables for two distinct genetic data sets: 1) Fst genetic distance based on data from 10 microsatellite loci (Roy et al. 1994); and 2) mitochondrial DNA restriction fragment length polymorphisms (RFLP) (Wayne et al. 1992).

MARGINAL TESTS

Variable set	F	P	%var
Fst (microsatellite)			
Distance	1.822	0.0878	31.29
Temperature	0.794	0.6795	25.39
Rainfall	1.136	0.3679	11.20
Habitat type	0.683	0.6625	7.05
Water Barrier	1.669	0.1789	15.65
Climate	1.594	0.1953	78.81
Vegetation	2.393	0.0168	70.53
Fst (mtDNA RFLP)			
Distance	4.929	0.0094	45.10
Temperature	0.793	0.6117	17.77
Rainfall	0.324	0.7160	2.43
Habitat type	3.783	0.0437	22.54
Water Barrier	1.394	0.3329	9.68
Climate	2.725	0.0429	73.16
Vegetation	4.112	0.0116	75.51

trophic specialists, which is contrary to the generally accepted concept that wolves, and large carnivores in general, are habitat generalists (see Noss et al. 1996). The contradiction could be in some measure explained by the importance of prey selection in wolves and by considering prey species as habitat components.

Hybridization

All members of the genus *Canis* can potentially hybridize (see Coppinger et al., this volume, for a different viewpoint), but only matings between gray wolves and domestic dogs (Vilà & Wayne 1999; Verardi et al. 2006 but see Adams et al. 2003b) and gray wolves and other wolf-like canids of the Great Lakes Region of North America (Lehman et al. 1991; Wilson et al. 2000) are likely to be important from a conservation perspective. In addition, hybridization between the red wolf (*Canis rufus*) and coyote (*Canis latrans*) has affected the genetic uniqueness of red wolves in the past and currently, the single reintroduced population in Alligator River in North Carolina (Jenks & Wayne 1992; Roy et al. 1996; Hedrick et al. 2002; Miller et al. 2003). Distinguishing between pure forms and their various hybrid generations has been challenging in the past. However, more sophisticated Bayesian-based assignment methods have shown great power to identify even multigeneration hybrids between red wolves and coyotes (Adams et al. 2003a; Miller et al. 2003). In Italy, wolves have been observed to roam with dogs and there are reports of interspecific hybridization (see Andersone et al. 2002). However, the overall influence on the genetic integrity of the wolf population was uncertain. The use of assignments tests with a large sample of dog and wolf populations clearly identified individuals of mixed ancestry and some of these individuals had unusual phenotypes (Andersone et al. 2002; Randi & Lucchini 2002). Similar analyses identified a wolf-dog hybrid in Sweden, but critically, these authors used sex specific markers in addition to microsatellite loci to identify the sex of each species in the cross (Vilà et al. 2003b). More recently, the use of physically linked microsatellite loci enhanced the discrimination and classification of dogs and wolves and their hybrids in Italy (Verardi et al. 2006).

Assignment tests have been used to identify hybrids between wolf-like canids. In Algonquin Park in Ontario, Canada, the resident wolf may be a distinct species of North American wolf, *Canis lycaon* (Wilson et al. 2000, 2003, Kyle et al. 2006). This species hybridizes with coyotes and gray wolves. Study of the park population suggested it was genetically distinct and assignment analysis found five migrants, some of which were phenotypically distinct and had some coyote ancestry (Grewal et al. 2004). Similarly, hybrids between coyotes and red wolves in the wild, identified through assignment tests, permitted hybrids of ¼, ½, and ¾ red wolf to be correctly assigned (Miller et al. 2003). Such identification is critical to management because the primary threat to the small red wolf population is hybridization with coyotes. Control of coyotes and hybrids on the population boundary can theoretically maintain the genetic integrity of the population (Fredrickson & Hedrick 2006). Finally, such hybridization may leave a long genetic legacy in a population, for example, mtDNA analysis of coyotes from the American Southwest showed that a dog mtDNA haplotype was common, suggesting ancient hybridization with Native American dogs (Adams et al. 2003b). In general, hybridization between discrete taxa may be a conservation concern if it has anthropogenic rather than natural causes (Wayne & Jenks 1991; Allendorf et al. 2001; Wayne & Brown 2001). In this regard, hybridization among Great Lake wolf-like canids primarily may represent habitat loss and predator control efforts by humans since coyotes only invaded the area early in the last century when wolf numbers were controlled to a low level (Moore & Parker 1992). Consequently, genetic management of Algonquin wolves may be justified given that red wolves may have benefited from plans to manage coyotes (Stoskopf et al. 2005; Fredrickson & Hedrick 2006; Murray & Waits 2006).

Historical diversity

Most molecular population genetic studies use current patterns of genetic diversity to infer historical processes. However, recent studies using DNA extracted from specimens over the last 50,000 years have questioned the accuracy of such inferences (Hadly et al. 1998; Leonard et al. 2000; Barnes et al. 2002; Shapiro et al. 2004). Historical levels of diversity may not be adequately represented by current genetic patterns, especially if there have been recent population changes (Roy et al. 1996; Wilson et al. 2003; Leonard et al. 2005). Museum collections are a DNA repository in this regard, as specimens from past populations (also including populations that are now extinct) can be typed and the effect of recent population changes can be evaluated (Wayne et al. 1999). For example, genetic analysis of two historic wolves from the northeastern U.S. found they contained mtDNA sequences similar to those of the current Algonquin or New World wolf, supporting the notion that it is a separate species with a formerly larger geographic range (Wilson et al. 2003).

Gray wolves of the historic American West suffered whole scale extermination and by 1940 were largely eliminated from western states. However, populations in southwestern Canada that are likely closely related were much less affected and presumably contained much of the genetic diversity lost in the western U.S. wolves. Genetic analysis of historic specimens from the western U.S. suggested otherwise (Leonard et al. 2005). Two-thirds of mtDNA haplotypes in the historic population were unique, and levels of diversity in the historic population were considerably higher than in their modern Canadian conspecifics. Further, the haplotypes closely related to the Mexican gray wolf had a much broader geographic range than suggested by subspecific accounts (Fig. 1.1.4). The higher diversity of American wolves is likely due to the role of the West as an Ice Age refugium from which wolves colonized Canada more recently. Thus, Canada and Alaska contain only a subset of this refugial diversity. The larger geographic distribution of the Mexican wolf implied by the genetic results provides a mandate for more extensive reintroduction with allowance for mixing between them and northern gray wolves. In general, the use of old specimens from wolves elsewhere across their historical and current geographic range will more clearly test ideas about isolation, recolonization, and population changes that have occurred in the recent past.

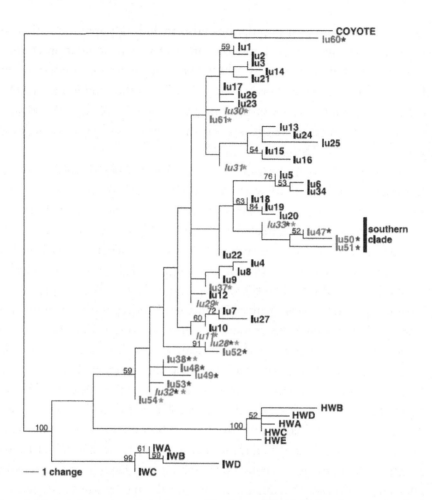

Figure 1.1.4. A phylogenetic analysis of grey wolf haplotypes Worldwide based on mitochondrial control region sequence data (Leonard et al. 2005). The phylogeny shows that current and historic North America (grey letters) haplotypes do not define a single cluster and are instead grouped with those from Europe and Asia (black). However, a cluster exclusive to North American is defined by haplotype lu33 and historic haplotypes lu47, lu50 andlu51 (the southern clade). Haplotypes lu33 and lu47 are found only in samples of current and historic Mexican wolves whereas haplotypes lu50 and lu51 are found in historic samples of gray wolves from Utah to Nebraska and are intermixed with haplotypes common in northern gray wolves. The wide distribution of the southern clade suggests that gene flow was extensive across the recognized limit of the Mexican subspecies providing a wider mandate for reintroduction. Further, the large diversity of historical haplotypes reflects the greater diversity in the American Ice Age refugial population (see text).

NON-INVASIVE MONITORING

The use of DNA from trace remains of organisms, such as blood, urine, feces, or feathers, offers a powerful tool to characterize genetic variation in species that are rare or difficult to capture (Waits & Paetkau 2005). In wolf-like canids, feces are a ready source of material from which genetic information as well as information on parasites and diet can be obtained (Kohn & Wayne 1997; Kohn et al. 1999a). Despite concerns about genotyping error and the accuracy of population estimates (Creel et al. 2003), studies with coyotes that used both genetic and radiotelemetry information (Fig. 1.1.5, Kohn et al. 1999a; Prugh et al. 2005) have clearly shown that fecal DNA can be used to estimate population size and trace individual dispersal. Additionally, pedigree, kinship, and population relationship information can potentially be derived from fecal DNA (Kohn et al. 1999a; Lucchini et al. 2002; Adams et al. 2003a; Lyengar et al. 2005; Prugh et al. 2005; Randall et al. 2007). Prugh et al. (2005) specifically demonstrated the accuracy of population monitoring and were able to assess sources of error. They showed that the size of an Alaskan population of coyotes could carefully track, with a time lag, the population size of hares and reviewed the general use of fecal, non-invasive population monitoring for carnivores. Finally, fecal monitoring of hybridization between red wolves and coyotes in combination with global positioning coordinates of fecal samples proved to be a sufficient monitor of hybridization between the two species (Adams et al. 2003a). Given population declines in many areas and the difficultly of capturing wolves, especially in natural reserves, fecal genotyping will likely be increasingly used in the future (Kohn et al. 1997; Waits & Paetkau 2005). However, technical issues must be carefully addressed (Randall et al., in review).

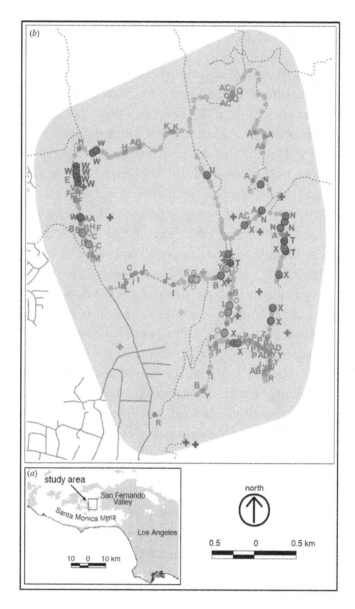

Figure 1.1.5. Study location (a) in the Santa Monica Mountain near Los Angeles where coyote presence was deduced by fecal genotyping and radiotelemetry (b). Multilocus fecal genotypes that matched those of captured coyotes and their nearest telemetry locations are presented as circles identified with letters and matching symbols with matching shade of grey, respectively. Dark-gray circles represent feces with genotypes that did not match any of the captured coyotes. Light-gray circles represent the remaining sites where feces were collected.

THE FUTURE

New molecular markers and population probes

Three applications of new molecular markers have demonstrated their utility over past studies that used microsatellites or mtDNA. First, studies using sex chromosome markers, such as X- or Y-chromosome microsatellite loci, have revealed differences in sex specific migration rates and effective population size (Sundqvist et al. 2006). For example, Y-chromosome analysis of the Scandinavian wolves found only two haplotypes suggesting minimally, two males founded the small population (Sundqvist et al. 2001). Combined use of microsatellite loci, mtDNA, and Y-chromosome markers identified the parents of a suspected dog-wolf hybrid as a female wolf and male dog (Vilà et al. 2003b; this volume). Second, new marker classes such as SNPs can provide a test of demographic hypothesis based on other genetic loci. For example, the pioneering use of SNPs on Scandinavian wolves reaffirmed conclusions from previous analyses such as the genetic distinction of individual Scandinavian wolves from each other and from other populations (Seddon et al. 2005; Andersen et al. 2006). Finally, the study of genes under selection that are important in adaptation and fitness is an elusive goal of population genetic studies (Crandall et al. 2000; Wayne & Morin 2004; Kohn et al. 2006). In this regard, wolves have been well characterized for MHC variation, a candidate class of genes under selection (see above). These studies tested the hypothesis of natural selection on genes and regulatory elements as well as showing that red wolves share gray wolf and coyote ancestry, with a more close relationship with the latter (Seddon & Ellegren 2002; Hedrick at al. 2002; Seddon & Ellegren 2004; Berggren & Seddon 2005).

Themes

Two themes are likely to dominate future genetic research on wolves. The first theme stems from the recent emergence of whole genome sequences in dogs (Kirkness et al. 2003; Lindblad-toh et al. 2005). As a result of these efforts, an array of markers will be developed that can potentially be used to identify adaptive, neutral, and deleterious variation in populations of wolf-like canids including differences in gene expression (Kohn et al. 2006). This information will address long-standing questions such as the importance of genetic variation to fitness and population persistence. Answers to these questions will greatly assist conservation management (Kohn et al. 2006). Even long-standing issues such as effective population size, gene flow, and historical demography will be better addressed by the addition of new genetics markers that will number in tens of thousands rather than less than a dozen. The >100,000 SNP genotyping chip to be released in fall of 2007 is the most promising tool now available, but expression arrays and other genomic tools are on the horizon. New technologies such as high throughput sequencing may enable direct assessment of variation in hundreds of genes in natural populations (Margulies et al. 2005; Stiller et al. 2006). Secondly, non-invasive techniques that address genetics, disease, diet, hormone levels, and even age (Waits & Paetkau 2005; Dennis 2006) will permit an extensive characterization of wolf populations not previously possible, all through the use of discarded biological remains. These are exciting frontiers that more than ever before must involve a tight collaboration between geneticists and those who study the natural history and ecology of gray wolf populations.

1.2 What, If Anything, Is a Wolf?

Raymond Coppinger, Lee Spector, and Lynn Miller

> "In short, we will have to treat species in the same manner as those naturalists treat genera, who admit that genera are merely artificial combinations made for convenience. This may not be a cheering prospect; but we shall at least be freed from the vain search for the undiscovered and the undiscoverable essence of the term species." – Charles Darwin (1859, 1903)

INTRODUCTION

Species can be considered as moving targets. In every generation, there should be an adaptive response of a population of animals to an inconstant environment. This biological perspective, which is the core of the theory that has unified biology ever since Darwin proposed natural selection, is sometimes forgotten in the face of practical management decisions. For example, in the U.S. the federal Endangered Species Act (ESA) provides protection for species, subspecies, and populations. This protection, preservation, and restoration of a species, subspecies, or populations could imply that the essence (*sensu* Aristotle, Linnaeus) of the species is conserved. However, it should not imply that the phenotype or genotype is eternally fixed.

Management problems in restoration programs quite often centre on the genetic purity of the species being conserved. In North America, red wolves (*Canis rufus*) to be released from captivity into the wild are thought to be hybrids of gray wolves (*Canis lupus*) and/or coyotes (*Canis latrans*) (Wayne & Jenks 1991). Even though the restorers believe their animal has the "essence" of red wolf, geneticists say the species is not pure, or is a hybrid (O'Brien & Mayr 1991). The ESA does not provide protection for hybrids – even hybrids of severely endangered species. However, such ESA principles are not applied in the red wolf case. In other cases, some opponents of restoration plans object that the animals that were reintroduced are not the original subspecies or population and should therefore be removed.

For those of us interested in the conservation and restoration of wild canids there are several problems illustrated in these examples. The first is that definitions of species, subspecies, populations, and hybrids are unclear (O'Brien & Mayr 1991). Not only are species moving targets, but the definitions of species are ephemeral. The second and perhaps major problem is that we do not have a satisfactory methodology for identifying species, subspecies, and populations. Taxonomists do not agree with each other, and morphometric techniques do not agree with the genetic evidence. Thus, attempting to provide species, subspecies, or populations with legal definitions that can be used to define conservation plans becomes overwhelmingly difficult and often contentious.

At the simplest level one wants to preserve an endangered species because it is perceived to have intrinsic value. At a second level, there is the effort to preserve the ecosystem. It is the ecosystem that has an intrinsic value, and the various individual organisms behave synergistically to create that whole. At a third level, the attempt is the preservation of biodiversity, to maximize biodiversity as is elegantly laid out by Wilson (1999). Important to our discussion here, "species and subspecies" are the units of measurement of biodiversity. A world with two species is more complex, more "whole" than a world with one species. In each of these three conservation goals, there is the underlying assumption of the fixity of species. There is a number of species now, and our job as wildlife managers is to discover, describe, and preserve as many of them as possible.

We often practice wildlife management or endangered species management as if species are a fixed value and if they were clearly separate entities. In the red wolf recovery program, animals to be released into the wild have been genetically fingerprinted with the aim of testing subsequent generations and removing animals that show signs of hybridization. In preparation for their release, the environment was cleared of other members of the genus *Canis* in order to prevent hybridization. In the case of the Ethiopian wolf, which interbreeds with domestic dogs (*Canis familiaris* or *Canis lupus familiaris* [see below]; Wayne & Gottelli 1997), the proposal is to kill or sterilize the larger population of dogs in order to preserve the endangered canid species (Laurenson et al. 1997). Thus, it appears that the belief of the wildlife managers in both projects is to regard only the endangered species as having intrinsic and important value while the common species are considered as just vermin to be removed. In both of these cases it is the assumed fixed nature of a species, and a pre-eminent loss of biodiversity that drives the management plan. There is no consideration that dogs or coyotes may be the more highly evolved forms or that hybridization between these "species" might be the source of the variability necessary for red wolf or Ethiopian wolves to evolve and to adapt to the changing ecosystem (Reyer 2008).

The next question is: who is qualified to define these animals as an endangered species? Are the managers of so-called endangered species free to choose among the various taxonomic systems and pick one of the many species definitions available? For example, why should wildlife managers believe the geneticists who claim that red wolves are hybrids? Have we studied their methodologies and their definitions? Have they thought out the implications of what they are saying? Even if morphometricians or geneticists could reliably determine hybridization, who says that the new hybrid essence is not good enough or does not perform adequately in the ecosystem, or reduces biodiversity?

DIFFICULTIES IN SPECIES IDENTIFICATION

"...while we must make do with the terminologies of Aristotle and Linnaeus, we need not take them too seriously." – Haldane 1956

Many years ago, palaeontologist Albert Wood (1957) wrote a paper entitled: "What, if anything, is a rabbit?" Rabbits are lagomorphs. A debate ensued among famous palaeontologists (e.g., Albert Wood, George Gaylord Simpson) about whether rabbits were related to rodents. "Related" could mean they were descended from rodents, or that rodents and lagomorphs are descended from a common ancestor, or perhaps that rabbits were the ancestors of the rodents.

The 'rabbit debate' exemplifies how experts may shift back and forth, changing their minds about ancestries—based on new evidence, and sometimes upon re-analysis of existing data. In the last 50 years, molecular biology has steadily grown in technique, and enabled new insights to many evolutionary questions. For example, Graur et al. (1996) demonstrated that rabbits were descendants of primates. It is the kind of discovery that could not have been made through morphometric analysis alone (e.g., comparison of skulls and teeth), since such phenotypic characteristics might be confounded by convergent evolution.

Having a good definition of species and other taxonomic groups and their evolutionary history is necessary for management policy. In fact, without a proper well-defined name, wildlife law as it applies to endangered species becomes impossible.

Watch a 20 kg wild *Canis* moving across a field in New England or Quebec and ask the experts, "What is it?" and you could get several answers. Some wildlife biologists still call it a coydog (a supposed hybrid between a coyote and domestic dog; Silver & Silver 1969); others think it is a subspecies of coyote (*C. latrans* var.; Lawrence & Bossert 1967; Lawrence & Bossert 1969), while still others think it might be an Algonquin wolf (*C. lupus lycaon*). And maybe it is *C. lycaon* and more closely related to the red wolf (*C. rufus*) than it is to the gray wolf (*C. lupus*; Wilson et al. 2000; Kyle et al. 2006). Still others have argued that it might be a hybrid between the gray wolf (*C. lupus*) and the coyote (*C. latrans*; Lehman et al. 1991). A similar confusion can also be noticed for canids living in the Great Lakes regions of Canada and the U.S. (Leonard & Wayne 2007, Wheeldon & White 2009).

An animal's nomenclature is critically important in the twenty-first century because, for example, if the animal is a gray wolf (*C. lupus*) or red wolf (*C. rufus*) you cannot shoot it in the U.S. because they are on the endangered species list. If it is *C. lupus lycaon*, you can shoot it in Quebec, Canada, but not in the northeastern U.S. because technically it is a gray wolf. However, if it is *C. lycaon* it is unclear what the rules are in the northeastern U.S. In addition, if it is a coyote, you can shoot it. If it is any of the canids listed above or even a coydog, you cannot capture and keep it in Connecticut because it is considered a wild animal and a permit is required. However, in Massachusetts anything with dog in it is considered a dog and you can cage it. (Ironically, since the domestic dog is technically *Canis lupus fam.* (i.e., a subspecies of wolf), one could make the case that dogs be covered under the ESA. Can a species be endangered and its subspecies not?) But why is it so hard to identify our animal and why do so many people disagree?

Every species of the genus *Canis* has similar morphological features and it is somehow difficult to tell the differences among them. All *Canis* species are karyotypically identical, that is, all have identical chromosome numbers, sizes, shapes, and even banding patterns (Todd 1970; Chiarelli 1975; Wayne et al. 1987). All members of the *Canis* genus are inter-fertile. Hybrids are easily produced in the laboratory for study. In addition, there are growing numbers of wolf/dog hybrids and dog/jackal hybrids kept for pets. Finally, coyotes, wolves, dogs, and jackals hybridize "naturally." (Lehman et al. 1991; Vilà et al. 1997). In fact, the only barriers to reproduction among all these species are size differences, social organizations that tend to restrict reproductive access, and of course, geographic isolation.

MORPHOMETRIC SOLUTIONS TO THE SPECIES PROBLEM

"Taxonomy is written by taxonomists for taxonomists;... It is the most subjective branch of any biological discipline and in many ways is more of an art than a science." – Cowan 1971

Traditionally, as with the rabbit/rodent problem, differentiation was based on measurement. The underlying assumption is that statistical differences in phenotype may also reflect differences in genotype. The larger the differences in phenotype, the more distantly related are the two forms.

It is an assumption, however, that phenotype represents genotype. When that assumption is used to determine species as sexually isolated populations, it is often inadequate to the task. For example, dogs probably have the greatest morphological deviations (breeds) in the mammal world (Sutter et al. 2007). However, dog breeds are not distantly related one to another, and are not different species one from another. In dogs, very minor changes in onsets and offsets and allometric growth ratios can result in enormous differences in the resulting head shape. Similarly, very small allelic differences among dog breeds allow for large differences in size between breeds (Sutter et al. 2007).

Schneider (unpublished data; Coppinger & Schneider 1995) compares the skulls from five "species" of *Canis* and a number of dog breeds for differences in shape. Skull shapes were measured electronically for size-independent differences. If these two charts based on dorsal and ventral views (Fig. 1.2.1) are interpreted as phylogenetic trees, one sees immediately the problem with using morphometrics. The most diverse shapes are represented by breeds of dogs. Species such as coyotes, golden jackals, and side-striped jackals, which live continents apart, have almost identical head shapes, but change relationships dramatically depending on whether one is looking at the dorsal or ventral view. Wolves also change relationships depending on the view. In canids, differences in head shape may have little relationship to phylogeny and one cannot infer genetic relatedness or construct a phylogenetic tree using morphometrics only.

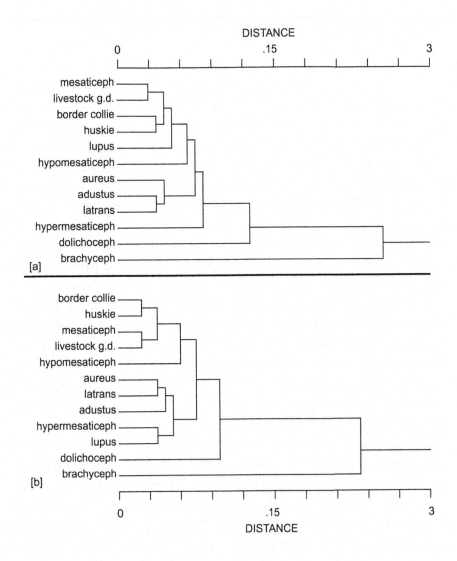

Figure 1.2.1. Cladograms of five species of the genus *Canis*, also including assorted breeds of dogs, based on (a) dorsal and (b) ventral morphometric views of adult skulls.

GENETIC SOLUTIONS TO THE SPECIES PROBLEM

In the past thirty years, molecular geneticists have entered the species debate. Their intent is to find DNA sequences that will show relationships between species, and finally to apply coalescent methods to date the origins of those species (Avise 2000). If speciation is the gradual shift of allelic frequency over time, it is assumed that populations with similar allelic frequencies are more closely related, while those with radically different allelic frequencies are more distantly related. The larger those genetic differences are, the longer the time since the two species diverged.

The geneticist argument starts with the neutral mutation theory (Kimura 1968). The neutral mutation theory is based on the observation that there are genetic mutations which are neutral to selective processes; they are not deleterious nor are they advantageous to the organisms that inherit them. For example, there are mutations that appear not to affect any changes in phenotype. The neutral mutation hypothesis predicts that these random mutations do not affect fitness, and thus they will not be selected against, or for, and therefore will accumulate over time. Leonard et al. (2002) and Savolainen et al. (2002) have applied such an approach to the problem of dog origin from wolves.

The flaw in this reasoning derives from the fact that populations are always finite in number. The corollary is that there is a limit to the number of haplotypes that can possibly accumulate. There must always be fewer haplotypes in a population than the number of individuals in the population. In addition, many individuals will die before reproducing and many neutral mutations will be lost by chance alone (genetic drift). It is therefore not obvious that heterozygosity will increase uniformly until saturation.

We hypothesize that the omission of this consideration in previous work may be partly responsible for the failure of previous calculations to predict the heterozygosity that is actually observed in empirical studies and in natural populations. For example, some studies find that the number of neutral haplotypes in natural populations is "orders of magnitude" less than theory predicts (Avise 2000).

We created a simple computational model to illustrate the dynamics of neutral mutation heterozygosity. Felsenstein (1971) derives rates for the loss of haplotypes in a mutation-free model, but we are unaware of analytical investigation of this question in models with both mutation and a finite population size.

OUR SIMULATION OF THE SPECIES PROBLEM

Our method was to simulate populations of genomes of length 750 base pairs (bp) that were reproduced asexually. This approach simplified calculations and still represented some inheritance mechanisms in nature, because mitochondrial DNA (mtDNA), for example, is transferred through the maternal line in mammals, without sexual recombination (Avise 2000). In canids, mtDNA analysis is widely used to support inferences about speciation. Source code for this simulation is available from http://hampshire.edu/lspector/whatwolf under 'The mitochondrial DNA (mtDNA) simulation (written in C)'.

During reproduction, the probability of random base substitution (mutation rate) was of 1 in 50,000 or 1 in 100,000 bp. The genome length was chosen to be similar to lengths of regions commonly used for molecular dating, for example the 672 bp hyper-variable region of the mtDNA D-loop in dogs and wolves (Tsuda et al. 1997). The mutation rates were chosen to be of the same order of magnitude as empirically determined rates, for example the rate of 1 in 85,190 bp determined by Heyer et al. (2001; they observed 0.0079 substitutions per generation per 673 bp), or the rate of 1 in 20,130 bp determined by Parsons et al. (1997; they observed 0.0303 substitutions per generation per 610 bp).

For each simulation, we began with a fixed number of clones of a randomly generated individual founder of the population. We then generated the same fixed total number of offspring in each subsequent generation, with the single parent of each offspring chosen randomly from the members of the previous generation. This produced a Poisson distribution of litter sizes with a mean of one. We continued this process for 5,000 generations while tracking the number of distinct haplotypes and the number of genomes identical to the founder.

We conducted a total of 64 simulations. Two simulations were run using different random number generator seeds for each combination of mutation rates (above) and the following population sizes: from 5,000 to 20,000 (in increments of 5,000) and from 50,000 to 600,000 (in increments of 50,000). (Note that the present-day population of wolves, worldwide, is probably between 200,000 and 300,000; also see Table of Wolf Populations in 2000 [Boitani 2003]). These were computationally intensive simulations, six of which terminated early due to system problems and were not rerun; we report on the results of the 58 simulations that terminated normally. The first result was that the founder haplotype was lost early in our simulations of reproductions. The founder's haplotype was extinct as early as generation 365 and never survived to generation 2,000 (Fig. 1.2.2). The founder had the highest probability of lasting for the most generations since the first several generations consisted almost entirely of its clones; haplotypes that arose later from mutations generally became extinct more quickly, and they rarely lasted 1,000 generations.

The second result of our simulations was that the increase in number of haplotypes (a proxy for heterozygosity) attenuated in early generations. The generation in which the number of haplotypes stabilized depended on the mutation rate and on the population size. We calculated the "stabilization time" to be the first generation in which the number of haplotypes in the population was within one standard deviation of the mean number of haplotypes over the last 1,000 generations of the simulation. Figure 1.2.3 shows that in all cases stabilization occurred long before the window over which the final mean of number of haplotypes in the population was calculated (generations 4001–5000). Stabilization occurred after fewer generations when populations were small (<200,000 individuals in Fig. 1.2.3). The populations in our simulations had no geographic structure; that is, the parent for each offspring was chosen randomly, without regard to geographic location. If geographic structure were added, then the "effective population size" (Avise 2000) would be lower and stabilization would be correspondingly more rapid.

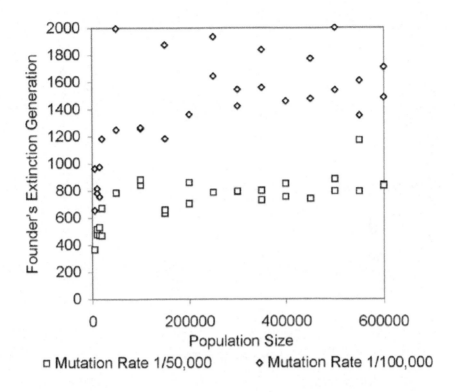

Figure 1.2.2. Extinction generations of initial founders in simulations of neutral mutation with fixed, finite population sizes.

The third result of our analysis was that the mean number of haplotypes, averaged over the final 1,000 generations, rose linearly with the fixed, finite population size of that particular simulation (Fig. 1.2.4). In fact, after stabilization the number of unique haplotypes in a population was a function of the population size, but not of the number of generations.

One unrealistic aspect of our primary simulations was that our population sizes were held constant throughout each run, whereas natural populations are subject to niche size fluctuations and periodic population crashes due to food scarcity, disease, or other cataclysmic events. To determine the effect of such events we conducted additional runs in which the population size was varied from generation to generation. We started

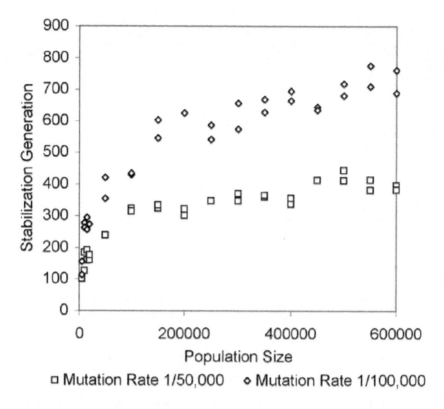

Figure 1.2.3. Stabilization generations of number of haplotypes in the population calculated with simulations of neutral mutation with fixed, finite population sizes.

with populations of 50,000 and each generation changed the population size by a number chosen from a uniform distribution between -1,000 and 1,000, maintaining a minimum population size of 100 and a maximum of 100,000. A plot of population size versus number of haplotypes for all runs was created by sampling the data at 100-generation intervals from generation 2,000 to 3,000 (Fig. 1.2.5). A linear relationship was maintained even with population size fluctuation (R^2 >0.9982, p < 0.001 for the runs with mutation rate 1/50,000; R^2 >0.9918, p < 0.001 with mutation rate 1/100,000).

THE WORLD OF WOLVES

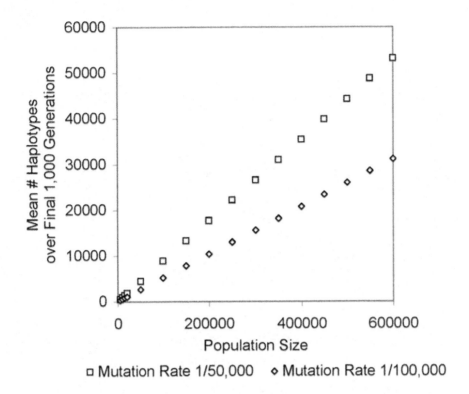

Figure 1.2.4. Mean number of haplotypes in the population over the final 1,000 generations (generations 4001-5000) calculated with simulations of neutral mutation with fixed, finite population sizes.

In analyzing the results listed above, we concluded that they have negative implications for the use of mtDNA to infer cladistic relationships, places of origin, and times of divergence. For example, Aggarwal et al. (2003) argue that Indian wolves are of ancient origin, suggesting 1–2 million years ago (ya). Vilà et al. (1997) contend that dogs diverged from wolves 135,000 ya. Wilson et al. (2000) hypothesize that *"DNA profiles of eastern Canadian wolf and the red wolf provide evidence for a common evolutionary history independent of the gray wolf,"* and over a million years ago. How is it that these papers can suggest such ancient origins when theory

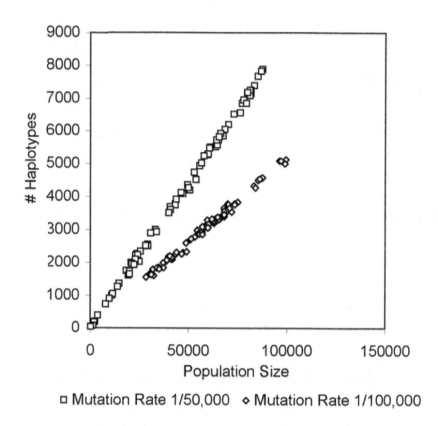

Figure 1.2.5. Number of haplotypes in the population sampled at 100-generation intervals from generation 2,000 to 3,000 during simulations of neutral mutation with variable population sizes.

would predict that all haplotype information is lost within a thousand generations (in the case of wolves, 2,000–3,000 years)?

In another classical example of canid research, Savolainen et al. (2002) claim that since the greatest diversity of mtDNA haplotypes of dogs now exists in East Asia, this must be the area of origin. Similar considerations are employed in human research when Ingman et al. (2000) reason that the higher diversity of mtDNA haplotypes in African populations *provides compelling evidence of a human mtDNA origin in Africa.*" However,

Templeton (1999) has criticized such arguments with the observation that mtDNA diversity within Africa is higher in food-producing groups than in hunter-gatherers. He argues (we think correctly) that differences in genetic diversity in humans are likely to be due to differences in population size and growth rates. More generally, these results may help to explain the reason for some long-debated discrepancies between theoretically predicted and empirically observed levels of heterozygosity (Lewontin 1974; Avise 1994).

In our opinion, the neutral mutation theory is seriously flawed in determining species, phylogenetic relationships, time of divergence, or the place of origin in canids, at least when mtDNA is used to obtain such inference. The best one can glean from these studies is that all the members of the genus *Canis* share haplotypes, indicating that they are simply subspecies of one another. Many biologists, including Darwin, tried to warn us of a commitment to the designation of species (see opening quote). The caveat may still exist. For example, Wilson et al. (2000) and Kyle et al. (2006) wrestle with both a genetic and a morphological solution to the question of species of eastern North American wolves. What the data showed could be that the eastern wolves were not a sexually isolated population, nor were any of the populations that surrounded it: gray wolves, coyotes or red wolves. Indeed the data could illustrate that these are subspecies or races within the genus.

SUBSPECIES, ADAPTATION, CLINES

Mallet (2001) traces the history of taxonomy from Linnaeus to the present, discussing the different motivations for taxonomists to use a trinomial nomenclature (e.g., dog: *Canis lupus* subsp. *familiaris*). A subspecies is a non-random distribution of alleles, geographically based. A subspecies also is a variety (breed, race) within the sexually isolated species, but not in itself sexually isolated from other subspecies.

It is assumed that the observable phenotypic variation in morphology, defined by the allelic distribution, is the result of local adaptations. The

Darwinian belief is that varieties, races, or subspecies are incipient species and are on the path to becoming true and new species. However, such an assumption has not a guaranteed outcome. Richard Goldschmidt (1933, as cited in Gottlieb 1992) selected for allelic differences for 25 years, trying to create a new species, and was never able to produce anything except subspecies, varieties, or races of gypsy moths.

This is not to say that on large continents, subspecies could not become species after separation for thousands of years, or that in some sense sympatric speciation could not happen (see Berlocher & Feder 2002), but rather that it has not been clearly demonstrated. To us, the emergence of dogs surrounded by the ancestral population of wolves might be a good example, but dogs are technically not a new species, and they are not reproductively isolated from the rest of the genus. But, whether considered species or subspecies, they do demonstrate extreme divergence from the genus, obviously derived sympatrically.

There is a tendency for a genus (or a species) such as *Canis* to grade morphologically from one end of its range to another. Many mammalian species tend to grade from large sizes in the northern, polar regions to smaller size in equatorial latitudes. Single genus clines are typical of a number of North American taxa, e.g., the cervids, ovids, bovids, and of course the canids. Each of the locally adapted populations (ecomorphs) of the *Canis* cline has been subdivided into numerous species, subspecies, and geographical races (Brewster & Fritts 1995) which are dwarfed by the sheer numbers of domestic dogs. It is often easier for ecologists to deal with the various ecomorphic forms as if they were species – even if they are not. For example, it would be difficult for us to think of the red wolf, which is often considered as a species, as having been geographically isolated from all other 'species' of *Canis* for some Darwinian time span, and having become a sexually isolated population as a result.

Although the larger members of the genus *Canis* exist in the northern or cooler latitudes, small populations of >20 kg animals can exist as historical remnants of past climatic eras. These relic populations are not different species than the <20 kg morphs that now surround them. There is no need to think of size or coat colour as species specific, or even as adaptive, without other evidence. Such characteristics may have been adapted to an earlier climatic regime and/or simply the result of local founder effects (Geist 1992).

Wolves, meaning populations of *Canis* which are >20 kg, are going extinct in Georgia, Alabama, and northward, and are being replaced by a healthy population of <20 kg *Canis*. The few remaining red wolves are not a different species than the coyotes replacing them, and indeed they breed with them, leaving their genes in a smaller ecomorph. Whatever environmental niche the red wolf morph was adapted to 5,000 years ago continues to change locally. Restoring that morph to its niche (which may no longer exist) might not be possible.Our Simulation of Founder Effects in the Subspecies Problem

Founder effects in geographically dispersed populations can be illustrated with simulations that depend upon various parameters, which were arbitrarily selected here. We modelled animals as marbles that roll around on a tabletop that represents a species niche. The tabletop is initially empty, corresponding to a niche that has recently been opened for colonization, for example by a receding glacier, or some cataclysm that locally wiped out all the previous occupants. Source code for this simulation is available from http://hampshire.edu/lspector/whatwolf under 'The "marbles on a tabletop" simulation (written for the *breve* simulation environment)'.

Each marble is characterized by three genes, each of which has four alleles. For the sake of visualization we map the values of the genes to colour components of the marbles, with the three genes determining the amounts of red, green, and blue. So, for example, if the alleles are labelled [0,1,2,3] and if these map to the amounts of colour [none, a little, a lot, full], then a marble with the genotype "000" would be coloured with no red, no green, and no blue (that is, it would be black), whereas a marble with genotype "102" would be coloured with a little red, no green, and a lot of blue (i.e., it would be dark purple).

Neither the genes nor the colours affect fitness, and both are neutral with respect to selection (neutral mutation theory). Our marbles are not inert, however. The simulation proceeds in small units of time called "time steps" and at each time step, each marble exerts a small random force in a random direction, so that the marbles tend to wander around the niche. Each marble also has a small probability (1/150 in the simulations reported here) of producing offspring. The offspring appears above the parent and usually hits the parent as it falls to the table, with the result that the parent and the offspring roll away from one another.

We explored two conditions of inheritance. In the first condition the offspring's genes are copied from the single parent's genes and each gene is then mutated with a probability of 1/100. Mutation is performed by changing a gene to a randomly chosen allele, which has a 1/4 probability of being the same as the original allele. This corresponds either to asexual reproduction or to single-sex propagation of genetic material, as occurs with mitochondrial DNA. In the second condition we permitted hybridization: a "mate" is chosen randomly from the nearby marbles and each gene is taken (with possible mutation) either from the parent or from the mate, each with a probability of 1/2.

A marble "dies" and is removed from the system if it reaches the age of 250 time steps, and it "ages" an additional 10 time steps each time it collides with another marble. This aging process helps to ensure that the population will spread across the table, since tightly grouped marbles will die more quickly and will therefore produce less offspring. This feature can be considered a model of a simple local resource, open space.

We begin each simulation with a single marble and we observe the dynamics of the system as offspring are produced and the population grows. If all of the marbles die out, which is rare with the parameters that we used except near the start of a simulation, then we start over. We limit the population to 1,000, but in the simulations reported here the populations grew only to about 800 and the limit was never reached.

Early in each simulation one observes a small and nearly homogeneous population with a few individuals having different genotypes that were produced by mutation (Fig. 1.2.6). After a few thousand time steps the population will have spread across the tabletop and several geographically distinct and genetically unique subspecies will be evident (Fig. 1.2.7).

Ecologists have developed a variety of tools with which to measure the emergence of geographically distinct subspecies (for example see Hubbell

Figure 1.2.6. Early snapshot of a "virtual marble" simulation demonstrating founder effects, with colours reduced to shades of gray. A small and nearly homogeneous population can be observed with a few individuals having different genotypes that were produced by mutation.

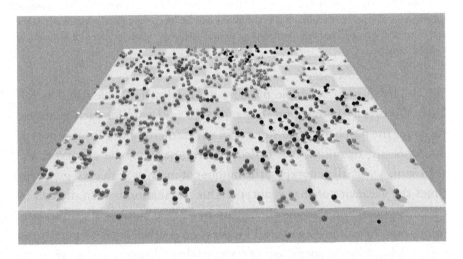

Figure 1.2.7. Later snapshot of a "virtual marble" simulation demonstrating founder effects, with colours reduced to shades of gray. A comparison with Fig. 1.2.6 shows that the population has spread, and subspecies can be identified as geographically and genetically distinct groups of individuals.

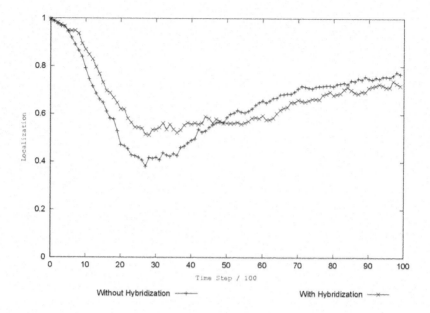

Figure 1.2.8. Localization coefficient values for ten "virtual marble" simulations run for 10,000 time steps (five with hybridization, averaged together, and five without hybridization, averaged together). Localization was initially 1, as the initial founder was geographically localized. At the end of simulations, the marbles, representing individuals, were again localized demonstrating founder effects.

1997). Here we use a simple measure of "localization" calculated as follows. We divide the tabletop into a 10 x 10 grid, and for each genotype we count the number of grid squares in which marbles with that genotype do not occur; this number is called the "vacancies" of the genotype. We then sum, across all genotypes, the number of marbles with each genotype times the vacancies of that genotype. This summation is then divided by the total population size and then again by 99 (the number of grid squares minus one) to produce an overall localization coefficient that ranges from 0 to 1. A localization coefficient of 0 means that all genotypes occur everywhere across the table top, while a localization coefficient of 1 means that each genotype occurs only in one grid square. In general, the localization coefficient can be thought of as the percentage of the territory in which a typical marble's genotype will not be found.

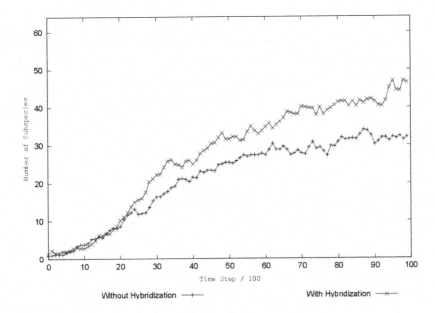

Figure 1.2.9. Numbers of subspecies obtained for ten "virtual marble" simulations run for 10,000 time steps (five with hybridization, averaged together, and five without hybridization, averaged together). Results of Figure 1.2.8 and this figure indicate how geographically distinct subspecies emerge, even without adaptive selection. The hybridization condition produced more subspecies.

We plotted the localization coefficient values of ten simulations (five with hybridization, averaged together, and five without hybridization, averaged together) each of which was run for 10,000 time steps (Fig. 1.2.8). Localization was always initially 1, as the initial founder was perfectly localized. It dropped as the population grew and spread, but it rebounded. At the end of each simulation the approximately 700 marbles were segregated geographically. We also plotted the numbers of subspecies in the same simulations (Fig. 1.2.9). Our primary observation from running these simulations was that geographically distinct subspecies readily emerged, even without adaptive selection of any sort. This has also been shown in human populations (Novembre et al. 2008). Also note that the hybridization condition produced more subspecies in our simulation.

The model illustrates why there can be so many subspecies represented in any population of animals with worldwide distributions such as those of the genus *Canis*. It also illustrates that the gene frequency at any given location is continuously changing in response to population shifts. If the local population does not go to zero, vacancies will be repopulated by individuals that do not represent the entire genetic spectrum of the individuals that are being replaced (founder effects).

HYBRIDIZATION IN NATURE AND PHYLOGENETIC WEBS

> "…[there is] every reason to believe that new species may arise quite suddenly, sometimes by hybridization, sometimes perhaps by other means. Such species do not arise as Darwin thought, by natural selection." – Haldane 1956

> "…most speciation involves natural selection; natural selection requires genetic variation; genetic variation is enhanced by hybridization; and hybridization and introgression between species is a regular occurrence…" – Mallet 2007

Just as the term species gets misused, it is much the same with hybridization. In the classic biological literature, species hybridization is characterized by a karyotypic change. The offspring or the new species is a polyploid or an alloploid of the parent species (Mallet 2007). In the *Canis* literature we tend to use the term hybridization in the agricultural sense of the word, where it is the crossing of races or breeds. In that sense the product is a mongrel but not a new form in the species sense because it never leads to sexual isolation the way karyotypic change does. In the *Canis* literature the term hybrid gets used in the agricultural sense but with the consequences of the biological usage.

For those of us involved in *Canis* conservation, each time two of the presently described "species" hybridize, the fear is that we will lose the "species" with the smallest population. But what is being lost is the pheno-type. The genes of the individual are being passed on. The smaller popula-tion could become unrecognizable phenotypically, but that does not mean they have genetically disappeared.

Coyotes breeding with gray wolves (Mech 1970), and coyotes breeding with red wolves (Nowak & Paradiso 1983) are cases where the authors are concerned that continued hybridization will lead to the demise of the species they are trying to protect and/or restore. Boitani et al. (1995) argue that hybridization between the 200–500 wolves in Italy and the 800,000 stray dogs may be a threat to that recovering wolf population, because of not only genetic contamination, but also competition for resources. Wayne and Koepfli (1996) report that 15% of Simien wolf/jackals contain evidence of hybridization with domestic dogs. Wilson et al. (2000) report that three red wolves, one Algonquin wolf, and four southern Ontario wolves have the same mtDNA haplotype as Texas coyotes. Twenty-five percent of the animals they are trying to differentiate have coyote haplotypes. For Vilà et al. (1997), nearly 20% of their dog breeds have wolf mtDNA. Lehman et al. (1991) found wolves with coyote mtDNA, and Wayne and Jenks (1991) identified "all" their red wolf population as containing coyote and/or grey wolf mtDNA.

Each genetic study of a *Canis* species seems to have to deal with the hybrid problem. In each study there is the *a priori* assumption that their animal is a true species and qualifies for the binomial nomenclature given to them. In each case it is assumed that sharing haplotypes is evidence of hybridization of the "species." However, we propose two different conclu-sions: 1) these are not true species, but rather subspecies of one another, and/or 2) the various methodologies cannot discriminate between them. As subspecies the expectation is that they will have a gene flow between them. In the true agricultural sense of the word hybrid there will be inter-breeding between the various races, breeds, varieties, and subspecies of the species. And because they are hybridizing, the ability of neutral mutation theory to discriminate between them is impossible. In addition, as in our diagram on skull shapes (Fig. 1.2.1), cladistic mitochondrial relationships may not be evidence of phylogenetic relationships, but rather of local founder effects.

Lorenzini and Fico (1995) cited several works of Boitani and his colleagues in Italy, who *"consider the interbreeding with domestic dogs one of the major threats to the integrity of the gene pool of the Italian wolf."* At a canid conference, one reporter outlined a project that was designed to keep red wolves pure (Adams et al. 2001). The founding red wolves in the recovery program were genotyped using microsatellite loci, so that wildlife managers will be able to sample the recovering population and weed out any red wolf offspring that show coyote or dog mtDNA. A similar approach has been proposed for the Ethiopian highlands, to neuter local dogs and reduce the flow of genes to the Ethiopian wolves (Laurenson et al. 1997).

However, there is a growing literature that suggests that hybridization might be a major source of genetic variation in nature (Reyer 2008). In fact, right from the beginning of Darwin's theory of transmutation of species by natural selection, critics argued that natural selection would decrease the variation from which further selection would proceed (Mivart 1871). The argument that natural selection decreases phenotypic variability – Darwin's theory is based on phenotypic variability – persisted until the twentieth century discovery of genes and then gene mutation. The increase in genetic variability comes from two sources – recombination and chance mutation. Hybridization maximizes recombination.

Lewontin and Birch (1966) suggest that hybridization is a major source of variation for adaptation to new environments. (New environments can be changing environments.) Haldane (1956) goes further in suggesting that hybridization can be a source of new species. Mallet (2007) concludes that *"hybridization can contribute to adaptive radiations..."*. (An adaptive radiation is a rapid evolutionary process characterized by an increase in the morphological and ecological diversity of a single, diversifying lineage.) Coppinger and Coppinger (2001) suggest that hybridization is a way to create forms that are phylogenetically bizarre. Almost all of our modern breeds of dogs in their most divergent forms are creations of sub-specific hybridization. Arnold (1997) summarizes a large literature on natural hybridization, giving many examples from the literature on plant, insect,

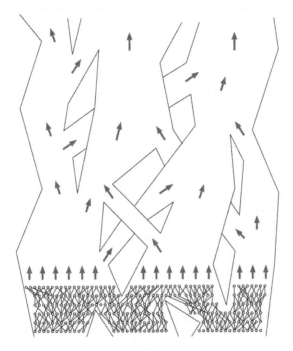

Figure 1.2.10. Schematic, conceptual diagram illustrating a potential phylogeny of a taxon, the genus *Canis* for example. Lines represent apparent boundaries between species; lines connecting circles (individuals) represent family trees from one generation to the next (time progresses upward); arrows represent family trees diverging into separate species or converging into lumping species.

lizard, mammal (coyote, wolf), and bird hybridization. Most important, he attacks the philosophical notion originated by Darwin and promoted by Mayr (1982) and others that hybrids must always be irrelevant to evolution. In fact, Arons and Shoemaker (1992) demonstrate the idea of novel phenotype as a product of hybridization.

In any restoration program, the success or failure is partly the ability of the restored animals to adapt to the habitat. The population being restored is small or rare, meaning a small gene pool and founder effects. Hybridization may increase the individual's fitness and create novel behaviour patterns, which allow for novel adaptation to new habitats (Arnold 1997; Doolittle 2005). Since hybridizing processes are occurring naturally in the genus *Canis*, it could prove counter-productive to their genetic survival to try to further isolate them from diversifying through hybridization with peripheral (and successful) forms (Kyle et al. 2006).

Once one realizes that existing "species" can swap genetic material and use that material in adaptive ways, the idea of a phylogenetic tree may become obsolete (Doolittle 2005). For those of us trying to understand the evolution of the various forms within the genus *Canis*, it all of a sudden becomes clear why constructing cladograms and phylogenetic trees is so difficult. These organisms are sharing genetic material and probably have for the last 5 million years. Within the genus very little radiation has taken place. They change size constantly, but essentially the phenotype is very conservative (Radinsky 1981). In fact, the various forms of *Canis* may not be monophyletic species as is indicated in our Fig. 1.2.10.

CONSERVATION MANAGEMENT

The genus *Canis* presently is divided into seven or eight species. All were named before Darwin's theory of evolution. The now-designated species do not come up to the criteria of species designation for sexually isolated populations. The members of the genus *Canis* are karyotypically identical and they interbreed, producing viable offspring in the wild. Morphometric measurements indicate phenotypic differences, but those differences rarely are indicators of species differences. Genetic studies have shown a gene flow between existing populations and species.

From the point of view of conservation management, *Canis* could be recognized as subspecies. Restoration programs could encourage viable populations of the genus *Canis* in the habitats they wish to restore. From a practical point of view, if there is still the wish to call these populations wolves, or red wolves, or Algonquin wolves (see above), for popular or political reasons, then so be it. Subspecies may be protected too, as it is exemplified by the Endangered Species Act in the U.S.

Hybrids may be classified as good subspecies and should not be necessarily discriminated against in conservation programs. Experimental evidence using mtDNA and cladistic statistics models demostrate that gene flow is constant and "pure" species are wishful thinking. In *Canis*, hybridization may increase genetic variability and in some instances create phenotypic novelties. Thus, hybridization should not be artificially prevented in restoration programs. Small populations of animals need genetic diversity for adaptation to occur. They also need genetic diversity to avoid deleterious bottlenecks that are the inevitable result of the restriction of gene flow.

The five noted biologists who are quoted at the tops of sections in this chapter were unencumbered during their years of investigation by the need to determine how a species should – or must – be preserved. In fact, they understood that the binomials and trinomials existed only as convenient labels, abstract concepts, approximations of reality. The species of the genus *Canis* in the world are the results of standing before Haldane's (1932) "tribunal of natural selection." The wolf – in whatever morphological or genetic phenotypes it has achieved – has maintained its Aristotelian essence in spite of our management.

ACKNOWLEDGMENTS

This material is based upon work supported by the United States National Science Foundation under Grant No. 0308540 and Grant No. 0216344 to L.S. Any opinions, findings, and conclusions or recommendations expressed in this publication are those of the authors and do not necessarily reflect the views of the National Science Foundation. Thanks are due to Lorna Coppinger for technical and creative editing.

1.3 Wolf Community Ecology: Ecosystem Effects of Recovering Wolves in Banff and Yellowstone National Parks

Mark Hebblewhite and Doug W. Smith

INTRODUCTION

Community ecology is the study of interactions between species in a food web in a particular ecosystem. Early community ecology studies were often descriptive and focused on detailing how species interacted with each other. Within the last few decades community ecology has shifted to a more experimental nature, especially in aquatic systems that were amenable to experimentation or natural perturbations (Paine 1969; Carpenter et al. 1985; Estes et al. 2004). Through experiments, researchers showed the counterintuitive effects of species changes on the structure of entire food-webs. For example, the freshwater lake experiments of Carpenter (1985) showed dramatic effects of predator exclusion on whole-lake ecology. And the now famous examples of sea-star (*Pisaster* spp.) exclusion on community structure led to the concept of a keystone species (Paine 1969). Similarly, Estes and Duggins' (1995) work on sea otter (*Enhydra lutra*)–sea urchin (*Strongylocentrotus* spp.)–kelp forests revealed an order of magnitude release in sea urchin density following otter removal. Anthony et al. (2008) demonstrated how such food-web pathways could affect up to five species and also link one apex predator (sea otter) to another (Bald Eagle, *Haliaeetus leucocephalus*). These studies confirmed that predators

69

can have strong community impacts beyond the species they directly prey upon. Progress in ecology regarding the impacts of predators in terrestrial systems has been slower, however, perhaps because of greater experimental difficulties (Minta et al. 1999; Schmitz et al. 2000), or a more auteco-logical focus.

The recovery of wolves (*Canis lupus*) throughout North America (Bangs & Fritts 1996) has prompted an interest in the ecosystem effects of wolves on terrestrial communities. Unfortunately, wolf research can provide little direct guidance for predicting community impacts because of an historic focus on autecological questions (sociality, reproduction) or predator-prey dynamics (e.g., Ballard et al. 2003). A quick review of the literature reveals that before wolf reintroduction to YNP in 1995, few studies outside of Isle Royale tested wolves' ecological role in ecosystems, and those that did focused almost exclusively on ungulates. The keen interest in ungulates arose primarily from hunting management concerns, not ecological. And while debate still swirls around whether wolves limit or regulate ungulate prey (*sensu* Sinclair 1989), a consensus seems to be emerging that wolf preda-tion, especially in concert with predation by other species (bears, humans), can limit and regulate ungulates such as moose (*Alces alces*) to low densities (Gasaway et al. 1992; Messier 1994; Hayes et al. 2003). Whether wolves can exert the same influence on elk (*Cervus elaphus*) appears to vary among systems, from uncertain or weak effects (Vucetich et al. 2005) to strong top-down limitation and regulation to low densities (Jedrzejewski et al. 2002; Hebblewhite et al. 2005).

If wolves can exert such strong impacts on prey, they should exert strong top-down forces on the entire community (Polis et al. 2000). Ac-cording to Hairston et al.'s (1960) green-world hypothesis, a world with wolves should be green. The scant evidence for terrestrial trophic cascades linked to wolf predation is weaker than marine systems, however, perhaps because of food web complexity, prey digestibility, and other negative feed-backs to predation efficiency (Polis & Strong 1996; Schmitz et al. 2000; Shurin et al. 2002; Tessier and Woodruff 2002; Schmitz 2006). Evidence has also been slower to accumulate because of the difficulty of conducting well-controlled experiments in wolf-prey systems (Boutin 1992). Regardless of the interest in trophic cascades, they are only one type of possible inter-action within terrestrial communities following wolf recovery (Estes et al. 2004). For example, trophic cascades can arise because of the avoidance of predation by prey species (Schmitz et al. 1997), and indirect interactions, such as competition, can occur between species.

Thus, the main objectives of this chapter are twofold. First, we provide a brief review of key community ecology concepts to provide a framework for understanding the types of food-web interactions that might be altered following wolf recovery. Second, we review evidence for the ecosystem impact of wolves through trophic interactions drawing on two case studies: one in Banff National Park (BNP), where wolves naturally recolonized the system in the mid-1980s (Paquet et al. 1996), and the second in Yellow-stone National Park (YNP), where wolves were reintroduced in 1995 and 1996 (Bangs & Fritts 1996). We rely on the results of previously published studies and provide new data on species interactions from both case studies where possible. We also take advantage of differing experimental designs in the two case studies, a pseudo-experimental design in BNP, and a time-series approach in YNP, to draw attention to problems facing the study of wolf effects in ecosystems. Finally, we draw comparisons between the ecosystem effects of wolves in the two study areas, and other systems, and conclude by making recommendations for future studies of wolf commun-ity ecology.

WOLF COMMUNITY ECOLOGY

The first comprehensive theory of food-web dynamics recognized the critical role for predation in structuring ecosystems (Oksanen et al. 1981; Fretwell 1987), building on the seminal work of Hairston et al. (1960). In the green-world hypothesis of Hairston et al. (1960), top-down control by predators on herbivore density results in increased plant biomass. Pre-dictions of the trophic cascade hypothesis are alternating correlations in abundance between trophic levels (Paine 1969; Fretwell 1987), which were coined 'trophic' cascades. Figure 1.3.1a represents hypothesized conditions

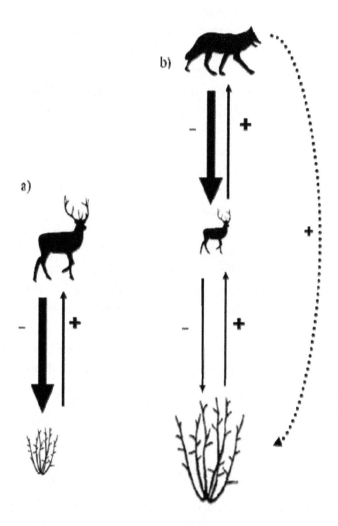

Figure 1.3.1. Simplified three trophic level model a) and b) after wolf recolonization given a strong trophic cascade effect of wolf predation on herbivore (elk) populations showing direct effects (solid lines) between trophic levels and their strength by thickness. Dashed lines indicate an indirect effect of wolves on plants. The trophic cascade hypothesis is tested by comparing the strength of wolves experimentally between systems without (a) and with (b) wolves, the effect of wolves can be determined on herbivore abundance (predicted negative effect) and on plants (predicted positive effect).

before wolf recovery, where herbivore density, released from predation by wolves, increases and herbivory subsequently reduces plant biomass. Following wolf recolonization in Figure 1.3.1b, predation causes a top-down trophic cascade with declining herbivore density, releasing plant biomass from herbivory. Distinguishing between *direct* effects and *indirect* effects between species is important in this simplified food-web model (Estes et al. 2004). Direct effects occur when there are no intermediary species between two interacting species, for example, through predation (or herbivory). Indirect effects are mediated by an intermediate species, such as the indirect effect of wolves on plants mediated by wolf-caused changes to herbivore density in Figure 1.3.1b.

Indirect effects of predation can also arise because of behavioural changes by herbivores in addition to direct effects of predation on herbivores. In a well-known test of these 'behaviourally-mediated' indirect effects, grasshoppers showed behavioural avoidance of spiders that were rendered experimentally ineffectual predators. Yet presence of these ineffectual spiders still resulted in a 40% grasshopper population reduction, compared with 70% reduction in the control with effective spider predators (Schmitz et al. 2000). These exciting results prompted a host of studies examining behaviourally mediated indirect effects in terrestrial systems, including areas recently recolonized by wolves (Fortin et al. 2005). Unfortunately, whether the results of small-scale experimental treatments can scale up to large-scale community dynamics remains unknown (Schmitz 2005). It seems certain, however, that indirect effects will interact following wolf recolonization to reshape terrestrial ecosystems.

Effects of wolves will go far beyond trophic cascades, however (Estes et al. 2004). Perhaps the most important non-predation form of direct interaction is competition, where at least one of two (or more) interacting species has negative effects on the other species (Fig. 1.3.2, H1 and H2). Three main forms of competition are recognized in community ecology (Holt 1977): *interference* competition, where two species on the same trophic level kill, but do not consume, each other; *exploitative* direct food competition, where two species consume the same resources; and predator-mediated *apparent* competition, whereby two prey species share a common

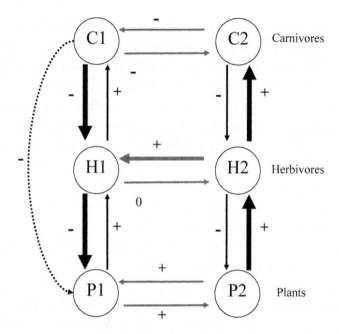

Figure 1.3.2. Three trophic level food web illustrating direct (solid) and indirect (dashed) interactions between carnivores, herbivores, and plants. Predation and other direct interactions are discriminated by black and gray lines, respectively. Direction and sign of the arrow indicates a benefit (+) or reduction (-) for the species at the arrow terminus, arrow width indicates effect strength. The left side of the figure shows a top-down trophic cascade, whereas the right side illustrates stronger bottom-up effects of plants on food-web structure. Interactions with both a + and - between consumer and resource represent predation (e.g., between P1 and H1), a + and + mutualism (P1 and P2), a – and 0 exploitative competition (H1 and H2), and a – and – competition (P1 and P2). Commensalism (+ and 0) is not shown. Finally, the dashed line between C1 and P1 illustrates an indirect effect of carnivores on plant density. Note for simplicity only some direct and one indirect effect is shown, but the number of indirect effects are far greater than direct effects.

predator species (Fig. 1.3.2). Note that only interference competition is a direct effect; exploitative and apparent competition are indirect effects mediated by a shared food or predator. Another form of indirect interaction is mutualism, where both species benefit from an interaction (e.g., cowbirds (*Molothrus ater*) on bison (*Bison bison*)). An even rarer form of species interaction is commensalism, whereby one species benefits without costing or benefiting another (Fig. 1.3.2). Scavenging is an important indirect interaction mediated by (in this case) wolf-killed ungulates (Vu-cetich et al. 2004; Wilmers et al. 2003; Stahler et al. 2002). Scavenging can either be a form of indirect competition or commensalism, based on the strength of the indirect interactions between the carnivore (+ effect on scavengers) and scavenger (– effect on predator, e.g., (Vucetich et al. 2004)). Recent reviews have reminded ecologists that direct effects are but a fraction of the potential species interactions possible in even a simple food-web (Bascompte et al. 2005; Estes et al., 2004). For example, in Fig. 1.3.2, the total number of direct interactions between the six species is 30, whereas the number of indirect species interactions is 1,920! (see (Estes et al. 2004) for calculations). Thus, the focus to date on trophic cascades in wolf systems seems almost myopic, and will surely be eclipsed in the future by studies of the indirect effects of wolves.

WOLF COMMUNITY ECOLOGY CASE STUDIES

We now explore community impacts of wolves in two ecosystems: Banff and Yellowstone National Parks. We provide background information for each study area, review the history of wolves and scientific methods, and review the ecosystem effects of wolves in both examples.

Case study 1: Banff National Park

Study area description

Banff National Park (BNP) is Canada's oldest National Park, established in 1886. It is 6641 km^2 in area, and lies on the eastern slope of the Canadian Rocky Mountains (51°15' / 116°30') where topography is extreme (1400 m to 3400 m) and valleys narrow (2–5 km). Climate is characterized by long, cold winters with infrequent warm weather caused by Chinook winds, and short, relatively dry summers. Most studies of wolf community effects oc-curred in low elevation winter elk range in the Bow Valley, one of the most important winter ranges for ungulates in BNP (Hebblewhite et al. 2002). Mean snow pack depth was 43 cm but increased in side valleys and higher elevations. Two towns (≤ 10,000 people), the national railway and highway, secondary roads, and human developments fragment the study area. More than 5 million visitors use the Bow Valley annually, and this high level of human activity arguably may influence all ecosystem effects of wolves reviewed here. Vegetation is dominated by coniferous stands of lodgepole pine (*Pinus contorta*), Engelmann spruce (*Picea englemanni*), and subalpine fir (*Abies lasiocarpa*) stands grading into alpine meadows at elevations above 2200 m. Grassland, riparian, and deciduous trembling aspen (*Populus tremuloides*) communities are rare but critical vegetation communities for biodiversity (Holland & Coen 1983). Riparian willow communities are dominated by *Salix maccalliana*, *S. planifolia*, *S. bebbiana*, and *S. commutate* (Holroyd & Van Tighem 1983).

Wolves coexist in a diverse large carnivore guild of seven species: cougars (*Felis concolor*), coyotes (*Canis latrans*), grizzly bears (*Ursus arctos*), black bears (*Ursus americanus*), lynx (*Lynx lynx*), and wolverine (*Gulo gulo*). Red fox (*Vulpes vulpes*) and bobcat (*Lynx rufus*) are uncommon and not considered here. Humans are the eighth large carnivore (Kay 1994) because of transboundary hunting and other human-caused mortality. Wolves' number approximately 35–40 in BNP during winter (Hebblewhite 2006) and grizzly bears number approximately 65–70 (Herrero 2005). Little is known of cougar, coyote, lynx, wolverine, or black bear density, although approximate Parks Canada estimates place numbers of black bears at 50, coyotes at 100–200, and wolverines at 25. Rough estimates of cougar density near BNP are ~10/1000km² (Kortello 2005). Thus, approximate predator densities for BNP are 60–70 carnivores/1000km².

Seven species of large ungulates are available to wolves in BNP: elk, white-tailed deer (*Odocoileus virginianus*), moose, mule deer (*O. hemionus*), bighorn sheep (*Ovis canadensis*), mountain goat (*Oreamnos americanus*), and a small (5-8) threatened population of woodland caribou (*Rangifer tarandus*); bison are extirpated. Elk are the most abundant ungulate in BNP, and comprise 40–70% of the diet of wolves (Huggard 1993b; Paquet et al. 1996). Elk exist in three main elk herds in BNP and between 1985 and

2005 numbered 1000–3500 during summer (Hebblewhite 2006; BNP, unpublished data). The largest of these three elk herds, the Ya Ha Tinda herd, migrates outside of BNP during winter and numbers between 800 and 2200 elk (Hebblewhite et al. 2006). The other two elk herds winter in BNP. Mule and white-tailed deer occur at low density, where moose, bighorn sheep, and mountain goats are rare and spatially separated from wolves in winter (Holroyd & Van Tighem 1983). Moose populations are estimated to be 50–60 (Hurd 1999), bighorn sheep approximately 1500–2500, and mountain goat 50–100 (BNP, unpublished data). Estimates for mule and white-tailed deer are unavailable. Thus, rough densities of ungulate prey in BNP during our study were ~600–700/1000km². See Hebblewhite et al. (2002) for a detailed description of the study area.

Wolf recolonization and experimental design

Wolves recolonized BNP via dispersal from populations to the north in the early 1980s (Paquet 1993). In 1985, they denned for the first time in 30 years in the Bow Valley. Wolf numbers in BNP quickly grew to a peak of ~60 wolves around 1992, and has been subsequently stable at approximately 35 wolves (Hebblewhite 2006). In the Bow Valley, numbers peaked around 24 in 1995, and then declined to 4–6 wolves in 2005. High human activity surrounding the townsite of Banff displaced habitat use by wolves from an approximately 43-km² area (Paquet et al. 1996; Hebblewhite et al. 2002). While other carnivores such as grizzly bears and cougars were also displaced, neither was extirpated. Thus, the recolonization of wolves represented the major ecological perturbation to this system. This perturbation enabled the study of the effects of wolf predation in areas of high human activity (low wolf use) and 'control' (high wolf use) areas outside of the zone of influence of the high human activity (Hebblewhite et al. 2002). The study design in BNP approximated a before-after-control-impact (BACI) design (Minta et al. 1999). Because of this natural experimental design, Hebblewhite et al. (2005) tested for effects of wolf exclusion using the log-response ratio (Schmitz et al. 2000). The log-response ratio is log (X_{p+}/X_{p}) where X_{p+} is the variable of interest (elk density) in the high wolf density area, and X_{p-} is the area in the 'experimental' low predator density area (Osenberg et al. 1997; Shurin et al. 2002). Log-response ratios have the statistically attractive feature of proportional correspondence to changes in population size, irrespective of variation in abundance (Osenberg et al. 1997). Variance in log-response ratio is calculated following Hedges et al. (1999). Thus, predictions of a trophic cascade are significant negative responses by herbivore density to presence of predators and positive responses to predators at the plant level (Fig. 1.3.1). Drawn from the community ecology literature, the use of log-response ratios is most appropriate in experimental predator manipulation experiments, and reporting of them aids meta-analyses of community-level impacts (Schmitz et al. 2000; Shurin et al. 2002).

BNP research methods

Collaborative research was essential. Studies of predators and ungulate prey relied on radio-telemetry during 1985–2005. Wolves, cougars, and grizzly bears were intensively studied via telemetry during the study period. Wolves, cougars and grizzlies were captured using foothold traps, Aldrich foot snares, hounds (cougars), or aerial darting or net gunning (Hebblewhite et al. 2004; Herrero 2005; Kortello et al. 2007). Captured animals were outfitted with VHF, or more recently, GPS collars. Collared wolves were used to study predation by entire wolf packs, and the main packs inhabiting the Bow Valley study area have been collared since 1985 (Paquet et al. 1996). Winter wolf-kill rates were estimated using snow backtracking methods during 1986–2000 following Hebblewhite et al. (2004). Snow tracking and GPS-location analysis methods were used to study wolf-cougar interactions (Kortello et al. 2007) during 2001–2004. Observations of wolf-grizzly interactions were recorded during aerial and ground telemetry during 1989–1996 (following methods of Paquet 1993; Herrero 2005). Wolf-coyote interactions were not studied. Of the seven species of ungulates, only elk, moose, and caribou have been the subject of research regarding effects of wolves. Ungulates were captured and handled using aerial darting or net gunning, ground darting, and corral trapping, and radio-collared with VHF or GPS collars. Effects of wolf predation on elk were the subject of two main radio-telemetry studies; one early (1984–1986) (Woods 1991) and one late (1997–2000, McKenzie 2001; Hebblewhite et al. 2005) in wolf recolonization. Hurd (1999) studied recruitment, and cause-specific mortality of radio-collared moose, as well as exploitative competition between moose and elk using extensive pellet surveys, fecal diet analyses, and analyses of spatial overlap. While no field studies have examined elk-caribou apparent competition, Hebblewhite et al. (2007) used a modelling approach to examine wolf-elk-caribou dynamics (Hebblewhite et al. 2007). Studies of vegetation response to wolf recolonization focused on aspen and willow, and measured indices of plant damage (browse) and gross and net primary productivity or recruitment (net current annual growth, CAG, or sapling density, Nietvelt 2001; White 2001; White et al. 2003) in plots located in areas with and without wolves.

Direct effects

PREDATION AND TROPHIC CASCADES

Hebblewhite et al. (2005) compared adult female elk survival and recruitment between the low and high wolf areas during 1997–2000 to test the trophic cascade hypothesis. To this comparison we add adult female survival and calf recruitment rates from Woods (1991) during the first two years wolves recolonized the Bow Valley (1984–1986) for a before-after-control impact (BACI) comparison. Survival modelling methods for the two study periods were similar, as were spring calf recruitment surveys (Woods 1991; McKenzie 2001). Adult female survival and calf recruitment from the low- and high-wolf areas were compared for elk for these two periods, and population growth rates (lambda, λ) were estimated following Hatter and Bergerud (1991). We tested for differences in wolf-caused mortality using chi-square tests, and analysis of chi-square residuals to test for differences in wolf-related mortality (Haberman 1973). During early wolf recolonization, elk mortality was mainly human-caused, with only 16% of mortality caused by wolves (Table 1.3.1). Adult survival and recruitment rates were high (0.90, Fig. 1.3.3b), resulting in a 20%

population growth rate. However, after wolf recolonization, adult survival had declined by 30% and calf recruitment was 40% less than before wolf recolonization (Table 1.3.1, also Fig. 1.3.3b), causing rapid population decline. However, in the low-wolf (control) area, survival, recruitment and population growth rate were identical to before wolves (Table 1.3.1, Fig. 1.3.3b). The main difference in survival was attributed to a tripling of mortality by wolves after wolf recolonization in the high-wolf area, from ~16% to 56% (Table 1.3.1). A chi-square test of the combined before and control (which were not significantly different) vs. the after mortality causes confirmed mortality was different between the pre/low and high wolf areas ($X^2_{df=14}$=27.1, P=0.021), which was driven by the residual difference of only wolf-caused mortality (P=0.03). Higher wolf-caused mortality was entirely consistent with the 3-times higher wolf-kill rate of elk in the high wolf area (Fig. 1.3.3a). This BACI comparison further strengthens inferences that wolves caused elk populations to decline (and hence caused the trophic cascade) (Table 1.3.4).

These strong differences in mortality and demography in BNP lead to an order of magnitude lower elk density in the high-wolf zone (Fig. 1.3.3c, Table 1.3.4). Certainly, other variables influenced population growth rate of elk, including climatic variation (Hebblewhite et al. 2005). In multivariate analyses between the low and high-wolf areas, Hebblewhite (2005) showed the combination of wolf predation and winter severity reduced elk, not human caused mortality or other factors. The comparison between zones strengthened the usually weak correlative inferences possible from time series studies because winter severity had no impact in the areas without wolves. Thus, in BNP, it seems clear that recolonization of wolves reduced elk well below their pre-wolf abundance.

Table 1.3.1. Comparative demography of elk and moose in the Bow Valley of Banff National Park, Alberta, Canada, before (1984-87) and after (1994-1999) recolonization by wolves. Percent mortality causes, adult female survival (with SE), calf recruitment (SE), and population growth rate (lambda) are reported for each study.

	Elk pre-wolf 1984-87	Elk high-wolf 1997–99	Elk low-wolf 1997-99	Moose high-wolf 1994-96
n collars, # radio-years	33, 72	17, 40	28, 45	45, 82
Mortality Causes	%	%	%	%
Wolf	0.18	0.56	0.14	0.56
Grizzly	0.00	0.00	0.00	0.07
Cougar	0.00	0.11	0.14	0.00
Parasites/Disease	0.12	0.00	0.00	0.15
Other	0.18	0.11	0.29	0.07
Human – highway	0.29	0.11	0.29	0.07
Human – railway	0.18	0.11	0.14	0.00
Human – hunting	0.06	0.00	0.00	0.07
Total Mortalities	17	9	7	27
Adult female survival (SE)	0.9 (0.05)	0.62 (0.06)	0.89 (0.06)	0.71[c] (0.03)
Calf recruitment (SE)	0.26[a] (0.02)	0.15[b] (0.02)	0.27[b] (0.016)	0.23[c] (0.075)
Lambda[d]	1.21	0.73	1.23	0.92

a – Pre-wolf elk recruitment averaged over 5 years (Woods 1991).

b – Elk recruitment during 1997-99 is the 14-year average including the pre-wolf period (Hebblewhite et al. 2005).

c – Adult moose survival did not differ between sexes; recruitment was an average of 3 years with a SE calculated assuming binomial confidence intervals (Hurd 1999).

d – Lambda calculated using the approximation of Hatter and Bergerud (1991).

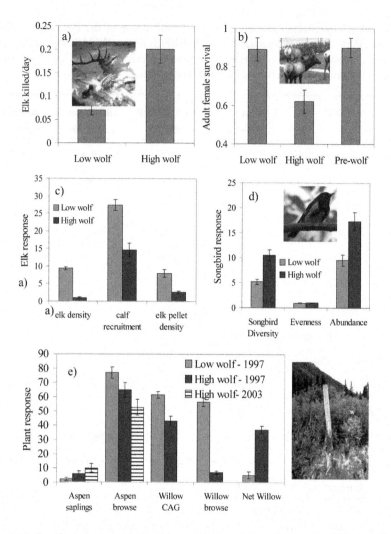

Figure 1.3.3. Pseudo-experimental test of the trophic cascade hypothesis in Banff National Park, Alberta, Canada, comparing areas with low and high wolf density (adapted from Hebblewhite et al. 2005) for differences in; a) wolf kill-rate of elk, b) adult female elk survival rates pre-wolf as well as the low and high wolf areas (see also Table 1.3.1), c) elk density, calf recruitment and elk density, d) songbird diversity, evenness and abundance, and e) aspen sapling density and browse intensity as well as willow current annual growth (CAG), browse %, and net willow production. For aspen, sapling density and browse intensity data from 2003 is also shown in e). All comparisons were statistically different except aspen sapling and browse rates between 1997 low and high areas; however, by 2003 aspen browse and sapling recruitment were statistically different than in 1997. See text for details.

Table 1.3.2. Response predicted by trophic cascade hypothesis for wildlife species following wolf reintroduction to YNP. A naïve log-response ratio [log (X_{p+}/X_{p-})] analysis of wildlife species response to wolves before $(X_{p-}$, 1985– 1995) and after wolf recovery $(X_{p+}$, 1995–2005) is shown for illustrative and discussion purposes.

Species	Predicted response	Log$(X_e/X_c)^a$	SE	P-value	'Wolf' effect	Consistent?
Elk	Reduce	-0.175	0.037	P<0.01*	Reduce	Yes
Bison	Increase	+0.020	0.010	P>0.7	None	---
Mule deer	Increase	+0.001	0.003	P>0.5	None	---
Pronghorn	Increase	-0.369	0.025	P<0.001*	Reduce	No
Bighorn	Unknown	+0.017	0.159	P>0.50	None	---
Coyote[b]	Reduce	-0.211	0.042	P<0.05*	Reduce	Yes
Cougar	Reduce	+0.242	0.006	P<0.01*	Increase	No
Grizzly bear	Unk/Reduce	+0.239	0.004	P<0.01*	Increase	No
Songbirds	Increase	+0.017	0.021	P>0.15	None	No

Log-response ratios were calculated using the mean of the time-series for each pre- and post-wolf period (see text for details). Positive log response ratio's indicate wolf recovery increased abundance, whereas negative ratio's indicate increased abundance.

Table 1.3.3. Riparian songbird abundance, species richness and diversity in willow sites that were completely protected from herbivory, sites that were recently released from herbivory, and sites with no recent growth under heavy herbivory in Yellowstone National Park (YNP), 2003. The log response ratio X_{p+}/X_{p-} of released (X_{p+}) to suppressed (X_{p-}) sites is also shown for comparison.

	Protected Sites Willow (SE)	Released Sites Recent Willow Growth (SE)	Suppressed Sites No Recent Growth (SE)	P Value	Log response ratio
Mean # Birds	12.2 (0.9510)	12.6 (0.7546)	9.6 (0.6602)	0.016	+0.12[a]
Richness	6.9 (0.5232)	6.3 (0.3293)	4.8 (0.3717)	0.0013	+0.16[a]
Shannon index	1.7 (0.1203)	1.7 (0.0513)	1.3 (0.0886)	0.004	+0.12[a]

All response ratios are statistically different than 0, P<0.05.

Table 1.3.4. Comparison of effects of wolves on elk and plants in BNP and YNP using log-response ratios [log (X_{p+}/X_{p-})].

	BNP	YNP
Elk	-0.99	-0.175
Coyote	N/A	-0.211
Willow songbird diversity	0.31	0.12
Willow songbird abundance	0.26	0.12
Aspen – 1997	0.42	0.06
Aspen – 2003	0.64	N/A
Willow (general)	0.87	0.33
Willow species #2	N/A	0.19

Sources are Hebblewhite et al. (2005) for BNP and aspen data presented herein: for YNP, Table 7 for elk, coyote, Table 4 for songbirds, Ripple et al. (2001) for aspen, and Beyer (2006) for the two willow species. N/A refers to not applicable or available.

Behaviourally mediated cascades

Although elk showed fidelity to low- and high-wolf zones during these studies, some adaptive movement between zones occurred following a risk-sensitive forage strategy (McKenzie 2001). However, while few direct studies tested for behaviourally mediated foraging strategies in BNP, several lines of evidence support this interpretation. McKenzie (2001) found that even the most habituated urban elk still spent about 15–25% of their time foraging in the areas near the urban refuge surrounding the town of Banff. Indeed, this is where all predator mortality for low-wolf elk occurred (Table 1.3.1). Furthermore, Kloppers et al. (2005) found that elk were closer to refuge areas when wolf activity was higher, but up to 2 km distant when wolf activity was zero. Huggard (1993b) also found elk recently attacked by wolves fled much more readily than elk that were not attacked by wolves within the past week (elk flight response of 57.1m before vs. 104.1m after). These observations suggest that behaviourally mediated effects occurred in BNP, although their population-level impacts on elk are unknown.

We review previous studies and provide new evidence for interspecific competition between wolves and cougars in BNP. It is important to note that wolf-cougar interactions were studied only late in recolonization (2000–2004), which may have missed different dynamics early in wolf recolonization. First, we estimated the rate at which two wolf packs usurped cougar kills during one winter (2000/01) using the methods of Hebblewhite et al. (2004) by backtracking wolves in snow. Two wolf packs were monitored for 93 and 111 days out of a 185-day winter period. Wolves in the two packs scavenged 0.032 (±0.006 95% CI) and 0.009 (+0.0001) kills per day from cougars, or 5.7 and 1.6 cougar kills per winter by these two packs. During this same period, cougars scavenged no wolf kills. These results were confirmed in more detail by Kortello et al. (2007), who studied multi-scale interactions between wolves and cougars during 2001–2004. In terms of habitat use, Kortello et al. (2007) found cougars consistently avoided wolves at fine spatial scales. At kill sites, cougars never usurped wolf kills (n=152), but wolves usurped 12% of all cougar kills, scavenged 25% of all cougar kills, and cougars scavenged wolf kills only 4% of the time. In terms of total predation impact, Kortello et al. (2007) found wolves were removing 16–21% of the elk population vs. cougars who removed 1–4%, confirming an asymmetry of competitive ability. And during elk population declines (caused in part by wolves), cougars switched their diet from 70% elk in 2000/01 to 70% mule deer and bighorn sheep in 2003/04. This switch occurred one year before wolves switched following elk declines, further suggesting asymmetric competitive ability. We expanded this diet analysis by examining 389 wolf-killed and 70 cougar-killed prey located from 1987 to 2000 following methods of Huggard (1993c) and Hebblewhite et al. (2004). Cougars killed significantly more bighorn sheep and deer than wolves, who killed more elk (Fig. 1.3.4, overall $\chi^2_{(d.f.=5)}$ = 467.1, p<0.00001; elk, sheep, and deer were significantly different). Finally, Kortello (2005) documented 17% of collared cougar mortality (one of six deaths) were caused by wolves (i.e., direct interference competition), and starvation as a cause of death in at least two of the other mortalities. Based

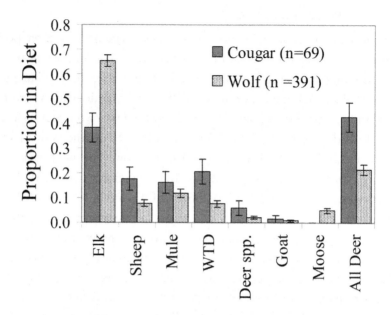

Figure 1.3.4. Proportion (+/–1 S.E.) of prey species killed by wolves and cougars during the winter in the Bow River Valley and tributaries from 1987/87 to 1999/00. Prey species composition differs by species ($\chi^2_{(d.f.=5)}$ = 467.1, p<0.00001).

on these studies, wolf recolonization in BNP negatively affected cougars asymmetrically through both interference competition (direct mortality) and exploitative competition through kleptoparasitism by wolves of cougar kills. Cougars appeared to respond by shifting their diet from elk to deer and sheep.

In terms of wolf-grizzly competition, 35 observations of interactions at carcasses of large ungulate prey were recorded in BNP and the surrounding region during 1989–1996 (7 ground, 28 aerial; P. C. Paquet, unpublished data). Out of these observations of conflicts for possession of carcasses, the following outcomes were observed: three (9%) cases where wolves killed cubs (interference competition) with no attack observed on the female; 19 (54%) cases of wolves successfully usurping kills made by single bears (the sex of which was unknown); 6 (17%) adult bears pushing packs of <4 wolves off wolf-killed carcasses (larger wolf packs were never pushed off);

3 (9%) cases of carcass defence by wolves where bears were intercepted at a distance (>1km) from the kill, and 4 (11%) neutral or undetermined outcomes. Moreover, in regional studies of radio-collared wolf survival, no cases of grizzly-caused mortality were ever discovered (n>100 wolves; (Callaghan 2002); M. Hebblewhite, unpublished data). Therefore, in BNP, wolves seemed capable of out-competing grizzlies through interference and exploitative competition.

Indirect effects

INDIRECT TROPHIC CASCADE EFFECTS

To test for cascading effects of wolves on vegetation communities, Hebblewhite et al. (2005) compared aspen recruitment (# saplings / 100m^2), aspen browse intensity (%), willow current annual growth (g/m^2), willow browse removed (g/m^2), and net willow production (g/m^2) between low and high wolf areas in 1997–1999. Indirect effects of wolves on willow were statistically significant, showing 7 times greater net willow production in high wolf areas as a result of reduced browsing rates (Fig. 1.3.3e, Table 1.3.3). Indirect effects of wolves on aspen recruitment or browse pressure were not statistically significant by 1999, although the trend was for higher aspen recruitment in areas with more wolf predation. To examine whether this trend continued for aspen, we resampled the high-wolf area in summer 2003 (n=40 plots, following Hebblewhite et al. 2005). The low area was not sampled in 2003 because preliminary sampling showed sapling densities were very similar to 1997 (BNP, unpublished data). We tested for differences in aspen recruitment and browse among the three treatments (1997 low- and high-wolf, 2003 high-wolf) using ANOVA adjusting for multiple comparisons. Both aspen sapling density ($F_{2,127}$=2.98, P=0.04) and aspen browse intensity ($F_{2,36}$=3.9, P=0.04) differed among treatments, but the only significant differences were between the 1997 low-wolf and 2003 high-wolf treatments for sapling density (P=0.019) and recruitment (P=0.02, Fig 1.3.3e). Moreover, the increased variation in aspen sapling recruitment in the high-predation area between 2003 (SE = 3.10) and 1997 (SE = 1.9) showed that the effect of wolves on aspen was spatially variable.

Hebblewhite et al. (2005) tested the consequences of wolf predation on songbirds between low- and high-wolf areas. Songbird diversity and abundance were roughly double in high-wolf areas as compared to low-wolf areas (Fig. 1.3.3d). Songbird evenness, a measure of change in species dominance, did not change between areas, indicating a wholesale community shift, not just changes in one or two key species. Indicator species that were absent in low-wolf areas included American redstarts (*Setophaga ruticilla*), Tennessee warblers (*Vermivora peregrina*), Orange-crowned warblers (*V. celata*), and least flycatchers (*Empidonax minimus*) (Nietvelt 2001), confirming the critical importance of tall willow and songbirds that depend on such habitat for nesting and reproduction.

This tie between willow and other species extended to perhaps the ultimate keystone species – beaver (*Castor canadensis*) (Naiman et al. 1986). Whereas beaver lodge densities were not available in either low- or high-wolf areas, Hebblewhite et al. (2005) found a strong negative relationship between beaver lodge density and elk density in the low-wolf area between 1986 and 2000. Detailed studies by Nietvelt (2001) strongly support the hypothesis that exploitative competition between elk and beaver caused declines in beaver densities (see below). Elk and beaver competed directly for tall willow. At high enough browsing intensity, elk herbivory prevented willow from becoming tall, reducing the availability of suitable willow for beaver (Nietvelt 2001). Because wolf predation reduced elk densities in the Bow Valley, the number of active beaver lodges has apparently increased (Parks Canada, unpublished data).

APPARENT COMPETITION

Hurd (1999) undertook a 4-year study (1993–1997) of competition between moose and elk to understand causes for moose declines that were correlated with wolf recolonization. Predictions of exploitative competition were that moose and elk 1) spatially overlap but their abundance is negatively correlated, 2) dietary overlap is asymmetric with elk diet broader, and 3) elk reduce abundance of the more limited food resources for moose. In n=236 pellet plots, patterns of spatial overlap between moose and elk were asymmetric, with elk overlapping moose (15%) far less than vice versa (71%). This asymmetry was reflected in abundance because moose and elk pellet counts were negatively correlated (Spearman rank correlation $r_s = -0.45$, n=178, P<0.001). Moose and elk diet during winter significantly differed, with elk using 14 plant species regularly vs. six for moose. Diet comparisons confirmed continued asymmetry. Moose diet overlap with elk was 0.31 whereas elk overlap with moose diet was 0.87. Moreover, evidence strongly suggested that elk, not moose, abundance was high enough to negatively reduce abundance of the most important browse species for moose, willow. For these reasons, Hurd (1999) concluded that at fine-spatial scales, elk were exploitatively out- competing moose because of their greater diet breadth and higher abundance.

Apparent competition can also result in similar spatial patterns between elk and moose. If so, wolf predation should be the main cause of moose mortality and should be sufficient to cause moose to decline. We test the latter prediction here by comparing Hurd's (1999) moose demography with the demographic patterns of elk before and after wolf recolonization. Indeed, wolves were the leading cause of moose mortality (Table 1.3.1), causing 56% of all moose mortality. Adult moose (male and female were the same) survival rates were very low, and combined with low calf recruitment (most likely a result of predation); moose populations were certainly declining because of wolf predation. Moose and elk in the high-wolf area had similar demography, evidencing the strong top-down effect of wolf predation (Table 1.3.1). Thus, Hurd (1999) concluded that apparent competition was occurring in combination with exploitative competition in a negatively 'additive' fashion, and was responsible for declines of moose populations following wolf recolonization.

Apparent competition between elk and federally threatened woodland caribou has important conservation implications in BNP and Jasper National Parks, where caribou population size is <5 and ~150, respectively. Whereas exploitative competition could be a factor, elk and caribou diet differ sufficiently to avoid competition for forage. In the absence of field data, Hebblewhite et al. (2007) used a modelling approach to show that apparent competition could be driven by the strong numeric response of wolves to primary prey density (elk). Even with extremely low wolf kill-rates of caribou, wolf predation could lead to unsustainable levels of caribou mortality at even moderate elk densities (Messier 1995a; Wittmer et al. 2005; Hebblewhite et al. 2007). This occurred because wolves continue to kill caribou even at low caribou density because of abundant elk, leading to inverse-density dependence in predation rate on caribou (Wittmer et al. 2005). This ignores the role of bear predation on caribou as well, which would only exacerbate effects of wolf predation. With current densities of wolves and elk in BNP, the Banff caribou population will almost certainly become extirpated (Hebblewhite et al. 2007). Even in Jasper, where caribou densities are quite higher, high elk densities could lead to caribou declines. Evidence for apparent competition in this example of an endangered species indicates that wolf predation can have unanticipated negative consequences for an endangered species. Ultimate causes for caribou declines thus include unnaturally high elk densities supported by urban predation refugia surrounding townsites in both Parks, high elk densities outside National Parks, and human infrastructure that increases wolf predation efficiency (i.e., Alberta Woodland Caribou Recovery Team 2005). Despite the lack of empirical studies, woodland caribou throughout boreal and mountainous regions of Canada are endangered by apparent competition mediated by moose (Alberta Woodland Caribou Recovery Team 2005; Wittmer et al. 2005).

SCAVENGING

To document the occurrence of scavenging on wolf kills in BNP to allow inferences from YNP's more detailed scavenging studies, we recorded the number of scavengers found at 221 ungulate prey carcasses between 1995 and 2000 that were killed by wolves. We tallied a minimum of 20 different species that used wolf-killed prey carcasses during the winter months. We found an average of 2.2 (range 0 to 9) species of scavengers on each kill, the most common of which were common raven (*Corax corax*) (present at 96% of all kills), coyote (51%), black-billed magpie (*Pica pica*) (19%), pine marten (*Martes americana*) (14%), wolverine (8%), and bald eagles (8%); other species included (in descending order) gray jay (*Perisoreus canadensis*), golden eagle (*Aquila chrysaetos*), long- and short-tailed and least weasel (*Mustela* spp.), mink (*Mustela vison*), lynx, cougar, grizzly bear, boreal and mountain chickadee (*Parus* spp.), Clark's nutcracker (*Nucifraga columbiana*), masked shrew (*Sorex cinerus*), and great gray owl (*Strix nebulosa*). When present, an average of 12.7 (range 1-55) ravens, 2.1 (range 1-4) coyotes, 2.6 (range 1-7) magpies, 1.1 (range 1-2) martens, 1.2 (range 1-3) wolverines, and 1.6 (range 1-3) bald eagles fed on carcasses when these scavengers made use of wolf-killed prey.

Case study 2: Yellowstone National Park

Study area description

Situated in northwestern Wyoming, Yellowstone National Park (YNP) is the world's oldest formally protected National Park (1872), and covers a large (8991 km^2) mountainous and ecologically diverse area. Elevations range from 1500 to 3300 m, creating a range of habitat types. Numerous highways and trails bisect the park, several human settlements <500 inhabitants are found inside YNP, with three larger towns immediately bordering the park. Over three million humans visit YNP each year, emphasizing the importance of humans to trophic interactions similar to BNP. Major habitats include from low to high elevation: grassland-sagebrush steppe, Douglas fir (*Pseudotsuga menziesii*), lodgepole pine, subalpine fir and Engelmann spruce, whitebark pine *(Pinus albicaulis)*, and alpine environments (Despain 1990). Riparian willow communities (including over 20 species of *Salix* spp.) are rare and aspen and cottonwood (*Populus* spp.) are uncommon and declining in the northern part of the park (Larsen & Ripple 2003). The lower elevation 'northern range' (NR) in the Lamar and Yellowstone river valleys provides large open grassland areas, whereas the interior areas of the park are more forested and higher elevation. Geothermal areas occur throughout the park, especially in the interior areas, providing year-round snow free conditions. Most wildlife throughout YNP are migratory, so seasonal use of these habitats is the norm.

Diversity and abundance of carnivores is high. The wolf population on the northern range is dense (50–100 wolves/1000 km^2), but lower in the park interior (10–20 wolves/1000 km²). Winter wolf diet is constituted primarily of elk (92%; Smith et al. 2004), but use of bison for interior wolves is increasing (Smith 2005). Summer diet is more variable with use of mule deer and other smaller prey augmenting kills of elk (Smith et al. 2006). Besides wolves, there are grizzly and black bears, cougars, and coyotes. Approximately 150–200 grizzly bears reside within the park and about 20–30 grizzly and black bears reside on the northern range (K. Gunther, personal communication; Schwartz et al. 2006). Cougar distribution is variable, with 20–25 concentrated in the northern range (T. Ruth, personal communication). Coyotes are common and number ~150 on the northern range (Crabtree & Sheldon 1999). Thus, a preliminary estimate of large carnivore density on YNP's northern range is 288–308 carnivores/1000km², but lower across the whole park.

All ungulates occurring in the Rocky Mountains are present in YNP and have been preyed upon by wolves (Smith 2005): elk, bison, moose, mule and white-tailed deer, pronghorn antelope (*Antilocapra americana*), bighorn sheep, and mountain goat (which are exotic to YNP, Lemke 2004). Elk and bison dominate the ungulate system. Summer elk numbers from eight different herds are estimated at 25,000–35,000, but only one-third to one-fourth winter in the park as six herds migrate beyond the park each winter (Keiter & Boyce 1991). The northern Yellowstone herd is the largest at 10,000–20,000, winters in the northern range, and is also partially migratory (Lemke et al. 1998). One elk herd, the interior dwelling Madison-Firehole herd, is non-migratory (White & Garrott 2005). Bison dominate in this area, especially in winter because bison migration is truncated at the park boundary for political reasons. Bison numbers range from 3,000 to 5,000 park-wide and are strongly influenced by human removals (1,100 in 1997 and 1,000 in 2005; Gates et al. 2005). Mule deer are the third most abundant ungulate in YNP, and are migratory (T. Lemke, personal communication). Population estimates are only available for mule deer that use the NR and are estimated at 2,000–3,000, but they are widespread during summer in YNP. Moose are rare on the northern range, estimated to number less than 200 (Tyers 2003) and ~500 park-wide. The other ungulates within YNP are rare, not surveyed, but are rarely killed by wolves. Thus, ungulate densities during summer in YNP are approximately 3,900–4,500 ungulates/1000 km².

Wolf recovery and experimental design

Yellowstone has a rich scientific record, making it an excellent site to examine consequences of wolf reintroduction and other major ecological perturbations on ecosystem dynamics. Upon park establishment in 1872, wolf eradication was congressionally mandated park policy (Pritchard 1999). By 1926 the last wolf in YNP had been killed (Weaver 1978) and wolves were ecologically absent from then until reintroduction. Forty-one wolves were reintroduced from Alberta, British Columbia, and north-west Montana in 1995 and 1996 (Bangs & Fritts 1996). The population grew rapidly for approximately 10 years, averaging a 20% annual increase (Smith 2005). Population growth peaked in 2003 at 174 wolves in 14 packs but then declined (due to intra-specific competition and disease, Smith, unpublished data) to 118 wolves in 11 packs by 2005. In addition to wolves, population estimates for many wildlife species date back to the late 1800s and early 1900s. Changes in populations can be correlated to major ecosystem perturbations like forest fires, elk removals, severe winters, and reintroduction of wolves. This strong science approach is rare for national parks because park policy typically does not allow manipulative experiments and because wolf-ungulate-vegetation ecosystems occur at large spatial scales that are difficult to study via replicated experiments (Boutin 1992).

The experimental approach in YNP was time-series based (Boyce & Anderson 1999; Minta et al. 1999), with pre- and post- wolf comparisons on population counts of species (Fig. 1.3.5), instead of using the log-response ratio between areas with and without wolves as used in BNP. Because there is no control area, however, inferences about cause and effect are more difficult to address (Walters 1986; Minta et al. 1999) because confounding variables could also have also changed pre- and post- wolf, such as climate. Cause and effect are more difficult to address conclusively with time-series approaches, but inferences are strengthened with more mechanistic studies (e.g., of ungulate foraging ecology). In some settings,

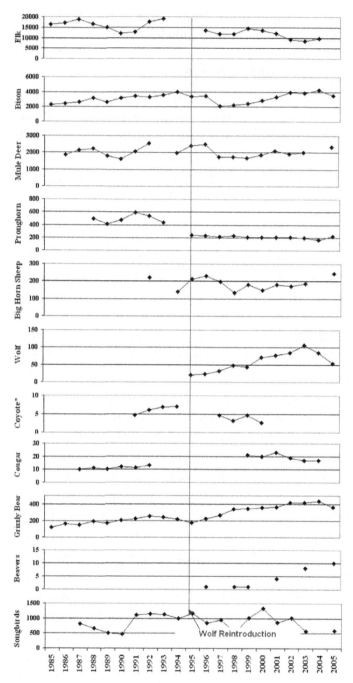

Figure 1.3.5. Population sizes for selected animal species ten years prior to and ten years after (1985–2005) wolf reintroduction to Yellowstone National Park. Data are from the northern range of Yellowstone except for bison, wolves, grizzly bears, and songbirds. Data sources: elk (Northern Range Working Group, unpublished data), bison (YNP, unpublished data), mule deer (T. Lemke, unpublished data), pronghorn antelope (P. J. White, unpublished data), bighorn sheep (P. J. White, unpublished data), wolf (Smith 2005), coyote (Gese et al. 1996, S. Grothe, unpublished data, A. Switalski, unpublished data), cougar (Ruth 2004), grizzly bear (Schwartz et al. 2006), beavers (Smith 2005), songbirds (unpublished data, USGS Patuxent Wildlife Research Center 2006).

control areas do exist, for example for vegetation such as aspen and willow using elk exclosures. In these settings, log-response ratios between variables measured inside and outside exclosures can reveal the effects of elk removal, but not necessarily wolf reintroduction, on vegetation. We illustrate and discuss more aspects of the study design afforded by wolf recovery in YNP below.

YNP research methods

Studies of wolf ecosystem effects in YNP resulted from co-operative efforts of multiple independent researchers. Most mammal studies in YNP relied on radio-telemetry. Initially all the reintroduced wolves were collared (Bangs & Fritts 1996), but recent efforts have maintained collars on 30–40% of all wolves (with ≥ 1 collared wolf per pack). Researchers maintained approximately 40–60 collared grizzly bears annually, with fewer collared black bears (Schwartz et al. 2006). Intensive cougar studies on the northern range were conducted pre-wolf from 1987 to 1996 (Murphy 1998), and then resumed from 1998 to 2005 (Ruth 2004). Most cougars on the NR were collared during this study. Coyotes were radio-collared in two different NR areas (Crabtree & Sheldon 1999; Gese et al. 1996) in a manner that allowed comparison of pre- and post-wolf effects. Intensive studies of elk, bison, and pronghorn also employed radio-collars (White & Garrott 2005; Mao et al. 2005). Moose were radio marked but less intensively, but surveyed annually from 1985 to 2001 (Tyers 2003). Bighorn sheep and mule deer were surveyed on an approximately annual basis, and mountain goats bi-annually (White & Garrott 2005). Capture techniques were similar to BNP, and depending on objective, VHF, GPS, and ARGOS satellite tracking collars were all deployed. Other researchers surveyed beavers (Smith 2005) and songbirds (Hansen et al. 2005). Vegetation sampling was accomplished through a wide array of independent researchers on aspen (Larsen & Ripple 2003; Ripple et al. 2001), willow (Bilyeu 2006; Beyer 2006; Despain 2005), and cottonwood (Ripple & Beschta 2005). Plant studies used ground sampling and manipulative experiments like artificial beaver dams, exclosures, and elk feeding experiments to explore community consequences of wolf predation.

Overview of ecosystem effects of wolves in Yellowstone

Wolf restoration to YNP has generated debate over what the wolf impacts on the ecosystem were, or will be in the future, after the first decade. Most researchers seem to agree at least qualitatively that YNP will be different after wolf restoration. Work from other national parks like Banff and Isle Royale (McLaren & Peterson 1994) attest to the changes wolves can bring about affecting both animals and plants. But what will happen in Yellowstone? Many long-time Yellowstone workers emphasize the uniqueness of the park, especially the northern range. Some have cautioned that wolf effects may be dependent on a minimum wolf density or on how other factors interact with wolves (Berger & Smith 2005; Garrott et al. 2005).

Examination of Figure 1.3.5 suggests several species abundances may have changed between the pre- and post- wolf periods. Naively considering these data as 'experimental', we can adopt the log-response ratio analytical approach described above for predator exclusion experiments (Table 1.3.2). Adopting this approach would lead us to conclude that mean abundances of elk, pronghorn, and coyote all declined following wolf recolonization, whereas cougar and grizzly bear abundances all increased (Table 1.3.2). Clearly, however, interpreting cause-and-effect from this simple analysis, borrowed from true replicated experiments, is insufficient, and a more detailed examination is required to disentangle wolf effects in YNP.

Direct effects

PREDATION AND WOLF-ELK RELATIONSHIPS

Wolves may limit or regulate only three of the eight elk herds in YNP: the northern herd (White & Garrott 2005; although see Vucetich et al. 2005), the Madison-Firehole in the interior (Garrott et al. 2005), and to a lesser degree, the Gallatin elk herd (Creel & Winnie 2005). The other five herds migrate outside of YNP during winter, escaping year-round wolf predation. We restrict our review mostly to the northern Yellowstone elk herd with some references to the Madison-Firehole elk herd. Population fluctuations of the northern Yellowstone elk herd have been a topic of debate for a century (Houston 1982; Kay 1998). Ironically, since wolf reintroduction the debate has switched from their being too many elk to too few. The northern Yellowstone elk herd has declined by about 40% since wolves were reintroduced in 1995, the causes of which we review below. Before wolves in 1995, NR elk density was 13–15 elk/km^2, one of the higher elk densities reported in the literature. By 2004, winter NR elk numbers had declined by 40% to 6–7 elk/km^2, still much higher than the areas surrounding YNP (Smith et al. 2003). Therefore, when we discuss ecosystem effects due to lower elk density on the northern range, elk density is still high compared to other elk populations.

To understand the role of wolves in these declines, Vucetich et al. (2005) conducted the type of time-series analysis outlined above where changes in elk population growth rate were correlated to wolf predation, snow depth, summer drought, and human harvest rates. Winter climate, drought, and especially human harvest were all worse for elk than occurred in the preceding decades, and explained 64% of the variance in elk numbers without requiring wolf predation. As a result, wolf predation appeared mostly compensatory, in comparison to 'super-additive' human harvest (Vucetich et al. 2005). Other modelling work also suggests that wolf predation is compensatory (Varley & Boyce 2006). An alternate view argues instead that wolf predation is mainly additive because of effects of wolf predation on prime-aged females (White & Garrott 2005). However, Vucetich et al. (2005) compared elk dynamics pre- and post- wolf in time series analyses, and strongly supports a compensatory role of wolf predation, at least in the first 10 years post-wolf. Regardless of the discussion over direct effects of predation in the future, wolves could be reducing elk densities through the underappreciated interaction with winter severity (Hebblewhite 2005). In addition to direct effects, they could be influencing trophic relationships by changing behaviour of elk.

BEHAVIOURALLY MEDIATED TROPHIC CASCADES

In comparison to BNP, research on elk behavioural changes due to wolves was extensive, both on Yellowstone's northern range and in other nearby systems. Virtually all of the work showed elk behaviour has changed since wolf restoration, both spatially and temporally. Mao et al. (2005) found elk moved to higher elevations in summer and used burned areas more than unburned areas on the northern range. The burned areas had numerous downed trees that, in theory, could impede wolf travel/chases of elk. However, these changes were potentially confounded by the large fires of 1988, and so cannot be entirely attributed to wolves. In winter there was no differences in elk habitat selection post-wolf (Mao et al. 2005). In the same area Fortin et al. (2005) found elk less likely to travel into aspen stands when wolves were present; while wolves were present elk travelled more frequently into conifer forests. Adjacent to YNP, on the Gallatin River, Creel and Winnie (2005) found elk reduced herd size far from cover on days wolves were present but were in larger groups the days wolves were absent. In the same area, Creel and Winnie (2005) showed that in the presence of wolves elk retreated into forest cover, whereas when wolves were absent elk foraged in the open grassland. Other research in the Madison River showed a strong landscape effect on wolf predation. Bergman et al. (2006) found wolves' most successful killing elk in areas of habitat transition (e.g., thermal areas, forest edges), not in areas of highest elk density. In other words, certain landscape features predisposed elk to wolf predation. And Gude et al. (2006) found that in the broad lower valley of the Madison River elk responded to wolf presence, even though wolves were at low density, by moving away from wolves and thereby diluting elk effects on vegetation.

INTERSPECIFIC COMPETITION

The most dramatic example of interference competition was the 50% reduction of the coyote population by wolf predation (Crabtree & Sheldon 1999). Most of the reduction was from direct killing at wolf kills where coyotes attempted to scavenge and were killed (Crabtree & Sheldon 1999; Ballard et al. 2003). Wolves rarely consumed the coyotes. Coyotes visit virtually every kill made by wolves and wolves do not prevail only when coyotes outnumber a lone wolf. Most wolf-caused coyote mortality occurred at kills in YNP (Ballard et al. 2003). Recently, however, coyotes appear to be adapting to wolf presence through changes in use of the landscape (e.g., spatial) and socially by living in smaller group sizes (J. Sheldon, unpublished data). The pre-wolf number of coyote packs in Lamar Valley was 11, after wolves were released this declined to 6, and has recently increased again to 12 (R. L. Crabtree & J. Sheldon, personal communication), which may be a result of the recent decline in wolf numbers (Fig. 1.3.5). Exploitative competition does not seem to be occurring between wolves and coyotes.

Unlike wolf-coyote interactions, there is evidence for both interference and exploitation competition between wolves and cougars. Wolves are dominant to cougars, probably because of large pack size, and wolves have killed seven cougars in YNP, whereas cougars have only killed two wolves (Ruth 2004). Cougar and wolf researchers have used GPS collars to document kills made by cougars that were usurped by wolves (Ruth 2004). While cougars and wolves in YNP use prey and habitat differently in a manner expected to reduce competition, spatial restriction in space-use of cougars has occurred since wolves were reintroduced, suggesting asymmetric competition (Ruth 2004). Exploitative competition between wolves and cougars appears to be minimal as cougar prey selection and kill rates have not changed compared with pre-wolf monitoring (Murphy 1998; Ruth 2004). However, should prey continue to decline and become more limiting, future competition for prey cannot be ruled out.

Both interference and exploitative competition between wolves and grizzly bears is an important intra-guild change following wolf reintroduction. In terms of interference competition, wolves have not killed adults, but have killed grizzly bear cubs (Ballard et al. 2003; Gunther & Smith 2004). Female grizzly bears with cubs rarely use carcasses, but this might not be because of wolves, but to avoid infanticide from males (Swenson et al. 1997). To examine the relative strength of exploitative competition, we observed 122 interactions of wolves and grizzly bears at carcasses from 1996 to 2006, 63 of which were aerial and 59 ground observations. Out of these observations for possession of the carcass, we observed the following: 4 (3%) cases where wolves killed grizzly bear cubs (direct interference competition); 2 (2%) cases of wolves usurping kills made by bears; 30 (25%) with bears pushing packs of <4 wolves off wolf-killed carcasses; 23 (19%)

bears pushing packs of >4 wolves off wolf-killed carcasses; 8 (7%) cases of adult bears usurping carcasses from wolves that died of unknown causes; 2 cases (2%) of packs of <4 wolves usurping carcasses from bears that died of unknown causes; 3 cases of packs >4 wolves usurping bears off of carcasses that died from unknown causes and 50 (41%) cases of neutral or unknown outcome. In summary, of the known outcomes bears prevailed in 61 (85%) of 71 encounters with wolves at carcasses. Moreover, in one area of YNP, Pelican Valley, where grizzly bear densities are very high, every kill made by wolves from March through October was usurped by grizzly bears (YNP Wolf Project, unpublished data). The effects of this on the pack are unknown, but reproductive failure has occurred twice since 1996, a higher rate than for northern range YNP wolf packs. This pack is also plagued with low pup survival, though a direct link to kleptoparasitism by grizzly bears is yet to be established.

Indirect effects

INDIRECT TROPHIC CASCADE EFFECTS

YNP has a long interest in elk-vegetation interactions stemming from historic concerns about overgrazing that resulted because of early-twentieth-century extirpation of carnivores that led to increasing elk populations. From 1932 through 1968, approximately 75,000–80,000 elk were killed or removed to protect the vegetation (Houston 1982). Ungulate removals were directed by a park management plan heavily influenced by range management practices intended to control ungulate numbers below the forage carrying capacity. Predation by wolves was considered unimportant (Pritchard 1999). The results of this policy are still debated, but one clear outcome was that woody vegetation did not respond to the ungulate reductions. This meant that willow, aspen, and cottonwood were suppressed by ungulate browsing through most of the twentieth century (Houston 1982; Kay 1990; Pritchard 1999). Control of elk was ended in 1968 when the elk population of the northern range was 3,000–4,000 (Houston 1982). After 1968, the population increased rapidly (Fig. 1.3.5), reaching a high in the late 1980s, declined after a severe winter in 1988–89, and increased again to an all-time high of >20,000 only to decline again from another severe winter 1996–97 (Lemke et al. 1998). Just before the second decline from the severe winter, wolves were reintroduced (Bangs & Fritts 1996). Around 1998, in the presence of wolves and after nearly a century of suppression from elk browsing, willow growth exceeded browsing levels and the first release of willow occurred. This release happened despite elk densities three to four times higher than elk densities in the 1950s, when willows were still suppressed by elk browsing. The correlation with wolf reintroduction caused some to propose the trophic cascade hypothesis that willow growth was triggered by wolf predation limiting elk and affecting elk foraging behaviour.

However, in addition to a trophic cascade, the following alternative hypotheses should be considered: 1) climate, 2) winter severity, 3) geomorphology, 4) willow water balance, and 5) moose population decline. Evidence for these alternative hypotheses comes from a variety of sources. The number of days >0° C for the active period of willow growth (May–July) was an average of 11.8 days (23% increase) higher during 1997–2004 compared with 1985–1996 (Despain 2005). Relatedly, winter severity from 1997 to 2005 was amongst the mildest on record with the lowest snow pack (Farnes et al. 1999; P. Farnes, personal communication). This would allow a wider distribution of wintering ungulates, greater availability of non-willow forage, and therefore reduced browsing intensity of willow meadows. From a geomorphology perspective, the spring floods of 1996 and 1997 might also have altered water availability for willows. Another significant factor could be the loss of beavers in the 1930s, which could have changed water tables sufficiently to prevent willow recovery (Singer et al. 1994, reviewed in Bilyeu 2006). And finally, the 1988 fires reduced available moose (an obligate winter willow browser) habitat and thus population size (Tyers 2003), and reduced moose densities might have released willow.

Two main studies on elk-willow relationships on the northern range tested multiple working hypotheses for willow regeneration. First, Beyer (2006) followed a time-series approach from 1989 to 2001 to test for the effects of wolves on willow regeneration. In two separate analyses, Beyer

(2006) related willow growth to browse rates and to wolf presence, while controlling for the effects of climate (including precipitation, drought severity, snow depth and the North Pacific Oscillation winter severity index), elk population size, and watershed. Previous year's growth and the percent browsed by elk had the strongest influence on willow growth rate – snow depth had minimal effect on willow. In the best models, the presence of wolves positively affected willow growth over and above the effects of precipitation and winter climatic severity (Beyer 2006). For example, winter severity without wolves was <500 times as likely to be the best model as one that included wolf predation, strongly discounting the winter severity hypothesis. Moreover, the neutral effect of the drought index casts similar doubt on the climate hypothesis. Because increased elk browsing decreased willow, wolf presence increased willow, but elk numbers were unrelated to willow growth (Beyer 2006). This led Beyer (2006) to argue for a behaviourally mediated cascade, not a direct effect of wolf reduction of elk population size, at least not yet. In addition to this time-series investigation, other correlative studies have found similar relationships between wolf recovery and willow regeneration (Ripple & Beschta 2006).

In a second study of willow recovery, Bilyeu (2006) used an experimental approach to test for feedbacks between lower water tables, reduced willow productivity, and beaver absence. By using experimental beaver dams, Bilyeu (2006) found that under low browsing but inadequate water, willows did not grow as much as willows that had adequate water and were not protected from elk browsing. Stream incision due to loss of beaver in the 1930 has lowered the water tables, increasing the water stress of willow making them less able to cope with browsing (Bilyeu 2006). Without an increase in available water brought about by the restoration of beavers, regardless of browsing level, Bilyeu (2006) contend that willows will remain suppressed and limited in distribution. Thus, beaver are the 'keystone' that could switch between stable states in YNP. Moderate browsing may serve to stimulate willow growth, so it is possible that with adequate water and some browsing suitable conditions for beaver recovery could occur. In addition, partial beaver recovery on the northern range (see below) suggests willow is recovering at least enough (due to reduced browsing) to encourage beaver population growth. Bilyeu's (2006) study is promising in that it tested multiple factors (water balance, browsing, beaver dams) using an experimental approach and suggests that even partial beaver recovery may interact with these factors to cause the increased willow growth.

Neither the geomorphology nor moose hypotheses were considered by these studies, but we consider evidence for them weak. If the spring floods of 1996 and 1997 increased willow growth, why was there not an expansion in willow distribution at the same time as growth? And for the role of moose declines, the timing of the fires (1988) and willow release (~1998) cast doubt on this explanation. Moose are also subject to wolf predation, and thus behavioural changes like elk. Moreover, moose occur at extremely low densities relative to elk on the NR and it is unlikely that moose browsing could exceed that of the numerically dominant elk (see also Hurd (1999)'s study in BNP in Table 1.3.1). Other hypotheses, such as increased temperature stimulating higher concentrations of plant-defence compounds in willow, were not tested (R. Renkin, personal communication). However, if this has occurred, it has not influenced beaver population growth (Smith 2005), despite their sensitivity to defensive chemicals (Basey 1999). To summarize, reductions in willow browsing occurred because wolf predation on elk reduced numbers and/or changes in behaviour. However, elk herbivory interacts with winter climate (especially) and the interaction between beaver recovery and water table height. Thus, in the future, if even modest increases in beaver occur in the northern range, we predict a widespread recovery of willow could occur mediated through these positive indirect pathways.

These elk-willow studies were echoed by more limited investigations of effects of elk herbivory on aspen. One early study found taller aspen suckers in mesic aspen stands with high wolf but low elk use (Ripple et al. 2001), but this result was ephemeral and did not translate to aspen recruitment (M. Kauffman, unpublished data). Other work found increased cottonwood germination, but similarly scant sapling recruitment (Beschta 2003). Overall, aspen and cottonwood growth has continued to be suppressed. The failure of aspen and cottonwood to recruit successfully following wolf recolonization casts doubt on the occurrence of a wolf caused trophic cascade for these plant species. Thus, there is an emerging agreement among researchers that willow, but not aspen and cottonwood, has been released from elk herbivory after decades of suppression since 1998. Importantly, all researchers show that the response has been non-uniform, and studies have suggested that it vegetation response will be linked to spatial variation in wolf predation risk (Ripple & Beschta 2006).

WHAT ARE THE CONSEQUENCES OF TALLER WILLOWS?

Taller willows benefit a variety of songbirds (Baker & Hill 2003). Preliminary results from a study led by A. Hansen and L. Baril from Montana State University in 2005 showed stands of "released" and protected (willows that were never suppressed and have always been tall) willows had a greater abundance and diversity of songbirds than did suppressed stands (Hansen et al. 2005, Table 1.3.3). This represents only one year of data but the study is continuing. Restored riparian habitats will likely affect other animals and plants as well. Fishes, reptiles and amphibians, and small mammals have all been shown to benefit from wetland restoration. Boreal chorus frogs, for example, use beaver ponds extensively in YNP (C. Peterson, personal communication).

APPARENT COMPETITION

During the first 10 years of wolf recovery, wolf predation was primarily focused on elk in winter and elk and deer in summer (Smith 2005). Bison have been a minor component of the wolf diet. In interior YNP during winter, we speculate that preferential use of elk by wolves despite greater bison numbers may have reduced the elk population and put them at a competitive disadvantage to bison for forage resources. On the northern range of YNP, bison numbers have been increasing while elk have been declining. Although present conditions are inconclusive, preferential predation of wolves (and cougars) on elk will likely give bison a competitive edge. Further research will be necessary to tease out this relationship but human removals of bison may also affect the relationship altering any predation affects due to wolves.

Twelve different scavengers (similar to those found in BNP) have been recorded using wolf kills (Wilmers et al. 2003) and five visit virtually every kill: coyotes, ravens, magpies, and golden and bald eagles. Cougars cover and conceal their kills, greatly reducing availability and the number of scavengers that use them. Bears also make kills but much less frequently than wolves or cougars, do so only during spring, summer and fall, and like cougars, usually conceal their kills. Wilmers et al. (2003) showed wolf-killed carrion is spatially and temporally more available to scavengers post–wolf recovery. This differs from pre-wolf conditions where carrion abundance was significantly more pulsed in late winter/early spring and in the fall in areas with human hunting (Wilmers et al. 2003). Wolf predation provided carrion more evenly year round and more spatially dispersed than human hunting. Although if wolves reduce elk numbers, less total carrion might be available, it is more even spatial and temporal distribution might compensate for any negative effect of reduced biomass of carrion. Wilmers and Getz (2005) also concluded that wolf-killed carrion might moderate impacts to the scavenger community incurred via global warming because milder winters result in less winter-kill, whereas wolf predation will still maintain carrion for scavengers. They argue that biotic regulation of carcasses by large carnivores will be more resistant to perturbations than abiotic events linked to global climate change.

Scavenging may have played a role in the evolution of group living in wolves as a strategy to reduce losses to scavengers (Vucetich et al. 2004) because the per-capita amount of food lost to scavengers' declines with increasing wolf group size. In winter, ravens rely on wolf kills and located wolf-killed elk within minutes of wolves making the kill versus days for non-wolf killed prey (Stahler et al. 2002). Average number of ravens per kill was 28 with as many as 135 being recorded (Stahler et al. 2002). Add other scavengers and a substantial amount of meat can be stolen from wolf kills, possibly contributing to the formation of packs so their kin can use more of the food.

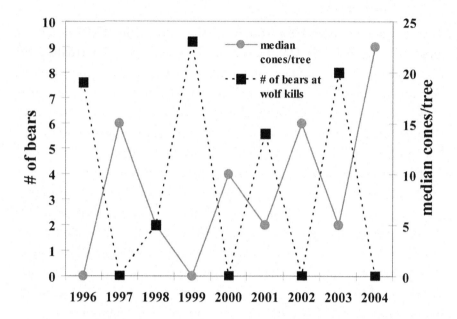

Figure 1.3.6. Number of grizzly bears observed during summer on wolf kills as a function of the median number of whitebark pine cones/tree as a measure of whitebark pine nut production in the northern range of Yellowstone National Park, 1996 to 2004. Median number of whitebark pine cones/tree were obtained by the interagency grizzly bear team (see Schwartz et al. 2006) for methods).

Besides avian scavengers, many mammals also scavenge wolf kills. Black bears are subordinate to wolves at carcasses (Ballard et al. 2003), although lone wolves or young wolves can be at a disadvantage to large black bears. Grizzly bears benefit from wolf-killed prey throughout the year, whereas prior to wolf restoration, carrion was seasonally pulsed only in late winter. Carcasses may also be important to bears during falls when other food sources fail or are episodic, like the availability of whitebark pine nuts (Fig. 1.3.6). Poor and good pine nut years were defined by the Interagency Grizzly Bear Study Team (Schwartz et al. 2006). Grizzly bear use of wolf-killed ungulates carcasses strongly increased ($r = +0.83$, $n=9$) during poor whitebark pine nut years. The number of bears on elk carcasses killed by wolves during September and October (the time when use of pine nuts is typically highest) were significantly greater (t = 2.776, P = 0.011, n = 9) in poor (mean = 6.3 bears observed on wolf kills) than in good pine nut years (mean = 1.2 bears observed on wolf kills). The frequency of flights per month was approximately equal for all years. This example illustrates an unanticipated indirect pathway between grizzly bears and whitebark pine mediated by wolves.

There are other scavengers besides vertebrate ones, and also indirect effects of wolf predation on flora and soil nutrients. Research in YNP is just beginning on this topic, but more species of beetles use carcasses than all vertebrates put together. Sikes (1994) found 23,365 beetles of 445 species in just two field seasons using wolf-killed carrion. Obviously, this underestimates the number of decomposers such as insects, mites, invertebrates, bacteria, and fungi, which likely number in the thousands. In addition, even longer-term effects of carcasses are the localized nutrient surges they cause. Bump and Peterson (personal communication) found elevated levels of nutrients around elk carcasses killed by wolves. Using paired soil samples, one at the carcass site and one away from it, they found 20–500% greater nitrogen (ammonium and nitrate), phosphorous, and potassium at the carcass site. Soil nutrients relative to control sites appear to increase since time of mortality. Bump and Peterson attribute this to direct nutrient leaching from carcass remains and indirectly to urine and feces from carnivores and scavengers. With an estimated >2,500 carcasses generated by wolves, cougars, and other carnivores on the northern range of YNP the amount of nutrients becomes significant.

DISCUSSION

We found evidence for pervasive effects of wolves via direct and indirect pathways in both Yellowstone and Banff National Park. Direct effects in both systems included limitation or regulation of elk by wolves, behavioural avoidance of wolves by elk across spatial and temporal scales, and intra-guild competition (both exploitative and interference) with other large carnivores. Indirect effects included the influence of wolves on willow and aspen growth, species that also relied on these plants such as riparian songbirds and beavers, and apparent competition between elk and alternate prey such as bison, moose, and caribou mediated by wolf predation. However, it is clear that the most numerous indirect interactions occurred between wolves and the scavenger guilds in both systems. Between 12 and 20 vertebrate scavengers made use of wolf-killed prey, a number that was vastly outstripped by the 445 species of just beetle scavengers in YNP. Present studies certainly underestimate the number of invertebrates and other genera that benefit from wolf-killed prey via indirect pathways. This emphasizes that the 5 or 6 direct species interactions linked to wolves is certainly small in comparison with the hundreds of indirect species interactions in ecosystems with wolves (Estes et al. 2004).

Regardless of the prevalence of indirect effects, the dominant interaction that currently mediates almost all other species interactions in both ecosystems is the between wolves and elk. In BNP, a clear BACI study design provided strong experimental evidence that wolf predation reduced elk survival and population growth rates to cause the population to decline to less than 25% of their pre-wolf abundance (Table 1.3.1). To compare results from YNP and BNP, it is important to note that without the low wolf control for comparison, Hebblewhite et al. (2002) would have determined wolves were uncorrelated with elk declines in the high wolf area in time-series correlation analysis. This was because of insufficient variation in wolf predation rates in the one time-series, and followed others (Boyce & Anderson 1999; Minta et al. 1999) by recognizing this as a limitation of single time-series analyses. Only by comparing time-series between zones (in effect, a cross-sectional time-series, e.g., Wooldridge 2001), were Hebblewhite et al. (2002) able to elucidate the strong limiting effects of wolves on elk. This agrees with advice from Minta et al. (1999), who cautioned against inferring top-down control from time-series models alone, and argued for experimental studies in areas with and without wolves.

Against this background, we consider the arguably weaker evidence for top-down effects of wolves on elk in YNP. Key ecological differences between BNP and the northern range add caution to over-interpreting results from BNP, the most notable of which is the certainly higher habitat quality and primary productivity of YNP (see below). Another large difference is the additive effects of the late winter hunt by humans in YNP (Vucetich et al. 2005) – human-caused mortality is much lower in BNP (Hebblewhite et al. 2002). We agree with Vucetich et al. (2005) that human-caused mortality appears to be driving recent declines in elk populations in YNP in combination with climate. By comparison, human-caused mortality was unrelated to elk population growth in BNP in the presence of wolves (Hebblewhite et al. 2002). However, one difference between the time-series analyses in BNP and YNP is that in BNP, the effect of winter severity on elk differed with and without wolves. Without wolves, winter severity reduced elk density only at high density, whereas with wolves, wolf predation interacted with climate, with kill-rates increasing in deeper snows (Huggard 1993c), to reduce elk density more. By not considering the interaction of predation with climate (Lima et al. 2002), the effects of snow in Vucetich et al. (2005) may include effects of wolf predation. Certainly, demographic studies of elk before and after wolf recolonization are needed. Nonetheless, we believe the real test in YNP will occur once the northern herd experiences some combinations of favourable winters and spring precipitation. Under these conditions, wolf predation could become less compensatory, especially if human hunting continues (White & Garrott 2005). If this is true, then in the next decade a strong a signal of wolf limitation of elk should emerge in YNP as in BNP. An experimental reduction of the late-season hunt, the purpose of which was to prevent overgrazing (now a moot point, White & Garrott 2005), could provide a powerful adaptive management experiment (Walters 1986) to test the degree of compensatory mortality caused by wolves. And finally, the relatively higher predator:prey ratio in BNP (~0.10 carnivores:ungulate prey, see study area descriptions) compared with YNP (~0.07) suggests stronger predation impacts should be expected in BNP. Conditions in YNP may still be in transition, however, to the higher predator:prey ratio observed in BNP.

Regardless of debate over the lethal effects of wolves, there was evidence from both systems of behavioural changes in elk in the presence of wolves. Elk reduced group sizes and moved into forested cover in the presence of wolves, changed habitat selection patterns to avoid wolves in summer, and avoided aspen stands with higher predation risk in YNP. In BNP, elk were closer to predation refugia when wolf activity was higher, and were warier following attack by wolves. This agrees with results from YNP and suggests that there may be population consequences of anti-predatory behaviour that could indeed translate to lower trophic levels.

The negative effects of wolf predation on elk, whether through changes in elk density and/or distribution, cascaded down to lower trophic levels consistent with the trophic cascade hypothesis in both systems. The return of wolves to BNP led to reduced elk densities, which caused higher willow growth rates and cascading indirect effects on riparian songbirds and beavers. Clearly, the effects of wolf predation were strongest on willow, which appeared to cross an herbivory threshold at about 5 elk $/km^2$ in BNP (Nietvelt 2001). In contrast, even by 1997, after 12 years of wolf predation, aspen sapling density was not significantly different between the low and high wolf areas. Aspen release did not statistically occur until 2003, almost 20 years following wolf recovery, at a point where elk densities were <1 elk$/km^2$ and close to the predicted threshold for aspen regeneration in the Canadian Rockies (White et al. 2003). Again, the control area in BNP made interpretations relatively straightforward in comparison with YNP, and helps 'fill' in some of the missing details likely occurring in YNP. Despite some debate over alternate hypotheses, the two largest studies in YNP confirm a plausible role and provide evidence for wolf predation increasing willow regeneration to a level that may support beaver recovery. Once beaver recover, dam building over decadal time-scales may be required to facilitate extensive willow recovery to the level that willow occurs as a dominant riparian cover type in BNP (Bilyeu 2006). Interestingly, as perhaps the only comparative evidence that behavioural effects may be stronger than direct effects of wolves in YNP, Beyer et al. (2006) found willow growth rates were independent of elk density, but not wolf presence. Teasing apart the relative contributions of lethal and non-lethal effects of predation on trophic cascade effects will likely require difficult experiments or comparisons across a gradient of wolf recovery (Schmitz 2005).

Intra-guild competition was common between wolves and coyotes, cougars, and grizzly bears, in both systems. Similar to African ecosystems, where intra-guild competition shapes life-history strategies of carnivores (Creel et al. 2001; Caro & Stoner 2003), wolf recovery has clearly returned an important ecological process to both systems. Intra-guild competition with wolves certainly has the same potential as in African systems to reduce carnivore densities, as exemplified by African wild dogs (*Lycaon pictus*) bearing the brunt of the costs of competition with lions (*Panthera leo*) (Creel et al. 2001). Certainly, coyote populations were reduced because of wolves in YNP. Although no information was available on coyote–wolf competition in BNP, similar observations of coyotes being killed by wolves (M. Hebblewhite, unpublished data), suggests similarities with YNP. The degree of intra-specific competition between wolves and other carnivores differed in strength between cougars and grizzly bears between systems. In YNP, there seemed to be only weak competition between cougars and wolves, whereas in BNP, competition appeared more acute, and led to an apparent diet separation with cougars focusing more on deer and sheep as prey. We believe the difference in degree between systems could also be a function of time. In another 10 years post-wolf in YNP, based on studies in BNP (Kortello et al. 2007), we predict competition between wolves and cougars to increase to a degree that could reduce cougar densities.

The relative strength of wolf-grizzly competition also varied between systems. In BNP, contests between wolves and grizzlies appeared relatively balanced, with 54% of disputes at carcasses won by wolves. Pack size appeared to mediate these conflicts as bears rarely usurped wolf kills from >4 wolves. In contrast, wolves bore the brunt of stiff competition from grizzlies in YNP, and this competition may have increased over the last 10 years. Wolves lost 85% of all carcass disputes to bears in YNP. In addition, anecdotal observations suggest the rate at which wolf kills are kleptoparasitised by grizzlies is higher in YNP. We consider two main reasons for these differences. First, bear densities are approximately 2.5 times higher in YNP (~25/1000km² in YNP vs. ~10/1000km² in BNP). Second, body size of adult grizzlies in YNP from 1975 to1989 averaged 134 kg for females and 193 for males compared to 96 and 148, respectively, in BNP (Schwartz et al. 2003; Herrero 2005). And the elevated frequency of conflicts over carcasses in YNP may also be due to 3–4 times higher wolf densities, which would increase encounter rates between species. Alternately, wolves may not be food limited yet in YNP compared with BNP, and not willing to defend carcasses as vigorously as evidently the case in BNP. Regardless, the consequences of stiffer grizzly competition in YNP may have yet to be realized on population sizes of wolves, but could be expected in the future based on studies of African wild dogs (Creel et al. 2001). In comparison, competitive ability between wolves and the three main carnivores examined appear to follow from grizzly bear≥wolf>cougar>coyote, of course during the period when bears are not hibernating. Few data are available for black bears, but they appear ranked close to cougars in intra-guild competitive ability. Drawing on the African literature, the population consequences of intra-guild competition may follow a similar rank order.

Regardless of future consequences of competition between carnivores to population densities, the consequences for trophic dynamics may be similar. Many studies have reported higher system resilience where carnivore diversity is high in terms of trophic cascades (Snyder et al. 2006 and literature therein), similar to the effects of herbivore and plant diversity (Tilman et al. 2001). This raises an important point that has been often overlooked in the quest for wolf-caused trophic cascades, especially in YNP. Although wolves are clearly the largest change to the carnivore guild in the last 10 years in YNP, grizzly bear and cougar densities are both higher in the last 10 years, and increasing, as was the late season human harvest of elk. Disentangling the wolf predation effect from other predators in YNP will therefore be difficult. For example, grizzly bears were responsible for ~55% of elk calf mortality post-wolf in YNP (Barber-Meyer 2006). Moreover, despite a better experimental comparison, this problem affects inferences from BNP to a lesser degree. As competition between wolves and grizzlies increases in the future, their may be some functional redundancy in wolf and grizzly densities in terms of community dynamics (Miquelle et al. 2005; Woodroffe & Ginsberg 2005). Wolves, grizzlies, cougars, humans – as far as the indirect effects of predators on plants – it may not matter whose 'fault' it is as the synergistic effects of the whole guild operate to regulate elk densities to low levels (Messier 1994).

Despite functional redundancy in direct effects on elk, the indirect effects of wolves may far outstrip the direct effects in terms of their importance to ecosystem dynamics. Indirect effects (i.e., carrion production) may be the unique trophic contribution of wolves. No other species generates as much carrion over such a consistent temporal scale as wolves (Wilmers et al. 2003). Another unique trophic effect of wolves in both systems was their role as mediators of apparent competition between primary and alternate prey species, including moose, caribou, and potentially bison. In BNP, wolf recovery led to declines of moose and caribou populations because wolves were numerically buoyed by elk densities, and this increased predation rates on these rarer species. While evidence is weaker, wolf predation on elk appears to have the potential to increase bison numbers in YNP. The difference in the effects between systems is likely a function of differential prey vulnerability to predation. Moose and caribou are amongst the most selected prey species in multiple-prey systems (Huggard 1993a; Dale et al. 1995; Lessard 2005), likely due to their relatively high profitability and vulnerability, respectively, to predation once encountered. In contrast, Bison are amongst the most formidable prey of wolves, and attacking and killing bison incurs large risk (MacNulty 2002).

We suspect that the most important potential indirect interactions remain unstudied. Changes in the distribution and density of elk will have far-reaching effects on more than just willow and aspen components of the plant community in YNP. Elk exert strong indirect effects in grassland ecosystems on nutrient cycling, disturbance regimes, and net primary production over and above their direct effects of herbivory (Hobbs 1996). Elk herbivory changes litter quality and nitrogen mineralization, which combines with fecal and urinary nitrogen deposition to amplify heterogeneity in nutrient cycling (Hobbs 1996). With increased spatial heterogeneity in elk distribution caused by wolf predation, heterogeneity in nutrient distribution and hence primary productivity may be expected to increase (Hobbs 1996; Frank 1998). This will have dramatic potential consequences for grassland net primary productivity, will change ungulate foraging patterns (Wallace et al. 1995), and could reduce the carrying capacity of the northern range by increasing the amount of lower productivity areas (Hobbs 1996, Frank 1998). This could have important bottom-up effects then on wolf density, revealing the complexity of disentangling top-down from bottom-up processes (Hunter & Price 1992). Furthermore, many herbivory processes are mediated by changes in plant composition, and Schmitz (2006) shows that weak trophic cascades can yield much larger changes in plant species diversity through such indirect interactions. Given the dominance and importance of the grassland communities to Yellowstone's northern range (Frank 1998), the lack of studies investigating potential effects of wolves on these indirect pathways seems an oversight. Another rich area of potential indirect effects includes the effects of predation on prey populations mediated by diseases such as Brucellosis (*Brucella* spp.). While empirical evidence for this in BNP or YNP is scant, it is reasonable to expect that density-dependent disease prevalence in ungulate populations may be reduced by wolf predation effects (Packer et al. 2003), although in some circumstances, predation may actually increase disease prevalence (Holt & Roy 2007). Regardless, given the increased conflicts between disease and wildlife, especially in the greater Yellowstone ecosystem (Bienen & Tabor 2006), future research on the indirect effects of disease-predation interactions will be fruitful.

In comparison with the wider trophic cascade literature, the effects of wolves are similarly weaker than trophic cascades in aquatic systems and by invertebrate predators (Schmitz et al. 2000; Shurin et al. 2002). Despite the limitations of small sample sizes of the numbers of interactions, we compared the relative effects of wolves on herbivores and plants from YNP and BNP (Table 1.3.4) to results of reviews by Schmitz et al. (2000) and Shurin et al. (2002) in Figure 1.3.7. First, both direct and indirect effects were of greater magnitude in BNP relative to YNP, and while YNP was closer to the mean of 18 trophic cascade studies in terrestrial systems by Shurin et al. (2002), BNP had stronger effects than Shurin et al.'s (2002), but the same as Schmitz et al.'s (2000) reviews. In addition, in BNP, direct effects attenuated on plants; that is, effects of wolves on plants were less than wolves on elk, as seen in Fig. 1.3.7 by BNP being below the 1:1 line.

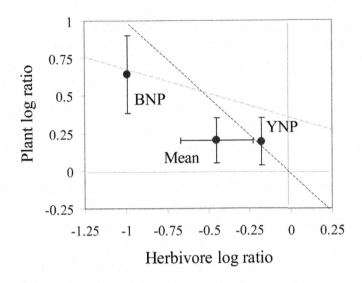

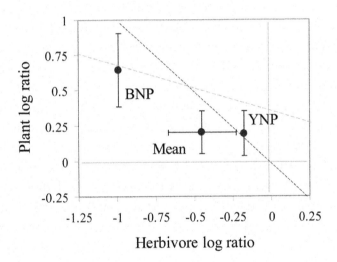

Figure 1.3.7. Comparison of the effect size (and 95% confidence interval) of predators on herbivores and plants measured using the log response ratio (log[X_{p+} /X_{p-}]) in Banff and Yellowstone National Parks versus the mean of 18 terrestrial trophic cascade studies (Shurin et al. 2002). 95% confidence intervals could not be calculated for YNP and BNP because only direct effects on elk were considered. The black dashed line represents the 1:1 line where herbivore and plant effects are equal; below the line, indirect effects of predators on plants attenuate. The gray dashed line is the mean of 97 terrestrial and aquatic trophic cascade studies (Shurin et al. 2002).

In contrast, direct effects and indirect effects were equal in YNP. In fact, indirect effects were slightly, if not statistically, greater than the direct effects observed (Fig. 1.3.7). Both YNP and BNP were relatively close to the slope of the relationship between plant and herbivore effects from Shurin et al.'s (2002) review. The stronger effects in BNP, we believe, may be a result of a longer time period required for the effects of wolves to equilibrate on elk (Hebblewhite et al. 2005), especially because many variables, such as aspen recruitment, experienced significant time lags in their response. If this is true, then we predict the indirect effects on plants might not change appreciably as the system shifts more to the left along the herbivore effect axis following the general cross-system relationships revealed by Shurin et al. (2002) (Fig. 1.3.7). Alternately, the slightly higher predator and prey diversity in YNP could be contributing to reduced strength of trophic cascades, as predicted by trophic theory (Polis et al. 2000), although the mechanisms for diversity mediation in trophic cascades are still under question (Schmitz et al. 2000). However, the differences in attenuation between systems point to what may be an important difference between systems. Several studies in YNP have pointed to the importance of behavioural mediation in trophic cascades (Fortin et al. 2005; Beyer 2006), and the relatively stronger indirect effects of wolves on plants in YNP supports this hypothesis. Regardless, this comparison emphasizes the strong insights available when trophic cascades are studied using an experimental approach. If more studies presented such data summarizing response variables in areas with and without wolves (including standard errors), meta-analyses of the ilk of Shurin et al. (2002) and Schmitz (2000) would present wolf ecologists with exciting opportunities for syntheses.

RECOMMENDATIONS FOR FUTURE STUDIES

Our comparison of in BNP and YNP illustrated the benefits of an experimental approach to understanding of wolf effects. Indeed, Estes et al. (2004) and Walters (1986) comment that an understanding of community dynamics is not possible without natural experiments. Replicated control areas that provide temporal baselines are critical in these studies. However, experimental designs will be difficult to conduct in 'real' systems of large enough spatial scales. Studies in YNP suffered from a lack of control; BNP from a lack of replication. Therefore, researchers will need to take advantage of 'natural' experiments – areas that wolves do not recolonize – to provide the best BACI design (Sinclair 1991). Alternatively, gradient approaches where researchers compare a response across the wolf recolonization 'front' may be useful. Because many studies will be correlative in nature, path analyses or structural equation models that aim to disentangle direct and indirect effects will help provide syntheses (Shipley et al. 2002). Another approach that we believe will be useful given the constraints imposed on 'natural' experiments will be cross-sectional time series approaches (Woolridge 2001). By collecting multiple time-series (panels) of elk, willow, aspen, etc., abundances in areas with differing wolf recovery dynamics, cross-sectional time-series analyses will provide opportunities to test for the broad, region-wide influence of wolves. Regardless, confounding of indirect and direct effects of wolf recolonization in community dynamics is likely to pose problems for interpreting mechanisms of ecosystem impacts. Examples of where this will be important include wolf regulation or behaviourally mediated trophic cascades – which is 'more' important; or in studies of exploitative vs. apparent competition. Finally, while the temptation may exist to claim studies summarized herein constitute evidence that wolves are a keystone species, we side with Mills et al. (1993) in urging caution. The data required to truly test if wolves are a keystone species remain elusive and require comparative experimental tests of the relative importance of wolves, bears, cougars, humans, etc., all on elk (and plant) density (Power et al. 1996). To date, only a handful of studies have presented data of sufficient rigour to even be used to test the trophic cascade hypothesis for wolves. As more researchers present data that will be useful in meta-analyses, a future test of the keystone species hypothesis for wolves may be possible, but at present, we conclude there is insufficient evidence to test the keystone species hypothesis for wolves.

MANAGEMENT IMPLICATIONS

Recovery of wolves in both national parks compared here seems to bolster the support for ecosystem management and the role of carnivores for restoring many important ecological processes required by both countries Parks' legislation. Decades of debate about overgrazing by elk on YNP's northern range (Kay 1998) may be moot now if wolves, combined with a number of indirect species interactions, reduce elk densities and their behaviour to the point where long-term ecosystem states are maintained for species like willow, aspen, and beaver. In fact, wolf recovery emphasizes that most debates about the northern range of Yellowstone over the past half century occurred in a wolf-free environment. While critics of the national parks suggested human predation (elk removals) would be necessary to reduce elk densities (Kay 1998; Wagner 2006), they seemed to discount or fail to recognize the potential influence of wolf predation on maintenance of long-term ecosystem states. So in the modern YNP environment, with a strong effect of the late winter hunt (Vucetich et al. 2005) and a complete large carnivore guild, elk densities are sure to be maintained at levels low enough for potentially willow, and likely (in the future) aspen restoration.

However, the restoration of wolves may not always yield 'positive' ecosystem effects. They may even have undesirable ecosystem impacts such as evidenced by the near-extirpated BNP caribou population potentially due to apparent competition mediated by wolves (Hebblewhite et al. 2007). Caribou conservation raises the thorny issue of the potential need for wolf control, presently underway in Alberta to recover caribou (Alberta Woodland Caribou Recovery Team 2005). It also raises the issue that elk could not have existed at even moderate densities over long time scales or caribou populations could not have persisted. In this respect, caribou viability and aspen sapling recruitment may all be indicators of the same long-term ecosystem state for the Rockies. We encourage researchers not just to investigate 'positive' ecosystem effects of wolves, but also potential 'negative' direct and indirect effects. This will ensure an unbiased scientific approach to wolf community ecology, and acknowledges that ultimately, the value of wolves in ecosystems is a result of human perceptions and attitudes.

As an example, management implications of wolves will often differ between jurisdictions. These changes may be interpreted as positive by humans who orient toward ecological or preservationist oriented values, but could be viewed as negative by others who value maximum sustained yield of trophy bull elk, for example, in areas adjacent to parks. Moreover, subtle differences may exist even between parks. In Yellowstone, the goal of the National Parks Service is to re-establish and protect ecological processes, with no targeted population level for any animal or plant, and to minimize effects of humans. YNP has to date avoided managing for specific 'targets' of densities for key indicator species by minimizing human intervention (Cole 1971; Boyce 1998). In Banff, Parks Canada follows a similar management objective focused on maintaining ecological integrity, also through a process-oriented perspective. Nationally, Parks Canada observes a broader mandate of ecological integrity to include humans as a key ecological process through hunting, trapping, and prescribed fire. This is especially true throughout the northern national parks, where many recent parks were created with full co-management of First Nations people. As a result, Parks Canada has interpreted the scientific literature to manage for a more targeted range of key indicator species densities based largely on pre-European conditions, including the effects of human hunting and fires (White et al. 1998). Wolves fit into both management objectives, as predation by wolves is a key natural process in North American ecosystems and was present in both systems pre-European contact. The argument that YNP should manage for a particular state, one with fewer herbivores and lusher vegetation – one seen in early park photographs around the turn of the century – misses the point of these differing management objectives; neither is wrong, but their goals are different. Allowing natural carnivores to fluctuate over time will produce large swings in animal and plant populations, unlike in Banff, where plant and animal populations will fluctuate less. The consequences of differences between park policies need to be considered more carefully, for example, in the case of endangered species management. Regardless, restoration of wolves provides an opportunity to test whether national parks can truly function as ecological baselines in the context of human activities outside parks and in the future (Arcese & Sinclair 1997).

ACKNOWLEDGEMENTS

Support for the Yellowstone component was provided by Yellowstone National Park, the Yellowstone Park Foundation, the Tapeats Foundation, the Perkins Prothro Foundation, the California Wolf Center, an anonymous donor, and National Science Foundation grant DEB-0613730. D. Guernsey created the figures for the Yellowstone section and we appreciate the hard work of D. Stahler, R. McIntyre and numerous other volunteers and technicians of the Yellowstone Wolf Project. The wolf research in Yellowstone would not have been possible without these people and the many others who enthusiastically follow and help with understanding the wolves of Yellowstone. Support for research in BNP came from Parks Canada, Canadian Pacific Foundation, NSERC, Alberta Enhanced Career Development, John/Paul & Associates, Paquet Wildlife Fund, World Wildlife Fund, and many other funding agencies. Field assistants too numerous to count contributed to on the ground field efforts since 1987, including a number of graduate students whose work we summarize; A. Kortello, J. McKenzie, C. Callaghan, T. Hurd, C. White, C. Nietvelt, J. Woods, D. Huggard, among others. Wolf-grizzly observations were provided by M. Gibeau and P. Paquet. Strong scientific and administrative support for the research programme in BNP came from C. White, T. Hurd, and D. Dalman, Parks Canada biologists for BNP. Without their vision and guidance, none of the research reviewed in this chapter would have been possible. P.J. White and D. Bilyeu provided helpful comments on an earlier version of this manuscript. Finally, we thank Jonathan Shurin for providing advice on interpreting data from his manuscripts for Figure 1.3.5.

1.4 Will the Future of Wolves and Moose Always Differ from our Sense of Their Past?

John A. Vucetich, Rolf O. Peterson and M. P. Nelson

> "It is the principle involved, and not its ultimate and very complex results, that we can alone attempt to grapple with."
> – Sir D'Arcy Thompson (1942:643)

INTRODUCTION

The wolves (*Canis lupus*) and moose (*Alces alces*) of Isle Royale have been studied continuously and intensively for nearly 50 years. In the context of informal settings (e.g., public talks and discussions with managers and colleagues), we have long characterized the most general conclusion of this long-term research in two ways. First, even after 50 years of observation, each five-year period of the wolf-moose chronology seems to be significantly different from every other five-year period. Second, the longer we study the more we seem to realize how poorly we understand the population dynamics of Isle Royale wolves and moose. In this paper, we pursue these ideas in a more rigorous fashion. The result may be insight, derived from long-term research, about how ecological explanations are developed and judged.

BACKGROUND

Natural history

Isle Royale emerged from Lake Superior (North America) over 8 K years ago. Isle Royale is a long (72 km) and narrow (~7.5 km) archipelago with one main island (544 km2) and approximately 150 smaller surrounding islands (most <0.1 km^2). The island is located in Lake Superior, approximately 24 km from the Lake's north shore (Fig. 1.4.1). The island is almost completely forested. The topography is rough due to glacial scouring of ridges and valleys running the length of the island. Elevation ranges from 180 m to 238 m. The geologic history of Isle Royale is further described in Huber (1983).

The forest habitat is usefully characterized by three distinct regions. The northeast region is transitional boreal forest, dominated by spruce (*Picea glauca*), balsam fir (*Abies balsamea*), aspen (*Populus tremuloides*), and paper birch (*Betula papyrifera*). The middle region was burned over in 1936 and is currently dominated by 80-year old stands of birch and spruce. The southwest region is covered with mixed stands of maple (*Acer saccharum*), yellow birch (*Betula allegheniensis*), cedar (*Thuja occidentalis*), and spruce. Swamps and other wetlands are common in the island's numerous valleys. The vegetation of Isle Royale, especially as it relates to moose herbivory, is further described in Pastor et al. (1998).

Moose arrived to Isle Royale in about the year 1900. Archaeological evidence from camps of Native Americans, who had used the island for at least the past 3K years, suggests that this was the first time moose had ever inhabited Isle Royale. Without reasonable evidence to the contrary, it is presumed that moose swam to Isle Royale. For 50 years moose interacted with the forest without predation or significant human harvest. By the late 1920s the impact of moose on the forest had become noticeable and the population probably comprised two or three thousand moose (Murie 1934). By the mid-1930s many moose had died of malnutrition and the population declined to probably a few hundred animals (Hickie 1936).

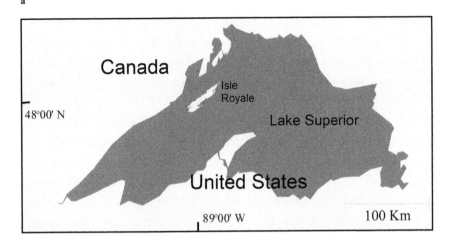

a

Canada

Isle
Royale

Lake Superior

48°00' N

United States

89°00' W   100 Km

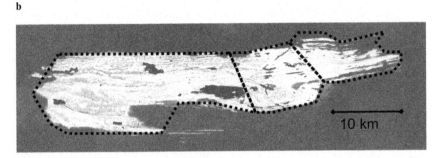

b

10 km

Figure 1.4.1. (a) The location of Isle Royale within Lake Superior, North America. (b) In this satellite image, Isle Royale is usefully divided into three regions. The middle region was largely burned in 1936, and is currently characterized by low moose density. The eastern third of Isle Royale and the western shoreline areas are transition boreal forest and characterized by higher moose density. The polygons denote the approximate boundaries of Isle Royale wolf packs in a typical year. Gray areas are inland lakes.

Murie (1934) suggested that the moose population be harvested or predators, such as wolves, be introduced as a means of controlling such boom and bust cycles. Murie (1935) was a strong advocate for wilderness preservation, and he believed neither of these interventions would be inconsistent with the notion of wilderness.

Isle Royale's moose density varies among the three basic habitat types. Typical densities in winter are 0.6 moose/km^2 in the island's middle region, and 2.5 moose/km^2 in the other portions of Isle Royale. For context, typical moose densities at other sites in North America tend to be <1.0 moose/km2 and commonly <0.2 moose/km^2 (Karns 1997). Coincidentally, Isle Royale moose are relatively small-bodied (360–400 kg for adult females and 425–450 kg for adult males). They also have the smallest antler size of all measured moose populations (Peterson & Vucetich 2002). Each January and February, the average proportion of the population constituted of calves is 0.15 (coefficient of variation = 39). During the 1960s, twinning rates (proportion of cows with calves that had twins) were high (0.25). In the early 1970s, the rate dropped to ~0.10. In recent decades, the twinning rate has been less than ~0.05.

Although there were plans and one attempt to introduce wolves to Isle Royale in the 1940s and 1950s, the attempt failed and other plans were never carried out. Wolves arrived on Isle Royale by crossing an ice bridge connecting Isle Royale and Canada in the late 1940s. This is presumably the first time in the island's history that a wolf population had become established. Analysis of mtDNA indicates that the Isle Royale population was founded by a single female (Wayne et al. 1991). Since being founded, the Isle Royale population has remained genetically isolated. Empirical and analytical assessments suggest that the Isle Royale wolf population is extremely inbred, has lost ~80% of it neutral genetic diversity since being founded, and continues to lose ~13% of its neutral diversity each generation (i.e., the effective population size is ~3 and one wolf generation is ~4 years; Peterson et al. 1998).

The ultimate impact of inbreeding on Isle Royale wolves is unclear. Although Isle Royale wolves exhibit high rates of skeletal deformities (Räikkönen et al. 2006), whether fitness is affected by such deformities is unknown. Isle Royale wolves have vital rates (survival and recruitment) that are comparable with other healthy wolf populations (mean pack size = 4.9 [CV=47] for 1967–2006; mean number of pups in mid-winter = 3.0 [CV=90] for 1997–2006; mean annual mortality rate = 0.28 [CV=60] for 1975–2006). However, since 1980 the number of wolves for every old (vulnerable) moose has been substantially less than before 1980 (Wilmers et al. 2006).

Humans do not harvest wolves, moose, or the forest. Although present on the nearby mainland, white-tailed deer (*Odocoileus virginianus*), coyotes (*C. latrans*), and black bear (*Ursus americanus*) are absent from Isle Royale. Winter wolf diet is ~95% moose, and summer wolf diet is >85% moose. Most of the remaining diet is beaver (*Castor canadensis*). The only significant causes of moose death are wolf predation and malnutrition, both of which are sometimes exacerbated by severe winters and winter ticks (*Dermacentor albipictus*). Between 40% and 60% of the moose winter diet is a single species (i.e., balsam fir). Compared with many large vertebrate communities, the Isle Royale wolf-moose system seems simple (Smith et al. 2003).

Moreover, the Isle Royale wolf-moose system is commonly characterized as a single-prey/single-predator system. However, the justification for this characterization is becoming increasingly difficult. The importance of other factors – such as canine parvo-virus (Wilmers et al. 2006), moose ticks (Peterson & Vucetich 2006), and winter severity (Vucetich et al. 2004) – have been made this clear.

Research history

Continuous research on Isle Royale wolves and moose began in the summer of 1958 (Fig. 1.4.2). At that time, the primary, long-term monitoring was an annual winter census of wolves and moose. Beginning in the early 1970s long-term monitoring expanded to include: 1) the key statistic that connects populations of predator and prey – the per capita kill rate, and 2) systematic and more concerted efforts to collect specific skeletal remains of dead moose (including skull, mandible, and metatarsus). Approximately one-third of all moose that have ever lived in the population are eventually collected, and currently we have skeletal remains of more than 4,000 different moose. By the mid-1990s, long-term monitoring had expanded again to include aspects of forest structure and demography (especially balsam fir tree-ring growth patterns, decline of canopy fir, and browse

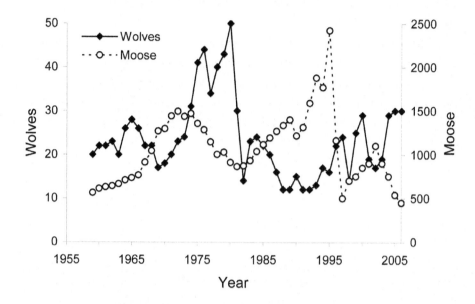

Figure 1.4.2. Population trajectories of wolves and moose on Isle Royale, 1959–2006. Each year the entire wolf population is counted from a small aircraft (details in Peterson & Page 1988). The number of moose is estimated from population reconstruction (before 1995, see Solberg et al. 1999) and aerial survey estimates (after 1995, details in Peterson & Page 1993).

rates). By 2005, long-term monitoring had expanded again to include annual monitoring of moose ticks, moose diet composition, and more intensive monitoring of wolf and moose genetics. Recently, we have also investigated the means by which moose forage quality and wolf intestinal parasites might be monitored annually. The greatest obstacle to continuing and expanding monitoring is limited funding, and the greatest resistance to improving the research is administrative.

NUMERICAL ANALYSIS

At the coarsest scale the interaction between wolf and moose populations can be characterized by the extent to which their abundances are correlated across years. Most generally, observational (i.e., non-experimental) ecological inquiry is fundamentally based on the observation and interpretation of covariation among temporally varying processes or entities. Undoubtedly, the interpretation can be complex and often entails autocorrelation and cross-correlation at various or multiple time lags (e.g., Pascual & Ellner 2000). Although we ignore such details in this analysis, we limit our inferences from this analysis (see below) to those we expect are robust to such simplification.

For no other purpose than as a heuristic, suppose that a simple explanation for a positive correlation is that prey largely determine predator abundance; a negative correlation may suggest that predators determine prey abundance, and weak correlation may indicate either a more complex interaction or weak interaction.

Between 1959 and 2006 the correlation between wolf and moose abundances was negative, but not strongly so ($r = -0.26$, $R^2 = 0.07$, $p = 0.08$). However, the estimated correlation has not always been such. Shorter-term correlations have fluctuated greatly throughout the first 50 years of the study.

To assess quantitatively how the estimated correlation has fluctuated over time, and how it has depended on the length of observation, we calculated a set of correlations, each depending on a different subset of the data. First, we estimated the correlation (and R^2) for each five-year, consecutive set of observations (e.g., 1959–1963, 1960–1964, ... 2002–2006). There are 44 such sets of data. Then we estimated the correlation (and R^2) for each 10-year, consecutive set of observations (e.g., 1959–1968, 1960–1969, ... 1997–2006). There are 39 such sets of data. We continued this procedure for sets of data that were 15, 20, 25, 30, 35, 40, 45, and 50 years in length. The result is depicted in Figure 1.4.3.

We appreciate that these data sets are not independent. We are careful to limit inferences drawn from this analysis (see below) to those that would be insensitive to this lack of independence. Our inferences are motivated by appreciating that one could have observed the wolves and moose of Isle Royale beginning in any year and continuing for any period.

Estimated values of r range from nearly –1 to 1, and instances of strong positive and strong negative correlation are common (Fig. 1.4.3a). The variation in *r* is substantially reduced for periods of observation that are 15 years and greater. The average R^2 declines with increasing periods of observation (Fig. 1.4.3b). Keep in mind, R^2 is sometimes taken as a measure of the explanatory power of a model.

Using the same subset of data described above, we also calculated estimates of the mean time to extinction (MTE) using a very simple model, requiring only knowledge about a population's past trajectory (Foley 1994). Our interest is not in MTE, *per se*. Rather, our interest in MTE is as a statistic that is sensitive to the estimated variance of a population's dynamics. Increased variance causes a decrease in MTE. The equation for MTE is (Foley 1994):

$$MTE = \frac{\exp(2ks)}{2sE[r]}\left(1 - \exp(-2sn_o)\right) - 2sn_o ,$$

(1)

where k is the natural logarithm of the carrying capacity (which we estimate as the maximum observed population to that point in the study), n_o is the natural logarithm of the most recent population size, s is the ratio $E[r]/\mathrm{Var}[r]$ or the ratio of the expected annual population growth rate to the variance in the growth rate. The expectation and the variance were replaced with their maximum likelihood estimates based on the data observed for the particular subset of data being considered.

The relationship between duration of observation and MTE is complex, because with increasing period of observation there is a tendency for $\mathrm{Var}[r]$ and k to increase (Arino & Pimm 1995). These factors have an opposing influence on MTE. Nevertheless, with increasing duration of observation the coefficient of variation in estimates of MTE decline

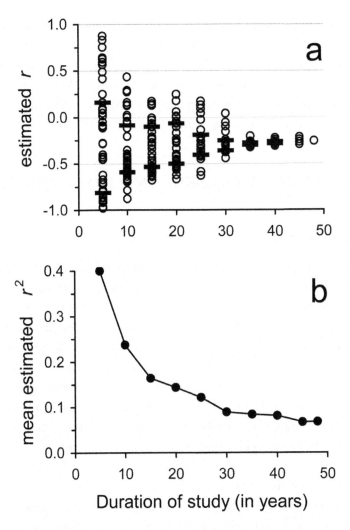

Figure 1.4.3. (a) Estimated correlation coefficient (r) between wolf and moose abundances across years (Fig. 1.4.2). Each estimate is based on a different subset from the time series of wolf and moose abundances. Each subset of data represents abundances from consequent years and is characterized by the number of years of observation (x-axis). Many of the data subsets are over-lapping, and therefore not entirely independent. Heavy bars represent the interquartile range for each duration of observation. (b) Mean value of estimates for r^2 for the various subsets of data representing different durations of observation. Insomuch as the r (panel a) represents a simple model of wolf-moose dynamics, r^2 represents the explanatory power of that simple model. Panel (b) suggests that with increased duration of observation, the explanatory power of this simple model tends to decline substantially over time.

dramatically (Fig. 1.4.4). A dramatic drop in variance occurs at 20 years of observation. This sudden decrease is likely attributable to the dramatic wolf decline that occurred in the early 1980s (Fig. 1.4.2). This decline accounts for a substantial portion of Var[r] in the 50-year chronology, and virtually all subsets of data representing >20 years contain this event, whereas shorter time series may or may not contain this event.

QUALITATIVE ANALYSIS AND DISCUSSION

Statistical explanations

The patterns described above are easily explained by statistical theory. Moreover, those intimately familiar with statistical theory may even have anticipated results like those depicted in Figures 1.4.3 and 1.4.4.

The pattern in Figure 1.4.4 arises from a complex interaction of processes. First, the estimated carrying capacity (k) tends to increase with increased observation, and MTE increases with increased k. Second, the estimated variance of a time series tends to increase the longer a time series is observed (Arino & Pimm 1995), and MTE decreased with increased variance. Any ecological or evolutionary parameter that depends on the variance will be prone to bias that arises from underestimates of variance, which arise from short periods of observation. For example, demographic-based estimates for the rate of inbreeding are affected by the temporal variance in population abundance (Vucetich & Waite 1998). For processes that are highly autocorrelated (i.e., time series with reddened spectra), very long periods of time (perhaps more than one hundred years) may be required to accurately estimate the variance (Arino & Pimm 1995).

Figure 1.4.3 is vaguely explained by virtue of the wolf-moose system having been, apparently, a non-stationary process. Because stationarity is defined (informally, though adequately) as a process whose means, variances, and autocorrelation patterns are the same over whatever time interval they are observed; this account of Figure 1.4.3 may be more of a statistical description than an explanation.

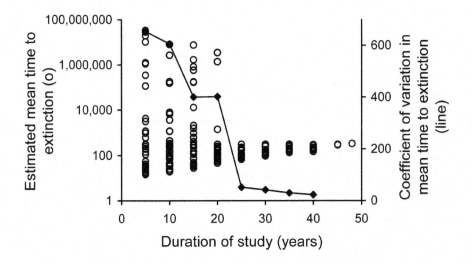

Figure 1.4.4. Estimated mean time to extinction based on population counts from the Isle Royale wolf population (Fig. 1.4.2) and a simple population model (Eq. 1). Each estimate is based on a different subset from the time series of wolf abundances. Each subset of data represents abundances from consequent years and is characterized by the number of years of observation (*x*-axis). Many of the data subsets are overlapping, and therefore not entirely independent. The solid line is the coefficient of variation for mean time to extinction estimates.

The low variance of responses (i.e., the *y*-axis of Figs. 1.4.3a and 1.4.4) for longer durations of observation is *partially* attributable to the longer time series being less numerous and more dependent on each other than the shorter time series (There are many five year segments with no data points in common). Variance for longer durations of observation could be higher than observed if more independent long time series were available. The explanation does not diminish the validity of the inferences we draw from Figs. 1.4.3 and 1.4.4 (see below).

Regardless of these statistical accounts, our observations are important for ecologists and managers whose sense of the world is more strongly influenced by empirical observation than by statistical theory. The critical question remains: how long does one have to observe an ecological system before it is stationary, before one can acquire a reliable sense of its functioning?

INDUCTION AND PREDICTIVE SCEPTICISM

We have studied only one 50-year period in the Isle Royale wolf-moose system, a system whose future is indefinite. The past 50 years have been characterized variously – in simple terms (e.g., Fig. 1.4.3) and in more complex terms (e.g., Vucetich & Peterson 2004a, b). Are there other 50-year periods in the future whose characterization will contradict these past characterizations? The idea is not far fetched. We already know that wolf-moose dynamics during the 1960s and 1970s are remarkably different than during the 1980s and 1990s. For example, before 1980 wolf predation was an important influence on moose population dynamics, whereas after 1980 the influence of wolf predation appeared trivial, and the influence of winter climate and food availability became much more important (Wilmers et al. 2006). Also, before 1980 there were about ~7 old moose per wolf (moose >9 years of age tend to be more vulnerable to predation), and since that time there have tended to be ~19 old moose per wolf (Fig. 5 of Peterson et al. 1998). If the first two decades of wolf-moose dynamics were quite unlike the two decades that followed, is it not plausible (perhaps even likely) that the next 50 years will be quite unlike the past 50 years?

Figure 1.4.3 and the previous discussion suggest a need for critically reconsidering the role of inductive reasoning in ecological science. Certainly, the role of inductive reasoning for extreme cases is reliably understood: It is reasonable to infer inductively that the next severe drought in a particular ecosystem will cause reduced primary productivity *because* severe drought usually causes reduced primary productivity in most studied ecosystems. At the other extreme, it is unreasonable to infer inductively that pine martens (*Martes americana*), for example, have a top-down effect on their prey because perch (*Perca fluviatilis*) have a top-down effect on their prey. Between these extremes there may be a significant set of ecological circumstances whereby inductive inference seems (even after careful consideration) to be reasonable, when in fact it is not.

Explaining past ecological phenomena

If the sole purpose of and criterion for ecological science is not to develop an explanation that *predicts* phenomena in another system or in the same system at a different time, then how would we judge explanations intended to explain past ecological phenomena?

Ecological explanations are commonly represented by statistical models that are judged by their parsimony *and* on how well they fit observed data. Importantly, measures of fit are *absolute* (e.g., for normally distributed data, R^2 ranges from 0 to 1), and measures of parsimony are *relative* to the models being compared (Burnham & Anderson 1998). When prediction is one's primary purpose then parsimony is a relatively well-developed concept: among compared models, the most parsimonious entails a balance between variance and bias that achieves confidence intervals with minimal width and coverage at the approximate nominal level. Hereafter, we refer to this as *narrow parsimony*. Examples of narrow parsimony include adjusted-R^2 and Akaike Information Criterion. Narrow parsimony can be expressed mathematically and typically includes a term to describe how well a model fits the observed data and a term to describe the model's complexity. Parsimony increases with increased fit and decreased model complexity.

Parsimony also has a more general sense, whose precise meaning is more difficult to isolate (e.g., Plutynski 2005). Explanations of past ecological phenomena ought to exhibit *general* parsimony, which may or may not correspond precisely with narrow parsimony. Below we discuss three Isle Royale examples that illustrate the issues that arise when explaining the past, rather than predicting the future, is the primary goal.

(1) Vucetich et al. (2002) compared several models aimed at explaining past patterns of the per capita rate at which wolves kill moose during winter. The most important comparisons were among these models:

prey-dependent model: *kill rate* $= \alpha N/(\beta + N)) + \varepsilon$, (Eq. 1a)

ratio-dependent model: *kill rate* $= \alpha(R)/(\beta + (R)) + \varepsilon$, (Eq. 1b)

predator-prey-dependent model: *kill rate* $= \alpha N/(\beta N + P - \gamma) + \varepsilon$, (Eq. 1c)

where N is moose abundance, P is wolf abundance, R is the ratio of moose to wolves, ε is an error term, and other Greek symbols are parameters estimated from data. Vucetich et al. (2002) concluded that the ratio-dependent model was the most parsimonious.

Conventionally, when narrow parsimony is quantified, model complexity is judged exclusively by the number of model parameters (i.e., dimensionality). However, a model's complexity also has a structural or conceptual component, which is not reflected by its dimensionality. Although the prey-dependent and ratio-dependent models are equally complex in terms of the numbers of parameters, the ratio-dependent model is conceptually more complex insomuch as the predictor variable (i.e., the ratio of moose to wolves) is an interaction term. Because a bivariate predictor variable contains more information than a univariate predictor variable, the ratio-dependent model ought to (and does, in fact) outperform the prey-dependent model. The ratio-dependent model has a similar built-in advantage when compared to the model with both predator and prey abundance. Although both models account for the influence of wolves and moose, the ratio-dependent model does so with one fewer parameter. Does this set of candidate models represent a general strategy for developing better ecological explanations? That is, if two or more variables are expected to interact, should one combine them in some appropriate manner and omit the original univariate predictor variables? Such an approach would, if appropriate, be broadly applicable. Any related set of variables (e.g., climate variables) can be combined (using, e.g., principle components analysis) into some sort of interactive term. Is this a cheater's way of forcing more into a model without being penalized for the extra parameters, or is this a legitimate strategy for developing better explanations?

More generally, is it appropriate to compare the parsimony of a linear model (e.g., $y=a_0+a_1X$) with any of the various non-linear models that possess the same number of parameters as a linear expression (e.g., hyperbolic, inverse, exponential, or other such functions), or ought one to compare the linear model to a second order polynomial? The opportunity to express nonlinearity in X with one less parameter may allow one to justify an explanation with an additional predictor variable. For example, the expression, $y=(b_0X_1/(b_1+X_1))+b_2X_2$, is nonlinear, has two predictor variables, and only three parameters (not including the variance of the error term), whereas a second order polynomial has the same number of parameters, but only one predictor variable. If one has good *a priori* reason to consider a simple linear model (with two parameters), then is special theoretical justification required to consider a nonlinear model (also with two parameters)? If such justification is available, would that not count as justification against considering the linear model? In this case the reason for tending so closely to the *a priori* considerations is that the non-linear model has a built-in advantage (i.e., it has increased complexity that is not accounted for by narrow parsimony).

An important sense of general parsimony is reflected by a corruption of an aphorism traditionally credited to Einstein: Scientific explanations ought to be as simple as possible, but no simpler. Under what conditions should a model (perhaps a model that exhibits narrow parsimony) be excluded from consideration as a useful explanation because it is too simple or ecologically inappropriate?[1] When should the seemingly objective, quantitative rational considerations associated with narrow parsimony be overridden by conflicting rational considerations?

Some think the prey-dependent model is a poor explanation, regardless of its empirical fit, because it implies certain properties that are undesirable (e.g., Akcakaya et al. 1995). Others think the same of the ratio-dependent model (e.g., Abrams 1994; see also Abrams & Ginzburg 2000). Perhaps the most critical shortcoming of the ratio-dependent model is that

---

1 Burnham & Anderson (1998:140) discuss some negative consequences of even considering models that are inappropriate on a basis of a priori rational considerations.

it predicts that predators can persist in the presence of vanishingly small prey populations. In reality, there is some lower limit of prey below which a predator population cannot be supported. This pathology can be corrected by subtracting the lower limit (τ) from N (i.e., *kill rate* $= \alpha((N-\tau)/P)/(\beta+(N-\tau)/P)) + \varepsilon$). Although the data to which the model is being fit and the principles of narrow parsimony do not justify the inclusion of τ, it can be justified on the basis of observing, estimating, or guessing this lower limit from other knowledge. Is this a sensible means by which to develop an ecological explanation? Ecologists do not seem to agree on this matter (cf., Turchin 2003 and Boyce 2000 with Abrams 1994). The disagreement is fundamental and concerns understanding the proper balance between empirical observation and rational consideration in the development of explanations. Although rational considerations are a critical element of any explanation, the extent of their influence is not always easily identified, can be difficult to judge, and is prone to subjectivity.

(2) Vucetich and Peterson (2004a) examined two models that aimed to explain annual population growth rate in Isle Royale wolves. One model was more directly mechanistic (i.e., the predictor variable was per capita kill rate) and explained little observed variation (i.e., $R^2=0.22$). The other model was less directly mechanistic (i.e., the predictor variable was number of old, vulnerable moose) and explained more observed variation (i.e., $R^2=0.42$). If the purpose is to predict the future, clearly the second model seems more promising. However, if the purpose is to explain the past, how does one compare the explanatory value of a more mechanistic model that provides a poorer fit with a less directly mechanistic model, which happens to provide a better fit? Similarly, but more generally, consider a spectrum of modelling styles: from those relying more heavily on the inclusion of extra-empirical, though rationally justified, elements (e.g., Turchin 2003) to those focusing more on the development of inferences that can be supported primarily by the data upon which the model is primarily built, even if such data do not appear to exhibit aspects that may be rationally justified (e.g., Murdoch et al. 2003). Do they represent different kinds (of equally valid) ecological explanation, or does one style usually produce better or more useful ecological explanations?

If predicting the future is not a primary goal, then either/or approaches may not be the most appropriate means of developing ecological explanations (about past phenomena). If true, we may need a better understanding of how to develop unified explanations about ecological phenomena from various models and other bits of empirical information that seem incommensurable (Chapter 4 of Burnham & Anderson [1998] offer important advice about this issue, although it is limited to sets of models developed from exactly the same sets of data.)

(3) Vucetich and Peterson (2004b) attempted to explain how wolves, forage abundance, and climate affect the dynamics of moose. They used time series of moose abundance and other presumably related covariates (e.g., wolves, annual balsam fir growth, and climate). Given this context, compare:

$$moose_{t+1} = f(wolves_t, forage_t, climate_t) + \varepsilon_t \qquad \text{(eq. 2a)}$$

with

$$moose_{t+1} = f(wolves_t, forage_t, climate_t, moose_t) + \varepsilon_t. \qquad \text{(eq. 2b)}$$

Suppose that inclusion of $moose_t$ (i.e., density dependence) affects the model in some important manner (e.g., increases the fit to the data and/or changes the parameter estimates associated with $wolves_t$, $forage_t$, and $climate_t$). If one's goal is to explain the past, rather than to predict the future, how, if at all, should the model with $moose_t$ even be considered? We do not dispute that understanding patterns of density dependence may be useful for certain purposes (e.g., predicting the future or comparing dynamics of different populations). However, if the goal is to understand how past patterns of moose abundance had been affected by predation or forage abundance, the inclusion of density dependent terms *could* result in a poor explanation for two reasons: (i) In advance we know that density-dependent dynamics are a necessary property of populations that persist and do not grow to infinity (Royama 1992). Consequently, in this context density dependence is a highly phenomenological process, without much potential to explain anything beyond the population's persistence. (ii) Resource abundance and predation *may often* affect a population in an importantly density dependent manner. If so, density dependent terms will be confounded with resource and predation terms. Suppose one felt justified in giving primacy to the influence of *wolves*$_t$, *forage*$_t$, and *climate*$_t$ but still wished to judge whether previous moose abundance explained any additional variation in subsequent moose abundance. In this case, one might consider: *i*) fitting equation (2a) to the observed data, *ii*) fitting the time series of residuals from equation (2a) to the time series of previous year's moose density (i.e., fit this equation: $\varepsilon_t = g(moose_t) + \varepsilon'_t$), and (*iii*) combining the two models: $moose_{t+1} = f(wolves_t, forage_t, climate_t) + g(moose_t) + \varepsilon'_t$. For emphasis, the parameters associated with *wolves*$_t$, *forage*$_t$, and *climate*$_t$ would be unaffected by $g(moose_t) + \varepsilon'_t$. This approach would assume that most density dependence in a population arises from interaction with predators and resources, rather than from territorial behaviour or interference intra-specific competition that is unrelated to food or predation.

This example reflects a very general issue concerning models that include sets of variables representing multiple levels of mechanism. To see the generality, suppose winter climate *per se* has little direct influence on moose population dynamics. Rather, suppose climate's effect is primarily indirect and affects moose through nutrition (food intake) and predation. In this case, one might construct a model that could be represented as: $moose_{t+1} = f(wolves_t, forage_t, climate_t) + h(climate_t) + g(moose_t) + \varepsilon''_t$. This approach is not obviously correct or incorrect, and not obviously better or worse than the kind of model represented by equation (2b).

When prediction is not the primary purpose of judging an explanation, then explanations may be primarily concerned with understanding causation. The notion of causation is surprisingly complicated (Skyrms 1980; Cartwright 1989; Pearl 2000). If severe winter climate causes moose to be more vulnerable to predation, and if predation causes moose abundance to decline, can we say that climate causes moose to decline? If one aims to develop ecological explanations in terms of cause and effect, then one must address how to combine the explanatory influence of variables that operate at different mechanistic levels.

Testing data or testing explanations?

Ecological data are difficult to collect. It is also often difficult to know when ecological data are collected with adequate precision or accuracy. Consequently, ecologists may often not know whether we are testing the adequacy of an ecological explanation, or testing the adequacy of data.

For example, how adequate is our perceived influence of balsam fir on moose population dynamics (i.e., Vucetich and Peterson 2004b; Wilmers et al. 2006)? We represent balsam fir by an annual index of tree-ring growth, which is thought to reflect annual primary productivity. Do we underestimate the influence of balsam fir because tree-ring growth is a poor indicator of balsam fir availability? Do we overestimate the influence of balsam fir because fir growth is highly correlated with the availability of other unmeasured forage?

Similarly, if adequate ecological explanations are relatively complex (recall Einstein's aphorism), then the development of adequate explanations requires data from numerous potentially related processes collected over long periods. This is an important issue, because we do not know if adequate ecological explanations are relatively complex (cf., Burnham & Anderson 1998:12 and Kareiva 1994), and the data necessary to test relatively complex explanations is remarkably sparse.

There is a huge difference between testing data and testing explanations. In many cases, one gets the sense that ecologists believe we are testing explanations, when in fact we are confirming the inadequacy of our data to test potentially adequate explanations.

Ecological explanations and historical explanations

The timing and circumstances of the collapse of the Soviet Union were unpredicted. Nevertheless, there are reasonable explanations for the cause of the collapse. Human history is importantly represented by events that were unpredicted but were subsequently provided with reasonable explanations. The history of the Isle Royale wolf-moose chronology is comparable. The severity of the wolf collapse of the early 1980s was not predicted (Fig. 1.4.2). Nevertheless, introduction of canine parvovirus is a reasonable explanation for the decline (Peterson et al. 1998). The severity of the moose collapse in the mid-1990s was not predicted. Nevertheless, there is a reasonable explanation (i.e., convergence of severe winter, moose tick outbreak, lack of forage, exceptionally high moose density).

If pure predictive ability is not the sole (or primary) determinant of what counts as a good ecological explanation about past ecological phenomena, then this may be one way in which ecology differs fundamentally from a science like physics, where prediction is generally treated as necessary and paramount. Good explanations of past ecological events may be like good explanations of past events in human history. Epistemologically, ecology may be like a hybrid of physics and systematic investigations of human history.

Importantly, the criteria for good explanations in history may be quite different than is the case for physics. An important, caution-raising implication of relating ecology to history is that the primary purpose of explaining human history may be fundamentally political and ethical – that is, for the purpose of prescribing how we ought to behave and relate to other humans (Staloff 1998; Lemon 2003). Is the general and fundamental purpose of explaining ecological phenomena to prescribe how we ought to interact with nature? If it is, should it be? Can it be otherwise? Is the prescriptive dimension of ecological explanations substantial and inescapable – as is often the case for historical explanations?

Certainly, consulting an ecologist about how to manage natural resources (i.e., science-based management) is analogous to consulting a physicist about how to build a spacecraft. However, to what extent is such ecological consultation analogous to consulting a historian about how to run a government? The nature of the physicist's advice depends only on her knowledge. The nature of the historian's advice depends on the historian's knowledge, political tendencies, and ethical attitudes. Arthur Schlesinger, Jr., William F. Buckley, and Arthur Herman are all highly qualified historians/political scientists, but each would have critically different views on how to run a government. No respectable politician should defend his or her use of a historian's advice on the sole basis that the historian is knowledgeable about history. How exactly ought natural resource managers relate to ecologists?

Predicting future ecological phenomena

If inductive reasoning about future ecological phenomena is *sometimes* unreliable, and if we have a poor *a priori* sense for knowing when induction is and is not unreliable, then how ought natural resource managers interact with ecological systems? We are not championing an extreme notion of scepticism, whereby inductive reasoning about future ecological phenomena is always unreliable. Our claim is that for a significant set of cases, inductive reasoning will not be reasonable, though it may seem so. The Isle Royale chronology illustrates this possibility insomuch as there are numerous five- and ten-year periods whereby one would have gotten the false sense that wolf and moose abundance is strongly correlated (Fig. 1.4.3).

In principle, natural resource managers conventionally rely on two tools for decision making in the face of uncertainty, adaptive management (AM; Walters & Hilborn 1978), and risk analysis (RA; Varis & Kuikka 1999; Byrd & Cothern 2000). What kind of tool is AM, if the future is often unlike one's empirical sense of the past? If one's sense of the past is based on short periods of observation,[2] then AM may not be particularly useful. Conversely, AM would not seem all that effective a tool if reconsideration of a management action were held off until a reliable sense of its effect is available, which may take 30, 50, or more years of observation. If one has good reason to think that the future is often unlike one's empirical sense of the past, then RA is difficult to employ because there is little empirical basis for judging the probabilities of various outcomes, given various actions.

Although AM and RA may be necessary components of reliable management, they may not be sufficient. The Isle Royale experience, like many other experiences, suggests that the Precautionary Principle (deFur & Kaszuba 2002) is also necessary. Because we often have a poor sense of

---

2 Imagine an adaptive management program where the evaluation of management required 50 years of observation.

the magnitude of our ignorance, the Precautionary Principle may be necessary when uncertainty and ignorance are thought to be great *and* when they are thought to be unimportant. To quote Oliver Wendell Holmes (Simmons 1992): *"Certitude is not the test of certainty. We have been cocksure of many things that are not so."* Consequently, the challenge presented by the Precautionary Principle is not understanding when it should be applied – it should always be applied. Rather, the underappreciated challenge of the Precautionary Principle is to understand what it suggests that we actually do (see Majone 2002; Conko 2003; Goldstein & Carruth 2005). Better understanding of the Precautionary Principle will require committed collaboration amongst sociologists, environmental philosophers, political scientists, and ecologists.

Finally, the Precautionary Principle may often be motivated by fear that mismanagement of natural resources will be detrimental to human "welfare" and enterprises. Ethical considerations (e.g., Taylor 1986; Naess 1989; Callicott 1999) and the influence on the emotional intellect (Goleman 2005) of many people who reflect on the Isle Royale ecosystem (personal observation) suggest that even the Precautionary Principle, because of its relation to fear and focus on human welfare, could be inadequate for developing a right relationship with nature. A reasonable case can be made that a right relationship with nature requires "natural resource management" that arises from respect for and wonderment at nature's intrinsic value (Moore 2005), rather than fear of nature's revolt against humanity. Differences between a management based on fear and one based on wonder and respect are liable to be substantial.

Extreme events and causal explanations

Extreme events (e.g., so-called "100-year droughts") may have substantial impacts on a population, especially if relationships are highly nonlinear at extreme ends of a predictor variable's range. Understanding the impact of extreme events may be difficult, because extreme events are thought to occur only rarely.

However, the frequency of extreme events depends on one's perspective. One could recognize numerous types of independently occurring extreme events, each of which are able to influence a moose or wolf population's dynamics (e.g., summer temperature, timing of green-up, annual snow fall, a few types of disease, etc.). If there are 10 independent variables and the probability of a single extreme event is 2% (e.g., extremely severe *or* extremely mild winter), then some kind of extreme event (i.e., something comparable to, say, a "100-year drought") occurs, on average, about once every 6 years. Moreover, two extreme events could co-occur in the same year. Co-occurring extreme events could have similar or opposing influences on the population, and may or may not interact (in the statistical sense of the word). If there are 10 independent variables and the probability of any single extreme event is 4% (e.g., extremely severe *or* extremely mild winter), then two extreme events (i.e., each comparable to, say, a "50-year drought") co-occur, on average, about once every 20 years.

In nearly five decades of observing the wolves and moose of Isle Royale, we are aware of several extreme events. In the early 1980s, the wolf population crashed in response to canine parvovirus. In the mid-1990s, the moose population crashed during the coincidence of an extremely severe winter, extremely low forage abundance, and a moderate outbreak of ticks. In the early 2000s, moose were negatively affected (and wolves were positively affected) by what may turn out to be a severe multi-year outbreak of ticks. In 2005, moose may have been adversely affected by an extremely hot summer.

The challenge presented by extreme events is: Because a particular type of extreme event occurs rarely, its impact is difficult to understand. This creates substantial difficulty in knowing whether a population is primarily affected by many different types of extreme effects or by moderate variation in a few key effects. This alternative represents a very basic feature of a population's dynamics, about which ecologists seem to have divergent opinions (cf., Burnham & Anderson 1998:12 and Kareiva 1994). Using conventional principles of model selection, a fair empirical comparison of this alternative is not possible unless a system has been observed for a very long time. For organisms in seasonal environments, a long time (measured in years) is about ten times the number of possible effects. The inability to assess this alternative empirically heightens any insight that might arise from a conceptual assessment.

The *number of effects* required to adequately describe a population depends not only on the contingent, empirical nature of the population, but also on the purpose of the model (i.e., predicting future or explaining past) and the logical constraints implied by the *kind of effects* that one considers. When one's purpose is prediction of unobserved (future) events, then conventional model selection strategies based on narrow parsimony are appropriate. In this case, models with fewer parameters will usually be selected in favour of modes with more parameters, not because the simpler models are adequate, but because the sample size is small (duration of observation is short).[3]

When one's purpose is to explain the past, model development is more complex. As an illustration, compare this set of models:

$$r_t = \alpha_0 + \alpha_1 m_t + \varepsilon_t \qquad (3a)$$
$$r_t = \alpha_0 + \alpha_1 w_t + \varepsilon_t \qquad (3b)$$

where r_t is moose population growth rate in year t, m_t is moose density, w_t is wolf density, ε_t is usually referred to as the error term, and the alphas are coefficients estimated from the data.

Equation 3a is the simplest, least mechanistic, and most general model in population biology. The first two terms of equation 3a describe how the population is *affected* by numerous density-dependent *effects*, and the third term describes the affect of numerous density-independent effects. Logically, all possible effects are accounted for (albeit phenomenologically) by the two mutually exclusive sets of terms. Even if the so-called model fit is low (i.e., low R^2), the model is perfectly adequate for explaining how

---

3   Sample size limits the number of parameters that can be estimated with reasonable precision (i.e., reasonably small standard error). When a parameter estimate is associated with a large standard error, the estimate may be a poor reflection of the truth.

past dynamics have been influenced by density-dependent and density-independent effects.

Although equation 3b entails more mechanism than equation 3a, it is odd in a certain way. The first two terms of equation 3b describe the effect of predation, and the third term accounts for effects that are not predation. Although this set (predation and not predation) is mutually exclusive and covers all possible effects, it is an odd way to sort the universe of possible effects. Conceptually, it may be necessary (and possibly sufficient) to account for moose forage if one accounts for predation. If so, the universe of possible effects is divided and completely covered by three categories: predation, forage, and other effects. If accounting for predation requires accounting for other effects representing a similar level of mechanistic detail, then failure to do so may result in a misspecified model (i.e., a model that omits an important variable). Misspecified models have biased parameter estimates, unless the omitted variable(s) is completely orthogonal (uncorrelated) to the observed variable(s) (Phillipi 1993).

The comparison of equations 3a and 3b suggests that the number of variables needed to describe adequately a population depends importantly on how one divides the universe of possible effects, as opposed to depending exclusively on empirical, contingent aspects of the population being analyzed. Inclusion of a mechanistic term may imply the need to include all mechanisms occurring at that level of detail, if biased estimates of model coefficients are to be avoided. It also seems likely that mechanisms that are more detailed will be associated with a larger set of other mechanisms that operate at the same level of detail.

This comparison of equations 3a and 3b also implies a conceptual deficiency with an equation like $r_t = \alpha_0 + \alpha_1 m_t + \alpha_2 w_t + \varepsilon_t$. Consider this equation to be an elaboration of equation 3a. If predation has elements that are density-dependent and (or) density-independent, then the terms of this equation do not represent a set of mutually exclusive categories. The result is a confounded set of parameters.

Our assessment of equation 3b showed that mechanistic models might be vulnerable to biased parameter estimates. Although a model with biased parameter estimates may fit observed data well, such a model would, by definition, provide a distorted sense of causal influence. Moreover, an accurate sense of causal influence would seem an essential component of a good explanation, especially if prediction is not paramount. However, the conceptual nature of causation is sufficiently elusive, especially for observational data gathered in an ecological context, that a more sophisticated appreciation is needed. There are good reasons for thinking that formal experimentation is the only practical means by which causation may be determined (e.g., Havens & Aumen 2000; Fowler et al. 2006; cf. Pearl 2000), and for thinking that causation does not even exist unless there is an external manipulator (e.g., Russell 1913; Holland 1986). The best explanations of the Isle Royale wolf-moose system may not be primarily concerned with an external manipulator. Because causality is a sufficiently vexing concept, it seems reasonable to admit explanations of past ecological phenomena that do not depend importantly on any notion of causation. Good explanations of past ecological phenomena may entail no more than a model that is rationally reasonable and provides a good empirical fit – regardless of its causal accuracy (or narrow parsimony) (Thompson 1942; Keller 2002).

The development of ecological explanations

Scientific explanations may be usefully characterized by their degree of simplicity or complexity. The virtue of complex explanations is our belief that nature is complex. The virtue of simple explanations is their comprehensibility, testability, and applicability. Scientific explanations also arise from a dialectic between *a priori* rational considerations (i.e., theories) and empirical observation.[4] The duration of empirical observation may generally limit the complexity (or simplicity) of many ecological explanations. The Isle Royale study may illustrate something general about how ecological ideas develop.

4　This view is consistent with most modern philosophers of science (e.g., Kuhn 1962; Laudan 1990; Brown 2001; Rosenberg 2005). This view contrasts with K. Popper's (1959) view, that science entails two highly distinct stages: hypothesis generation and hypothesis testing. Hypothesis testing is a purely empirical affair, and hypothesis generation could arise from any rational (or irrational) process.

The relationships illustrated in Figure 1.4.3 suggest that short-term research (e.g., studies <10 years) would often promote belief in simple ideas (e.g., a strong bivariate correlation and high R^2). Moreover, short-term research would tend to preclude the development of complex ideas; because, in the context of multiple regressions, detecting the influence of even moderately important predictor variables requires about ten observations per predictor variable (i.e., a model with five predictor variables may require upwards of 50 observations).

In the parlance of Frequentist statistical theory, precluding the development of a complex idea is analogous to a Type II error, and belief in simple ideas is analogous to a Type I error. Unfortunately, short-term research can foster errors of both types simultaneously. By contrast, long-term research may allow for the development of more complex ideas, and usually discredits belief in simple ideas. One guard against becoming overly convinced about the appropriateness of a simple idea is to calculate and report confidence intervals for R^2 (Neter et al. 1989). Although this is rarely done, it can be illustrative. For $n=50$, the 90% CI for $R^2=0.5$ is approximately [0.32, 0.65]. For $n=25$, the 90% CI for $R^2=0.5$ is [0.24, 0.71]. This method of calculating CI's is not advisable for $n<25$.

A similar sense about the influence of duration of observation is implied by comparing ideas that have arisen at various points in the history of the Isle Royale study. After observing Isle Royale wolves and moose for less than five years, Allen and Mech (1963) concluded: *"Our studies thus far indicate that the moose and wolf populations on Isle Royale have struck a reasonably good balance."* Today, "reasonably good balance" seems like an inadequate description of the Isle Royale system. More recently, the Isle Royale dynamics have been characterized by comparison to "discordant harmonies" (Botkin 1992).

After a few years of observation, Mech (1966) concluded that wolf predation reduced moose abundance to levels below which resources limited moose populations. After about 15 years of observation, Peterson (1977) concluded that food limitation did affect moose population dynamics, as did annual fluctuations in winter severity. Only after nearly 50 years of observation has disease been implicated in affecting long-term dynamics of Isle Royale wolves and moose (Wilmers et al. 2006). Most recently, we are beginning to suspect that moose ticks also play an important role in long-term wolf moose dynamics (Peterson & Vucetich 2006). We are just now attempting to develop means for long-term monitoring of forage quality and summer forage for moose.

Beginning about 70 years ago, a central tenet of predation ecology has been that the kill rate is largely determined by biological processes (i.e., prey abundance or the ratio of prey to predator), and is the primary predictor of predator growth rate. Based on approximately 30 years of observation, Vucetich et al. (2002) and Vucetich and Peterson (2004a) concluded that Isle Royale wolf kill rate was: (*i*) poorly predicted by moose abundance or the number of moose per wolf and (*ii*) did not provide a good basis for predicting population growth rate of Isle Royale wolves.

D'Arcy Thompson and the nature of explanation

The distinction we make between predicting the future and explaining the past for population ecology is, at the very least, congruent with D'Arcy Thompson's view on the nature of biological explanations. Thompson is known as the father of mathematical biology and for his magnum opus, *On Growth and Form* (1942). *On Growth and Form* is a classic because its depiction of what counts as a biological explanation is attractive to some and bewitching to, but not easily dismissed by, others (Keller 2002). The most succinct expressions of Thompson's (1942) view on the nature of biological explanations seem to be: *"It is the principle involved, and not its ultimate and very complex results, that we can alone attempt to grapple with."* Thompson (1942) also writes (p. 75):

> "We must learn from the mathematician to eliminate and to discard; to keep the type in mind and leave the single case, with all its accidents, alone; and to find in this sacrifice of what matters little and conservation of what matters much one of the peculiar excellences of the method of mathematics."

Thompson (1942) seems to have thought that (Keller 2002): "The representation of living processes in mathematical form might have utilitarian value, but it could also be viewed as an end in itself." Keller (2002) explains Thompson's mathematical end-in-itself this way:

"[Thompson] may have faulted the founding father of morphology [Goethe] for ruling "mathematics out of place in natural history," but he was more than sympathetic to Goethe's criticism of the constraint exerted on man's ability to understand the world of nature by the "compulsion to bring what he finds there under his control." In [Thompson's] view, the best and highest uses of mathematics lay well beyond the range of that compulsion; indeed it was mathematics that would lead us along the path that Goethe himself had advocated – to a proper appreciation of the "variety of relationships livingly interwoven" [Thompson quoting Goethe].

Keller (2002) also describes Thompson's view on explanations in terms that imply the reality of particulars (whose complex results cannot be grappled with) and the less certain nature of principles that can be grappled with:

"For Thompson, the goal of explanation appears to have been primarily one of sufficiency – in only a few instances did he argue for logical necessity, and virtually never for empirical necessity. He said in effect, this is how it could happen, not how it need happen, and certainly not how it does happen in any particular instance. One might say that what he found most compelling about mathematics was not so much its deductive power as its power to lead our imagination away from the particular instances found in the real world and toward that which the particular is a mere instance."

Keller (2002) concludes:

> "In comparing Thompson's explanatory goals with those of classical geneticists, I remarked on the different values placed on necessity and sufficiency... Such differences, I claim, demarcate distinctive epistemological cultures in the practice of science."

Keller's evidence suggests that recent and contemporary science is comprised of various epistemological cultures. More specifically, the value of various kinds of explanation varies among scientific cultures. Despite the divergence, each view is a scientific view, by virtue of being held by a scientific community. In this sense it may not be all that valuable to consider whether the epistemological culture of applied ecology is scientific. However, it is critical to ask whether the epistemological culture of applied ecology – a culture confident in its aim to predict future ecological phenomena – is one that promotes a flourishing relationship between humans and nature.

CONCLUSION

Hypotheses about the wolves and moose of Isle Royale have been generated by observing that system (e.g., Mech 1966). These hypotheses have been rejected by continuing to observe the wolves and moose of Isle Royale (e.g., Peterson 1977). This process of observation and rejection causes us to wonder about the limits of inductive reasoning in population ecology and whether the future of Isle Royale wolves and moose will always differ from our sense of their past. In plainer language, albeit with the loss of some important detail: even after 50 years of observation, each five-year period of the Isle Royale wolf-moose chronology seems importantly different from every other five-year period (Fig. 1.4.1). More strikingly, the first two decades of observation (1959–1980) are characterized by markedly different dynamics than those of the following two decades (Fig. 5 of Peterson et al. 1998; Wilmers et al. 2006).

Nearly 50 years of observation were required to conclude that long-held cornerstones of quantitative predator-prey theory are inadequate for predicting future Isle Royale wolf-moose dynamics. Specifically, per capita kill rate is not well predicted by prey density (Vucetich et al. 2002), and wolf growth rate is not well predicted by kill rate (Vucetich and Peterson 2004a).

Our characterization – that the longer we study the wolves and moose of Isle Royale the more we learn how little we understand – seems reasonable if understanding is judged primarily on the ability to make reliable, nontrivial predictions about the future dynamics of populations. When predictive ability is the judge of knowledge, the growth of ecological knowledge may be a process of discovering ignorance.

Because, as the Isle Royale system suggests, inductive reasoning about ecological systems may frequently be unreliable, it may be necessary to distinguish two types of ecological explanation: those entailing predictive ability and those entailing non-predictive explanations of the past.

When the value of an explanation is not based solely on predictive ability, its value is judged on a delicate mixture of empirical observation and rational consideration. The rational considerations will, at times, seem (at least, to outside observers) to be subjective conclusions of researchers and (or) peer-reviewers. The meaning of empirical observations is deeply dependent upon rational and theoretical presuppositions that are not always easily identified or justified to the point of excluding conflicting presuppositions.

With respect to explaining the past, much understanding has been gained. We have learned that wolves are selective predators (Peterson 1977), social structure is an important determinant of predation rate (Thurber & Peterson 1993), a disease-induced reduction in wolf abundance was followed by increased moose abundance and reduced growth of balsam fir (McLaren & Peterson 1994), and raven scavenging may favour sociality in wolves (Vucetich et al. 2004). Although this knowledge may have limited value for predicting the future, it seems necessary and sufficient for providing a reasonable (albeit, incomplete) explanation of the past. They lead us, in the words of D'Arcy Thompson and Goethe, to *"a proper appreciation of the variety of relationships livingly interwoven."*

ACKNOWLEDGMENTS

We thank L. Vucetich for comments on previous draft of this manuscript. This work was supported in part by the U. S. National Science Foundation (DEB-9903671 and DEB-0424562) and Isle Royale National Park. This chapter does not necessarily reflect the views of the NSF or Isle Royale National Park.

Wolves' Role in Wildlife
Management Planning:
Human Impacts in Protected
Wolf Populations, Hunting,
and Removal of Wolves

2.1 Influence of Anthropogenically Modified Snow Conditions on Wolf Predatory Behaviour

Paul C. Paquet, Shelley Alexander, Steve Donelon, and Carolyn Callaghan

INTRODUCTION

The influence of human-caused landscape alteration on wildlife populations is of growing concern among conservationists. Most studies, however, have focused on long-term and permanent modification of habitat caused by industrial activity (e.g., forestry, mining, recreational developments). Although seemingly minor human influences can affect an animal's probability to survive and reproduce, the potential effects of seasonal and temporary landscape modifications caused by removal or compaction of snow have received little serious consideration. This chapter uses gray wolves to understand the effects of anthropogenically modified snow conditions on the species and on its predatory behaviour.

With regard to wolves, very few studies of have accounted or controlled for the effects humans have on wolf behaviour and ecology (Boitani 1982; Paquet et al. 1996; Ciucci et al. 1997; Theuerkauf et al. 2001; Musiani & Paquet 2004; this volume). This is a serious omission, considering that these influences include behavioural avoidance of some areas and roads (Thurber et al. 1994; Paquet et al. 1996), reduction of genetic variability (Leonard et al. 2005), altered hunting patterns (Paquet et al. 1996), confounded predator-prey relationships (Seip 1992; Hebblewhite et al. 2002), and distorted patterns of travel (Musiani et al. 1998; Duke et al. 2001; Ciucci et al. 2003; Whittington et al. 2004). Almost certainly, incomplete and inaccurate information has obscured our understanding of wolves and their role in large mammalian systems.

Most North American wolves spend winter in a snowy environment. Accordingly, snow is a seasonal environmental variable that affects wolves' decisions on where and how to search for prey. Where deeper snow conditions make travel and hunting more difficult, the movements of wolves are partly related to a search for favourable snow conditions. Foraging theory suggests a predator's diet, including prey choice, will be the product of many foraging episodes or searches, which try to maximize energy gain in a minimal amount of time (Krebs & Davies 1993). Decisions made during a given foraging episode entail costs and benefits to the individual predator, or hunting group (Krebs & Davies 1993). To travel efficiently in deep snow, wolves use existing wildlife trails or other packed trails made by humans (Thompson 1952; Mech 1970; Bergerud et al. 1984), as wolves have difficulty moving in snow deeper than 40–50 cm (Formozov 1946; Kelsall 1969; Pulliainen 1982). Where trails are unavailable, wolves will travel in areas of low snow, such as creeks and lakes, coniferous forests, and windswept ridges (Mech 1970; Paquet et al. 1996; Kuzyk & Kuzyk 2001).

When large mammals are grouped into regional faunas, those with morphological adaptations to snow occur in more snowy regions. Within a local area, species adapted to their environment and each other, survive in winter by living and feeding in different habitats based on snow conditions (Telfer & Kelsall 1984). Snow coping abilities, however, vary among these sympatric species, with wolves showing morphological adaptation to snow surpassed only by caribou (*Rangifer tarandus*) and moose (*Alces alces*). Winter survival strategies of wolves and their prey reflect co-evolved relationships and adaptations that developed over millennia. Accordingly, wolves as important predators on ungulate populations appear to have influenced the evolution of ungulate behaviour in snow (Telfer & Kelsall 1984).

Predators can have a considerable influence on the use of resources by their prey (Brown 1988, 1999; Lima & Dill 1990; Lima & Bednekoff 1999). In theory, prey species need simultaneously to find high-quality patches of food and reduce the risks of predation. Because predators often focus their activity in areas where prey are compelled to feed (Kunkel &

Pletscher 2001; Lima 2002), habitat selection by herbivores should balance loss of fitness due to predators and fitness gain due to improved access to forage (Fryxell & Lundberg 1997; Darimont et al. 2007). Elk, for example, commonly respond to an increase in predation risks by intensifying their use of forested areas (Wolff & Van Horn 2003; Mao et al. 2005), and by decreasing the time spent in aspen stands (White et al. 2003). Caribou reduce their vulnerability to predation by wolves by spacing out or spacing away from areas where wolves concentrate their travel (Bergerud et al. 1984; Bergerud 1985, 1992; Bergerud & Page 1987).

Compaction of snow caused by human activities (e.g., skiing, snow-mobiling etc.) creates a dense base in the snow pack, which can mimic the effects of a road. Compression or removal of snow along roads, trails, and seismic lines creates winter travel routes into previously inaccessible areas. Accordingly, these travel routes increase the range and speed of wolf movements during snow cover, which results in increased rates of predation. In Riding Mountain National Park, Manitoba, wolves killed coyotes (*C. latrans*) more frequently during winters with deep snow than winters with shallow snow (Carbyn 1982), usually along compacted snowmobile trails (Paquet 1989). Murie (1944), observed wolves in Denali National Park, Alaska using ploughed roads to hunt sheep in areas that were difficult access. Zalozny (1980) reported that road networks cleared of snow allowed wolves to travel farther, which increased access to prey over a larger area. In areas where forest cover and human activities adjoin, travel routes that are efficient to follow may attract wolves to agricultural and urban areas. Wolves in the central part of Eurasia moved seasonally from mountains where snow was deep to valleys with shallow snow, and preferred to use ploughed roads (Formozov 1946; D. Bibikov, personal communication). In Poland, wolves travelled faster on trails and roads than off-road (Musiani et al. 1998), whereas wolves in Sweden, avoided high snowfall areas above 1,000 m and travelled primarily along valleys with ploughed roads and across windswept plateaus (Bjarvell & Isakson 1982).

Varying seasonal snow depths can affect prey distribution (Mech et al. 1971; Mech et al. 1995), wolf predation rates (Peterson & Allen 1974; Peterson 1977; Nelson & Mech 1986; Fuller 1991a, 1991b; Huggard

1993c; Smith et al. 2004), vulnerability of ungulates to predation (Nelson & Mech 1986; Mech et al. 1995; Hayes et al. 2000), diet composition (Bobek et al. 1992; Huggard 1993c), and scavenging (Huggard 1993c). Few studies, however, have addressed the effects snow conditions have on the movements of wolves and functional responses (e.g., search time) of wolves to prey (c.f. Formozov 1946; Telfer & Kelsall 1984; James & Stuart-Smith 2000). None we are aware have assessed whether compaction or removal of snow by humans alters movement patterns and indirectly influences relations of wolves with prey, other predators, and humans. Documenting these patterns is important because most packed and snow-free trails result from human activity. In the past 40 years, numbers of people engaged in winter recreation and industrial activities have increased dramatically. At the same time, the mobility of winter recreationists, the size of industrial operations, and extent of travel networks have expanded, exposing previously inaccessible areas to potential disturbance by humans.

Studying the behaviour patterns of wolves hunting and killing ungulates is important for understanding wolf-ungulate systems. If human-caused changes in snow conditions affect movements and predatory behaviour of wolves, ecologists need to assess implications for prey species, other predators, and wolf-human relationships. Herein, we use tracking information collected during 16 years of wolf ecology studies to test the general hypothesis that changes in snow conditions caused by human activities alter the travel behaviour of wolves and thus wolf-prey relationships. We examine associations between snow conditions, use of snow-covered landscapes by wolves, human activities that modify snow conditions, and wolf-prey interactions.

STUDY AREA

We collected information used in this study in Riding Mountain National Park, Manitoba; Jasper National Park, Alberta; Banff National Park, Alberta; Peter Lougheed Provincial Park, Alberta; Yoho National Park,

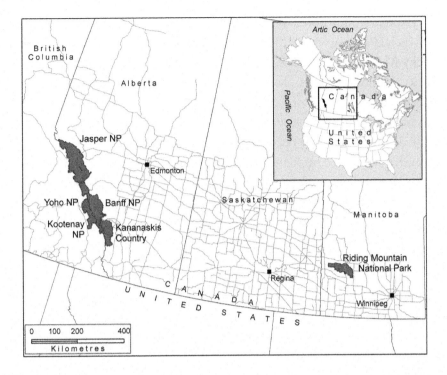

Figure 2.1.1. Study Area Map. The areas of research are identified in black shading, including: the National Park complex (Banff, Jasper, Kootenay and Yoho) and the Kananaskis Provincial Park in the Central Rocky Mountains to the west, Riding Mountain National Park to the east.

British Columbia, Kootenay National Park, British Columbia, and Pukaswka National Park, Ontario (Figure 2.1.1).

Riding Mountain National Park (RMNP) is in the forest-agricultural zone of southwestern Manitoba (Hill 1979), where elevations range from 319 to 756 m. The weather is dry continental, typical of the prairie provinces of Canada (Carbyn 1982). January is the coldest month, with a mean daily temperature of –20.4° C. Permanent snow usually appears in mid-October and melts in early May. The snow depth usually exceeds 80 cm and peaks in mid-March. During our study, snow accumulation was moderate with maximum thickness usually not exceeding 110 cm. Ungulate prey include elk (*Cervus elaphus*), moose (*Alces alces*), white-tailed deer (*Odocoileus virginianus*), and mule deer (*O. hemionus*).

Jasper, Banff, Kootenay, and Yoho National Parks, and Peter Lougheed Provincial Park are within the Continental Ranges of the Central Canadian Rocky Mountains. Henceforth, we refer to these parks collectively as the Rocky Mountain Parks. Topographic features include rugged mountain slopes, steep sided ravines, and flat valley bottoms. Snow accumulations vary according to slope, elevation, aspect, and vegetation cover. Maximum snow depths (> 100 cm) occur in November-December, and March-April (McGregor 1984). Ungulate prey includes elk, moose, white-tailed deer, mule deer, mountain sheep (*Ovis canadensis*), mountain goats (*Oreamnos americanus*), and caribou (*Rangifer tarandus*).

METHODS

Movements of wolves were examined using radio-telemetry and snow tracking. We captured wolves using modified leghold traps and by darting from helicopters (see Carbyn 1983; Huggard 1993c; Paquet et al. 1996; Hebblewhite et al. 2003).

During periods of permanent snow cover (>10 cm), we ground-tracked wolf packs by snowmobile, cross-country skis, snowshoes, and on foot. We followed the tracks continuously and only short sections were obscured by fresh or windblown snow. When packs separated, we followed the group with the most animals. Distances were recorded by odometer (snowmobile) and pedometer. Location data were recorded to the nearest 100 m as Universal Transverse Mercator (UTM) coordinates. We transferred locations to digitized 1:50,000 Ecological Land Classification (Holland & Coen 1982, 1983) and National Topographic Survey base maps (1927, 1983 Datum). Travel routes and environmental variables were digitized as Geographical Information System (GIS) layers and overlaid with a 100×100 m pixel grid to census environmental attributes.

In RMNP, we selected trails opportunistically (Lehner 1979) when fresh wolf tracks were encountered (1–2 days after snowfall). In the Rocky Mountain Parks, we located wolves using radio-telemetry and intercepted their tracks by following a compass bearing to their estimated position.

Usually, 5 km constituted a tracking session. Nonetheless, we recorded all sessions >1 km if tracks were lost or obscured before 5 km. The interval between tracking sessions was >24 hrs.

We classified wolf travel routes as; 1) human-modified trails, made by snowploughs, snow machines, track-setting equipment, skis, dog sleds, and snowshoes; and 2) natural trails, made by wolves and other wildlife. At the beginning of a tracking session, we measured width of trail and depth of wolf tracks in the snow to the nearest 1 cm. After that, we measured trail width and track penetration every 100 m or each time cover type changed. The depth to which an animal sinks reflects a combination of foot-load (ratio of body mass to foot area), snow depth, resistance (hardness), and density (Formozov 1946; Nasimovich 1955; Telfer and Kelsall 1979). One metre perpendicular to the trail, we also measured penetration of a cylinder that generated 110 g/cm^2 when dropped onto the snow from 1 m. An adult wolf of 35–50 kg has a foot-load (ratio of body mass to foot area) of 89–114 g/cm^2 (Formozov 1946; Nasimovich 1955). Thus, the penetration of the cylinder approximated the depth a walking 45 kg wolf sinks in the snow. We assumed that off-trail measurements reflected general snow conditions in areas the wolves travelled. We did not record these data for tracks made by running wolves or tracks made by wolves chasing ungulates. For analysis, we divided data into 6 categories of snow penetration, 10–20 cm, >20–30 cm, >30–40 cm, >40–50 cm, >50–60 cm, and >60 cm.

While tracking, we recorded the 9 following dominant cover types, which varied from completely open to nearly closed canopy: rock and ice, open ridges, open forest edges, meadows and clearings, riparian areas characterized by willow (*Salix* sp.) and alder (*Alnus rugosa*) scrub, marshes, and ericaceous bogs, open forest with <50% coniferous canopy, closed forest with >50% coniferous canopy, and aspen (*Populus tremuloides*) forest with >50% deciduous canopy. Frozen water bodies and streams were classified as frozen waterways. In the Rocky Mountains, we also recorded elevations every 100 m travelled using altimeters (Avocet® Vertech) and by reconstructing travel routes on topographic maps.

Species, age, sex, and an estimate of biomass consumed were recorded for each ungulate killed by wolves (Carbyn 1983; Paquet 1992). We estimated biomass available for consumption at each kill using ungulate weights obtained from hunter kills in RMNP and highway kills in the Rocky Mountain Parks. We assumed average weights of 30, 58, and 20 kg for elk calf, moose calf, and deer fawn, respectively.

When possible, we also measured the length of chases that resulted in a kill. Ungulate carcasses investigated by wolves were classified as carrion if no evidence of a kill was apparent or if the kill was confirmed previously. Kills and carcasses found within 200 m of a trail were assigned to modified or natural trails if tracks to the kill were continuous and signs of a chase obvious (Paquet 1992).

In RMNP, 2 trails leading to winter range of adult male elk were intentionally created by snow machine during 2 winters when unsettled snow depth exceeded 60 cm. We used aircraft to monitor movements and activities of wolves and the response of elk before and after trails were created.

In RMNP, we used aerial surveys to obtain density, age, and sex counts of elk and moose within the territories of the 5 study packs. From 1982 through 1986, classified counts were conducted twice monthly in November, December, January, February, and March. However, recognizing elk calves from the air was increasingly difficult as winter progressed, so we do not include the March surveys in this report. Confidence limits were established using statistical tests reported by Czaplewski et al. (1983).

We tested whether snow conditions on wolf trails were independent of snow conditions next to trails. Our null hypothesis was that track penetration would be the same on and off-trail. We also tested whether natural and modified trails traversed landscapes of equivalent cover types and snow conditions. We postulated that cover and snow conditions would be the same for both trail types. For the Rocky Mountains, we also compared distribution of trail types by elevation. Lastly, we compared selection of prey, rates of predation, biomass available, biomass consumed, length of chases, and condition of prey on modified and natural trails.

We tested data for normality using the Shapiro-Wilk test. Tracking and elevation data were analyzed by means of the G-test for goodness-of-fit and independence and adjusted with Williams' correction for continuity (Sokal & Rohlf 1995). The z-test was used to compare means of track penetration, corrected for multiple comparisons. We used Bartlett's test and the F-test to determine homogeneity of variance in cover data. The Kruskal-Wallis test was used to compare track variation in penetration of tracks among cover types (Sokal & Rohlf 1995). We used the Wilcoxon rank sum test to assess predation related variables. Results of statistical tests were considered significant at an α level 0.05. Statistical analyses were performed using SAS (SAS Institute 1995) and SYSTAT® (Systat 2002).

RESULTS

We surveyed 8,430 km of wolf trails in RMNP, and 7,332 km in the Central Rocky Mountains. Six wolf packs were monitored for 5 years and 5 packs for 7 years, respectively. Mean pack size as determined from tracks was 5.1 (sd = 2.2) in RMNP and 7.2 (sd = 2.8) in the Central Rocky Mountains. For analyses of snow and cover characteristics, we randomly sub-sampled 755 km of trail in RMNP and 901 km in the Rocky Mountain Parks.

Wolves travelled on harder snow and used compacted trails more frequently than trails covered in soft snow, thereby reducing sinking depths. Wolves in all areas used travel routes where foot penetration in snow was significantly lower than penetration measured 1 m off the trail (RMNP $G = 2526$, df = 6, $P < 0.001$, Jasper National Park $G = 2526$, df = 6, $P < 0.001$, Banff National Park/Peter Lougheed Provincial Park $G = 2526$, df = 6, $P < 0.001$, respectively). Modified trails of compacted snow in all study areas were used more often than natural trails (RMNP $G = 1503$, df = 1, $P < 0.001$, Jasper National Park $G = 352$, df = 1, $P < 0.001$, Banff National Park/Peter Lougheed Provincial Park $G = 977$, df = 1, $P < 0.001$, respectively).

Wolves used modified travel routes where snow was shallower than it was near the trail. Most wolf tracks penetrated 10–20 cm (43–68%). Overall, fewer tracks occurred in snow conditions where foot penetration exceeded 40–50 cm. We found track penetration next to human-modified trails was deeper than on-trail penetration (G = 977, df = 1, P < 0.001), resulting in greater mean sinking depths of wolf limbs. Track penetration on and off natural trails, however, was similar (P > 0.05). On human-modified trails, 16–27% of wolf tracks traversed areas where off-trail track penetration was >60 cm. In comparison, only 1–7% of wolf tracks on-trail penetrated >60 cm. That is, by staying on compacted trails wolves traveled areas where deep snow would likely impede movements.

Use of elevations

In the Rocky Mountains, the movements of wolves were most abundant at low elevations where snow was shallow; although wolves used areas at all elevations where snow was shallower than average. Overall, 81% of wolf movements were restricted to lower elevation valley bottoms during periods of snow, with occasional forays to higher elevations on human-modified trails. Human-modified trails used by wolves occurred at significantly higher elevations than natural trails (G = 101, df = 5, P<0.001). A combination of ploughed roads, snowmobile trails, and ski trails constituted 97% of trails used by wolves while traversing upper elevation mountain passes that connected valleys.

In the more homogeneous topography of RMNP, movements of wolves also reflected seasonal and annual variations in weather conditions and snow depths (Paquet 1989). Wolves predominantly used the same areas in winter and summer, but movement patterns changed in winter when wolves travelled on frozen lakes and waterways compacted by wind (Paquet 1989).

Use of cover

Use of cover on natural and modified trails was similar in all areas (P > 0.05). Thus, we pooled data from all regions for analyses by cover type.

The frequency that wolves used cover types on natural and modified trails differed significantly (G = 85.9, df = 8, P < 0.001). The depth wolves sank within cover types also varied for natural (Kruskal-Wallis H = 361.6, df = 8, P < 0.001) and modified trails (Kruskal-Wallis H = 264.1, df = 8, P < 0.001). In most paired comparisons of cover types, the depth wolves sank on natural trails was higher than on modified trails (Table 2.1.1). Notable exceptions were riparian and closed forest areas.

Overall, wolves on natural trails traveled habitats where snow was shallower and harder than habitats traversed on modified trails. They used areas with low snow and vegetative cover and habitats favoured by deer and elk more than expected, based on occurrence. Wolf movements on natural trails showed a strong avoidance of meadows and exposed areas of all types including habitat edges. Wolves travelling natural trails favoured riparian areas and cover types with high snow-intercept characteristics such as closed coniferous forests, using habitats with high snow depths less frequently (Table 1.5.1). Distances tracked on natural trails in riparian (R^2 = 57, P = 0.05) and closed coniferous (R^2 = 57, P = 0.05) habitats increased as snow depth increased, whereas the use of deciduous cover (R^2 = 57, P = 0.05) and open meadows decreased (R^2 = 57, P = 0.05). In areas where off-trail snow depths were > 40 cm, travel in open habitats occurred most frequently on modified trails (G Williams = 108.63, df = 8, P < 0.001).

Use of prey

While snow tracking, we found 1,578 ungulates killed by 11 wolf packs and an unknown number of solitary wolves. After removing solitary kills and standardizing annual tracking distances, 783 kills remained for analyses (Table 2.1.2). On natural trails, elk and deer densities had a strong effect on the sites where wolves travelled and made kills, with wolves concentrating their movements and hunting in wintering areas of elk and white-tailed deer. Rates of kill on modified trails in RMNP (t = 2.75, df = 66, P = 0.008) and the Rockies (t = 5.22, df = 57, P < 0.001) were significantly higher than on natural trails, although travel on modified trails appeared unrelated to ungulate densities (Table 2.1.3). Elk and deer killed

Table 2.1.1. Winter use of cover types by wolves on natural and modified trails in Jasper National Park, Alberta; Banff National Park, Alberta; Peter Lougheed Provincial Park, Alberta; and Riding Mountain National Park, Manitoba. Double asterisks indicate difference in mean track penetration on natural and modified trails was highly significant (P ≤ 0.001).

	MODIFIED TRAIL			NATURAL TRAIL		
HABITAT	Mean Track Penetration (cm)	±SD	Rank by Use	Mean Track Penetration (cm)	±SD	Rank by Use
Frozen Waterways**	5.2	2.5	8	3.8	2.1	4
Rock & Ice**	7.2	4.1	9	9.4	1.6	9
Closed Forests	15.8	4.5	6	15.2	2.2	3
Open Ridges**	12.1	4.5	5	21.1	4.7	2
Riparian	20.2	7.1	7	21.5	6.4	1
Open Edges**	11.2	5.0	4	31.0	3.6	5
Open Forests**	14.1	3.8	3	32.2	6.7	6
Aspen**	17.3	4.4	2	37.2	8.6	8
Meadow**	17.6	3.9	1	41.8	9.2	7
TOTAL	13.4			23.7		

Table 2.1.2. Comparison of kill and consumption rates on natural and modified trails. Data were collected in Riding Mountain National Park (RMNP) and the Central Canadian Rocky Mountains (Rockies) while ground tracking 11 wolf packs in snow.

STUDY AREA	Kill Rate (Kills/Km)	Biomass Available/kg	Biomass Consumed/kg	Mean Pack Size	Kg/Wolf/kg
RMNP Natural	0.07	13.04	8.43	5.06	1.67
RMNP Modified	0.16	33.24	10.12	5.06	2.00
Rockies Natural	0.08	13.99	11.54	7.20	1.60
Rockies Modified	0.18	38.33	15.99	7.20	2.22

Table 2.1.3. Comparison of prey species killed on natural and modified trails. Data were collected in Riding Mountain National Park (RMNP) and the Central Canadian Rocky Mountains (Rockies) while ground tracking 11 wolf packs in snow.

STUDY AREA	PREY SPECIES				
	Caribou	Elk	Deer	Moose	Sheep
RMNP Natural		58	24	6	
RMNP Modified		148	20	46	
Rockies Natural		101	39	5	
Rockies Modified	9	181	93	27	26

by wolves on or near modified trails occurred after shorter chase lengths than on natural trails. The combined mean kill rate/km for all parks was positively associated with increased off-trail snow depth (R = 0.68, P = 0.039). Rates of kill were not associated with trail width in either study area (P = 0.561). Percentage of available biomass consumed on natural trails was higher than on modified trails in the Rocky Mountains (t = 7.7, df = 57, P < 0.001) and RMNP (t = 4.39, df = 66, P < 0.001).

Composition of species killed by wolves differed significantly on modified and natural trails for RMNP (Chi-square = 21.65, df = 2, P < 0.001) and the Rocky Mountains (Chi-square = 5.58, df = 2, p = 0.05). In the mountain parks, all adult moose, sheep, and caribou kills were associated with trails established and maintained by humans. In RMNP, comparatively more adult male elk and calves were killed on modified trails than natural trails.

Lastly, the combined mean kill rate/km for all parks was positively correlated with increased off-trail snow depth (R^2 = 0.68, P = 0.039). Chase lengths associated with kills near natural trails were greater than chase lengths associated with kills near modified trails in RMNP and the Rockies (P = 0.0174 for RMNP; P < 0.0001 for Rockies). Percent femur fat was similar for kills associated with both trail types in RMNP and the Rockies.

DISCUSSION

Our results show that snow conditions influence how wolves move about, where they travel, the rates at which they kill prey, and their use of prey. Ease of travel is a critical determinant of landscape use by wolves during periods of moderately deep snow cover. Where opportunities exist, wolves improve the efficiency of travel by using networks of snowmobile trails, ski trails, and winter roads, thereby reducing negative effects of snow on movements. Travelling packed or snow-free routes, wolves traverse otherwise inaccessible areas where snow conditions naturally preclude or restrict movements (> 40–50 cm). Using these trails confers benefits to wolves, especially where snow conditions exceed their morphological threshold. Specifically, human-modified trails reduce energetic costs associated with travel, provide wolves access to areas that are otherwise unavailable or difficult to reach, and improve chances for predation.

Predator and prey

More than 60 years ago, Formozov (1946) suggested that snow conditions directly influence wolf use of habitat by affecting prey availability and by making portions of habitats unusable or undesirable in some seasons. Subsequent research has shown that certain combinations of snow depth and density differentially impair the mobility of wolves (Nasimovich 1955; Fuller 1991a) and their ungulate prey (Pruitt 1959, 1960; Peterson & Allen 1974; Telfer & Kelsall 1979), thereby influencing community structure, and composition (Pulliainen 1982; Okarma et al. 1995). Studies in North America (Mech et al. 1971; Kolenosky 1972; Peterson & Allen 1974; Nelson & Mech 1986; Paquet 1992; Huggard 1993c), Europe (Bobek et al. 1992; Okarma et al. 1995), and Asia (Fedosenko et al. 1978) suggest hunting success and kill-rate by wolves is higher in winters with deep snow because wolves have a lighter foot loading than most ungulates (Nasimovich 1955; Telfer & Kelsall 1984) and canids often travel on crusted snow that will not support their prey (Paquet 1989).

Our results indicate that during periods of snow cover, prey are more vulnerable to wolves under certain trail conditions and wolves select for these conditions. For example, kills per km on trails unrestricted by snow averaged 2.5 times more (range 2–3) than on natural trails. In addition, some prey species, as well as sex and age classes, show an increased risk of predation along human-modified trails. In the mountain parks, all adult moose, sheep, and caribou kills were associated with trails established and maintained by humans. In RMNP, more adult male elk and calves were killed on modified trails than natural trails. This is strong evidence that human modified winter trails can alter predator-prey dynamics, which may ultimately affect the availability, vulnerability, distribution, abundance, and structure of prey populations (Schmitz et al. 2000). The lesson is that ecologists need to relate the short-term effects of anthropogenic activities to their long-term consequences.

Consumers often forage in spatially complex environments where resources are distributed unevenly among patches that differ in productivity, size, isolation, and other physical traits. From an optimal foraging perspective (Stephens & Krebs 1986), "patch choice" is an important aspect of foraging ecology because it is the first decision determining where to feed. The choice of sites, and ultimately fitness, is determined by foraging opportunities and security from predators. Maintaining trails and roads free of snow increases wolf hunting efficiency by expanding the speed and range of wolf movements, which reduces search time and results in increased rates of predation, thereby changing the functional response of wolves to ungulate prey (cf. James & Stuart-Smith 2000). Prey are forced to respond by finding predator free or predator secure foraging opportunities (Stephens & Peterson 1984; Ripple & Bechsta 2003; Creel & Winnie 2005). Consequently, in some human dominated ecosystems the long-established relationships that have governed predator-prey interactions for millennia might now be irrelevant or seriously distorted. Accordingly, increased wolf use of winter caribou habitat via artificial trails, and thus high predation risk and rates of predation, has been invoked as an explanation for the precipitous decline of caribou in Alberta and British Columbia (Seip 1992; James & Stuart-Smith 2000; Dyer et al. 2001). Likely, from the perspective of caribou (and other herbivores), adaptation of new and effective anti-predator strategies lag far behind a rapidly changing landscape.

Physiographic effects

Mountainous topography modifies climate, which creates substantial differences in regional snow conditions. Vertical changes in elevation often produce significant variation in snow conditions. Because of the morphological constraints imposed by deeper snow at higher elevations, wolves in mountainous areas typically select for easier travel routes in the prey rich valley bottoms as snow depths increase (Huggard 1993c; Paquet et al. 1996). During winter, wolf populations compress at lower elevations, preying on species such as elk and deer, which also seek areas with shallow snow-packs (Paquet et al. 1996). In pristine environments, the high-elevation, winter ranges of moose, caribou, and sheep are rarely used by wolves because travel into these areas is difficult. In our mountain study areas, however, wolves used a network of ploughed roads, snowmobile trails, and ski trails to traverse upper elevation habitat with deep snow conditions, often crossing mountain passes that connected low elevation valleys. By staying on compacted trails, wolves travelled areas where deep snow would likely impede movements. Notably, all documented predation of caribou and sheep occurred along or near these trails. Human activities that improve access to these winter refugia appear to negate the anti predator advantages conferred by these normally inaccessible areas.

CONSERVATION AND MANAGEMENT IMPLICATIONS

Understanding animal movement in increasingly human-dominated landscapes is essential for the persistence of many wolf and prey populations (Noss et al. 1996). Individuals, species, biological communities, and ecosystems all respond differently to human-induced changes. Consequently, minor changes in behaviour at any of these levels can cause distortions in relationships that differ significantly from conditions that preceded the change. Identifying, assessing, and addressing these distortions is a fundamental issue for conservation.

As summit predators, wolves can have a profound influence on other species and the dynamics of biological systems (Terborgh et al. 1999; Hebblewhite et al. 2005). Although our study did not directly address the ecological significance of modifying "natural" movement patterns of wolves, our observations suggest strongly that the potential for system wide alteration is high (Schmitz et al. 2000). The established relationships among habitat use, prey accessibility, and topography can be seriously perturbed; dispersal patterns and use of travel corridors altered; access to winter ungulate ranges unknowingly facilitated; and movements of wolves outside protected areas into agricultural zones encouraged. These relationships combine to determine the selective landscape for wolves and their prey, and ultimately fitness. Consequently, many evolutionary traits are influenced, including physiology, morphology, and behaviour (Darimont et al. 2007). We should not forget that human ecological impact has evolutionary consequences and can greatly accelerate evolutionary change in the species around us (Palumbi 2001).

Our findings indicate that, for the most part, wolves benefit from snow-free and compacted trails, taking advantage of less energetically demanding travel routes to kill prey more efficiently and frequently. Wolves, however, may be disadvantaged in other circumstances; for example outside protected areas, where anthropogenically modified trails bring wolves in contact with humans, which might result in wolf mortality increases (Mech 1995, Mech et al. 1988). In comparison, our results suggest that ungulate prey may suffer increased rates of predation by wolves. We believe the influence of human activity on winter wolf movements may have particularly adverse consequences for prey species such as caribou (Hebblewhite et al. 2007).

Where wolves are present, managers need to assess effects of roads, recreational trails, service trails, snowmobile trails, or human activities that modify snow cover and ease travel for wolves. Development and implementation of comprehensive access, recreation, and settlement plans are essential in occupied wolf habitat to maintain a low density of people, particularly in those areas where human activities put wolves and their prey at risk. In addition, future ecological studies of wolf and prey interactions should include the potential confounding influence of human-modified snowy landscapes.

ACKNOWLEDGMENTS

We thank Parks Canada, the Canadian Wildlife Service, and World Wildlife Fund Canada for providing logistic and financial support. We appreciate the very helpful and insightful reviews of earlier manuscripts by H. Okarma, M. Hebblewhite, M. Musiani, B. Miller, and J. Vucetich.

2.2 The Recolonizing Scandinavian Wolf Population: Research and Management in Two Countries

Olof Liberg, Åke Aronson, Scott M. Brainerd, Jens Karlsson, Hans-Christian Pedersen, Håkan Sand and Petter Wabakken

INTRODUCTION: TWO COUNTRIES WITH SIMILAR NATURAL BUT DIFFERENT CULTURAL, ECONOMIC, AND POLITICAL PRECONDITIONS FOR WOLVES

After a long period of persecution, the wolf (*Canis lupus*) has made a remarkable comeback in North America and Europe during the past few decades (Boitani 2003). An instrumental factor in this recovery has been an improvement in human attitudes toward wolves (Mech 1995). However, there is still a wide gap between the attitudes of urban and rural inhabitants toward this species (Skogen & Haaland 2001; Williams et al. 2002). The new challenge in wolf conservation is in striking a balance between both wolf and human interests, acceptable also to local people living with wolves and people living in cities (Mech & Boitani 2003a). This issue is especially critical in Europe, where there are no wilderness refuges large enough to harbour viable populations of large carnivores (Linnell et al. 2005a). Thus, wherever wolves settle on this continent, they will have to interact with humans (Promberger & Schröder 1993). If Europe is to accommodate its expanding wolf populations, we must find strategies that allow wolves and man to coexist (Linnell et al. 2001). Scientific research

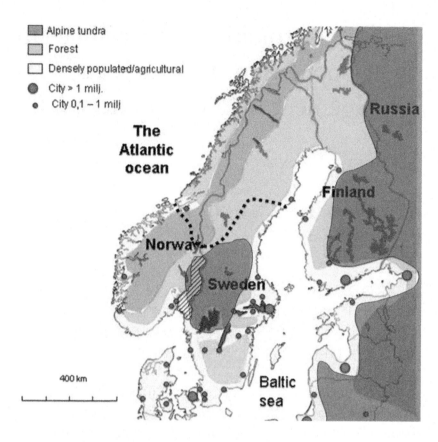

Figure 2.2.1. The Scandinavian Peninsula, with habitats and present distribution of the breeding wolf units (dark grey). The western portion of the range for the Finnish–eastern European wolf population is also indicated (in dark grey). The southern boundary of the reindeer grazing range in Scandinavia is indicated with dashed line. The Norwegian wolf zone is indicated by striped area.

has a key role in this process by providing a rational common ground for making difficult management decisions. However, this option has been poorly exercised thus far in Europe (Mech & Boitani 2003a).

Scandinavia and continental Europe share many common challenges regarding wolf recovery, although some aspects differ. Controversies with wolves and other large carnivores generally get worse in areas where they have been absent for extended periods before they return (Zimmermann et al. 2001), and this is also the case with Scandinavia (Wabakken et al.

THE WORLD OF WOLVES

2001; and see below). The Scandinavian Peninsula, shared by Norway and Sweden, might at a first glance seem well-suited for wolves. The human population density is low and there is a rich supply of wild ungulate prey and suitable habitat with forests comprising almost 60%, and alpine tundra another 25% of the Peninsula (Fig. 2.2.1).

However, most of these vast expanses are claimed by various stakeholders with potential or existing conflicts with wolves (Swenson & Andrén 2005).

In the north, the Sámi people continue their traditional rights to graze semi-domesticated reindeer (*Rangifer tarandus*) on 40% of the Peninsula, and claim that wolves are not compatible with this practice. In the west, Norwegian farmers release over two million sheep each spring to graze on the open range, with significant losses to predators (Swenson & Andrén 2005). Furthermore, most of the land in Scandinavia is private, with associated hunting rights of economic and social importance. Moose (*Alces alces*), the favoured prey of Scandinavian wolves (Olsson et al. 1997), is also the most important game species. Approximately 140,000 moose are harvested annually in Norway and Sweden (Lavsund & Sandegren 1989; Solberg et al. 2003), and the annual moose hunt is rivalled only by Christmas as the largest event of the year in rural communities. There is a conflict between hunters and wolves already around the competition for moose (Kojola 2000; Sand et al. 2006a), but the worst conflict is caused by the fact that wolves kill hunting dogs (Karlsson & Thoresson 2000; Ericsson & Heberlein 2003), as was found also in Finland, although there attacks on dogs were even more frequent near human residences (Kojola et al. 2004). Dogs for more than 100 years constituted a central part of the Scandinavian hunting traditions, and 10–20 dogs have been killed annually by wolves in recent years. This is not only an economic loss to the owner, but also an emotional. The violent death of what often is regarded as a dear family member, and in some cases a valuable hunting champion, is understandably a traumatic event.

Another important factor that influences the attitudes of rural inhabitants is the fear for human safety (Linnell et al. 2002; Skogen & Krange 2003). The mere presence of wolves has increased anxiety for the safety of women and children in particular. Today, many local inhabitants in the wolf range consider that the return of the wolf has seriously reduced their overall quality of life (Skogen & Krange 2003; Sjölander-Lindqvist 2006).

Scandinavian wolf management is further complicated by the fact that Norway and Sweden have rather different political and economic situations. Sweden is highly industrialized, and farming is strongly rationalized in large units, and rural society is proportionately small and thus of less political influence. Norway, on the other hand, has pursued a long-term policy of preserving and promoting its rural communities and culture by subsidies for small-scale agricultural practices. As a result, a greater proportion of the Norwegian population inhabits rural areas, and consequently is more politically empowered relative to its Swedish counterpart. In addition, Sweden is a member of the European Union and is bound to its strongly protective legislation for large carnivores, whereas Norway is not. Consequently, Norwegian wolf policy is more influenced by rural interests and less by those of nature protectionists as compared with Sweden.

These different situations in the two countries have led to different large predator policies. The Swedish wolf management policy is regulated by the Predator Act "En sammanhållen rovdjurspolitik" passed by the Parliament in 2001 (Swedish Ministry of Environment 2000). The Act states that a preliminary national goal is to reach a minimum of 20 breeding packs, and before this goal is reached, control of wolves (e.g., to reduce depredation or mitigate conflicts in other ways) should be kept to a minimum. Wolves shall be allowed to occur all over the country wherever there is suitable habitat, but with a restriction that breeding packs must not be tolerated in the reindeer summer grazing range (mainly the alpine areas). Norwegian predator policy is regulated by the Predator Act "Rovvilt i Norsk Natur" (Norwegian Ministry of the Environment 2003), passed by the parliament in 2004. The Act states that wolves primarily shall be tolerated within a specified "wolf zone" in southeastern Norway, along the Swedish border (Fig. 2.2.1). Within this zone there shall be allowed a minimum of three breeding packs, not including packs that partly use Swedish territory. When this goal is reached, control of additional wolves in the zone might be allowed if local authorities find it necessary to mitigate conflicts. Outside the zone, local governments may allow removal of wolves after they have received complaints, irrespective of whether the goal inside the zone is reached or not.

Because both countries share the same wolf population, these different policies have at times led to some political tension between the countries. On top of this, biological restrictions, including small population size (roughly 150 animals in spring 2006) and genetic vulnerability of this isolated wolf population, limit options available to managers.

In spite of these political differences, we have been fortunate to achieve a very close scientific co-operation between Norway and Sweden, which has been formalized through project SKANDULV. In this chapter we will first provide an overview of the results from our biological research on the Scandinavian wolf population, and then describe the efforts made to integrate these results into management of this population. There is also an extensive social science research on large carnivore issues in Scandinavia (e.g., Andersson et al. 1977; Bjerke et al. 1998; Kaltenborn et al. 1999; Skogen & Haaland 2001; Williams et al. 2002; Ericsson & Heberlein 2003; Skogen & Krange 2003; Sjölander-Lindqvist 2006), to which we refer whenever needed, but a separate treatment of this research is beyond the scope of this paper.

RESEARCH STRATEGY AND METHODS

The small Scandinavian wolf population has been continuously monitored by snow tracking since the first solitary wolves were detected in the late 1970s, at first by volunteers and later by professional field personnel (Wabakken et al. 2001). The need for close coordination of research activities in Norway and Sweden resulted in the establishment of the Scandinavian Wolf Research Project (SKANDULV) in January 2000, two years after scientific research was first initiated. SKANDULV is a consortium of independent projects based at seven universities in Sweden and Norway. A research coordinator facilitates close co-operation and the flow of information internally and externally. Field efforts are closely coordinated and all data are shared within the consortium. One Swedish and two Norwegian ecological projects comprise the core of SKANDULV, along with associated projects focusing on genetics, population modelling, veterinary medicine and pathology, sociology, and depredation. SKANDULV also has close co-operative ties with Finnish wolf researchers (Aronson et al. 1999; Pedersen et al. 2005; Wabakken et al. 2006).

Each winter 10–20 wolves are captured and equipped with radio-collars. Wolves are located by ground tracking on snow and then darted from a helicopter. Between 1998 and 2006 we have instrumented a total of 76 wolves, representing 110 "wolf years" (number of years each wolf was instrumented summed up for all wolves). The first wolves were fitted with VHF transmitters; however, we have exclusively used GPS transmitters since 2003. We have programmed GPS transmitters to record a minimum of 1–6 positions/day, and up to 54 positions/day for intensive predation studies. For genetic analyses, we have taken blood and tissue samples from live-captured wolves and from retrieved dead wolves, and faeces found during tracking (Liberg et al. 2005). We use telemetry and snow-tracking as primary methods in our research, including the annual population estimates. Analysis of mortality, movements, and predation is based on radio-telemetry (for details see Wabakken et al. 2001; Liberg et al. 2005; Sand et al. 2005, 2006a; Zimmermann et al. 2007).

MONITORING

Monitoring of wolf numbers and distribution is based on snow tracking (3000–4000 km each year), since 1998/99 complemented with telemetry, and since 2002/03 with DNA-analyses of primarily scats (Liberg et al. 2005; Wabakken et al. 2006). Snow tracking has been performed each winter from 1978/79 to present. This work started as a purely voluntary effort, and gradually became more organized and official with co-operation between Norway and Sweden beginning in 1981. In both countries, monitoring efforts have been financed by the governments. In Sweden, since 2002 the regional county boards (Sw. "länstyrelserna") have been officially responsible for these counts in their respective jurisdictions. In Norway, Hedmark University College has been subcontracted by the Norwegian Institute for Nature Research to census stationary wolves while personnel of the Norwegian Nature Inspectorate record non-stationary wolves.

An effort is made to find and distinguish all wolves in the population through the tracking work, but with an emphasis on stationary wolves. Over 100 field personnel, employed both full-time and part-time, search actively for wolf tracks on snow during the census period (1 October–28 February), and follow several thousand kilometres of wolf tracks each season. These are also assisted by volunteers and aided by reports from hunters and from the general public. Wolves are classified either as family groups (packs), scent-marking pairs, solitary stationary wolves, or solitary non-stationary (vagrant) wolves. We count the total number of wolves in each pack, and infer reproduction through the presence of pups. We employ DNA and telemetry techniques to distinguish between wolves in adjacent territories. Census data are entered into a government owned data base in Norway ("Rovbasen") and Sweden ("Rovdjursforum") respectively. In co-operation with SKANDULV, the monitoring institutions in each country have produced annual Scandinavian wolf status reports since 1999 (e.g., Aronson et al. 1999; Wabakken et al. 2006). Through co-operation with colleagues in Finland, data on Finnish wolf packs also were included in these reports.

GENETICS AND BREEDING HISTORY OF THE POPULATION

Breeding history and the construction of a pedigree

The Scandinavian wolf population is small and isolated, with a gap of 800 km between it and the nearest neighbouring wolf population in eastern Finland (Liberg 2005; Linnell et al. 2005; Fig. 2.2.1). These are typical preconditions for genetic problems (Shaffer 1981; Ebenhard 2000). Genetics thus have been central within this study from its start. Fortunately the DNA-technique was already well developed at that time. One of the first tasks of SKANDULV was to track the kinship relations of the population. Unfortunately, DNA-material from the early days of wolf re-colonization in the 1980s was scant. However, we combined records from snow tracking and other field data with DNA-profiles from the few wolves that were sampled during that era. Only one of these early samples belonged to a breeder, and the genotypes of the other breeders were reconstructed with aid of DNA from putative offspring. Thus, we reconstructed the breeding history of the population, starting from the first founders to present (Liberg et al. 2005). The result was one of the first complete pedigrees of a wild mammal population ever constructed (Fig. 2.2.2).

Wolves disappeared from the Scandinavian Peninsula by the end of the 1960s or early 1970′s (Wabakken et al. 2001). The last confirmed breeding occurred in 1964, in northernmost Sweden. However, in the end of the 1970s there were persistent reports of wolves from the south-central part of the Peninsula, and in 1983 biologists recorded the first litter here. DNA analyses later revealed that both wolves in the breeding pair were immigrants from Finland/Russia (Vilà et al. 2003a; Liberg et al. 2005). The same pair continued to produce litters until 1985, when the female was killed by a sheep farmer. She is the only breeding wolf born before 1995 for which DNA material was preserved and later genotyped (Fig. 2.2.2). Her mate, whose tracks were distinguishable due to a deformed paw, disappeared the following spring. However, wolves again reproduced in this territory two years later, and genetic evidence implies that these breeders were siblings, offspring from the first breeding pair. Incestuous breeding by a sequence of various constellations of wolves continued within this pack until 1991, when we observed the first mating outside the original territory. A female, descended from the original pair, had dispersed northeast 250 km in 1985 (almost half the distance to the Finnish population), settled there and finally mated and bred there with an unrelated male ("Gh" in Fig. 2.2.2). We were able to reconstruct the genetic make-up of the two breeding wolves from DNA obtained from their offspring, and determined that the male in this pair was a new immigrant from the east

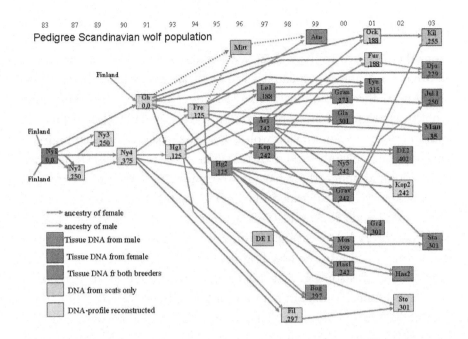

Figure 2.2.2. Pedigree of the Scandinavian wolf population. Abbreviations inside squares indicate the identity of the pair, figures indicate inbreeding coefficient (F) for the offspring of that pair. Arrows indicate the ancestry of the male and female in each breeding pair. Dashed lines indicate less secure ancestries. Arrangement of breeding pairs according to the time scale on top indicates first year of breeding for each pair. This figure and findings by Liberg et al. are also described by Wayne (see this volume, page 24).

(Liberg et al. 2005). He was the last wolf from the outside taking part of the Scandinavian breeding population. Thus, the Scandinavian wolf population is composed of the genes from only three founders, all from the larger Finnish/Russian population (Vilà et al. 2003a; Liberg et al. 2005). From this point onward, the number of breeding pairs increased rapidly (Fig. 2.2.2), although we so far have not been able to confirm any new immigrants (Liberg et al. 2005).

From 1998, when the wolf marking programme started, we got DNA directly also from breeders (Fig. 2.2.2). Four years later we started extracting DNA also from scats. This latter source has proven to be a very valuable tool that has enabled us to continually update the pedigree by genotyping almost every new breeder in the population.

Inbreeding depression

From the pedigree we have calculated inbreeding coefficients for almost all litters born, and documented a strong negative correlation between inbreeding coefficients and litter sizes (Liberg et al. 2005). This inbreeding problem is already limiting the growth of the population (see below). In addition to this, Scandinavian wolves tend to display an unusual high degree of presumably inherited malformations in the population (Räikkönen et al. 2006), although these have not been directly linked to inbreeding. Refined analysis have revealed that there is a strong selection ($i = 0.245/$ generation; Lande & Arnold 1983) against the most homozygous wolves, such that for each level of inbreeding it is the most heterozygous wolves that are recruited into the breeding population (Bensch et al. 2006). The conclusion of this study is that this mechanism will retard the deteriorating effects of inbreeding, but not prevent them (Bensch et al. 2006). Thus, eventually there will be a need for further immigration of wolves from the Finnish/Russian population to our own. Although the distance is great (see above), we have recorded several dispersals matching the gap, including an 1100 km dispersal of a Scandinavian female to northern Finland near the Russian border. A significant barrier to interchange between these populations is the reindeer husbandry zones in Fennoscandia, since national policy in Norway, Sweden, and Finland and local cultures do not tolerate their presence or establishment due to depredation risks (Swedish Ministry of Environment 2000; Norwegian Ministry of the Environment 2003). We have identified several immigrants in northern Scandinavia by DNA analysis of scats and tissue samples, but so far all of these disappeared within a short time, most likely poached, before they could contribute to our gene pool. However, lethal control sanctioned by the government has also removed potential immigrants. In 2005, an immigrant wolf was killed by the Swedish management authorities only 200 km north of the current Scandinavian wolf breeding range. A possible remedy to this stalemate is by trans-locating wolves from Finland to Scandinavia – however, this is a controversial issue and is presently the subject of hot debate in Sweden.

DEMOGRAPHY

The Scandinavian wolf population is expanding in an environment that is favourable concerning resources (space and prey) but hostile concerning human tolerance. These aspects, as well as genetic problems, strongly influence its demography.

Reproduction and pack sizes

Number of reproducing packs per year has increased from one in 1990 to 15 in 2005 (Wabakken et al. 2006). Litter sizes are recorded on snow during winter. We limit our estimates to first-born litters only as it is impossible to differentiate between pups of the year and older siblings from tracks (Wabakken et al. 2001). For the whole study period 1983–2005 the average winter litter size was 3.9 (range 0–8). During 1991–1997 the average winter litter size was 4.2, which is in the lower part of the range reported in the literature (Fuller et al. 2003). Thereafter, the average litter size however has declined, to 3.9 during 1998–2001, and later to 3.4 for the period 2002–2005. This decline is most likely the result of ongoing inbreeding depression (Liberg et al. 2005). Winter pack sizes have averaged 6.1 wolves (range 3–11, pairs not included) for the entire study period, which corresponds well to the average reported for a large number of North American wolf populations living on deer and moose (Fuller et al. 2003), but is well above the level reported for another newly established expanding wolf population (Wydeven et al. 1995).

Survival

Our survival estimates are based on 76 wolves that we have radio-marked since December 1998. Overall annual survival was 0.67 for the period 1999–2006 (n = 110 "wolf years"). This does not include pup survival between birth and the winter marking period in January–March. Territorial animals had a survival rate of 0.78, while subordinate adult pack members had a survival of 0.61 and survival of dispersing animals was as low as 0.22. Poaching was the strongest single mortality factor, causing

58% of total mortality, while legal killing comprised 14%, traffic 11% and natural causes (disease, age, trauma) another 17% of total mortality. We could not find any time trend in the survival estimates during the period 1999–2006. However, based on annual population and recruitment estimates, we could deduce an annual overall survival rate for the pre-marking period of 1991–1999. For this early period we cannot differentiate between mortality factors, but the total survival of 0.79 was clearly higher than the 0.67 as estimated for the radio-monitoring period 1999–2006. The former figure is typical for a non-harvested wolf population, (Ballard et al. 1987; Hayes & Harestad 2000), while the latter corresponds well to the average for many wolf populations in North America (Fuller 1989a; Fuller et al. 2003), although well above the level typical for declining populations (Ballard et al. 1987).

Population Growth

The winter population size has grown from 2–4 animals in 1982/83 to 150 animals in 2005/06 (Fig. 2.2.3). For our calculations of annual growth rate, we have not included the period 1983–1990, when only a single family existed and the population was stagnant. After the second pair bred in 1991, the wolf population grew nearly continuously with an average annual lambda over the whole period of 1.17. During the 1991–97 period this rate was 1.31 but declined to 1.16 during 1997–2002 and further to 1.12 during 2002–2006. Considering the situation of this wolf population, with adequate prey and large tracts of unoccupied habitat (Wabakken et al. 2001; Sand et al. 2006b), a steadier increase in growth rate could be expected. We believe the main reason is a combination of the reduced survival rate due to illegal killing, and declining litter sizes due to the progressing inbreeding (see above). However, preliminary population simulations, based on these data, predict continued positive population growth over the next 30–40 years if no additional problems occur, e.g., an increase in the rate of illegal killing, or more inbreeding effects than those already accounted for (Forslund et al., unpublished data).

DISPERSAL – TERRITORY ESTABLISHMENT

Typically, Scandinavian wolves disperse at an early age and may disperse long distances. By May 2005, we had radio-collared 17 pups for which we also have information until 3 years of age. Out of these 17 young wolves, 15 (88%) dispersed, all of them as pups (13%) or yearlings (87%) (Fig. 2.2.4). Nine (60%) of these 15 dispersed from their natal territory as 10–14 months old, i.e., during March–June. The two non-dispersers (female siblings) budded as yearlings from their natal pack after their father was illegally killed and their mother failed to hold the territory without a new partner. Dispersal ages of Scandinavian wolves are similar to what was found for dispersing wolves in Finland (Kojola et al. 2006) and north-eastern Minnesota (Gese & Mech 1991), but are lower than reported in most North American studies, where the average dispersal age ranged between 2.5 and 3 years (Mech & Boitani 2003b).

A record straight-line dispersal distance of nearly 1100 km was set by a female wolf which traversed across Fennoscandia from southeastern Norway to the northeast part of the Finnish-Russian border. However, long range dispersers (> 300 km; N=23) were predominately males (87%), and most of them did not succeed to reproduce. Among 68 successful breeders (even sex ratio), there was no significant difference in dispersal distance between females (130 km, range 15–345 km) and males (167 km, 34–422 km). The low dispersal age and the long distance dispersals of Scandinavian wolves may be explained by low wolf densities, good supply of ungulate prey, and large expanses of vacant habitat (Wabakken et al. 2001).

So far, no group dispersal is confirmed, and no disperser has been verified to join an already established pack in Scandinavia. An individual disperser settles in a vacant area or a territory already established by an individual of opposite sex. In most cases, the female settles before the male.

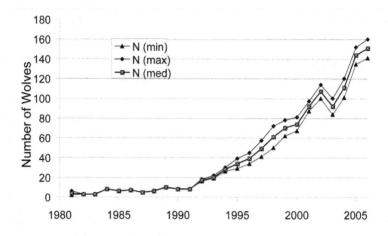

Figure 2.2.3. Dynamics of the Scandinavian wolf population 1981–2006. Data show number of wolves counted during winter.

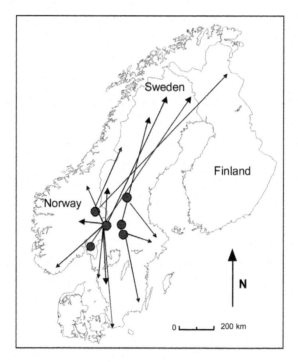

Figure 2.2.4. Long range dispersals in 15 wolves during 1984–2004 in Scandinavia. Black circles indicate natal territories. Arrows indicate the place where the wolf was found dead or where faeces were found that could be identified with aid of DNA-analyses.

PREDATION AND IMPACT ON WILDLIFE AND HUNTING

Prey choice

Several ungulate species are available for the wolf in Scandinavia. The moose (*Alces alces*) occurs in high densities (0.5–2.0 / km²) over most of the Peninsula, whereas the roe deer (*Capreolus capreolus*) reaches high densities (2–10/ km²) only in the southern half of it. Semi-domestic reindeer (*Rangifer tarandus*) only occurs in the northern third of the Peninsula, whereas the wild variant is limited to alpine habitats in southern Norway. Local populations of red deer (*Cervus elaphus*), fallow deer (*Dama dama*), and wild boar (*Sus scrofa*) are found in fragmented populations in southern Sweden, and red deer also occur on the west coast of Norway, all generally outside the present wolf range.

The moose constitutes the primary prey both in terms of numbers killed (>75%) and by kg biomass ingested (>95%) by wolves in Scandinavia (Olsson et al. 1997; Sand et al. 2005) (Fig. 2.2.5). The roe deer is the next most important ungulate prey and is the primary species consumed by wolves in territories where roe deer densities are high relative to those of moose. Wolves also consume small game species such as beaver (*Castor fiber*), badger (*Meles meles*), mountain hare (*Lepus timidus*), and capercaillie (*Tetrao urogallus*) and black grouse (*Tetrao tetrix*). In addition, wolves occasionally depredate livestock, primarily reindeer and domestic sheep (*Ovis aries*).

Moose calves comprise between 39% and 93% of all kills, depending on the pack sampled. Calf occurrence in diet was not correlated with the age distribution in the local moose population, which indicates that packs may learn different hunting strategies. The high proportion of calves in wolf kills during winter in Scandinavia compared with North American studies (13–56%; Mech 1966; Haber 1977; Peterson 1977; Peterson et al. 1984; Mech et al. 1998) may be explained by both a stronger selection for this age class and a higher proportion of calves in the living winter population (15–30%). Compared with human harvest, more calves, less prime-aged

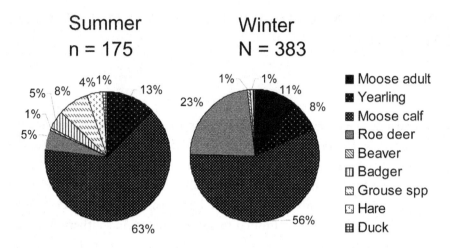

Figure 2.2.5. Number and type of wolf killed prey found during study periods in winter and summer 1999–2004 in Scandinavia.

(2–10 years), and older (≥11 years) moose were killed by wolves, whereas yearlings were killed in similar proportions by wolves and hunters. This pattern of age selection of moose by Scandinavian wolves corresponds well to results from North American studies (Mech 1970; Mech et al. 1998; Hayes et al. 2000).

Kill rates

We studied wolf predation behaviour in detail with the aid of GPS radio-transmitters in >15 packs in Scandinavia. We applied a novel technique based on combining downloaded GPS data with GIS analyses in order to find all ungulate kills during intensive study periods during both summer and winter by using a schedule of hourly (winter) or half-hourly (summer) positions.

Winter kill rates of moose in Scandinavia was almost two moose killed per week/pack or 4–5 moose killed/wolf/100 days, which roughly corresponds to 5–10 kg biomass meat available/wolf/day (Sand et al. 2005). This kill rate in terms of *number of moose* killed per time unit during winter is higher (30–110%) than generally reported in the American literature

(Peterson et al. 1984; Ballard et al. 1987, 1997; Thurber & Peterson 1993; Messier 1994; Hayes et al. 2000). The higher kill rate in Scandinavia compared with North America may best be explained by the higher proportion of calves in the kill and thus a lower amount of consumable biomass per moose killed.

Few studies have reported wolf kill rates for the summer period (but see Jedrzejewski et al. 2002). By visiting the majority (>90%) of GPS positions received from one or both of the breeding wolves in various packs, and by using dogs in the field for finding prey killed, we were able to obtain data on kill rates for the summer period (June–Sept). During this season, wolves displayed an even higher preference (90%) for calves (1–4 month old) than during winter. Total kill rates were 56–73% higher than during winter, although decreasing with time as calves grew larger during the summer. Biomass available to wolves was on average of 5–6 kg/wolf/day. As a result of the high summer kill rate, as much as 40–50% of the total annual moose kill may occur during the 4-month period June–September. Since most calf predation during summer is additive in Scandinavia, this may be an important factor limiting moose population growth within wolf territories.

Interestingly, most moose carcasses were not totally consumed by wolves and were usually abandoned within 24–36 hours after killing (Sand et al. 2005). A total time of 1.25 days near their killed prey corresponds to approximately 10–70% of the average handling time reported for wolves preying on moose in North America (Fuller & Keith 1980; Messier & Crête 1985; Ballard et al. 1987, 1997; Hayes et al. 2000). Variation in pack size was not a likely cause to this variable pattern since the handling time of prey was not related to pack size in Scandinavia. Our GPS data indicated that the wolves tended to kill and feed upon larger prey such as moose mainly during the dark hours and that they normally rested during daytime several kilometres away from carcasses between feeding bouts. Thus, short handling time, incomplete consumption of carcasses, and resting far from killed prey is a typical pattern for wolves in Scandinavia. This may be an adaptation for minimizing encounters with humans in Scandinavia, previously and presently the main mortality factor of wolves. A dense forest road system (1–1.5 km/km^2) combined with a higher human population density makes wolf areas more accessible in Scandinavia compared with many wolf areas in North America. Alternatively, or additionally, this typical pattern may be caused by the high availability (density + behaviour) of their main prey species (see below). Several studies have shown wolves use carcasses less when prey is easy to kill (Carbyn 1983; Bobek et al. 1992).

Impact on moose population and harvest

The present knowledge of wolf predation on moose has mainly emerged from studies in North America (Ballard & Van Ballenberghe 1998). Wolf predation has been found to constitute everything from a slight (e.g., Ballard et al. 1987) to a major (Boutin 1992; Orians et al. 1997; Ballard & Van Ballenberghe 1998) limiting factor for moose populations. The varying impact may reflect a genuine variation among areas and years due to variation in moose density (e.g., Messier 1994), wolf pack size (Hayes et al. 2000), wolf/moose ratios (Vucetich et al. 2002), prey age structure (Peterson et al. 1984; Ballard et al. 1987), and varying supply of alternative prey (Messier & Crête 1985).

In most of Scandinavia, predation on moose by large carnivores (wolves and brown bears) has been absent during the last century. The lack of top-down limitation by large carnivores, combined with restrictive hunting regulations, resulted in a dramatic increase in the moose population during the twentieth century (Cederlund & Markgren 1987; Østgård 1987; Lavsund et al. 2003). Human harvest became the main limiting factor of moose during this time (Cederlund & Sand 1991; Solberg et al. 1999, 2003). Today the average density of moose in southern and central Scandinavia is >1 moose/km² with an annual population growth (λ) before harvest of 1.35–1.45 in most areas (Solberg et al. 2003).

The impact of wolf predation on the total Scandinavian moose population is at present very limited. In 2003 hunters harvested approximately 140,000 moose annually in Scandinavia. This represents about 25–30 % of the pre-hunt moose population (Solberg et al. 2003), which numbers about 450,000–500,000 moose. In 2005, 150 wolves distributed over 28 wolf territories were estimated to have killed approximately 3500 moose/

year in Scandinavia, which corresponded to approximately 2.5% of the total annual human harvest. In comparison, estimated traffic mortality (automobiles and trains) corresponded to 4–5% of the annual harvest.

In Värmland, the province of highest wolf density in Sweden (7 wolf packs or pairs with 34 wolves over 17 000 km^2 = 2 wolves/1000 km^2), wolves killed approximately 840 moose in 2005 compared with 9200 moose killed by hunters and an additional 400 moose killed by traffic. If we conservatively assume that mortality from other causes, such as malnutrition, disease, and bears, is equal in size to traffic mortality (probably an underestimation), harvest accounted for 82.5 % and traffic for 3.9 % of moose mortality in Värmland that year, whereas wolf predation was responsible for 9.7 % of mortality (probably an overestimation).

For local moose management in Scandinavia with wolf territories patchily distributed it may be more relevant to estimate the effects of wolf predation within actual wolf territories than over larger areas. At this geographical level, depending on factors such as the local moose density (0.5–2.0 km^2) and productivity, as well as wolf territory size (500–1500 km^2), wolf predation *per se* may account for 15–100 % of the total annual growth (λ) in the moose population. However, even within most wolf territories current estimates of predation does not exceed 50% of the annual production of moose.

Based on predator-prey studies from Scandinavia, Europe, and North America we argue that the expected impact of wolves on moose in the future will continue to be low compared with other human activities (harvest, traffic mortality). This assumption may be explained by a low density of wolves far below saturation and with relatively large, non-contiguous territories, partly resulting from an active management regime currently aiming at controlling the wolf population far below their biological carrying capacity. The assumption of low impact of wolves on moose is also corroborated by the fact that the moose population in most parts of Scandinavia continues to have a high density and productivity. However, locally in areas with low density and productivity of moose coinciding with high densities (small territories) of wolves, the impact from wolf predation may turn out to be the dominating mortality factor, sometimes even exceeding the annual production of moose.

Hunting success

Scandinavian wolves are highly successful moose predators. Average hunting success was 50–60% counted on moose groups attacked, and 26% counted on number of individual moose involved in the attack (Sand et al. 2006a). This is roughly 3–4 times higher than reported in North America (Mech 1966; Haber 1977; Peterson 1977; Peterson et al. 1984; Mech et al. 1998) (Fig. 2.2.6). Furthermore, Scandinavian moose seldom stand their ground when attacked by wolves as compared with their conspecifics in North America. Chase distances in Scandinavia were short (average 50–100 m) with some moose even being killed while lying down. We have found no evidence that moose have adjusted to wolf presence by changing their anti-predator behaviour even in areas where wolves have occurred continuously for 10–20 years since their re-colonization. It seems that moose behaviour toward wolves, but also toward humans, in Scandinavia differs from North America. Aggressive behaviour toward humans has frequently been reported for North American calf-rearing female moose (Geist 1963; Mech 1966, 1970; Peterson 1977; Franzmann & Schwartz 1998; Mech et al. 1998). In Scandinavia, aggressive behaviour by calf-rearing females toward humans is extremely rare (Ekman et al. 1992; Sand et al. 2006a). We conclude that Scandinavian moose have not regained an efficient anti-predator behaviour toward recolonizing wolves as swiftly as has been seen in North America. We argue that the reason for this difference is the longer period of separation between the two species in Scandinavia, the longer and much more intensive human harvest of moose compared with any North American area, and perhaps even the use of baying dogs as a common hunting method in Scandinavia (Sand et al. 2006a). Whether this will just cause a delay in readjustment, or whether selection and/or drift have completely eliminated some of the genetic basis for this behaviour in the Scandinavian moose population remains to be seen.

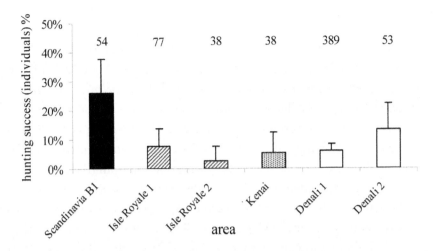

Figure 2.2.6. Wolf hunting success on moose (95% C.I.) based on the number of individual moose attacked in Scandinavia and North America; Isle Royale 1 (Mech 1966); Isle Royale 2 (Peterson 1977); Kenai (Peterson et al. 1984); Denali 1 (Haber 1977); Denali 2 (Mech et al. 1998). Sample size (*n*) for each study is given above bars.

DEPREDATION ON DOMESTIC STOCK AND DOGS

Conflicts between wolves and rural interests are directly related to land use practices in Sweden and Norway. Swenson and Andrén (2005) provided an excellent overview of the contrasting policies regarding rural communities, livestock and reindeer grazing, large carnivore management, and compensation schemes. The Norwegian situation is presented in detail in Andersen et al. (2003). Commonalities between Norway and Sweden include conflicts associated with depredation on dogs and semi-domesticated reindeer. The situation regarding other livestock, however, differs, with greater conflict and depredation on free-ranging sheep in Norway, where this activity is heavily subsidized by the government. In Sweden, this activity is not, and farmers must take measures to protect their livestock on fenced pastures near their homes.

Livestock

There are a total of 2.4 million domestic sheep and 236,000 cattle in Norway (Norwegian Ministry of the Environment 2003). About 2.1 million sheep are grazed annually on open range with little or no shepherding. Most other livestock, including 300,000 sheep, are grazed on pastures on or near farms. Total sheep mortality, due to all causes, averages 120,000 sheep/year (5%). During 1999–2006, the Norwegian government paid out on average €6.7 million per year in compensation for around 32,000 sheep killed annually by predators (golden eagle (*Aquila chrysaetos*), lynx (*Lynx lynx*), brown bear (*Ursus arctos*), wolverine (*Gulo gulo*), and wolf) (Norwegian Directorate for Nature Management 2005). Of these, approximately €202,000 was spent to compensate the loss of 995 wolf-killed sheep each year , or about 3% of total annual depredation loss in the country. On average, about 72% of all wolf-killed sheep occur in Hedmark county in southeastern Norway; however, most (nearly 90%) sheep in this county are killed by other predators such as brown bear, lynx, and wolverine (See Table 2.2.1). In 2008, the Norwegian government budgeted about €13.6 million for monetary compensation for livestock and reindeer depredation by large predators, in addition to about €6.7 million for measures aimed at reducing conflicts and preventing depredation (Norwegian Ministry of the Environment 2007).

In Sweden, there are approximately 500,000 sheep and 1.2 million cattle, of which the vast majority (99%) are grazed within fenced pastures. Livestock operations are generally small, and 92% of sheep farms have < 50 ewes. Between 100–200 sheep and 2–6 calves are killed by wolves each year. Since 1997, the government compensates for documented cases of depredation on livestock. This amounts to about €30,000 per year, with farmers receiving 1–2 times the market value for animals lost. In addition, the government invests about €100,000 annually on pro-active measures – aimed at reducing depredation by large carnivores, primarily through the construction of electric fences. In the core wolf area, wolves kill approximately 1% of the total number of sheep each year (Statistics Sweden 2006). Thus, wolf depredation on livestock is not considered to be critical for lamb producers in Sweden today.

Table 2.2.1. Number, species and age of ungulate prey found and classified as being killed (n=97), or probably killed (n=18), by wolves during five winter study periods in three wolf territories.

Type of prey	Tyngsjö 2002	Gråfjell 2001	Gråfjell 2002	Gråfjell 2003	Bograngen 2003	Total / Average
Moose adult	12	3	5	1	2	23
Moose calf	8	13	25	23	14	83
Moose of unknown age	0	0	2	0	0	2
Total moose	20–24	15–16	26–34	20–24	16–17	97–115
Roe deer	3	0	1	1	1	6
Total number of prey	23	16	33			72
Study period	84	70	133	62	62	411
No of days per moose	4.2–3.5	4.7–4.4	4.2	3.1–2.6	3.9–3.6	4.2–3.6

Semi-domesticated reindeer

In Norway, about 200,000 reindeer are grazed throughout the year on roughly 40% of the total land area, primarily in northern Norway. Although this area is outside the current boundaries of the breeding wolf population, wolves occasionally disperse into this region. On average, the government pays herders about €3.3 million for around 22,500 reindeer estimated to be taken by predators (mostly lynx and wolverine) each year. Herders received compensation for 213 reindeer killed by wolves during the seasons 1999/2000–2004/05. Wolf depredation varies greatly from year to year (0–114 animals), with compensation averaging about €8,500 annually (see Table 2.2.2).

In Sweden there are approximately 250,000 reindeer grazing year-round in the northern 40% of the country. As in Norway, there are no

Table 2.2.2. Depredation loss for domestic sheep in Norway, 1999–2004 (Source: Norwegian Directorate for Nature Management).

Year	Sheep depredation total	Sheep killed by wolves
1999	33109	622
2000	32034	837
2001	29891	788
2002	30920	1847
2003	31902	742
2004	30477	2408

resident wolves in this region. Dispersing wolves kill 50–200 reindeer annually. The government does not compensate for individual losses, but instead pays the Sámi villages for verified presence of wolves. Sámi villages receive €2,500 for confirmed wolf presence (tracks), and €50,000 for each established reproductive pair. About €10,000/year is paid to Sámi villages, primarily to cover costs associated with moving reindeer to areas with fewer predators.

Dogs

As the wolf population increased in Scandinavia, the incidence of wolf attacks on dogs increased concurrently (Fig. 2.2.7). During 1995–2005, 151 dogs (of which 80% were used for hunting) were classified as wolf-killed in both countries. In addition, many other dogs were either injured or suspected to have been killed by wolves. Norway has compensated owners for the actual value (as much as €5,000) of wolf-killed dogs since 1999. In Sweden, dog owners are compensated with €1,000, independent of the dog's actual value.

SKANDULV has actively co-operated with hunting organizations in both countries in testing and implementing various preventative measures. The most notable of these is the so-called "Wolf Telephone". This is a telephone answering machine which continually is updated with a very approximate position for the last radio location for each of our instrumented

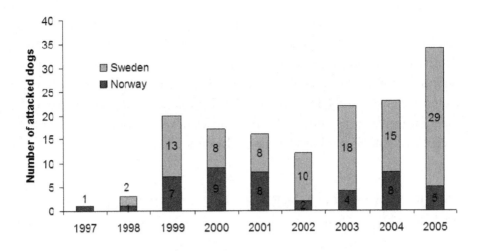

Figure 2.2.7. Wolf attacks on dogs in Sweden and Norway 1997–2005. Most of the attacks were fatal.

wolves during the hunting season. Hunters may then choose not to hunt in that area that day. The warning does of course not completely prevent wolf dog-encounters as wolves are very mobile and there usually are also non-instrumented wolves in the territory. So far we have not been able to detect any reduction in the number of wolf attacks in wolf territories with a "Wolf Telephone" compared with territories without a wolf telephone. This may however be due to an increased hunting frequency in territories with a "Wolf Telephone" as hunters might feel less worried for their dogs' security there. In a survey of 500 hunters (with hunting dogs) in five wolf territories, on average 98% wished to keep the "Wolf Telephone" (J. Karlsson, unpublished data).

Extent of wolf depredation in relation to other predators

In general, wolf depredation on domestic livestock and semi-domesticated reindeer is minimal in Norway and Sweden relative to depredation by other species of large predators (Table 2.2.3). However, when it occurs, it generates strong controversy and negative sentiments among rural dwellers. Indeed, wolf zoning policy in Norway is based to a large extent on the density of grazing sheep in order to prevent greater depredation loss by wolves. Depredation on dogs is very controversial among hunters in both countries, and is difficult to mitigate. Effective mitigation and management measures are essential in both countries if wolves are to gain broader acceptance among rural dwellers in both countries.

INTEGRATING RESEARCH INTO WOLF MANAGEMENT

The wolf management in Scandinavia is facing several challenges. In the typical European manner, the Scandinavian wolf population is completely limited to a multi-use landscape which it is sharing with humans and their activities (Breitenmoser 1998; Linnell et al. 2005). This inevitably has led to a number of conflicts with humans, including competition for prey, depredation on domestic stock and dogs, and an increasing number of complaints from people that have had direct confrontations with wolves. At the same time the wolf population itself is facing growing problems and its long-term viability is far from secured. Although the population has developed well since it first established itself in the 1980s, a heavy toll from poachers and a progressing inbreeding depression now is reducing the growth rate and eventually threatens to turn it negative (see above). We will here try to line out how the research sector has been, or could be, used to improve the wolf management and conservation.

The most obvious way in which research can support management is by providing data and analyses critical for management decisions or policies (Mech & Boitani 2003a). The identification of the two main limiting factors for the Scandinavian wolf population, illegal killing and inbreeding depression, are research results of high relevance for the management. Our quantification of the amount of poaching has led to the Government decision to allocate more resources into anti-poaching activities in both Norway and Sweden. SKANDULV personnel have also been called to

Table 2.2.3. Depredation loss for semi-domesticated reindeer in Norway (1999/2000–2004/2005) (Source: Norwegian Directorate for Nature Management).

Year	Reindeer loss (total)	Reindeer killed by wolves
1999/00	19468	1
2000/01	20033	0
2001/02	11532	81
2002/03	10720	4
2003/04	10400	13
2004/05	11400	114

court trials to witness in cases concerning poaching. So far, these efforts have not led to any measurable decrease of illegal wolf killing, but we believe that recognition of the problem and information on its magnitude are necessary preconditions for it being solved.

The detection and quantification of the inbreeding depression of wolf litter sizes has had profound effects for the wolf debate in Scandinavia. At almost every occasion where wolf management and conservation is discussed in Scandinavia, this issue is brought up. It has led to a strong lobbying for actively bringing in more wolves, and although the governments and the managing authorities in the two countries so far are not prepared to take such a step, they are aware of the option and are discussing it. They are also carefully following our ongoing demographic and genetic monitoring of the wolf population. Continuous updating of our wolf population simulation model with new data is providing us with an important early warning device, should the wolf situation turn critical. Before an allowance is given to kill a wolf for damage prevention, the normal routine now includes a DNA analysis of the targeted offender (mainly by collecting faeces from it) to evaluate its genetic value.

Our data on predation rates and impact on the moose population are frequently used in the debate on how much wolves compete with hunters. Moose densities within most of the Scandinavian moose range typically is above 1/km², (Solberg et al. 2003). At such densities, there is moose enough for both wolves and hunters (Andrén et al. 1999). One complication is that several large forest companies within the wolf range want to reduce moose densities down to 0.4–0.5/km^2 because of claimed damages on young trees, especially pine (Bergström et al. 1995; Glöde et al. 2004). At such low densities the competition between hunters and wolves will be intense. Our data do not solve this conflict, but they give the factual baseline from which to reach compromises.

Contacts between managing agencies and research are not limited to reading reports. There is a continuous communication between the two through numerous channels both formal and informal, often on a personal level. The SKANDULV coordinator updates agencies regularly on our research results and field work, primarily by electronic newsletters, as well as by telephone and/or meetings with managers. The financers of large carnivore research in Norway, Sweden, and Finland, both government institutions and non-governmental organizations, together with representatives from central management authorities in all three countries have formed a committee for coordinating large carnivore research in the three countries, and personnel from SKANDULV are frequently invited to its meetings. Also, SKANDULV has taken the initiative in a regular series of annual conferences where during three days scientists and managers meet, preliminary research results are presented and planned management actions are discussed. This is one of the few forums where officials from central managing agencies in Norway and Sweden regularly meet and get opportunity to discuss matters of mutual interest.

SKANDULV also arranges special scientific workshops with invited researchers and managers (e.g., Liberg 2006), and major research results are often presented at special meetings with Scandinavian managers prior to publication. Often (but not always) scientific personnel from SKAND-ULV are asked for background facts before large decisions are taken by the central authorities. SKANDULV scientists have provided reports to both Norwegian and Swedish governments as part of the larger process of large carnivore policies formulations (Andrén et al. 1999; Pedersen et al. 2005).

Involvement of stakeholders, including hunters, farmers, foresters, conservationists, local politicians, and even policemen, is a very important part of large carnivore management (Decker et al. 1996). To this end, managing agencies in Norway and Sweden have organized in each country a national committee with representatives from concerned stakeholders which meet three or four times a year to discuss management actions and policies with responsible officials. No scientists are formally attached to these committees, but they are frequently invited to their meetings to give factual backgrounds.

However, through our work on the ground in the wolf areas, scientists and field assistants in SKANDULV meet local people almost daily, which also has led to a developed network of contacts with key persons in the local communities. In each wolf territory where we put transmitters on wolves, we also organize a contact group with representatives from local stakeholders and politicians, and with one representative from SKAND-ULV in each group. We hold regular meetings, usually on a monthly basis, where we inform about the wolf situation and discuss any matter brought up. These groups have turned out to be very important for dampening of irritations and conflicts. The so-called "wolf telephone" (see above) was started on the initiative of SKANDULV, to warn hunters where it might be risky to let dogs loose. Since the research project began we have striven to involve local people in our activities. During the first years, much of the monitoring work was performed by local volunteers with whom we co-operated. Recently much of the managing responsibility for large carnivore management has been delegated from central to regional agencies in both countries and SKANDULV closely co-operates with these. We are often invited to their meetings, and frequently asked for advice on a large host of topics, from their regional management plans to how to deal with specific problem wolves. These regional agencies have a number of field personnel employed in two main tasks: inspecting depredated domestic animals as a prerequisite for damage compensation, and annual monitoring of large carnivore populations. Often these are the same people that were earlier co-operating with us in SKANDULV, and our involvement with them is continuing through participation in training courses and through frequent informal contacts. SKANDULV personnel travel to more than 100 local meetings annually in both countries, to inform about and discuss wolf matters.

Finally, we think it necessary to point out that, although closeinvolvement of research with management offers great opportunities, there are also risks involved. There are probably few fields of science where the separation and distinction between the roles of research and management are as easily confused as when working with large carnivores. Scientists can risk losing their credibility with stakeholders and with the general public by becoming too involved in management issues or by taking stands in conflict issues (Skogen and Haaland 2001). Managers, on the other hand, might be tempted to interfere in an unsound way with the research. There is also the risk of territorial disputes between management and research as to the proper borderline between the two. Also, irritation might occur when scientists fail to appreciate the political restrictions that limit management options or make their results comprehensible. Managers might annoy scientists by disregarding their results or advice, for prestige purposes or due to lack of understanding.

On the other hand, it is a privilege for researchers to work with an issue where the interest in their results is so intense and widespread, and it is a grand opportunity for managers to work so closely with science and be able to put brand new research results directly into practice. And if there is any area in resource management where there is a great potential for an adaptive approach, this is it. To successfully grasp the opportunities while avoiding the risks, both parties have to engage in a will to understand, a mutual respect for the professional skill of each other, and in frequent and open communication.

ACKNOWLEDGMENTS

We want to thank the large number of co-workers and assistants, both in the field and the laboratory, who have contributed so much to this study, and we would like to especially mention Per Ahlqvist, Henrik Andrén, Jon Arnemo, Staffan Bensch, Stein E. Bredvold, Michael Dötterer, Åsa Fahlman, Pär Forslund, Olav Hjeljord, Örjan Johansson, Ilpo Kojola, Erling Maartmann, Peter Segerström, Douglas Sejberg, Kent Sköld,

Linn Svensson, Sven-Olov Svensson, Ole K. Steinset, Thomas H. Strøm-seth, Camilla Wikenros, Barbara Zimmermann, Mikael Åkesson and Inga Ängsteg. We also want to thank all the management personnel on central and regional levels in Norway and Sweden with whom we have had the privilege to co-operate. The study was supported by the Swedish Environmental Protection Agency, The Swedish Association for Hunting and Wildlife Management, World Wildlife Fund for Nature (Sweden), Swedish University of Agricultural Sciences, Norwegian Directorate for Nature Management, Norwegian Research Council, Norwegian Institute for Nature Research, Hedmark University College, and County Governor of Hedmark.

2.3 Synthesizing Wolf Ecology and Management in Eastern Europe: Similarities and Contrasts with North America

*Włodzimierz Jędrzejewski, Bogumiła Jędrzejewska,
Žanete Andersone-Lilley, Linas Balčiauskas, Peep Männil,
Jānis Ozoliņš, Vadim E. Sidorovich, Guna Bagrade, Marko Kübarsepp,
Aivars Ornicāns, Sabina Nowak, Alda Pupila and Agrita Žunna*

INTRODUCTION

In Eastern Europe, wolves (*Canis lupus*) face as great a range of variation of environmental conditions as anywhere else in the world. Topographic features of the terrain change from vast lowlands with postglacial lakes, to hills and mountains. Density of human population and infrastructure is so variable that both large wilderness areas (ideal wolf habitats) and human-made cultural landscapes (unsuitable for large carnivores) occur in a large-scale landscape mosaic. Forest cover predominantly consists of commercial, managed woods dominated by Scotch pine (*Pinus silvestris*), but includes also substantial patches of well preserved, natural, and semi-natural forests. In various parts of the region, ungulate (the main prey of wolves) communities are dominated by small (roe deer, *Capreolus capreolus*), medium (red deer, *Cervus elaphus*), or large-sized species (moose, *Alces alces*).

Recent studies of population genetics of wolves in Eastern Europe (Pilot et al. 2006) have demonstrated that wolves displayed spatial genetic structure that was influenced by ecological factors. In Eastern Europe, five distinct subpopulations were delimited based on frequencies of mitochondrial DNA haplotypes, and two based on allele frequencies of microsatellite loci. Pilot et al. (2006) proposed that natal-habitat-biased dispersal could be an underlying mechanism linking population ecology of wolves with their population genetic structure. Interestingly, such genetic differentiation among local populations – without obvious physical barrier to movement – was correlated with ecological factors: climate, habitat types, wolf diet composition (dominant species of ungulates), and human activity. These results mirror recent studies showing similar ecological effects on genetic differentiation in the absence of isolation by distance among wolves in the Canadian Arctic, where barren-ground and forest wolves, though contiguous, were strongly genetically distinct (Carmichael et al. 2007; Musiani et al. 2007).

In addition to ecological factors that may promote genetic differentiation, the centuries-long and still-present human pressure (Bibikov 1985; Jędrzejewska et al. 1996; Andersone-Lilley & Ozoliņš 2005) is also certainly a strong influence on life history and ecological adaptations of wolves in Eastern Europe. The long history of intense persecution of wolves in Eastern Europe may contrast sharply with recent history (since the 1970s) in North America (Musiani & Paquet 2004). Eastern European countries have often resorted to organized predator control campaigns. Wolf control methods included (a) winter hunts employing 'fladry' (a technique by which lines of flags [fladry] are used to funnel wolves toward hunters; Okarma 1989); (b) late summer hunts during which wolves are lured by hunters who simulate wolf howling (Pavlov 1990); and (c) spring searches for wolf dens with the objective of killing pups (Sidorovich et al. 2007). Only in the recent decade has the extermination of wolves in Eastern Europe been abating and partial or full protection initiated. However, the protected populations may still be threatened by direct (poaching, road kills) and indirect (habitat fragmentation) human impacts.

In this chapter, we review the results of numerous recent studies not easily accessible to western scientists on wolf ecology conducted in five countries of Eastern Europe: Poland, Belarus, Lithuania, Latvia, and Estonia. We analyze the biological and ecological features of wolves that allowed them to adapt to the natural diversity of living conditions and successfully cope with the long-lasting and large-scale exploitation and other influences by humans. Throughout, we compare and contrast wolf ecology and management with North American literature, and propose several mechanisms for differences between European and North American wolves. Finally, we discuss the perspectives for sustainable management of wolf populations in the five countries and identify possible directions of future research on the species.

CHARACTERISTICS OF THE REGION

This study's five countries mostly occur in the East European Plain (the largest mountain-free part of the European landscape), with the mean elevation being about 170 m a.s.l. and the maximum elevation reaching 346 m a.s.l. The only exception is southern Poland, where hills and mountains (the Carpathians, up to 2,499 m a.s.l.) occur (National Geographic Society 1990). In total, the region stretches between 49°00'-59°40'N latitude and 14°10'-32°40'E longitude, and covers 684,600 km^2 (Poland – 304,510 km^2, Belarus 207,600 km^2, Lithuania 65,200 km^2, Latvia 64,100 km^2, and Estonia 43,200 km^2). Climate is transitional between Atlantic and continental types, with mean temperature of January ranging from –3.6°C in Belarus, where continental features prevail, to –2.4°C in Estonia, and –0.8°C in Poland. Mean temperature of July declines from 18.2°C in Belarus to 16.8°C in Estonia. Snow cover persists for 40–100 days in the Polish lowlands (but 175–230 days in the mountains) to 75–135 days in Estonia (http://www.climate-zone.com/continent/europe).

One-third of the region (33%) is covered with forests. The share of woodland increases in a southwest-northeast gradient from 28–29% of area in Lithuania and Poland, 34% in Belarus, 45% in Latvia, to 47% in Estonia. Forests largely belong to temperate continental type, and are dominated by Scotch pine, Norway spruce (*Picea abies*), birch (*Betula* sp).,.), and oak (*Quercus robur*), in southern parts with mixtures of lime (*Tilia cordata*) and hornbeam (*Carpinus betulus*) (Food and Agriculture Organisation of the United Nations [FAO] 2000). Wet areas are dominated with alder (*Alnus* sp.) woods. Temperate oceanic type forests (with beech, *Fagus sylvatica*) occur in northwestern Poland, and temperate mountain forests (with beech and fir, *Abies alba*) in southern Poland. The whole region, with the exception of hills and mountains in southern Poland, is rich in lakes and wetlands (Nivet & Frazie 2004). Total area of wetlands, mires, and river-flooded marshes (including forested mires) covers from about 6–9% of the country in Poland and Lithuania to 30% in Belarus and Estonia.

Communities of ungulates include two widespread species occurring throughout the whole region: roe deer and wild boar (*Sus scrofa*); two species inhabiting the major parts of it: the red deer, reaching its northern border of occurrence in Estonia, and moose, with a southwestern border of its range in Poland (Mitchell-Jones et al. 1999). Moreover, two other rare native species (European bison, *Bison bonasus*, and chamois, *Rupicapra rupicapra*) and three introduced aliens (fallow deer *Dama dama*, sika deer, *Cervus nippon*, mouflon, *Ovis ammon*) occur locally in small populations. Among medium-sized animals that play a role of secondary prey to wolves, the beaver (*Castor fiber*) and the brown hare (*Lepus europaeus*) occur in all countries, and the mountain hare (*L. timidus*) in the northern part of the region (Mitchell-Jones et al. 1999).

The human population of the five countries is 58 million inhabitants, but mean density varies greatly, from 29 person/km^2 in Estonia and 36/km^2 in Latvia, to 49 person/km^2 in Belarus, 55/km^2 in Lithuania, and as many as 155 person/km^2 in Poland. The level of human transformation of the landscape increases along north–south gradient, with improving environmental and climatic conditions for agriculture and animal husbandry. According to CORINE Land Cover data (Federal Environmental Agency, German Remote Sensing Data Center of the German Aerospace Center 2004), the share of agricultural areas increases from 32% in Estonia to 64% in Poland. The density of roads (an anthropogenic feature of habitat strongly avoided by wolves; Jędrzejewski et al. 2004a, 2005a) is similar in Estonia, Latvia, Lithuania, and Poland (1.12–1.35 km/km^2), and notably lower in Belarus (0.45 km/km^2) (International Road Federation 2006).

Domestic animals kept in open pastures from spring until autumn includes mainly cattle and sheep, with smaller numbers of horses and (rarely) goats.

STATUS, RANGE AND ESTIMATED NUMBERS OF WOLVES

The conservation and management status of wolves in the five countries is inversely related to wolf population size and occupied area. In general, the legal status of wolves improves with rarity (Table 2.3.1). In Poland, where wolves only permanently occur in the eastern and southern parts of the country, wolves have been fully protected since 1998, and occasional permits are issued by the Minister of Environment to shoot wolves that cause frequent, localized damage to livestock. In the Baltic States (Lithuania, Latvia, Estonia), the species was traditionally treated as a pest, but before the countries' accession to the European Union in 2004, hunting legislation was changed and wolves gained status as a game species with a fixed hunting season and annually planned hunting quota. In Belarus Republic, wolves are still regarded as a pest and intense harvest of their number is allowed year round, with most individuals shot during winter hunts and spring searches for the breeding dens with pups. Recently, a more rational approach to wolf management appeared in the local hunters' journal (Sidorovich & Nikiforov 2007), but immediately roused counter-arguments (Tyshkevich & Vostokov 2007).

In Poland, Lithuania, Latvia, and Estonia, large-scale censuses of wolves have been conducted. Censuses were organized and coordinated by scientists and conducted by local forestry and national park services, as well as hunters. The censuses were based on year-round mapping of wolf tracks and observations (Poland, Estonia), and/or one or two days of coordinated snow tracking in winter (Poland, Lithuania, Latvia). The census data are most extensive for Poland, where a national census of wolves began in 2000 (Jędrzejewski et al. 2002a, 2004a, 2005a), and Estonia, where it was initiated in 2003 (P. Männil, unpublished data). In Latvia, winter surveys of wolves began in 2004 and in Lithuania – in 2006 (J. Ozoliņš & L.

Table 2.3.1. Estimated population size of wolves (winter counts), hunting harvest, and legal status of the species in the Baltic states, Belarus Republic and Poland; data for 2005–2007. [a] Census conducted by scientists, forestry and national park services; [b] Data from official hunting statistics; [c] Only wolves frequently causing damage to domestic animals are culled.

	Characteristic of wolf population				
Country	Estimated numbers	Status	Annual harvest	Hunting season	Bounties paid
Estonia	230[a]	Game	16–40	1 Dec-28 Feb	No
Latvia	200-300[a]	Game	130	15 Jul-31 Mar	No
Lithuania	200-220[a]	Game	20	1 Dec-1 Apr	No
Belarus	1340[b]	Pest	~800	Whole year	Yes
Poland	650[a]	Protected	0-2[c]	-	-

Balčiauskas, unpublished data). No formal population surveys have been conducted in Belarus Republic to date.

Although no consistent information about wolf population size and distribution is available for the whole region, data derived from various sources present a first approximation of wolf populations in the region. First, the range of occurrence is fairly well recognized in all countries except for Belarus, where it could only be presented as an approximate (most probably overestimated) area based on professional opinion (Fig. 2.3.1). The range of wolves consists of numerous patches of various sizes and shapes in Poland and the Baltic States, and presumably larger patches or even contiguous areas in Belarus (Fig. 2.3.1). Thus, in Eastern Europe, wolves may function as a very large metapopulation. Some patches (e.g., in Belarus, western Latvia and northwestern Lithuania, northeastern Poland) may be large enough, notwithstanding locally high harvests, to support self-sustained populations. However, many small patches on the map of wolf range denote ephemeral packs or even transient individuals. Those parts of the wolf range are highly unstable from year to year.

THE WORLD OF WOLVES

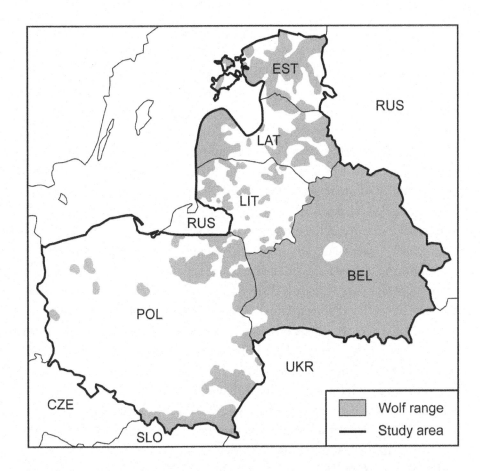

Figure 2.3.1. Range of wolf occurrence in Eastern Europe in 2005–2007. Data for the Baltic States and Poland are based on winter surveys conducted in the whole country, data for Belarus Republic are derived from various sources (records of harvested animals, interviews, and surveys in some regions). Note that the situation of the wolf in the region is dynamic and especially the location of small patches with wolf records may vary among years. Sources: Belarus – V. E. Sidorovich, unpublished data, Estonia – Männil and Kübarsepp (2006), Latvia – J. Ozoliņš, unpublished data, Lithuania – L. Balčiauskas, unpublished data, Poland – Jędrzejewski et al. (2004a, 2004b, 2005a) and W. J. et al., unpublished data.

Only a rough assessment of wolf population size in the region can be made. Available data suggest that 2600–2700 wolves might live in the whole region, with 50% of the population recorded in Belarus (Table 2.3.1). Unfortunately, it is not presently possible to verify the reliability of official statistics on wolf numbers in Belarus, which are not obtained from any standardized survey. Nonetheless, a very high annual hunting quota (Table 2.3.1) either indicates that wolf numbers are higher than estimated, and/or suggests wolves in Belarus could be declining (see data on sustainable mortality summarized by Musiani & Paquet 2004). In comparison to Belarus, in Poland, scientific censuses conducted in the first decade of the twenty-first century in Poland revealed that actual numbers of wolves were significantly lower than those reported earlier by the official statistics. The reason for the bias was the small size of the sample area used to determine hunting inventories (hunting districts average 50 km²), compared with the size of wolf territories, which average 210 km² (Jędrzejewski et al. 2007). Consequently, a pack of wolves recorded in adjacent units was often double- or even triple-counted, as official inventories usually summed the records from all units (Jędrzejewski et al. 2002a). The same problem was encountered in Latvia (Andersone-Lilley & Ozoliņš 2005), thereby casting doubt on the estimates reported in Table 2.3.1 for that country.

The annual legal harvest of wolves in the region ranges from near zero in Poland, to 5–10% of the winter estimate of numbers in Estonia and Lithuania, to 40–60% in Latvia and Belarus (Table 2.3.1). Such severe harvest of wolves in the two latter countries may cause a steady deficit of individuals (see Jędrzejewska et al. 1996), and suggests that despite their large range and size, those populations may function as a sink rather than source of wolves in the metapopulation. At the most extreme, populations in Belarus and Latvia may be in danger of local extirpation in the long term given these high harvests. Indeed, a recent study on gene flow between the local populations in Eastern Europe (including the European part of Russia) has shown that – contrary to expectations – the number of migrants from west to east predominated over migrants from east to west (W. J., unpublished data; M. Pilot et al., unpublished data). Similar phenomena were observed in the Western Carpathian Mountains (Polish-

Slovakian borderland), where intense harvest of wolves in Slovakia creates a mortality sink for wolves from the Polish side (Nowak et al. in press).

The spatial distribution of wolves in the region corresponds closely with the occurrence of large woodlands and natural or semi-natural marshes (comp. Global Land Cover Facility, http://glcf.umiacs.umd.edu/index.shtml). Forests are essential habitats of wolves in Eastern Europe. Indeed, high percentage forest cover along with low density of main motorways and human settlements were the best predictors of wolf occurrence in eastern Poland (Jędrzejewski et al. 2004a, 2005a). In this regard, factors influencing wolf distribution in Eastern Europe are most similar to the great lakes region in North America where wolf occurrence was well predicted by areas with low densities of roads and forest cover (Mladenoff et al. 1995, 1999). Only the southern populations of wolves in Poland were strong influenced in their spatial distribution by mountainous topography similar to that in western North America (Oakleaf et al. 2006).

It is unclear how much the range of wolves in Belarus and the Baltic States is determined by past and present control by people, and to what extent it is limited by available habitats. An analysis of the current wolf range in Poland and a GIS-based modelling of suitable habitats showed that there is a great potential for development of wolf range (W. J. et al., unpublished data). Wolves presently occupy about half the suitable habitat area, and large, contiguous patches of optimal habitats with abundant prey resources are available in western Poland. A major part of the potential wolf range had been occupied by the species soon after World War II, when wolves expanded in numbers and area after the war (Wolsan et al. 1992). Therefore, it needs to be determined what impedes the contemporary expansion of wolves to the West. Anthropogenic barriers to dispersal (agricultural fields, highways, cities etc.), high levels of human-caused mortality, and an Allee effect at low population densities may be the most likely factor. For example, the population spread rate of wolves through dispersal from Yellowstone was slower than expected based on movement models of recolonization because dispersing wolves had reduced probabilities of finding mates due to an Allee effect at the low densities of wolves present at the edge of an expanding population (Hurford et al. 2006).

Thus, in the early the twenty-first century, the metapopulation of wolves in Eastern Europe is still seriously affected by human exploitation and the existence of anthropogenic barriers to dispersal of wolves. Although the importance of hunting has declined in the recent two decades due to changing human attitude to wolves, dispersal barriers become more and more important with the growing density of transportation infrastructure.

PACK SIZE, REPRODUCTION, AND AGE STRUCTURE OF THE POPULATION

Similar to reviews of wolf population dynamics from elsewhere, as wolf harvest increases, both pack size and pack stability decrease, both the proportion of lone wolves in the population and the reproductive output of the population increase, and age structure becomes younger (Fuller 1989a; Fuller et al. 2003). Data from western Belarus (Belarussian part of Białowieża Primeval Forest, BPF) gave evidence that intense hunting from November till March (1980–1993) caused a regular decline in mean pack size from 4.0 wolves in late autumn, to 3.6 in mid-winter, to 2.3 in late winter. The proportion of lone wolves among all packs increased from 4% in the beginning of the hunting season to over 30% in late winter when the season ended (Jędrzejewska et al. 1996). Interestingly, molecular genetic techniques revealed that packs that had suffered great losses due to hunting were more likely to adopt non-related adult males (Jędrzejewski et al. 2005b). At the same time, pack size of wolves inhabiting the Polish part of BPF that were not hunted (though poaching did occur), varied from 4.2 in autumn to 3.6 in late winter, and the proportion of lone wolves did not exceed 15% of all recorded groups (Jędrzejewska et al. 1996).

In Estonia, where strict hunting regulations were introduced in 2003 (upper limits were set for annual hunting quota), the proportion of lone wolves in all wolf observations declined from 43% to 27% over four years (Table 2.3.2). Proportion of pairs among observations did not change, and the shares of packs with three or more individuals slightly (not significantly) increased (Table 2.3.2). However, these data reflect relative – and not absolute – measures of the pack size or social structure of the wolf population. A study conducted in 2004–2007 in southwestern Estonia, where wolves were rarely hunted, showed that undisturbed packs reach the size of up to 7–8 wolves (M. Kübarsepp, unpublished data).

Extensive data on pack size are available from Poland, where the wolf population has been protected since 1998. The national censuses of wolves (Jędrzejewski et al. 2002a; W. J. et al., unpublished data) yielded information on pack size for 79 to 122 packs each year (in total 591 pack-years) from autumn–winter seasons of 2000/2001 to 2005/2006 (Fig. 2.3.2). The mean pack size was 4.9 wolves (range 1–12), and packs of 5 individuals constituted 21% of all packs (lone wolves included). Little variation in pack size was observed, as 50% of all packs were those of 4 to 6 wolves.

The pack size of wolves increased significantly from south to north along a bio-geographic gradient, though the reason for that increase is not fully understood (Jędrzejewski et al. 2007). One of the essential factors determining wolf pack size may be the size of dominant prey: moose in the north, and deer in southern latitudes. Jędrzejewski et al. (2002b) proposed that the size of most frequently killed prey determines the pack size of wolves. Wolves neither guard nor hide their kills, so the optimal utilization of a kill (with minimal losses to scavengers) would be to consume it immediately. In Central Europe, red deer is the dominant and strongly preferred prey of wolves (Okarma et al. 1995), and a deer killed by wolves (most often a calf) is usually completely eaten by a pack of 4–6 within a few hours (Jędrzejewski et al. 2002b). No data on the pack size and prey consumption rates were available from northern parts of the study area (Estonia, Latvia), where red deer are rare or absent, and where more abundant moose could play an important role in the wolf diet (see below). Pack sizes of wolves in these northern areas would be expected to be greater than southern areas, similar to patterns in North America (Fuller et al. 2003).

Interestingly, wolf pack sizes in Eastern Europe are similar to those in the Great Lakes region of the Midwestern lower 48 states, Ontario, and Quebec, where wolf pack sizes averaged 4–6 (Fuller et al. 2003; Mech & Boitani 2003b), an area of similar latitude and vegetation communities

Table 2.3.2. Changes in the proportions of lone wolves, pairs, and packs including at least 3 individuals among all observation of wolves in Estonia, where upper limits were set for annual hunting quotas of wolves in 2003 (source: Department of Game Monitoring, Centre of Forest Protection and Silviculture, Estonia). Differences between years were statistically significant only for lone wolves (G = 4.01, df = 1, P < 0.05; G test for homogeneity of percentages).

| Year | Percentage of wolf observations | | | Sample size (n observations) |
	Lone wolves	Pairs	Packs ffl3 inds	
2003	43	34	23	447
2004	34	36	30	559
2005	31	35	34	709
2006	27	38	35	754

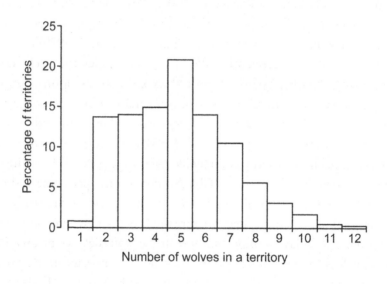

Figure 2.3.2. Frequency distribution of wolf pack size based on the data obtained during the national censuses of wolves (Jędrzejewski et al. 2002a, W. J. et al., unpublished data) in the autumn–winter seasons of 2000/2001 to 2005/2006. Sample size: 79 to 122 packs per year, in total 591 pack-years. The proportion of lone wolves is underestimated, as they were reliably detected only when occurring beyond the contiguous range of wolf population.

THE WORLD OF WOLVES

(productive hardwood forests), but with vastly lower ungulate species diversity. Wolves in the Great Lakes region of North America only occur with white-tailed deer (*Odocoileus virginianus*), and occasionally moose – compared to wolves in eastern Europe that occur with 3–6 ungulate prey species (see above). Thus, the effects of ungulate community diversity on wolf population dynamics and pack size in North America might not generalize to Eastern Europe. At the larger wolf population scale, in North America, the wolf numeric response to ungulate prey was greater in areas of higher ungulate diversity compared to single-prey wolf systems (Fuller et al. 2003). As we detail below, the negative numeric response between wolf density and ungulate biomass in Eastern Europe as a result of the periodically severe harvests over long periods contrasts with patterns in North America. Combined, the smaller pack sizes than expected based on ungulate diversity, and the decoupled wolf numeric response, both suggest an important role of the effects of long-term exploitation by humans on wolf life-history.

Breeding success of wolves in Eastern Europe was studied in several regions. The reproductive potential of wolves appeared high (the mean number of pups in a litter was about 6 in three regional studies; Table 2.3.3), but only about one-third of pups survived until the age of 1 year (Table 2.3.3), slightly lower than average wolf pup survival in North America (Fuller et al. 2003). In many regions, human removal of pups from the den is still common, either as an official method of wolf control (Belarus; Sidorovich et al. 2007) or as a traditional (though illegal) harvest practice (Poland; Jędrzejewska et al. 1996). Litter size of wolves varied predictably with changes in population density, as shown by the study in the Vitebsk region, northeastern Belarus (Sidorovich et al. 2007). In 1990–2003, wolf numbers were significantly affected by the hunting pressure by humans. Mean litter size was inversely density-dependent and varied from 4.8 to 7.7 pups among years. Interestingly, the increase in litter size with the declining density of wolf population concerned only female pups, whereas the mean number of male pups was not related to population density. Sidorovich et al. (2007) interpreted the sex-biased maternal investment in line with the advantaged daughter hypothesis proposed by Hiraiwa-Hasegawa

Table 2.3.3. Reproductive performance of wolves in Eastern Europe as determined by counts of placental scars (class *in utero*), visual observations of litters, and counts of pups in litters destroyed during predator control (age classes from newborns to 1-year old).

Age of pups	N pups in a litter		Region, years	Sample (n litters)	Source
	Mean	(range)			
In utero	6.4	(4–10)	Latvia, 1998–2005	32	Ozoliņš et al. (2001); J. Ozoliņš et al., unpublished data
0–1 month	6.1	(2–10)	N Belarus, 1985–2003	101	Sidorovich et al. (2007)
-	5.2	(3–8)	E Poland – W Belarus, 1975–1994	10	Jędrzejewska et al. (1996)
2–5 months	3.1	(2–5)	E Poland – W Belarus, 1975–1994	18	Jędrzejewska et al. (1996)
-	2.6	(1–7)	Poland, 2000–2001	43	Jędrzejewski et al. (2002a)
6–12 months	2.2	(1–2)	E Poland – W Belarus, 1975–1994	9	Jędrzejewska et al. (1996)

(1993). According to this hypothesis, a female-biased sex ratio of young is expected in species in which mothers are able to influence the reproductive success of their daughters through transmission of rank or some other quality. Indeed, population genetic studies have shown that in wolf packs, daughters often become successors of their mothers (Jędrzejewski et al. 2005b). Thus, in a heavily exploited population, producing more daughters may be an adaptive strategy. This evidence for a female-biased sex ratio contrasts with a sex ratio of parity across wolf studies in North America (Kreeger 2003) and suggests the intriguing hypothesis that long-term persecution by humans in Eastern Europe may have driven evolutionary adaptation by producing more female offspring (Milner et al. 2007).

A noteworthy feature of wolf breeding behaviour in Eastern Europe, especially when compared to protected wolf populations, is their frequent changes of denning sites, both between breeding seasons and within one season. In Eastern Poland (Schmidt et al. 2008), females rearing young used, on average, 2.25 dens during a 60-day denning period. The same breeding den was never used in consecutive years. Frequent moving of pups to a new location during the denning period was also reported from Ukraine (Gursky 1978), and the European part of Russia (Ryabov 1988). This contrasts with protected or lightly exploited North American wolf populations where wolves frequently re-use the same den from year to year (Fuller 1983; Fuller 1989b; Mech & Packard 1990). Therefore, such behaviour in wolves may either be an adaptation to a high-level disturbance by humans experienced by European wolves, or a function of loss of traditional knowledge of historical dens because of high population turnover.

Two other indices of wolf-human conflicts are the frequency of hybridization with dogs and population age structure. Hybridization between wolves and dogs is occasionally recorded in Eastern Europe in the regions of relatively high hunting pressure (e.g., Latvia; Andersone et al. 2002), and in the forefront of wolf expansion westward (Western Poland; W. J. et al., unpublished data). However, the overall incidence of wolf-dog hybrids among 353 individuals from Eastern Europe studied by molecular genetic techniques was rather small (1.7%, Pilot 2005). Age structure of wolf population (studied by examination of shot wolves) appeared significantly influenced by the level of hunting pressure (Table 2.3.4). In the extreme situations of very severe control, such as that in the Vitebsk region (northeastern Belarus), in years following heavy hunting, juveniles ≤1 year old may constitute over half (55%) of all wolves (Sidorovich et al. 2007).

The genetic study conducted by Jędrzejewski et al. (2005b) in the wolf population in Białowieża Primeval Forest (western Belarus and eastern Poland) showed that the intense exploitation of the population (through legal hunting as well as poaching) caused great instability of packs. Turnover of alpha males and females was rather fast, and persistence of pair bonds (n = 14 pairs) varied from 1 to 4 years, on average 1.8 years (SE = 0.2). In all cases except one, the cause of disruption was the death of one or both mates. Interestingly, high genetic polymorphism and heterozygosity excess occurred in this intensively hunted population. The most probable explanation for that result was the observed high immigration rate and recruitment of immigrant wolves to packs that suffered losses from hunting (Jędrzejewski et al. 2005b).

TERRITORY SIZE, SPACE USE, AND POPULATION DENSITY

The first European estimates of wolf territory size by repeated snow tracking during one winter season date back to the 1960s. Although underestimated as compared with results of radio-telemetry, the data showed a consistent south-north gradient in the wolf territory size. It varied from 82–120 km² in the Caucasus Mountains and the Polish Carpathians, to 141–191 km² in the European part of Russia, to 415–500 km² in Sweden (Haglund 1968; Kaleckaya 1973; Kudaktin 1979; Bjarvall & Isakson 1982; Kaleckaya & Filonov 1987; Śmietana & Wajda 1997). Furthermore, territories were larger in unsaturated, colonizing or recovering populations of wolves than in established ones (review in Okarma et al. 1998). Also the recent Polish, Belarussian, and Estonian studies, based on intense snow tracking and howling simulation, yielded similar results: territories of wolf packs ranged from 98–227 km² in southern Poland (Nowak et al. in press), 282–323 km² in central Belarus, 334–447 km² in northeastern Belarus (V. E. Sidorovich, unpublished data), to 430–520 km² in southwestern Estonia (M. Kübarsepp, unpublished data).

Only one population in Eastern Europe (inhabiting Białowieża Primeval Forest, E Poland) was thoroughly studied by intensive tracking of radio-collared wolves (Jędrzejewski et al. 2007). Annual territories of packs (minimum convex polygons with 95% of locations) covered 116–310 km² (mean 201), and their core areas (MCP 50%) embraced from 14 to 78 km² (mean 35). Inter-pack and between-year variation in the territory size were shaped by the abundance of wild ungulates, but it was not affected by the pack size (observed variation from 2 to 8 wolves in a pack). Very little

Table 2.3.4. Age structure of the wolf population in the Belarussian and Latvian populations in relation to the intensity of hunting harvest. Data from: Belarus – Sidorovich *et al.* (2007), Latvia – Ozoliņš et al. (2001), and J. Ozoliņš et al., unpublished data. Differences between percentage age structure in populations subjected to low and high hunting pressure significant for Belarus (G = 9.46, df = 2, P < 0.01), but not for the high harvests in two parts of Latvia (G = 3.71, df = 2, P > 0.1, G-test for goodness of fit).

Population	Hunting harvest	Percentage age structure of wolf population (years)			Mean age (years)
		ffi1	2–4	ffl5	
Northern Belarus	Low	34	46	20	2.8
Northern Belarus	High	55	34	11	1.5
Eastern Latvia	High	36	43	21	3.0
Western Latvia	High	49	32	19	2.6

overlap (on average 7%) of neighbouring territories was observed. The only exception was two packs that had recently split from one maternal pack (overlap up to 50%; Jędrzejewski et al. 2004b). Seasonal changes in the territory size and its utilization by wolves were driven by wolf reproductive biology. In spring–summer, when wolves' activities concentrated around denning sites, the territories covered 38–129 km² (mean 73), whereas in autumn–winter they expanded to 102–283 km² (mean 191) (Jędrzejewski et al. 2007). Wolf packs often temporarily split to divide labour in pup care, hunting, and food provisioning (Jędrzejewski et al. 2002b; Schmidt et al. 2008). Thus, home ranges of individual wolves belonging to the same pack somewhat differ. Ranges of subadult non-breeding females are about 30–40% smaller than those of adult breeding wolves (Jędrzejewski et al. 2007).

Wolves are very mobile animals. Their daily travels averaged 23 km (range 0.4–64 km) and the speed of their movement ranged from 0.3 to 7 km/h (Musiani et al. 1998; Jędrzejewski et al. 2001). Daily ranges covered by wolves were smallest in May (mean 9 km²), largest in January–February

(30 km²), and during the whole year they averaged 21 km², i.e., about 10% of the entire territory (Jędrzejewski et al. 2001). Wolves used their territories in a rotational way (Fig. 2.3.3). This was especially manifest during winter, when juveniles travelled with other pack members; wolves hunted in a new area each day, and returned to the same part of their territory every sixth day, on average (Jędrzejewski et al. 2001). The rotational use of space is associated with the need to patrol, defend, and mark the whole territory (Zub et al. 2003) but is also a strategy to minimize the evasive response of prey. Ungulates recognize the odour of large predators (Müller-Schwartze 1972) and become more alert when they perceive risk from wolves. Thus, wolves' hunting in various parts of their territory on consecutive days may help them cope with anti-predator adaptations of ungulates.

On the biogeographic (Holarctic) scale, mean wolf densities decline from 2.5–3 individuals/100 km² at latitudes 40-45°N to 0.7 individuals/100 km² at 60°N (Jędrzejewski et al. 2007). In Poland, where protection of wolves was introduced in 1998, the wolf densities are fairly stable from year to year. In various regions of the country, population densities were reported to vary between 2–5 individuals/100 km² (Śmietana & Wajda 1997; Okarma et al. 1998; Nowak et al. in press). However, in Eastern Europe, the hunting exploitation by humans rather than natural factors has been yet another important factor shaping population densities and dynamics of wolves. The longest available series (1847–1993) of wolf population dynamics from BPF (Poland and Belarus) showed four periods with high numbers of wolves, each occurring after wars or uprisings, and four phases of declines or near extermination (Jędrzejewska et al. 1996). Such fluctuations of wolf numbers with higher amplitudes as methods of predator harvest became more effective have been a typical feature of wolf ecology in Europe during the last centuries (Bibikov 1985; Pavlov 1990).

The most recent severe harvest of wolves occurred across all of Eastern Europe and the former Soviet Union, starting in 1946 and lasting until the 1970s (Bibikov 1985; Pavlov 1990). Wolf numbers reached the lowest numbers in the 1970s across Eastern Europe, and began to increase in the 1980s (Okarma 1993; Balčiauskas 2002; Andersone 2003; Andersone-Lilley & Ozoliņš 2005). Following the eradication of wolves, densities of ungulates

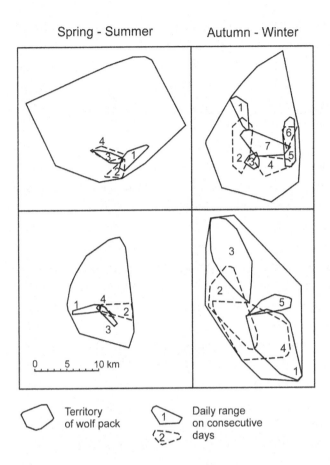

Spring - Summer   Autumn - Winter

Territory of wolf pack

Daily range on consecutive days

Figure 2.3.3. Examples of daily ranges of wolves in spring-summer and autumn-winter in the annual territories of wolf pack in Białowieża Primeval Forest, Eastern Poland (1997–1999). Daily ranges are minimum convex polygons comprising the daily movement routes of radio-tracked wolves. Numbers are consecutive days. Source: Jędrzejewski et al. (2001), modified.

began to grow at unprecedented rates (Filonov 1989; Jędrzejewska et al. 1997). Unintentionally, this created excellent conditions for wolf recovery as soon as persecution was stopped. Thus, patterns of wolf exploitation mirror North America, where wolves were heavily harvested and exploited through the 1940s to the late 1960s and 1970s, when population recovery began (Musiani & Paquet 2004).

A good example of relationships between wolves, humans, and wild ungulate abundance was provided by Sidorovich et al. (2003, 2007) from north-eastern Belarus (Vitebsk region). In 1990–2003, wolf density varied from 0.5 to over 3 individuals/100 km^2, as wolves numerically responded with 1–2-year time lag to varying hunting pressure by humans. The reasons for the intensified wolf control were as follows. In 1990–1996, a manifold decline in abundance of wild ungulates (moose, roe deer, wild boar) occurred, most probably due to uncontrolled exploitation of ungulates by humans in years of political transformation and economical regress (a phenomenon observed also in other regions in Eastern Europe during and after wartimes in the twentieth century; Jędrzejewska et al. 1997). This made wolves shift to predation on domestic animals, which resulted in these predators frequently appearing near and inside villages. Local people interpreted the growing rates of wolf damage as a sign of high numbers of wolves, and demanded that authorities and hunters fight the 'wolf plague'. In effect, the hunting impact on wolves increased and led to a marked reduction in wolf densities. Sidorovich et al. (2003) suggested that this scenario repeated in many areas of Eastern Europe in the last decade of the twentieth century – the years of political and economical transformation.

Indeed, human interference is the reason why in Central and Eastern Europe numerical relationships between wolf and their prey were often negative (with higher abundance of wild ungulates as wolves become exterminated; see Filonov 1989; Jędrzejewska & Jędrzejewski 1998), instead of a typical positive correlation between abundance of predator and biomass of its potential prey, reported from North America (review in: Fuller & Murray 1998). This further supports the general conclusions that intensive exploitation of wolves by humans in Eastern Europe creates key differences in ecology, behaviour, and potentially evolution.

FEEDING HABITS AND IMPACT ON PREY POPULATIONS

Wild ungulates are the main prey for wolves in Eastern Europe, constituting 80–98% of food biomass consumed, with little variation between summer and winter seasons (Jędrzejewski et al. 1992, 2000; Śmietana & Klimek 1993; Andersone 1998; Sidorovich et al. 2003; Andersone & Ozoliņš 2004; Nowak et al. 2005). In regions or in years with low abundance of wild ungulates, wolves may compensate for their shortage by frequent preying on livestock (up to 38% of food biomass in northeastern Belarus in 1994–1996; Sidorovich et al. 2003). Among medium-sized mammals, beaver may be an important supplementary prey to wolves in spring and summer (forming up to 13% of food biomass in Latvia; Andersone 1999; Andersone & Ozoliņš 2004), and hares year round (up to 17% of food biomass in northeastern Belarus; Sidorovich et al. 2003). Interestingly, medium-sized carnivores such as red fox (*Vulpes vulpes*), badger (*Meles meles*), and especially the alien species – raccoon dog (*Nyctereutes procyonoides*), are regularly reported as wolf kills (Jędrzejewski et al. 2000; Kübarsepp & Valdmann 2003; Sidorovich et al. 2003; Andersone & Ozoliņš 2004; Nowak et al. 2005; Valdmann et al. 2005). Wolves also frequently scavenge on carcasses of dead ungulates (Śmietana & Klimek 1993; Selva et al. 2003, 2005). Based on radio-tracking, Jędrzejewski et al. (2002b) estimated that scavenging on ungulate carcasses provided 8% of wolves' food biomass in BPF, eastern Poland.

In a south–north gradient, the Central European communities of wild ungulates vary in both species composition and densities. Roe deer and wild boar occur in the whole region, but their population density decline markedly toward the north (Melis et al. 2006; C. Melis et al., unpublished data). Red deer reaches its northern border of geographic range in northeastern Belarus and Estonia, whereas the moose has a southwestern limit of occurrence in central Poland (Mitchell-Jones et al. 1999). All this is reflected in the species composition of wild ungulates killed by wolves. Red and roe deer or red deer and wild boar dominate among wolf prey in

Poland, whereas moose, roe deer, and wild boar play important roles in Belarus and Estonia (Table 2.3.5).

Wherever red deer occurred in the community, it was invariably strongly selected by wolves from the available species of ungulates, and other coexisting species were avoided or taken proportionally to their abundance (Okarma et al. 1995; Jędrzejewska & Jędrzejewski 1998; Nowak et al. 2005). Where red deer was absent, wolves did not show any selectivity in their choice of prey, and killed roe deer, wild boar, and moose accordingly to their abundance in the local ungulate community (Sidorovich et al. 2003). This strong preference for red deer in multi-species ungulate communities is remarkably similar to North America, where every study that has examined multi-prey selectivity or diet composition shows that North American Elk are either the most or amongst the most preferred ungulate prey amongst wolves (Huggard 1993a; Weaver 1994; Hebblewhite et al. 2004; Smith et al. 2004).

The impact of wolves on prey populations was estimated in BPF, eastern Poland, based on 43 continuous (each lasting 2–9 days) sessions of radio-tracking combined with searches for kill remains (Jędrzejewski et al. 2000, 2002b). Mean daily food intake was 5.58 kg per wolf and per capita kill rate averaged 42.3 ungulates per year (63% of prey were red deer, 28% wild boar, and 4% roe deer). With the mean size of hunting groups being 4.4 individuals, wolf packs killed, on average, 0.513 ungulate prey per day, or one ungulate every second day. Kill rates on red deer significantly increased with deeper snow cover in winter, whereas kill rates on wild boar were notably higher in spring–summer, when piglets were present (Jędrzejewski et al. 2002b). Per capita kill rates decreased slightly with the increasing size of wolf hunting group (from 2 to 6 individuals). Interestingly, however, the amount of food acquired per wolf did not differ among small and large packs, because larger packs killed bigger prey (>100 kg) more often, and small prey (<50 kg) less frequently than did small packs (Jędrzejewski et al. 2002b).

Table 2.3.5. Regional (in a south–north gradient) variation in the ungulate prey of wolves (percentage of a given species in all ungulate specimens killed) in Eastern Europe, based on studies that identified prey remains to the species level. Data recalculated from: southern Poland – Nowak et al. (2005), eastern Poland – Jędrzejewski et al. (2002b), north-eastern Belarus – Sidorovich et al. (2003), south-western Estonia – M. Kübarsepp (unpublished data), and central Estonia – Kübarsepp and Valdmann (2003).

Prey species	Southern Poland	Eastern Poland	North-eastern Belarus	South-western Estonia	Central Estonia
Roe deer	45	4	10	67	15
Red deer	42	72	-	-	-
Wild boar	8	22	54	19	47
Moose	-	1	22	14	38
Domestic ungulate	4	1	14	-	-

Among prey species, wolves were an important cause of mortality only for red deer, taking annually 40% of the annual increase due to reproduction. Predation rate was inversely density-dependent. In fact, when red deer density decreased, wolf predation rate on the species increased and contributed to its population's growth to further worsening. Thus, wolves did not have a stabilizing effect on red deer numbers, and limited, but did not regulate its populations (*sensu* Sinclair 1989; Messier 1991). Moreover, red deer were also considerably affected by lynx predation and harvest by humans. Those three agents of mortality (wolf, lynx, and humans) were additive (Okarma et al. 1997; Jędrzejewska & Jędrzejewki 1998; Jędrzejewski et al. 2000). In accordance with the intense, short-term research, also the long-term data (covering over 100 years) showed that, whenever relieved from control by humans, wolves hampered the growth of deer populations and prolonged the time necessary to reach the carrying capacity of the habitat (Jędrzejewska et al. 1997; Jędrzejewska & Jędrzejewski 1998) that was itself set by bottom up drivers of primary productivity. Thus, in Eastern

Europe, the numbers of prey populations like red deer were a function of both bottom-up and top-down forces.

DAMAGE TO DOMESTIC ANIMALS AND INTERACTIONS WITH HUMANS

Wolf depredation on domestic animals occurs in all countries of the region (Table 2.3.6), although documentation of damage is done differently in every country. In Poland, where compensation for animals killed by wolves (for all farm species but dogs) is paid by the state, the records of wolf damage are believed to be reliable. In Lithuania, Latvia, and Estonia, where cases of depredation are voluntarily reported by livestock owners/ administrators and no regular compensations are paid for the losses, the numbers shown in Table 2.3.6 are underestimates, especially as regards smaller species of animals. In Belarus, no countrywide record of wolf damage is maintained. The main species of domestic animals targeted by wolves are sheep and cattle (Table 2.3.6). A specific feature of wolf damage in Eastern Europe is a high incidence of killing dogs, many of which are watchdogs (53% in the Belarussian sample – Sidorovich et al. 2003), often chained near houses.

Even considering the likely underestimation of the reported data, the extent of wolf damage in Eastern Europe is considerably smaller than in Southern Europe (e.g., Ciucci & Boitani 1998; Vos 2000). The main reason for the difference could be a short grazing season in the temperate and hemi-boreal latitudes. Damage occurs there from May to November, but most attacks are reported in summer and early autumn (Andersone et al. 2001; Balčiauskas et al. 2002; Nowak et al. 2005). For over six months per year, livestock is not available to wolves. In the lowlands of Lithuania and Poland, where pastures for cattle are located outside forests, damage has consistently been reported from habitats with sparse forest cover (Balčiauskas et al. 2002; Jędrzejewski et al. 2004a). In the mountains of southern Poland, most sheep pastures (small subalpine meadows) are located in the montane forest zone, so wolves kill sheep within well-forested

Table 2.3.6. Domestic animals reported as wolf kills in Eastern Europe in 2004 (year for which comparable data were available for all countries in the region). [a] Recorded as domestic animal killed by wolves; later interviews with administrators revealed that in most cases they were sheep. Data for Poland are well representative for the number of losses, whereas data for other countries are underestimates due to the lack of country-wide schemes of reporting wolf damage. Unpublished information provided by: W. Jędrzejewski (Poland), L. Balčiauskas (Lithuania), J. Ozoliņš (Latvia), and P. Männil (Estonia).

| | Number of animals killed by wolves | | | |
Species	Poland	Lithuania	Latvia	Estonia
Horse	4	-	-	-
Cattle	172	19	4	3
Sheep	547	24	17	106
Goat	18	-	5	-
Dog	12	2	1	59
Not specified	-	56[a]	-	-
Total	753	101	27	168

area (Jędrzejewski et al. 2002b). In Poland, most wolf packs (58%) did not cause damage to domestic animals, 27% of packs killed livestock occasionally (1–5 head killed per year), and 15% of packs caused notorious damage or even specialized in hunting domestic animals (W. J. et al., unpublished data for 2000–2002).

The major reason for wolf depredation on livestock is the local or temporal shortage of wild ungulates. Sidorovich et al. (2003) found that, in northeastern Belarus, human-caused decline in wild ungulate numbers made wolves kill domestic animals (cattle and dogs) very often. However, as soon as populations of wild ungulates recovered, the frequency of damage greatly declined because wolves shifted to preying on wild prey.

Contemporarily, wolf-human interactions in Eastern Europe are largely characterized by spatiotemporal segregation of wolves from and their avoidance of people (Theuerkauf et al. 2003). Well-documented recent cases of wolf attacks on humans are restricted to rare incidences of rabid wolves appearing in villages and challenged by people (Linnell et al.

2002; Sidorovich et al. 2003). A few cases of attacks by non-rabid wolves were described from Latvia (Linnell et al. 2002). However, as evidenced by a detailed analyses of historical sources from Estonia (Rootsi 2003) and Fennoscandia (Linnell et al. 2003), in the past (eighteenth–nineteenth centuries) the cases of rabid individuals attacking humans were more common than now and even specialized man-eaters (targeting mainly children) had periodically occurred in some regions.

PROSPECTS FOR WOLF STATUS AND RESEARCH NEEDS

This brief review of the status and ecology of wolves highlighted a diverse situation for the species in Eastern Europe. During the last decade, the management of wolf populations was improving toward rational conservation in Poland and the Baltic States, although increased efforts for wolf conservation are needed in Belarus. Furthermore, those countries have already implemented or have started to implement regular monitoring of wolf numbers and damage caused by wolves to domestic animals. In Poland and recently (2007) in Estonia, a system of financial compensation for wolf-induced losses in livestock was introduced. However, such changes in the management and attitude have not yet taken place in Belarus Republic, which harbours the largest population of the species in the region and a potentially unsustainable wolf harvest. As presented in this chapter, knowledge about wolf ecology is uneven throughout Eastern Europe. This situation calls for a new, large-scale approach to studying this highly mobile large carnivore. A joint international research effort with application of modern methodology (e.g., Global Positioning System [GPS] collars, molecular genetics, Geographic Information System [GIS]-based analyses) is clearly needed to fill the gaps in our knowledge on wolves in the region.

ACKNOWLEDGMENTS

The authors thank the European Nature Heritage Fund EURONATUR (Germany), the Latvian Forest Development Fund, Game Development Fund, the Science Council, State Forest Service, and Ķemeri National Park (all in Latvia), the Estonian Environment Investment Centre and Estonian Ministry of Environment, the Institute of Zoology of the National Academy of Sciences (Belarus Republic), International Fund for Animal Welfare IFAW, United Kingdom Wolf Conservation Trust, Wolves and Humans Foundation, and the Norwegian Research Council for financing various parts of the described research.

2.4 Wolf Ecology and Management in Northern Canada: Perspectives from a Snowmobile Wolf Hunt

H. Dean Cluff, Paul C. Paquet, Lyle R. Walton and Marco Musiani

INTRODUCTION: THE RENNIE LAKE WOLF HUNT CONTROVERSY IN THE NORTHWEST TERRITORIES

In February 1998, a Canadian national newspaper article (Mitchell 1998) raised questions and concerns about the killing of wolves (*Canis lupus*) for fur in the Northwest Territories (NWT), specifically in the 13,000-km^2 Rennie Lake area; about 175 km north of the Saskatchewan border (Fig. 2.4.1). Further news items, editorials, and letters to the editor criticized the hunt and generated strong public concern. Several other newspapers, radio, and television stations reported the story and it quickly became a contentious issue. This chapter presents new ecological data that we collected and analyzed on the Rennie Lake Wolf Hunt in the Northwest Territories of Canada, and sheds light on the controversy that arose from this event.

When the story unfolded, the hunt was still in progress. At that point, 460 wolves were reported killed in the area (Mitchell 1998). This figure was based on export permits issued to Aboriginal hunters (see Box 1) from northern Saskatchewan travelling northward to hunt wolf and wolverine (*Gulo gulo*) in the NWT. The number of wolves killed had climbed to 633 when the season ended in spring (Government of Northwest Territories (GNWT) news release 22 April 1998). An additional 125 wolves were estimated killed from areas adjacent to the Rennie Lake area during the hunting season (H.D.C., unpublished data). Although this hunt was not new, the number of wolves killed was large and members of the public and media expressed concern that killing this many wolves, in what was perceived to be a small geographic area, was not sustainable (Mitchell 1998; Parker 1998).

News media is an information source that helps the public form an opinion on a subject (Yankelovich 1991). Media coverage can also amplify interest in a topic (Bennett 1999). However, journalists tend not to be educators, and media coverage seldom delves into details or thoroughly evaluates issues raised (Yankelovich 1991). Drama is a frequent tool of media to highlight existing concerns, uncertainties, conflicts, and they rarely challenge the legitimacy of any source (Chartier & Gabler 2001). Therefore, information provided by one individual or agency is likely to be balanced against different opinions and consequently each information source is often presented on an equal footing with little or no analysis of technical accuracy (Yankelovich 1991; Chartier & Gabler 2001). How an agency responds to an environmental issue further influences public response, and this reality has spawned its own field of research into risk communication (Slovic 1986; Chess 2001). Consequently, it is not surprising the Rennie Lake wolf hunt became controversial. News media reports and government press releases have been the primary sources of information on a high-profile species that can evoke emotional debate. Furthermore, much of the public reaction occurred before the 1997/98 hunt statistics were complete or statistics from previous years were adequately reviewed.

Our objectives for this chapter were to present new data that we gathered on the Rennie Lake area wolf hunt activity, compare it with hunts from previous years and broader territorial kill statistics, and discuss the dynamics of the wolf-caribou (*Rangifer tarandus groenlandicus*) system. We also present new data on wolf movements and migration with caribou in the study area. We believe that understanding the relationship between wolves and barren-ground caribou in this region explains annual variation in the number of wolves killed and places the hunt into appropriate context.

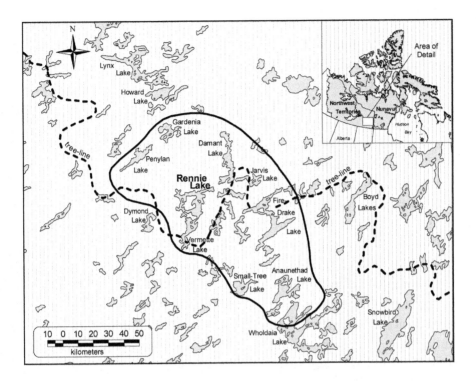

Figure 2.4.1. The 'Rennie Lake' wolf hunting area in the southeast corner of the Northwest Territories, Canada (since division with Nunavut on 01 April 1999). The 12,750 km² area straddles the boreal forest-tundra transition ('tree-line').

THE RENNIE LAKE AREA

The area where the 1997/98 wolf hunt took place has been informally dubbed the "Rennie Lake area" because this 328-km² lake is geographically central to most of the hunting and is easily identifiable on a map by its size and shape. The lake has also served as a base for one of the main wolf hunters there. This wolf hunt occurs in a region referred to in legislation as the "Border A" area, which is an 119,420-km² area at the southeast corner of the Northwest Territories (NWT), immediately north of Saskatchewan. The Rennie Lake area, where most of the Border A hunting has occurred, includes approximately 12,750 km² of the boreal forest and tundra ecoregions. About 15% (1,900 km²) of this area consists of lakes (Fig. 2.4.1). Rennie Lake straddles the boreal forest-tundra transition (treeline) with similar sized lakes (ranging from 168 to 614 km²) including Anaunethad, Damant, Firedrake, and Wholdaia lakes. Numerous smaller lakes are unnamed.

The actual geographic area used for hunting each year varies depending on the seasonal distribution pattern of caribou and wolves. People frequent the Rennie Lake area mostly during the winter hunting season but this has not always been the case. Up to 50 small or rudimentary wood cabins were once used in the area either as seasonal accommodations or as overnight shelters for hunters. Before the 1970s, 10 or more family units resided in the area for various parts of the year. This lifestyle, however, has declined rapidly (Müller-Wille 1974).

Aboriginal hunters from Fond-du-Lac, Black Lake, and Stony Rapids in northern Saskatchewan are traditional users of the Beverly-Qamanirju-aq caribou herds, which winter in the southeastern portion of the NWT. These hunters regularly cross into the NWT to hunt caribou, wolves, and wolverine for subsistence (Müller-Wille 1974). The NWT Wildlife Act (revised 1988) allows an applicant (normally an Aboriginal person) living in the northern half of Saskatchewan or Manitoba, who depends on hunting in the NWT for a livelihood (subsistence), to be granted an annual hunting licence restricted to a portion of the NWT immediately north of the border with Saskatchewan and Manitoba (NWT Big Game Hunting Regulations, NWT Wildlife Act). There is no fee for this licence.

PUBLIC REACTION AND PERCEPTIONS

Strong public reaction against the Rennie Lake wolf hunt was directed toward the GNWT, specifically the Department of Resources, Wildlife and Economic Development (RWED), now known as Environment and Natural Resources (ENR). Most letters from the public were sent in the first six months after the first newspaper article, but some continued to be received until the following year. The vast majority of letters were from

Defenders of Wildlife, probably because the wolf is a focal species for that organization, and a postcard-writing campaign was initiated. Most letters protested any killing of wolves and, in particular, the use of snowmobiles in the hunt.

The public was apparently led to believe that wolves were chased by snowmobilers to exhaustion and then shot (Mitchell 1998). However, there was no evidence to indicate this was common practice. Nevertheless, many people shared their concern, through letters, that current regulations did not do enough to prevent what they perceived as wildlife harassment. Others argued that the existence of laws did not guarantee compliance, especially in remote locations where enforcement is difficult. No letters supporting a ban on hunting wolves by snowmobiles originated from the NWT. This was not unexpected because of the utility of snowmobiles in the north. In the NWT (and Nunavut), most wolves are shot when encountered by hunters on snowmobiles (Hayes & Gunson 1995). Snowmobiles are common in the north and provide an essential mode of travel because of limited access to areas with few roads. Consequently, snowmobiles are routinely used to hunt a variety of wildlife. Although debate over use of snowmobiles by wolf hunters was part of the controversy, acceptance of the practice is largely an ethical matter, which we do not object nor discuss in this chapter.

People unfamiliar with the tundra–taiga ecosystem and caribou–wolf dynamics in the north may have also thought that far fewer wolves (e.g., <100) could be sustained in the area on a long-term basis, especially if they assumed a typical year-round density of about 5 wolves/1000 km^2 for northern ecosystems (Fuller et al. 2003). Understanding this northern ecosystem and its seasonal and ephemeral patterns of animal scarcity and super-abundance is critical to assessing the sustainability of this wolf hunt.

During the controversy, the government held community meetings to address the issue and committed to augmenting wolf research and monitoring efforts to assess the impact of the hunt. Tissue samples from wolves killed in the harvest were collected and analyzed for population structure (Musiani 2003). This study explored the genetics of wolves in the harvest and determined the geographical extent of wolves following migratory barren-ground caribou (Musiani et al. 2007).

REGULATIONS GOVERNING WOLF HUNTS

Wolves in the NWT are killed for fur. Wolves can be either trapped or hunted. Seasons and conditions are governed by laws and regulations specified in the NWT Wildlife Act. Most wolves in the NWT are killed by Aboriginal hunters who have subsistence hunting rights. Currently Aboriginal hunters are not subject to hunting limits, and do not require tags (see Box 1). However, wolf hunting and trapping seasons apply to all hunters when selling fur. Trapping seasons (01 November to 31 March or 15 April, for most areas) are restricted to times when fur is prime (i.e., when the new annual growth of hair follicles in winter is fully developed). Hunting season for wolves in the NWT opens 15 August in most regions, including the Rennie Lake area, and closes 31 May.

Although wolf hunting seasons in the NWT are liberal (273 to 310 days/year), the length of the hunting season has little influence on the number of wolves harvested. Long open seasons do not influence hunts for fur. Early hunting seasons serve primarily non-resident barren-ground caribou hunters who arrive in late summer or early fall to hunt barren-ground caribou and may hunt a wolf opportunistically for the trophy. Most wolf hunting occurs in winter and early spring when fur is prime to obtain highest market value. Timing of most wolf hunts is further influenced by the availability of large frozen lakes that provide access for hunters on snowmobiles. Few all-weather roads exist in the NWT. Some communities invest annually in ice-roads where snow is ploughed from the ice surface of frozen lakes and interconnecting portages. However, winter access to most areas in the NWT is facilitated by snowmobile.

HISTORICAL WOLF MANAGEMENT IN THE NWT

Historically, interest and techniques used in wolf hunting and management in the north have varied. Religious and cultural beliefs of some Aboriginal people coupled with the low commercial value of wolf hides resulted in few wolves being killed before 1924 (Freeman 1976; Heard 1983). In 1924, $30 bounties were introduced for wolves that were twice the average price of arctic fox (*Alopex lagopus*) pelts at the time (Soper 1928; Heard 1983). This added incentive to hunters and trappers significantly increased the wolf kill (Soper 1928). Higher fur prices also attracted additional trappers, many from Scandinavia and southern Canada (Usher 1971). Bounties were paid between 1924 and 1933 and 1937–39, and during each of these 13-year periods, about 1000 wolves were killed (Usher 1971). The wolf kill dropped when bounties were discontinued, trapping regulations were changed, and fewer trappers were on the land because of regulation changes and the onset of World War II (Usher 1971). Since 1938, trapping has been restricted to Aboriginal people with the exception of non-Aboriginal people who already held a trapping permit (Usher 1971).

In 1951, concern over declining caribou herds was high and the government responded by adopting strychnine poison as a predator control technique in many areas of the NWT. Government biologists and officers killed about a thousand wolves per year in addition to perhaps another 300 wolves/year killed by hunters and trappers and exported for fur (Kelsall 1968; Heard 1983). The Beverly caribou herd was among the herds of concern and consequently the poisoning effort against wolves included much of the Beverly caribou range, including the Rennie Lake area. Poisoning programs officially ended by 1964 although some unauthorized use occurred until 1970 (Heard 1983).

A $40 bounty for wolves was re-introduced in 1965/66 until payments ended in 1970, although legislation revoking that bounty did not occur until 1980 (Heard 1983). A $300/wolf incentive to trappers was given to trappers between 1977 and 1979 to reduce wolf predation on bison (*Bison bison athabascae*) in the Slave River Lowlands in southern NWT (Heard

1983). Only 34 wolves were taken that winter and the GNWT shot 10 additional wolves from a helicopter in March 1978 (Heard 1983). However, no aerial shooting occurred thereafter and the program ended in 1979 (Heard 1983). Today, there are no government predator control programs in the NWT.

Shooting is the preferred method for killing wolves for fur, with snaring a distant second (Cluff & Murray 1995). Snaring is considered ineffective for wolves on the tundra and near treeline. Snaring is more commonly practised in the forested areas where snares are easier to set and resident wolves can be targeted. The difficulty with trapping non-resident wolves within forested areas is predicting their re-use of trails given that the probability of repeated use of trails is low when following caribou on the move. Snares (and traps) also require repeated checks and would be vulnerable to disturbance by moving caribou. Consequently, opportunistic shooting of wolves when they are encountered is the most common of available techniques. Hunters sometimes may also revisit gut piles or where caribou were otherwise butchered and shoot wolves that may be scavenging there.

MONITORING THE WOLF HUNT

Documenting the NWT wolf kill over the last decade is complex because the NWT was divided into two separate territories, Nunavut and the NWT, on 1 April 1999. Nunavut was created because of land claim negotiations in 1992 with the Aboriginal people there (Inuit) and implementation of the resulting Nunavut Final Agreement (Nunavut Act, 1993, Statutes of Canada, Ottawa). Consequently, wolf kill statistics before 1999 include harvests from both territories. Kills reported after 1999 are reported separately by each jurisdiction. Nevertheless, we can distinguish kill statistics between the two territories for seven years before division because kill statistics have been reported by individual municipalities and communities since 1993.

Licences and 'tags' to hunt and possession ('bag') limits for wolves provide a means to monitor part of the hunt. Non-Aboriginal hunters residing in the NWT ("Resident hunters") and Canadian hunters residing outside of the NWT ("Non-Resident Hunters") may hunt wolves in the NWT but must purchase an annual licence to do so. These hunters are considered recreational hunters because they are not Aboriginal people hunting for subsistence. Until recently, non-resident hunters were limited to one wolf/year while resident NWT (non-Aboriginal) hunters may kill an unlimited number of wolves if they have purchased a tag before doing so. As of 2006, non-resident hunters can take two wolves/year depending on the area. The kill from these two groups combined has been about 25 wolves per year (Hayes & Gunson 1995).

Wolf pelts are typically sold through a fur auction, or private sale, or kept for personal use (e.g., pelts for show, parka trim). All pelts sold by auction require an export permit to leave the NWT. This requirement facilitates recording wolves killed by Aboriginal (subsistence) hunters when they decide to sell the fur. There is no requirement to report pelts sold through private sale or kept for personal use, and likely these kills go undocumented. Because private sale or personal use pelts are not reflected in annual kill data, export records must be considered minimum estimates.

Our conversations with hunters and general knowledge of their activity suggest export permits represent the majority of the wolves killed in the NWT, making export permits the single best method of quantifying the number of wolves killed annually. Fur auction sale records provide a second indicator of numbers killed. However, differences between export records and auction sale records occur when exported furs are not sold in the same year they are exported. Occasionally, wolf hunters keep pelts harvested in one year and export them to auction the following year, further confounding annual kill summaries. Although imperfect, collectively these estimates provide the best available information on annual territorial wolf hunts. Based on these data, the wolf kill in the entire NWT (pre-1999 boundaries) over the last 20 years has varied widely, but averaged 764 wolves/year (SE = 44.4) with a maximum kill of 1473 wolves in 1997/98 (Table 2.4.1). The mean (± SE) price per pelt (Canadian dollars) between 1980/81 and 1999/00 (values corrected to 1997 dollars) was $239.67 (± $9.67). About 45% of all the wolves killed annually in both the NWT and

Nunavut comprise about a third to half of the total killed during the last 10 years (Table 2.4.1).

WOLF HUNTING STATISTICS FOR THE RENNIE LAKE AREA

Annual records for the Rennie Lake area hunt have only been available since winter 1992/93, although the hunt has occurred before this date. For example, we are aware of one hunter who, until recently, has hunted wolves in this area each year since 1980. Since winter 1992/93, the number of wolves reported killed in the Rennie Lake hunt averaged 258 wolves (SE = 59.7, n = 10 years) annually (Table 2.4.1). As a proportion, the Rennie Lake wolf hunt has contributed from about one-third to three-quarters of the total annual kill in the NWT. Collectively, the median number of wolves killed in the Rennie Lake hunt over that last 10 years has been between 184 and 212 wolves, which is approximately one-third of the total annual NWT wolf kill.

The Rennie Lake wolf hunt is characterized by a small number (5–12) of Aboriginal hunters from Saskatchewan who kill a substantial number of wolves in a relatively small area (Table 2.4.1; Fig. 2.4.1). Not surprisingly, the number of wolves killed in a given winter hunting season depended in part on how many hunters participated. This relationship is supported statistically with a paired comparison between the number of hunters in a given year and the corresponding wolf harvest for that year (paired sample t-test = 4.228, df = 9, P = 0.002). Similar to Musiani et al. (2005), we used cross-correlation analysis (Box et al.1994) to evaluate the relation-ship between average wolf pelt price and number of wolves killed each year. We tested temporal cross-correlation at yearly intervals from 0 (no lag, equivalent to standard correlation) to ± 4 years. We calculated cross-correlation functions, which provided r-values that ranged between –1 and +1. We also calculated 95% confidence bands. Confidence bands indicated the level of correlation considered significant at the 95% significance level. If data were distributed randomly, auto-correlation or cross-correlation values

Table 2.4.1. Minimum hunting estimates of wolves killed in the Northwest Territories (NWT) and Nunavut, Canada. Records are from fur auction sales except for wolves taken in the Rennie Lake area, NWT, in which case data relate to export permits issued to Aboriginal hunters outside the NWT (specifically northern Saskatchewan). The number of Saskatchewan hunters participating each year in the Rennie Lake hunt is indicated in parentheses. The average values of pelts sold at auction are given except for the Rennie Lake area hunt where prices were not available. The Consumer Price Index (CPI) for Yellowknife, NWT is shown relative to 1997 for inflation adjustment. Values are in Canadian dollars.

	NWT	rest of NWT		Nunavut		Total	
Year	Rennie Lake	Pelts	Average $ value/ pelt	Pelts	Average $ value/ pelt	Pelts	CPI
1992/93	184 (9)	391	273.10	816	277.02	1,391	92.3
1993/94	45[a] (5)	346	310.22	781	275.24	1,172	93.9
1994/95	533 (12)	180	200.34	633	257.93	1,346	95.7
1995/96	88 (7)	171	255.74	556	254.67	815	98.3
1996/97	212 (7)	179	200.60	473	278.96	864	99.9
1997/98	633 (12)	184	200.92	656	227.12	1,473	100.0
1998/99	152 (6)	158	149.00	252	243.45	562	99.9
1999/00	314 (5)	107	136.30	555	195.66	976	100.9
2000/01	168 (8)	168	266.12	255	229.22	591	102.7
2001/02	247 (8)	160	274.63	465	245.80	872	104.3

[a] 1993/94 total underestimated because of missing records

should be near zero for most seasonal lags. We found that average wolf pelt price and wolves killed during a given hunting season were positively cross-correlated at yearly lags -2, -1, 0 and 1 ($0.496 < r < 0.747$, $P < 0.001$).

The cross-correlation plot (Fig. 2.4.2) indicated significant correlation for concurrent or adjacent events of price changes and changes in number of wolves killed (price increases and increases in wolf-killing concurrent or belonging to the subsequent years). In particular, pelt prices from the previous and the same year could contribute to determining number of wolves killed. More hunters would be expected to hunt the following year because of their expectation that high pelt prices the previous year being repeated (e.g., Flather et al. 1999). Fluctuations in the number of wolves killed and market value of furs might produce variability in annual income for wolf hunters. For example, one hunter from the Rennie Lake area reported earning more than CAD $70,000 in four months from wolf and wolverine pelts in one year, but in other years did not make enough money to pay for logistical costs (GNWT, unpublished data).

WOLF AND CARIBOU MIGRATION TOWARD WINTER HUNTING AREAS

Satellite collars were deployed on wolves and caribou as part of separate studies (Walton 2000; Gunn et al. 2001; Cluff et al. 2002; Musiani et al. 2007) coincident with the 1997/98 Rennie Lake wolf hunt. Caribou cows from the Bathurst range were first collared in April 1996 (Gunn et al. 2001), and between 10 to 20 collared caribou cows have been monitored each year since. These collars provided locations of caribou every five days to facilitate broad-scale monitoring of herd movement and yearly calving location. Although proportionally few caribou were collared, the collars appear to represent the general annual pattern of caribou migration and distribution (Gunn et al. 2001). Data collected from the collars and other caribou surveys demonstrate that caribou migration routes and winter ranges differ among years (Gunn et al. 2001).

Satellite collars were first deployed on wolves on the Bathurst caribou range in June 1997 after extensive aerial surveys of eskers the previous summer. Eskers are prominent ridges of stratified gravel and sand deposited during glacial melting and may extend for several kilometres (Banerjee & McDonald 1975). Wolves den in eskers and similar landforms because they provide a suitable place for wolves to dig a den in a landscape

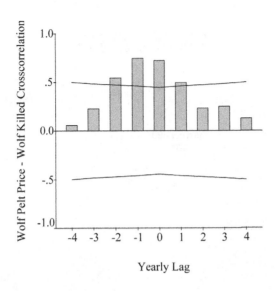

Figure 2.4.2. Cross-correlation for average wolf pelt price versus wolves killed (gray bars) for intervals lagged from 0–4 years in the Rennie Lake area of the Northwest Territories, Canada from the 1980–1981 to the 1999–2000 hunting season. Average wolf pelt prices and total wolves killed were calculated for each winter hunting season. Correlations were significantly different from zero when they crossed the 95% confidence bands (black lines).

dominated by bedrock, standing water, and permafrost (Cluff et al. 2002; McLoughlin et al. 2004).

Many of these collared wolves have travelled close to the Rennie Lake area from their capture sites several hundred kilometres away. In winter 1997/98, 8 of 12 satellite collared wolves (67%) captured about 400 km northwest of Rennie Lake during the previous summer travelled southward to the Rennie Lake area and the northern Saskatchewan border (e.g., Fig. 2.4.3). Wolves followed caribou to the winter range and travelled up to 600 km from their tundra den sites while doing so (Table 2.4.2, Fig. 2.4.3). Average movement distance of these 12 collared wolves from their den sites to their southernmost known location (Table 2.4.2) was 406.1 km (SE = 40.0, range = 241 km to 584 km).

In two winters of monitoring (1997/98 and 1998/99), dates when the greatest southward movements occurred differed by at least 92 days with

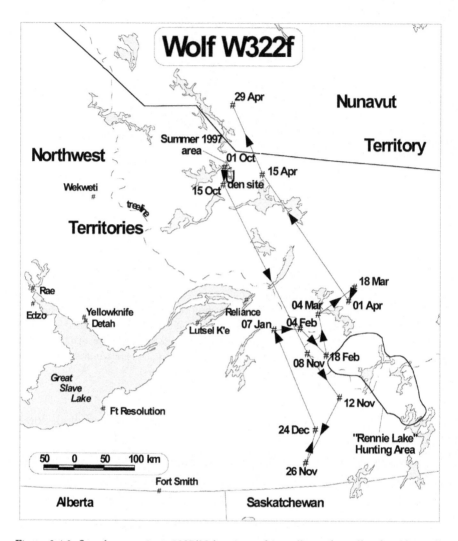

Figure 2.4.3. Sample-case winter 1997/98 locations of 1 satellite radio-collared wolf initially captured in the Bathurst caribou range area in June 1997. The "Rennie Lake" wolf hunting area is also indicated. The other 11 satellite radio-collared wolves followed similar migration routes to the Rennie Lake area that year.

Table 2.4.2. Straight-line distances between den sites of wolves from the Bathurst range fitted with satellite radio-collars to their southernmost known location of the following winter when they approached the Rennie Lake wolf hunt area. The date of the latter location is also indicated.

	1997/98			1998/99	
Wolf	kilometres	date	Wolf	kilometres	date
W303f	584	23 Dec 1997	W342f[a]	326	04 Dec 1998
W305f	573	09 Dec 1997	W344f	293	05 Dec 1998
W315f	513	25 Nov 1997	W347m	241	19 Feb 1999
W318f[b]	196	15 Dec 1997	W351m	262	22 Feb 1999
W320f	454	22 Nov 1997			
W322f	472	26 Nov 1997			
W311m	556	10 Dec 1997			
W327m	403	22 Nov 1997			

Mean = 406.1 km S.E. = 40.0 n = 12
Notes:
[a] satellite radio-collar failed after 08 December 1998.
[b] mortality site.

mean and median dates of 17 and 7 December, respectively (Table 2.4.2). Therefore, dates when wolves pass through a given area in winter can be difficult to predict. Nevertheless, hunters often hunt the area during December and return early in January (G. Bihun, personal communication). Whether hunters return again for subsequent hunts depends on the weather and the outcome of earlier excursions. Hunters usually return home by mid- to late February (G. Duncan, personal communication). Consequently, hunters can encounter wolves at the beginning of their winter migration southward or at southern extremes of the winter migration just before wolves return northward to the tundra.

Our wolf radio-collar data were consistent with surveys that demonstrate caribou migration routes and winter ranges differ among years. Based on weekly locations of radio-collared wolves and caribou, aerial tracking surveys in March, and *ad hoc* hunter and aircraft pilot reports, most caribou and wolves appeared to be situated north of Great Slave Lake in winter 1998/99, with fewer sightings in the Rennie Lake area. Our wolf radio-collar data were consistent with these surveys that demonstrated caribou migration routes and winter ranges differed among years. Of 11 satellite radio-collared wolves we captured earlier in June 1998 from the Bathurst caribou range in the Central Arctic, seven (64%) were found north of Great Slave Lake, four (36%) were northwest of the Rennie Lake area, and none were at Rennie Lake itself. The number of wolves killed that year in the Rennie Lake hunt was about one-quarter (152) that of the previous year (Table 2.4.1).

During the next winter (1999/00), Bathurst caribou wintered in the North Slave administrative region and in the Rennie Lake area, suggesting this herd wintered in two geographically separate areas (Gunn et al. 2001). The wolf harvest at Rennie Lake increased to 314 wolves that year (Table 2.4.1). In addition, that winter two radio-collared wolves from the Bathurst range were shot in the Rennie Lake area (December 1999), 424 km from their den site.

Unfortunately, our wolf monitoring capability was reduced after August 1999 when all satellite collars on wolves were removed (as planned) because their operational battery life was about to end. Although satellite collars were replaced by conventional VHF (Very High Frequency) radio-collars, subsequent winter locations could only be obtained by aerial radio-tracking flights, which occurred in March before the spring den survey. Regardless, the developing dynamic taking shape appeared that the location of caribou in winter influenced the location of wolves. Because annual migration routes of caribou and the wolves that follow vary among years, human hunters must respond to these changes or accept annual fluctuations in abundance.

CARIBOU-WOLF ASSOCIATIONS AND EFFECTS ON THE WOLF HUNT

Wolves from tundra regions of the NWT prey primarily on barren-ground caribou (Kuyt 1972). Barren-ground caribou are identified as herds that are defined and named by where they calve (Calef 1978). Some herds remain on the tundra year-round while others migrate south from calving and foraging areas on the tundra during summer to the winter ranges in the boreal forest (Kelsall 1968; Miller 1982; Gunn & Miller 1986; Fig. 2.4.4). Eight large migratory caribou herds have been identified as spending all or a portion of their annual cycle within current NWT boundaries (GNWT 2006). Local and scientific knowledge suggests that wolves regularly follow these caribou (Kelsall 1960, 1968; Heard & Williams 1992) and influence wolf movements. Wolves that follow migratory caribou from summer to winter ranges are also considered migratory (Parker 1973; Heard and Williams 1992; Walton et al. 2001a; Musiani et al. 2007).

Wolves are thought to associate with specific caribou herds, but this view remains largely untested. The area around Rennie Lake is normally used by the Beverly caribou herd. However, overlap in winter range between adjacent caribou herds is common, and can be 20% or more (Gunn & D'Hont 2002; A. Gunn, personal communication). Caribou herds that may overlap in winter with the Beverly herd include the Bathurst, Ahiak, and Qamanirjuaq herds.

Movements and distribution of caribou on the barren-grounds (tundra) and the wolves that prey on them confirm a tight predator-prey relationship. That is, barren-ground caribou feed primarily on lichens and migrate while doing so (Kelsall 1968). The caribou migration from the boreal forest and tree-line areas in winter to the calving grounds on the tundra is thought to be based on high-quality food optimization during spring calving, blood-sucking insect avoidance during peak lactation, and a possible predator avoidance strategy for their newborn calves (Kelsall 1968). Wolves follow caribou, but many breeding wolves appear to den at least 100 km south of the calving areas, which may serve to optimize the availability of caribou to breeding wolves (and their pups) when post-calving aggregations move southward in mid-summer (Heard & Williams 1992). After the rut in late October, caribou make their way southward beyond the treeline. Winter caribou concentrations vary and are likely influenced by snow-depth and food (lichen) availability (see Miller 1982). Precise locations of where caribou congregate in a given winter are poorly

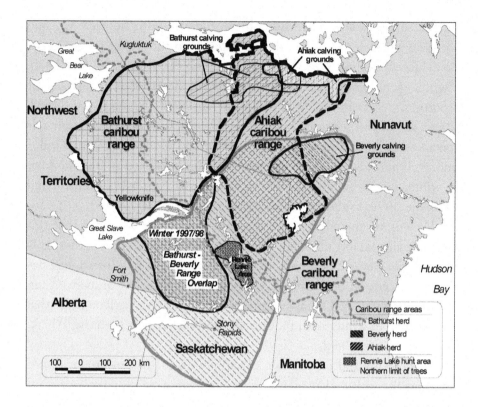

Figure 2.4.4. Typical range areas and summer calving grounds of the Bathurst, Beverly and Ahiak (formerly Queen Maud Gulf) caribou herds (modified from Gunn et al. 1997, 2000). The range overlap between the Bathurst and Beverly herds during the winter of 1997/98 is also shown. Overlap was determined by the movements of radio-collared caribou cows tracked by satellite (Gunn et al., 2001). Radio-collared wolves from the Bathurst caribou range also moved into the overlap area, which included Rennie Lake.

understood, but hunting mortality increases when these congregations are near Aboriginal communities.

During winter 1997/98, caribou from the Bathurst herd congregated east of their typical area and included Rennie Lake (Fig. 2.4.4). Although one satellite-collared caribou from the Bathurst herd crossed the border between the NWT and northern Saskatchewan, locations for the remaining satellite collared caribou stopped about 30 km short of the border (Gunn et al. 2001). Normally, Bathurst herd caribou winter predominantly north and northwest of Great Slave Lake. This was the first time a notable southeast shift in the winter range of Bathurst caribou was documented by telemetry, although references to similar shifts existed in oral history (Gunn et al. 2001). One of five satellite-collared caribou from the adjacent Ahiak caribou herd to the east was also present in the Rennie Lake area (Gunn et al. 2000).

It is likely that in winter 1997/98 wolves and caribou from the Bathurst, Ahiak, and Beverly caribou summer ranges all spent part of the winter in the Rennie Lake area, which historically has been primarily used by the Beverly herd and associated wolves. On occasion, some Qamanirjuaq caribou may also overwinter in the Rennie Lake area (Beverly Qamanirjuaq Management Board 1999). The unusual congregation of caribou likely resulted in a large number of wolves that normally associate elsewhere with either the Bathurst, Ahiak, and Beverly caribou, but concentrated in the Rennie Lake area during winter 1997/98.

Our data suggested the Rennie Lake wolf hunt included wolves from the Bathurst caribou range, which is consistent with Parker's (1973) observations. He described a close association between the distribution of wolves and caribou for a region adjacent to the Rennie Lake area and encompassing NWT, Nunavut, Saskatchewan, and Manitoba. Moreover, Parker (1973) commented on the interbreeding implications of cohabiting tundra and boreal wolves in the taiga-tundra transition during their winter breeding season because of the winter concentration of caribou.

Our radio-tracking data also support overlap in distribution of caribou and wolves on the winter range as a normal occurrence, although the area of convergence might change according to caribou movements. Wolves were abundant in the Rennie Lake area during winter 1997/98 because wolves from Bathurst, Beverly, and Ahiak (Queen Maud Gulf) caribou ranges (Fig. 2.4.4) moved into the area that year. An influx of animals to the area was also revealed by movements of several caribou and wolves fitted with satellite collars northwest of the hunt area (Gunn et al. 2001; Walton et al. 2001a, b). The influx of caribou and wolves to wintering grounds, including the Rennie Lake area, was corroborated by the dearth of caribou and wolves observed elsewhere in their range, and by poor success of local hunters (H.D.C., unpublished data).

Therefore, wolf and caribou location data suggests wolves concentrated in unusually high numbers in the Rennie Lake area during winter 1997/98 and this probably contributed to the high kill of wolves observed that year. This outcome was an example of a concomitant increase in the wolf kill resulting from migration of caribou and associated wolves to areas accessible to hunters (Hayes & Gunson 1995). Another documented shift in caribou winter range occurred during winter of 1978/79 near Kugluktuk, Nunavut (formerly Coppermine, NWT) on the northern coastline of mainland Canada (Coronation Gulf, Arctic Ocean). The wolf kill was heavy that year, when at least 850 wolves were killed near Kugluktuk (Hayes & Gunson 1995). Thus, in addition to pelt price, proximity of caribou and associated wolves to communities can influence fluctuations in annual wolf kill numbers.

In 1998–99, the Rennie Lake area wolf kill (152 wolves, Table 2.4.1) was about one-fourth that of the 633 wolves recorded the previous year. Hunters in the Rennie Lake area reported seeing fewer caribou and wolves during that winter. This is consistent with telemetry data, which indicated that only 2 of 16 satellite collared caribou (Gunn et al. 2001) and 4 of 11 satellite collared wolves travelled close to the Rennie Lake area that year. Instead, Bathurst caribou and wolves wintered farther northwest of Rennie Lake and beyond Great Slave Lake (Gunn et al. 2001; Walton 2000). In that area, Aboriginal hunters from the Tlicho First Nations mostly kill caribou and seldom hunt wolves, which may help explain the relatively low numbers of wolves taken in winter 1998/99.

ADDRESSING HUNTING SUSTAINABILITY

Wolves are considered abundant in northern Canada (above the 60th parallel; Heard & Williams 1992, Hayes & Gunson 1995) relative to other areas in North America, and populations can accommodate a moderate amount of human induced mortality (Hayes et al. 1991). The GNWT argued that the 1997/98 Rennie Lake wolf hunt was sustainable based on the large influx of caribou and wolves observed in the area that year and the resiliency of wolves to high kill levels (Keith 1983; Ballard et al. 1987; Fuller 1989a; Weaver et al. 1996). The resiliency of wolves to sharp declines in abundance has been documented in several jurisdictions. Wolf populations reduced by as much as 80% have rebounded in less than five years (Mech 1970; Peterson et al. 1984; Ballard et al. 1987; Boertje et al. 1996; Hayes & Harestad 2000; Hayes et al. 2003). In such extreme cases of wolf reduction, the most important factor influencing the rate of recovery, however, was immigration from neighbouring areas (Bergerud & Elliot 1998; Hayes & Harestad 2000). Thus, such reductions may not be sustainable in the long term.

Although the number of wolves in the NWT and Nunavut is uncertain, the population for both territories combined had been considered stable with about 10,000 wolves (Hayes & Gunson 1995). The proportion of wolves taken in the Border A wolf hunt compared with the rest of the NWT varies from about 32 to 77 per cent, disregarding the incomplete records of the 1993/94 hunt (Table 2.4.1). It appears that every 2–3 years the Border A wolf harvest exceeds 300 wolves and raises the proportion of the kill to three-quarters of the NWT total harvest.

Fuller et al. (2003) provides a recent review of sustainable mortality rates for wolves. These authors document how, depending on age and sex structure, wolf populations can sustain an annual hunting mortality of 30% of the winter population, as was also suggested by previous studies (Keith 1983; Fuller 1989a; but also see Haber 1996; Larivière et al. 2000; Paquet & Carbyn 2003). Assuming 30% winter mortality and a maximum kill of 760 to 800 wolves in the Rennie Lake hunting area, a population of approximately 2,700 wolves would be necessary in winter 1997/98 for the kill to be sustainable. The GNWT believed the wolf population from the combined Bathurst, Beverly, and Ahiak caribou winter ranges could constitute at least 2,700 animals. Unknown parameters include whether wolf populations from the Bathurst, Beverly, and Ahiak areas are interconnected and whether congregations occur frequently. Furthermore, the Bathurst caribou herd, estimated in 1996 at 350,000 caribou (Gunn et al.

1997), the Beverly herd, estimated in 1994 at 276,000 caribou (Williams 1995), and the Ahiak herd in 1996 at 200,000 caribou (Gunn et al. 2000) were all considered healthy then and likely provided sufficient prey for wolves. Recently, several barren-ground caribou herds have experienced a decline in numbers, including the Bathurst herd, currently estimated in 2006 at 128,000 ± 27,300 caribou (R. Case, personal communication).

Clearly, northern wolf-caribou dynamics, migratory behaviour, and their effects on the wolf hunt in the Rennie Lake area require further study and cannot be adequately portrayed just in cursory media articles. Since the wolf kill of 1997/98, the GNWT has collaborated with universities and non-governmental agencies to address the need for additional information. A genetic study of wolves killed in northern Canada analyzed relationships among wolf populations and characterized them as migratory or resident, both of which were likely killed in the Rennie Lake area (Musiani et al. 2001; Musiani 2003; Musiani et al. 2007). Results supported a genetic distinction between boreal forest (resident) wolves and tundra/taiga (migratory) wolves (Musiani 2003; Musiani et al. 2007). Such results indicate that any sustainability evaluation should account for impacts on both boreal forest (resident) wolves and tundra/taiga (migratory) wolves.

Genetic distinction at the landscape scale must be considered for management. Such a separation reflects enduring ecological mechanisms in this unique predator-prey system, in a landscape yet unfragmented by human encroachment. Understanding meta-population structure (Meffe & Carroll 1997) of genetic units should lead to wolf conservation approaches designed to preserve the diversity within and genetic interchange between population units (Wayne et al. 1992) while allowing for sustainable hunting and trapping.

Indeed, without the benefit of modern genetic techniques at the time, management of the wolf kill in NWT and Nunavut has historically distinguished between "boreal" wolves and "tundra" wolves. The distinction has been based on location. While conceptually based on wolves from the tundra versus the boreal forest, in practice the community or municipality recording the kill has determined the ecotype classification. Communities located on the tundra in the NWT and Nunavut record their wolf kill as "tundra wolves" while those communities well within the boreal forest record their kill as "boreal wolves". Rural settlements along the treeline or where these two wolf ecotypes overlap would rely on local personnel to assign pelts into the appropriate categories based on appearance. Assignment errors for these records likely vary annually depending on migration shifts of caribou and where the wolves originated that year. A collective effort to improve assignment of ecotype to the wolf harvest would benefit management because harvest levels could differ between them.

CONCLUSIONS

The Rennie Lake area wolf hunt case study indicates that in the NWT and Nunavut, Aboriginal hunters take most of the wolves killed. A variable, but significant portion of the total NWT kill (e.g., from ⅓ to ¾ of total) is taken by hunters from northern Saskatchewan (Table 2.4.1). This poses challenges in determining the exact number of wolf hunters involved, the number of wolves killed, and an assessment of the potential impact of the kill on the wolf population because recording of hunt statistics is incomplete.

The Rennie Lake wolf hunt is important to monitor because over one-third of tundra/taiga wolves (NWT and Nunavut combined) may be killed in a given year and the potential exists for exceeding this threshold commonly accepted for sustainability. However, determining what is sustainable is elusive because wolf population size must be estimated, an endeavour that is usually logistically difficult and prohibitively expensive. Fortunately, the wide variability in the annual wolf kill, largely because of annual variation in caribou migration routes, would mitigate an aberrant year and the overall wolf hunt could remain sustainable on a longer time scale.

Nomadic or semi-nomadic lifestyles have traditionally been an integral part of Aboriginal hunting in northern Canada (Müller-Wille 1974). In an ecosystem characterized by wildlife migrations, humans correspondingly adapted by also moving to where important resources, such as caribou, aggregated seasonally. With most Aboriginal hunting now originating from permanent communities and mobility to remote areas somewhat restricted by logistical costs, wide variations in annual hunt statistics that reflect changes in animal migration patterns might be expected. Whereas this may be the case for some areas, hunters from northern Saskatchewan have shown a willingness to travel long distances to hunt wildlife. Such hunters typically access the remote Rennie Lake area of NWT by aircraft. Nevertheless, our data regarding fluctuations in annual wolf kill statistics suggest migration patterns of animals significantly influenced this hunt. Whether the traditional economy continues to be viable, and whether access to hunting areas by aircraft continues to be affordable in the future, remains to be seen. A change in either factor will affect wolf hunt statistics in the Rennie Lake area.

The wolf hunt in Rennie Lake requires monitoring beyond solely determining sustainability of numbers harvested. This is important because the hunt can be of sufficient magnitude that any significant change can also influence dispersal patterns, pack structure, genetic diversity, and meta-population dynamics of wolves in northern Canada. Two wolf ecotypes, boreal and tundra/taiga, previously recognized locally, have been confirmed genetically (Musiani et al. 2007). Although harvest records distinguish between the two variants, communities subject to shifts in caribou migration routes should monitor annual migrations of caribou closely to facilitate accurate partition of the associated wolf kill into boreal and tundra ecotypes.

ACKNOWLEDGMENTS

We acknowledge the effort provided by wildlife officials from all regions in the NWT, Nunavut, and Saskatchewan for their wolf kill summaries. We thank A. Gunn for her comments and allowing us access to caribou movement data. G. Bihun, G. Duncan, R. Mulders, T. Berens, and L. Yonge assisted with compiling data for parts of this analysis. Their comments and those of anonymous referees on earlier versions greatly improved the manuscript. Funding for wolf satellite radio-collars was provided to the senior author by the Department of Environment and Natural Resources (GNWT), West Kitikmeot/Slave Study Society, World Wildlife Fund (Canada) Ltd., and industry partners.

Box 1. Aboriginal hunters are descendents of the founding peoples of Canada and have hunted for subsistence for thousands of years. Aboriginal people are distributed widely in tribes throughout Canada but comprise the largest proportion of Canada's population in the north. Most groups refer to themselves as 'First Nations' although the term is legally undefined. In 2001, approximately 1.3 million people (4.4% of Canada's population) reported having at least some Aboriginal ancestry (Statistics Canada 2003). In the Northwest Territories (NWT), 21,413 people (50% of the territorial population) were estimated with at least some Aboriginal ancestry in July 2005 (NWT Bureau of Statistics, http://www.stats.gov.nt.ca). The Aboriginal population continues to grow in the north and numbers now likely exceed their historical maximum (West Kitikmeot Slave Study 2007).

About 31% of Aboriginal people in Canada reside on reserves as a result of treaties established under Canadian law and this number has been declining gradually (Statistics Canada 2003). Other areas of Aboriginal residence include rural, non-reserve areas and urban centers. The proportion of Aboriginal people living in rural, non reserve areas has also declined slightly while a slow, but steady growth has been observed for Aboriginal people residing in cities (Statistics Canada 2003).

Canada entered into several recent land claim settlements with Aboriginal people who previously were without treaties or otherwise had incomplete ones. The first such settlement in the NWT was the Western Arctic Claim (Inuvialuit) in 1984. The catalyst for others that followed was the federal government's 1986 Comprehensive Land Claims Policy that guided the negotiation of Aboriginal claims based on the concept of continuing Aboriginal rights rather than extinguishment (Indian and North Affairs Canada, http://www.ainc-inac.gc.ca). In the NWT, these comprehensive claim settlements include the Gwich'in (1992), Inuit (1993), Sahtu (1994), and the Tlicho (2003) final agreements. Treaty Land Entitlement, land claim negotiation, and self government talks continue periodically for the remaining unsettled land claim areas within the NWT and its Aboriginal inhabitants. The main objectives of these land claim settlements are to establish greater certainty over the ownership and management of lands and its resources within Canada and avoid grievances in the future. Unlike the provinces, land and non-renewable resources are under federal jurisdiction in the NWT while some renewable resources are territorial responsibilities. The Rennie Lake wolf hunting area is currently situated in an unsettled claim area and is subject to negotiations for deferred Treaty 8 (1899) land entitlement provisions.

Subsistence hunting is a right of Aboriginal people across Canada and is recognized and affirmed in Canadian federal law (specifically, the 1982 Canadian constitution). This federal statute supercedes laws and regulations at the territorial or provincial level. Most mammals and non-migratory bird regulations are under the lesser territorial or provincial legislative authority. Consequently, Aboriginal people do not need a license to hunt and kill wildlife for subsistence or traditional purposes and are not subject to most restrictions that may apply to wildlife management except when conservation of the resource is adversely impacted. In these extreme cases, the duty of governments to consult with First Nations is paramount. Only after this consultation process has been completed can governments act to infringe upon subsistence rights.

Although Aboriginal hunters do not require a license for subsistence, a license is used when products from the harvest are sold or exported from the NWT. Consequently, a General Hunting License (GHL) is issued free-of-charge to subsistence hunters to facilitate these records and payment programs. Similarly, a "Border A" license is issued to those subsistence hunters residing outside the NWT but who hunt traditionally inside NWT boundaries (within specified limits).

2.5 Livestock Husbandry Practices Reduce Wolf Depredation Risk in Alberta, Canada

Tyler Muhly, C. Cormack Gates, Carolyn Callaghan and Marco Musiani

INTRODUCTION: PREDICTING SPATIAL OCCURRENCE OF WOLF ATTACKS TO PROTECT LIVESTOCK

Livestock depredation is the act of predation by wild predators, wolves (*Canis lupus*) for example, on domestic livestock. Conflict between humans and wolves often occurs where livestock production overlaps wolf range due to livestock depredation by wolves (Fritts et al. 2003). Depredation can have significant economic costs and cause emotional stress for individual livestock producers (Bangs et al. 1998; Bangs & Shivik 2001; Naughton-Treves et al. 2003). Lethal control of wolves is commonly practised in response to livestock depredation, whereas non-lethal methods are used sporadically as their efficacy under the local circumstances is often unknown (Smith et al. 2000a; Shivik 2006). As a result, wolf conservation can be particularly challenging in or adjacent to areas with livestock production. Spatial prediction of depredation occurrence and identification of husbandry techniques that diminish the rate of attack by wolves are useful ways to prevent livestock depredation and thus improve wolf conservation in agricultural areas (Treves et al. 2002; Fritts et al. 2003; Treves et al. 2004).

In Alberta, Canada, lethal control continues to be practised to manage livestock depredation by wolves (Gunson 1992; Musiani et al. 2005). Historically, there is a strong correlation between the number of livestock killed by wolves and the number of wolves lethally controlled in Alberta (Musiani et al. 2003). Currently, wolves are relatively abundant in northern and central Alberta (Musiani & Paquet 2004); however, wolves in southern Alberta are restricted to the foothills of the Rocky Mountains along the southwest forest and agricultural fringe (Alberta Sustainable Resource Development 2002). In this area the majority of wolves are killed in 'corrective' anti-depredation actions in response to depredation peaks (Musiani et al. 2005). Fewer wolves would be killed should depredation occurrence diminish. Identifying and employing non-lethal means to prevent livestock depredation by wolves in southwest Alberta may therefore be essential to maintain a viable wolf population in the area.

Several biophysical landscape factors (Meriggi & Lovari 1996; Ciucci & Boitani 1998; Linnell et al. 1999; Mech et al. 2000; Treves et al. 2004) and husbandry practices (Robel et al. 1981; Bjorge 1983; Tompa 1983; Bjorge & Gunson 1985; Fritts et al. 1992; Ciucci & Boitani 1998; Linnell et al. 1999; Mech et al. 2000; Smith et al. 2000a; Smith et al. 2000b; Musiani et al. 2003) have been identified as potentially affecting the occurrence of livestock depredation by wolves. In addition, specific factors might affect wolf depredation in certain areas and not in others, as factors' relationship to depredation is likely affected by interaction with other factors and the local biophysical, social, and economic environment. We visited and interviewed ranchers in southwest Alberta within the core area of confirmed wolf distribution (defined in Methods below) to record the location of depredation events and the husbandry practices on depredated and non-depredated ranches. We wanted to identify biophysical factors of depredation sites and husbandry practices of depredated versus non-depredated ranches that influence the probability of livestock depredation by wolves in the area.

ROLE OF BIOPHYSICAL AND HUSBANDRY FACTORS IN LIVESTOCK DEPREDATION

Human infrastructure (e.g., roads and buildings) is often used as an index of human density, and its avoidance by wolves has been demonstrated in various European and North American regions of the wolf range. Although wolves may use roads for travel (Thurber et al. 1994; Ciucci et al. 2003; Paquet et al., this volume), high road and human habitation densities are typically associated with low wolf densities (Thiel 1985; Mech et al. 1988; Mladenoff et al. 1995; Mladenoff & Sickley 1998). Therefore, it is expected that livestock grazed in remote areas (far from roads and buildings) should be at greater risk to depredation by wolves.

Although they are habitat generalists, wolves favour certain biophysical characteristics of the landscape. For example, in northern Italy wolves prefer travelling along routes at low elevations with mild slopes for ease of travel (Ciucci et al. 2003). Cattle favour flat terrain and proximity to water (Cook 1966; Roath & Krueger 1982). Biophysical factors favoured by both species, i.e., flat terrain, may result in increased encounter probability between the two species at locations with those characteristics. Therefore, depredation probability at those locations may be higher. However, depredation occurrence might depend upon other factors than habitat selection by wolves or livestock. Depredation might be more likely where biophysical and human factors allow. For example, some studies have hypothesized that depredation is more likely to occur in rugged terrain as those areas provide advantage to wolves over livestock, thus increasing the success of depredation for wolves (Dorrance 1982). We examined the relationship between slope and elevation (indicators of terrain ruggedness) and distance to water to depredation occurrence to determine whether terrain was a factor in depredation. Wolves use cover to avoid human detection and to stalk prey (Kunkel & Pletscher 2001; Ciucci et al. 2003; Chavez & Gese 2006). Forested areas may therefore be riskier habitat for grazing livestock (Dorrance 1982; Bjorge 1983; Ciucci & Boitani 1998). We examined whether depredation was more likely to occur closer to or within forest cover.

Wolf density is highly related to prey density (Messier 1995b; Messier & Joly 2000; Mech & Peterson 2003). Cattle grazed in productive wild prey areas may be more likely to encounter wolves. Treves et al. (2004) found higher densities of deer in townships that experienced depredation, but could not assess the causal explanation. We will test whether depredation occurs where there is greater density of wild prey to conclusively address this critical hypothesis. However, in Europe, wolves can persist in areas with little wild prey by preying on domestic livestock (Meriggi & Lovari 1996). Therefore, the relationship between wild prey density and wolf attacks on livestock might or might not be significant in our study.

Supervision of livestock by ranchers and herders may deter wolf attacks (Bjorge 1983; Bjorge & Gunson 1985; Linnell et al. 1999). We recorded the number of times a rancher supervised their cattle per week to determine whether depredation is more likely to occur when supervision rate is lower. In the study area, supervision of livestock might be reduced during the summer grazing period, as livestock is free ranging ('at large'; Musiani et al. 2004). Therefore, our research design testing for supervision effects accounted for seasonal changes. Several other husbandry practices may affect the occurrence of depredation. Carcasses from domestic animals can potentially act as attractants (Fritts et al. 1992; Mech et al. 2000; Chavez & Gese 2006). In our study, we determined whether ranches that do not dispose of carcasses had an increased likelihood of depredation. Younger cattle may be more susceptible to depredation (Oakleaf et al. 2003; Bradley & Pletscher 2005). We determined whether yearling cattle herds might prove more vulnerable to depredation then cow/calf herds, as yearling cattle herds may have poorer anti-predator behaviour (Bradley & Pletscher 2005). Dogs, particularly livestock guarding dogs, may be an effective means to prevent depredation (Coppinger & Coppinger 1995; Smith et al. 2000b); thus we also examined whether presence of dogs affected depredation risk. Our sample allows us to test the above relationships as it includes ranches that are different for: supervision rate (number of times per week livestock are patrolled by humans), carcass disposal (either removed or not), age of cattle (presence or not of yearlings and cow/calves), and dogs (presence or not).

INTERACTION OF LIVESTOCK DEPREDATION FACTORS

We used logistic regression and Resource Selection Functions (RSFs; Manly et al. 2002) to model probability of livestock depredation by wolves in southwest Alberta relative to the combination of biophysical landscape factors and the husbandry practices described above. Thus, we used an approach commonly employed for modelling species' distribution to model distribution of a behavioural pattern of two species. Specifically, we attempted to model distribution of wolf-livestock deadly interactions (similar to Kauffman et al. 2007 for wolves and elk), rather than wolf distribution or livestock distribution. However, we rely on the same fundamental assumption that makes RSF a valid approach: that if the distribution of resources is known, then the distribution and abundance of organisms can be characterized by RSFs (Boyce & Macdonald 1999). Our study deals with distribution of livestock depredation by wolves (i.e., not an organism). However, depredation too should depend upon distribution of resources relevant to wolves, to livestock. or to the occurrence of a deadly interaction.

RSFs have been widely used over the last decade to model probability of an animal using a resource unit (Manly et al. 2002; Johnson et al. 2006). Recently, the RSF approach has been criticized by Keating and Cherry (2004), who indicated major limitations in providing correct probability of use estimates, especially with the use-availability sampling design. Criticism of RSFs by Keating and Cherry (2004) were rebutted by Johnson et al. (2006), who pointed out how RSFs are still useful in predicting broad occurrence probability. Finally, a Special Section of the *Journal of Wildlife Management* contained nine papers describing in theory and in practice a wide range of applications of resource selection statistics (Strickland & McDonald 2006). Strickland and McDonald (2006) highlighted how the outcome of the section supports use of RSFs. Notwithstanding the debate on RSF methods, we explored its application to our context just to 'identify important habitat characteristics' related to depredation occurrence, an objective that can be met even according to Keating and Cherry (2004).

Our RSF approach belongs to the broader category of presence-absence methods (i.e., those that model a binomial response) used to model presence-only data, using samples of the background environment (random points throughout the study area), and of areas designated as "non-use" or "pseudoabsence" (Stockwell & Peters 1999; Boyce et al. 2002; Ferrier et al. 2002; Zaniewski et al. 2002; Keating & Cherry 2004; Pearce & Boyce 2006). We developed two models of wolf depredation occurrence, a biophysical and a husbandry model, relying on random points throughout the study area and on non-use points, respectively. Random points represented environmental variation in sites where depredation could occur in theory, whereas non-use points represented ranches where depredation did not occur but could also occur. We selected a study area and only those ranches that had confirmed wolf presence (defined below).

We produced two RSF models. The first model considered how wolf attacks on livestock were explained by biophysical landscape factors (elk density, slope, elevation, and distance to water, to forest cover, to roads, and to quarter sections with buildings). Our approach to modelling biophysical factors was not original, as other authors had similar methodology (Treves et al. 2004). However, we also produced a second model of husbandry practices (frequency of monitoring in the fall, winter, spring, and summer, carcass removal, age class of livestock herds grazed, presence of dogs, use of lethal control of wolves by ranchers and size of ranching operation). Although other authors also looked at whether wolf depredation occurrence had been correlated with husbandry practices (see Mech et al. 2000 for size of operation, calving locations, supervision rate, carcass disposal; and Bradley & Pletshcer 2005 for size of operation, cattle breed, cattle herd type, carcass disposal), this is the first study that uses husbandry practices to model and predict wolf depredation at the landscape level. Our approach, if validated, allows production of depredation probability maps indicating where depredation risk is higher and therefore management should be focused in the future.

STUDY AREA

The study occurred along the eastern slopes of the Rocky Mountains in southwest Alberta, Canada (Fig. 2.5.1). The Rocky Mountains occur along the western portion of the study area continuously from the northern to southern boundary. Toward the east, topography is less rugged, with rolling foothills that eventually level to flat prairie and agricultural lands.

Forested lands occur continuously in the western half of the study area and gradate into more open grasslands in the east. The most common tree species include lodgepole pine (*Pinus contorta*), white spruce (*Picea glauca*), and aspen (*Populus tremuloides*), with limber pine (*Pinus flexilis*), black spruce (*Picea mariana*), balsam poplar (*Populus balsamifera*), paper birch (*Betula papyrifera*), and balsam fir (*Abies balsamifera*) in less abundance. Ungulate species, including elk (*Cervus elaphus*), white-tailed deer (*Odocoileus virginianus*), mule deer (*Odocoileus hemionus*), and moose (*Alces alces*) occur throughout the study area. Carnivores (in addition to wolves) such as grizzly bears (*Ursus arctos horribilis*), black bears (*Ursus americanus*), cougars (*Felis concolor*), and coyotes (*Canis latrans*) also frequent the study area and can kill livestock.

Several small towns occur within the study area with populations of 300 to 3,665 people. Agricultural, forestry and oil and gas development occurs throughout the study area. Public recreation occurs particularly on public lands during the summer and fall. Livestock grazing remains a dominant land use on both private and public lands and cattle are the most common livestock grazed.

WOLF STATUS AND MANAGEMENT

Wolves in southern Alberta are not as abundant as in other parts of the province, and they represent a link between western Canadian and northwest U.S. wolves in Idaho, Montana, and Wyoming (Musiani & Paquet 2004). In Alberta, compensation programs are in place for losses of cattle, sheep, hogs, goats, and bison (Alberta Conservation Association 2002;

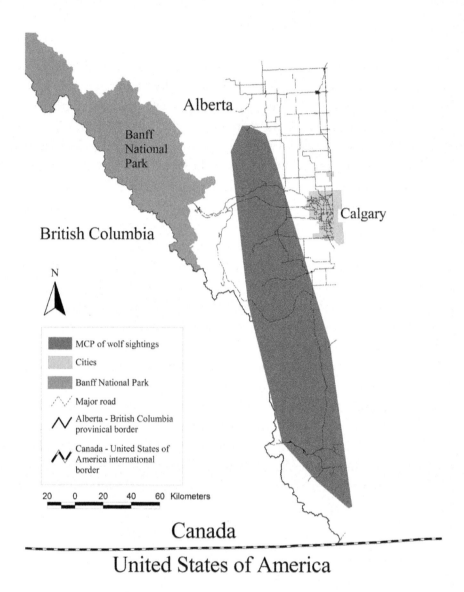

Figure 2.5.1. Map of the study area as indicated by the Minimum Convex Polygon (MCP) of wolf sightings by ranchers. The MCP defined the study area as where wolves and livestock overlap in southwest Alberta.

THE WORLD OF WOLVES

Musiani et al. 2003). However, given the importance of livestock production in southwest Alberta, Alberta Sustainable Resource Development, Government of Alberta, in partnership with various stakeholders, monitors wolf activity by placing Global Positioning System (GPS) and satellite telemetry collars on each wolf pack (Alberta Sustainable Resource Development 2002). If depredation by wolves is confirmed by telemetry data and site inspections, wolves may be culled. Wolf culling may be incremental; meaning wolves are culled one at a time to attempt to change depredation patterns without eliminating the whole pack. This incremental management response is aimed at maintaining a wolf population in southwest Alberta by allowing packs to maintain their territories. Nevertheless, lethal control is not entirely regulated as landowners or their delegates can kill wolves up to 8 km from their land if they feel wolves are a threat, and hunters are not required to carry a special permit to kill wolves (Gunson 1992; Musiani et al. 2003). Finally, trappers can kill wolves on registered trap lines (Gunson 1992).

METHODS

We limited our investigation to ranches no smaller than one section (approximately 2.6 km²) in size to avoid small "hobby farm" operations and residents not significantly involved in the livestock industry. We obtained the location depredation sites from the Government of Alberta, Sustainable Resources Development (SRD), Fish and Wildlife Division (FWD) and directly from ranchers. We arranged interviews on both depredated and non-depredated ranches by contacting ranchers in the study area by phone. The government of Alberta compiles information on sightings of wolves by the public. The resulting files include locations where inspection by wildlife officers confirmed presence of wolves. All ranches used in our sample were within the core area of confirmed wolf distribution. In addition, our respondents confirmed that wolves were permanently present in the area in recent years. If ranchers had experienced depredation, we collected the location of the depredation site(s) on their ranch using a handheld Global Positioning System (GPS; Garmin 12 XL).

We used logistic regression (Hosmer & Lemeshow 1989) and followed Manly et al.'s (2002) RSF approach to develop two livestock depredation probability models: one consisting of biophysical factors and another consisting of husbandry factors. For the biophysical model, we employed a used/available logistic regression RSF approach (i.e., depredated vs. available sites). For the husbandry model, we employed a used/unused RSF approach (i.e., depredated vs. non-depredated ranches). Use/availability was employed for the biophysical model because it was impossible to confirm that each available point had not been the site of a depredation event in the past. Conversely, ranchers are typically aware if depredation has occurred on their ranch, even if the exact location is unknown (Oakleaf et al. 2003); therefore for the husbandry model we could confirm that a ranch had not been depredated and non-depredated ranches were classified as "unused." Logistic regression provided β coefficient values for each factor, which indicate the increase in likelihood that the dependent factor (depredation) will occur (change from 0 to 1) given a unit change of the factor.

For the biophysical model, factors included: distance to cover (forest/shrub cover greater than 2 m tall), distance to quarter section with a building, distance to roads (divided into three classes, unimproved, gravel and paved), distance to water, elevation, slope, and density of elk. Nearest Features extension (Jenness 2003) in ArcView 3.2 (Environmental Systems Research Institute 1999) was used to calculate proximity of each site (depredated or available) to a factor of interest.

We used data from winter elk surveys collected by the Government of Alberta (Clark 2002; Jokinen & Jorgenson 2002) to calculate elk density throughout the study area. We calculated elk density because elk are likely the primary prey of wolves in the study area (Huggard 1993a; Hebblewhite et al. 2002). We averaged the yearly elk counts in each Wildlife Management Unit (WMU; Mean size: 1,405 km², Standard Deviation: 977 km²) and divided by the area of that WMU.

For a depredation event to occur, presence of both wolves and livestock is an obvious prerequisite. Livestock occurs throughout the study area. To establish areas frequented by wolves, and thus identify available locations for wolf depredation occurrence, we produced a 100% minimum convex polygon (MCP; Mohr 1947) using ArcView 3.2 (ESRI 1999) of all ranches surveyed that reported seeing wolves on their ranch (Fig. 2.5.1). All ranches in our samples were within the core area of wolf distribution and had wolf presence confirmed by government inspection (see above). We used MCP over other home-range analysis approaches (e.g., harmonic mean and kernel analyses) because intensity of use of an area was not important, as depredation could potentially occur wherever wolves and livestock overlap. Within the MCP, we generated 10,000 random points to sample the landscape of available sites to wolves using a random point generator (Jenness 2003) in ArcView 3.2. These available sites were compared with the used (depredation) sites in the biophysical logistic regression analysis.

Some ranches were affected by more than one depredation event. Forty-seven depredated ranches versus 45 non-depredated ranches were used to build the husbandry RSF model. Factors tested in the husbandry model included supervision rate during the summer, winter, spring, and fall, size of the ranch (km^2), whether the ranch was a cow/calf and/or yearling operation, whether wolf culling was practised on the ranch, whether dogs were present on the ranch and whether the rancher practised carcass removal.

Analyses were conducted separately to obtain a biophysical model and a husbandry model. We calculated Spearman's rank correlation for all factors (Zar 1984). If coefficients for any two factors were greater than 0.7, we considered them highly correlated and we removed from further analyses the factor that was least correlated to depredation (Manly et al. 2002).

We identified both a biophysical and husbandry set of candidate models that included different combinations of factors and compared them using Akaike's Information Criterion (AIC), an information-theoretic approach, to select the logistic regression model(s) that best predicted livestock depredation (Burnham & Anderson 1998; Anderson & Burnham 2002).

We validated the biophysical and husbandry RSF models separately using a k-fold cross validation approach, which allowed using all depredations data to build the model rather than withholding some data, then to be used for validation (Johnson et al. 2006). This option was ideal because (1) depredation is a relatively rare event and our sample size was limited; and (2) an independent, unrelated depredation dataset (to be used for validation purposes) was not available in the study area and period. The frequencies predicted according to our best model were calculated and compared with the frequencies observed in the data withheld at each iteration (n = 5 folds). Test statistics used to evaluate models included linear regression R^2 (values close to 1 preferred as they indicate fit), linear regression slope (values close to 1 preferred as they indicate predicted vs. observed 1:1 ratio), linear regression and Spearman-rank correlation significance. Test statistics were calculated for each iteration (i.e., each fold) and for the mean value of predicted and observed depredation frequencies of all iterations (the Overall value). Finally, if valid, we used the best biophysical and husbandry models, defined as above, to produce RSF-based depredation probability maps of the study area using Map Calculator in ArcView 3.2 (ESRI 1999).

We compared differences in surveillance rate of livestock by ranchers between depredated and non-depredated ranches across all seasons using a Kruskal-Wallis test and for each season (summer, fall, winter and spring) using a Mann-Whitney U test (Sokal & Rohlf 1995) to determine if ranches that experienced depredation had different supervision rates compared with ranches that did not experience depredation. We also compared whether supervision rate on all ranches differed between each season using a Mann-Whitney U test (Sokal & Rohlf 1995). We conducted all statistical analysis using SPSS 14.0 (2006).

RESULTS

Inspections by government wildlife officers confirmed wolf and livestock presence in an area of 10,100 km² of Southwest Alberta (MCP; Fig. 2.5.1). In this area, we visited 109 depredation sites, all located on ranches with confirmed wolf presence, at which wolf attacks occurred from 1981 to 2003. Domestic animals depredated included alpaca (3) and cattle (157). No two biophysical landscape factors (see above) were highly correlated with each other in depredated sites; therefore all factors were considered in logistic regression analyses. Frequency of monitoring in the summer and frequency of monitoring in the fall were correlated (r = 0.924) in the husbandry analysis. Frequency of monitoring in the summer was removed from the logistic regression analysis, as frequency of monitoring in the fall was more correlated with depredation occurrence (r=0.127 and r=0.120, for fall and summer, respectively).

Biophysical model

In AIC analyses, the best model explaining wolf depredation occurrence based upon biophysical landscape factors included five factors (Table 2.5.1). All of these factors were significant in the model (Table 2.5.2; p<0.034, Wald's Z>4.501), and the relative importance of each factor to predicting the occurrence of depredation, from highest to lowest, were elk density, distance to building, distance to road, slope, and distance to cover. In the model, depredation was more likely in areas with higher elk density, closer to buildings, further from roads, on flatter slopes, and closer to forest cover. The biophysical model did not adequately predict spatial occurrence of livestock depredation by wolves when tested with k-fold cross-validation (Table 2.5.3).

Table 2.5.1. A comparison of biophysical logistic regression models predicting the occurrence of wolf attacks on livestock in southwest Alberta. Models were assessed through the ranking of AIC values (Δ_i) and weights (w_i) describing the likelihood of the model. Model complexity (number of factors) is represented by K_i. Models with $\Delta_i < 2$ and the global model are indicated (following conventions by Burnham and Anderson 1998).

Model Ranking	Factors used	K_i	AIC	Δ_i	w_i
1	Elk density Distance to Building Distance to Dirt Road Slope Distance to Cover	7	1081.346	0	0.987
5	ALL (Global)	11	1096.44	15.094	0.0005

Table 2.5.2. Results for the biophysical model that best explains depredation, including standardized Beta coefficients, Beta coefficient standard errors, Wald statistics and Wald significance for each factor in the model. Significant values are indicated in bold.

Factor	Standardized Coefficient (β)	S.E.	Wald statistic (Z)	Wald Significance
Elk density	2.198	0.002	54.958	**<0.001**
Distance to Buildings	-7.181	<0.001	15.917	**<0.001**
Distance to Dirt Road	2.363	<0.001	13.031	**<0.001**
Slope	-3.455	0.018	9.967	**0.002**
Distance to Cover	-5.127	0.001	4.501	**0.034**

Table 2.5.3. Results of the validation of the best biophysical model for predicting livestock depredation by wolves. Factors in the model included elk density, distance to buildings, distance to dirt roads, slope and distance to cover. Validation statistics included linear regression R^2 value and significance, linear regression slope and Spearman correlation coefficient and significance comparing predicted depredation frequency to observed depredation frequency. Statistics for each k-fold group and for all groups (overall) are provided.

Group	Linear regression R^2 value	Linear regression significance (p-value)	Linear Regression Slope[*]	Correlation Coefficient (Spearman's rho)	Correlation Coefficient (p-value)
1	0.094	0.616	0.189	0.300	0.624
2	0.075	0.656	0.058	0.600	0.285
3	0.047	0.725	-0.165	-0.100	0.830
4	0.629	0.110	-1.756	-0.600	0.285
5	0.720	0.069	0.730	0.821	0.089
Overall[**]	0.206	0.442	-0.135	-0.500	0.391

[*] Values close to 1 are preferred as they indicate 1:1 ratio of expected vs. observed occurrences (Johnson et al. 2006).
[**] Overall calculated with mean values of predicted and observed in each bin of probability (n=5 folds; Boyce et al. 2002).

Husbandry model

The AIC-ranked top husbandry model to spatially predict wolf attacks also included five factors (Table 2.5.4). Four of these factors were significant in the model (Table 2.5.5; p<0.041, Wald's Z>4.192). Frequency of monitoring in spring was not significant, but was still a factor in the husbandry model. The relative importance of each factor to predicting the occurrence of depredation, from highest to lowest was wolf culling, yearling presence, and frequency of monitoring in winter, in fall, and in spring (Table 2.5.5). Ranches more likely to be depredated were those which practised wolf culling, had yearling cattle herds, and monitored livestock more frequently in the fall, whereas, ranches that monitored livestock more frequently in the winter and spring were less likely to be depredated.

Contrary to the biophysical model, the husbandry model predicted spatial occurrence of livestock depredation by wolves (Table 2.5.6). Linear regression between predicted and observed depredation events was significant ($R^2 > 0.937$, p=0.006, Slope=1.027). The Spearman-rank correlation between predicted and observed depredation event was also significant (Rho=1.000, p<0.001).

Despite its relationship with the depredation occurrence model, supervision rate of livestock across all seasons and in each season were not different between depredated and non-depredated ranches (Mann Whitney U>-1.765, p>0.078; Table 2.5.7). However, livestock supervision on all ranches (both depredated and non-depredated) was different across seasons (Kruskal-Wallis K=121.550, p<0.001) and between each season pairs (Mann Whitney U<-3.982, p<0.001) except for summer and fall (p=0.041, Mann Whitney U=-1.061). Therefore, in our study livestock supervision likely contributed to explaining depredation occurrence, but its seasonal variation likely resulted in varying effects on seasonal depredation occurrence.

A livestock depredation probability map for southwest Alberta was calculated using the husbandry RSF model (Fig. 2.5.2). The map spatially illustrates livestock depredation probability based on the husbandry practices on each ranch, i.e., wolf culling, yearling herds, and frequency of monitoring. As a sample case, we also produced a finer scale livestock depredation probability map for three contiguous ranches in the study area (Fig. 2.5.3) to illustrate how depredation probability maps can be used in depredation management, i.e., to determine high risk areas and where anti-depredation measures can be focused.

Table 2.5.4. A comparison of husbandry logistic regression models predicting the occurrence of wolf attacks on livestock in southwest Alberta. Models were assessed through the ranking of AIC_c values (Δ_i) and weights (w_i) describing the likelihood of the model. Model complexity (number of factors) is represented by K_i. Models with $\Delta_i < 2$ and the global model are indicated (following conventions by Burnham and Anderson 1998).

Model Ranking	Factors used	K_i	AIC_c	Δ_i	w_i
1	Yearling herds Wolf culling Frequency of monitoring in the fall Frequency of monitoring in the spring Frequency of monitoring in the winter	7	82.46	0	0.21
2	Yearling herds Wolf culling Frequency of monitoring in the fall Frequency of monitoring in the spring Frequency of monitoring in the winter Dogs on ranch	8	82.62	0.16	0.19
29	ALL (Global)	13	93.446	10.98	0.00086

Table 2.5.5. Results for the husbandry model that best explains depredation, including standardized Beta coefficients, Beta coefficient standard errors, Wald statistics and Wald significance for each factor. Significant values are indicated in bold.

Factor	Standardized Coefficient (β)	S.E.	Wald statistic (Z)	Wald Significance
Wolf culling	2.139	0.669	10.207	**0.001**
Yearling	1.335	0.614	5.166	**0.023**
Frequency of monitoring in winter	-0.121	0.155	4.254	**0.039**
Frequency of monitoring in fall	0.824	0.117	4.192	**0.041**
Frequency of monitoring in spring	-0.004	0.042	1.085	**0.298**

Table 2.5.6. Results of the validation of the best husbandry model for predicting livestock depredation by wolves. Factors in the model included wolf culling, yearling herds, frequency of monitoring in winter, frequency of monitoring in fall, and frequency of monitoring in spring. Validation statistics included linear regression R^2 value and significance, linear regression slope and Spearman correlation coefficient, and significance comparing predicted depredation frequency to observed depredation frequency. Statistics for each k-fold group and for all groups (overall) are provided, and significant values are indicated in bold.

Group	Linear regression R^2 value	Linear regression significance (p-value)	Linear Regression Slope[*]	Correlation Coefficient (Spearman's rho)	Correlation Coefficient (p-value)
1	0.902	**0.014**	2.806	0.918	**0.028**
2	0.967	**0.003**	1.274	0.894	**0.041**
3	0.881	**0.018**	0.793	0.975	**0.005**
4	0.834	**0.030**	0.819	1.000	**<0.001**
5	0.886	**0.017**	0.835	0.975	**0.005**
Overall[**]	0.937	**0.006**	1.027	1.000	**<0.001**

[*] Values close to 1 are preferred as they indicate 1:1 ratio of expected vs. observed occurrences (Johnson et al. 2006).

[**] Overall calculated with mean values of predicted and observed in each bin of probability (n=5 folds; Boyce et al. 2002).

Table 2.5.7. Comparison between seasonal supervision rates of livestock by ranchers. Mann-Whitney U tests indicate if the supervision rates were significantly different between depredated and non-depredated ranches and between each pair of seasons on all ranches; significant values are indicated in bold.

Season	Mean Supervision Rate of Ranches with depredation*	Mean Supervision Rate of Ranches without depredation*	Mann-Whitney U statistic (Z)	Significance (p)	Seasonal increase (Supervision on all ranches)	Mann-Whitney U statistic (Z)	Significance (p)
Summer	3	2	-1.680	0.093	Summer–Fall	-1.061	0.289
Fall	3	2	-1.555	0.120	Summer–Winter	-7.606	<0.001
Winter	6	7	-0.447	0.655	Summer–Spring	-8.511	<0.001
Spring	13	15	-0.160	0.873	Fall–Winter	-6.427	<0.001
All-seasons	6	5	-1.765	0.078	Fall–Spring	-7.732	<0.001
					Winter–Spring	-3.982	<0.001

*Supervision rate is the number of times per week the area where livestock are located is patrolled by ranchers.

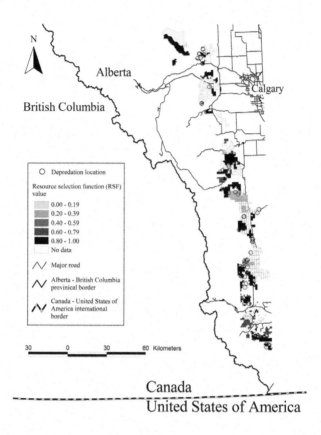

Figure 2.5.2. Map indicating the probability of livestock depredation by wolves in the study area as calculated using the husbandry Resource Selection Function (RSF). RSF values were calculated using the factors: wolf culling, yearling herds, frequency of monitoring in winter, frequency of monitoring in fall, and frequency of monitoring in spring. Darker areas indicate higher depredation probability.

DISCUSSION

This study aimed at modelling spatial distribution of wolf attacks on livestock and relied on two methodological approaches, one based upon husbandry practices, which was valid in predicting attacks, and the other based upon distribution of biophysical factors, which was not valid in predicting attacks. In particular, the husbandry model had strong and stable validation statistics (i.e., less variation in significance values between k-fold groups). Our findings therefore highlight the importance of husbandry factors in managing depredation risk. However, it is possible that the strong influence of intense husbandry in our study area obscures the influence of biophysical factors that might also contribute to depredation risk, as shown in other studies (Treves et al. 2004).

Established biophysical factors contributing to wolf attacks

In the biophysical model, depredation probability was correlated with factors known to affect wolf or prey presence or the success of the predation event. Livestock depredation risk was positively correlated with elk density, consistent with findings by Treves et al. (2004) and Bradley and Pletscher (2005). This relationship might suggest that, at the scale of our model, wolves in southwest Alberta establish packs in areas where wild prey populations are high, and are preying on domestic cattle that also occur within these ranges. However, the mechanisms influencing whether wolves prey on domestic or wild prey are likely more complex than what we could model from yearly wild prey distribution. For example, prey migration (Seip 1992; Hebblewhite & Merrill 2007) and snow depth (Mech et al. 2001) may affect predator-prey relationships in ways not identifiable by this study. Studying wolf-elk-cattle interactions at finer spatial and temporal scales may improve the validity of our models.

We also found that livestock depredation risk was higher closer to quarter sections with buildings, which seemed to contradict Mech et al. (2000) and Bradley and Pletscher (2005). However, in our sparsely-populated study area livestock too may be grazed in areas with higher human population and habitation density (Bourn 1978). The fact that depredation risk was lower closer to roads confirms that wolves may be avoiding human features (Thiel 1985; Mech et al. 1988; Mladenoff et al. 1995; Mladenoff & Sickley 1998). The relationship of flat terrain to depredation suggests attacks are occurring where livestock and wolves are most likely to overlap on the landscape. Cattle favour flat terrain when grazing (Cook 1966; Roath and Krueger 1982), and wolves are known to travel

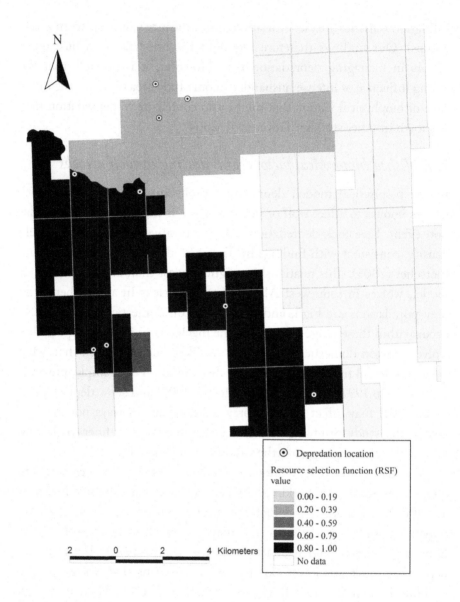

Figure 2.5.3. Map of a sample of ranches in the study area with their probability of livestock depredation by wolves as calculated using the husbandry Resource Selection Function (RSF). RSF values were calculated using the factors: wolf culling, yearling herds, frequency of monitoring in winter, frequency of monitoring in fall and frequency of monitoring in spring. Darker areas indicate higher depredation probability.

THE WORLD OF WOLVES

along easy routes, such as valley bottoms, as opposed to rugged and steep terrain (Ciucci et al. 2003). Finally, wolf habitat selection might explain our finding that depredation risk was higher close to forest cover. Forested areas allow wolves to avoid humans (Ciucci et al. 2003; Chavez & Gese 2006). In addition, liberal hunting and lethal control has limited wolves to forested areas in southwest Alberta (Alberta Fish and Wildlife Division 1991; Alberta Sustainable Resource Development 2002).

Predictive wolf attack model based on husbandry

We found a strong relationship between livestock depredation and wolf culling conducted on ranches, which was consistent with other studies that employed regression (Musiani et al. 2003; Shivik et al. 2003) and cross-correlation analysis (Musiani et al. 2005). These studies indicate that wolf control was corrective, not preventive, and therefore our findings cannot suggest increasing or decreasing wolf control levels to manage depredation. Culling of wolves has traditionally been a reactive measure to livestock depredation by wolves conducted by many individual ranchers and the government in southwest Alberta (Alberta Sustainable Resource Development 2002; Musiani et al. 2003); however, there is no evidence to indicate it is an effective long term solution, as depredation by wolves has been occurring in the study area for decades despite lethal control practices (Musiani et al. 2005).

Our finding that ranches that grazed herds of yearling cattle were more vulnerable to depredation than those that did not was consistent with other studies (Dorrance 1982; Bjorge 1983; Oakleaf et al. 2003; Bradley & Pletscher 2005). There may be behavioural characteristics of yearlings that make them more vulnerable to wolves (Bradley & Pletscher 2005). Also in our study, during interviews some ranchers described yearlings as having poor anti-predator behaviour (data not shown).

Supervision has previously been identified as an important husbandry method for preventing depredation (Bjorge 1983; Bjorge & Gunson 1985; Linnell et al. 1999), and our study largely supports this. During the winter and spring, ranches that supervised their livestock more frequently were less likely to be depredated. However, during the fall/summer those ranches that supervised livestock frequently were more likely to be depredated. It is possible that this relationship represents a response to depredation, similar to the relationship between depredation and wolf culling (see above). Conversely, the significant increase in supervision rate on all ranches during the winter and spring (Table 2.5.7) may contribute to lower attack rates on livestock at that time of year (see Musiani et al. 2005), as at this supervision level the relationship might become preventive.

APPLICATIONS FOR DEPREDATION MANAGEMENT

We found that a combination of husbandry factors was better at predicting livestock depredation by wolves in southwest Alberta, than biophysical factors. The added value of relying on husbandry factors is that these can be managed by people to prevent depredation, i.e., biophysical factors of the environment are not easily manageable. The majority of livestock operations in the study area in southwest Alberta are cattle operations; therefore it is important to note that the husbandry practices discussed in this chapter are not necessarily relevant to depredation of other livestock types such as sheep, for example.

Culling wolves might merely serve the role of a reactive measure (see this study's statistically positive relationship with depredation; Conner et al. 1998; Musiani et al. 2005), and therefore our study cannot provide recommendations on this. On the other hand, the positive relationship we found between depredation occurrence and presence of yearlings indicates that ranching operations that opt to graze yearling herds might be at risk. Depredation prevention measures could focus on protecting yearling herds. For example, yearlings could be grazed in areas outside of wolf range, in open, un-forested areas or in areas close to roads that wolves are known to dislike (Mech et al. 1988; Mladenoff et al. 1995; Mladenoff & Sickley 1998; Ciucci et al. 2003; Chavez & Gese 2006). Finally, our data indicate that increased monitoring of livestock might result in decreased risk in certain seasons (e.g., winter and spring). However, in other seasons (e.g., fall) monitoring might be ineffective as it potentially serves a reactive role. The intricate relationships between monitoring and depredation do not allow us to formulate specific recommendations regarding changes in livestock supervision. The correlative relationships (positive and negative) that we found between depredation and supervision suggest this warrants further investigation, as supervision appears to play a role in depredation.

Identifying factors that contribute to wolf attacks on livestock and using them to predict future occurrence of depredation is a useful management strategy (Treves et al. 2004). Depredation probability maps, such as those we produced for regions and for ranches in southwest Alberta (Fig. 2.5.2 and Fig. 2.5.3, respectively), may be useful to identify high risk areas where to focus prevention.

Recent findings by Chavez and Gese (2006) suggest that wolves do not actively hunt livestock in agricultural areas; however, they also believe that their wolves might not have developed a tendency to kill livestock yet. This implies that wolves might "switch" from hunting wild to domestic prey at some point. This switch might be due to a complex set of behavioural and environmental factors –for example, relative densities of wild and domestic prey. We speculate that the husbandry practices that played a role in wolf attack prevention in our study could also be used to prevent wolves from switching from wild prey to livestock.

In Alberta, ranchers are compensated 100% of the price of a killed animal for any confirmed livestock kills by wolves (Gunson 1992, Alberta Sustainable Resource Development 2002). In general, compensation programs might tend to become an additional form of subsidy, therefore encouraging a permanent state of conflict (Cozza et al. 1996). Thus, compensation programs should encourage preventive management (Poulle et al. 1997; Ciucci & Boitani 1998). In our interviews (T.M. et al., unpublished data), Alberta ranchers also indicated they felt current compensation was incomplete, as it does not consider the costs associated with preventive management (e.g., moving and/or supervising livestock). In addition to compensation, government policies should consider encouraging use of husbandry practices such as those that we found may prevent depredation.

ACKNOWLEDGMENTS

The authors would like to thank the ranching community of southwest Alberta for their involvement and collaboration in this study. We'd like to thank the Alberta Beef Producers, Alberta Sustainable Resource Development, Alberta Community Development, Alberta Conservation Association, the Calgary Zoo, Alberta Ecotrust, the Institute for Sustainable Energy, Environment and Economy, the Miistakis Institute for the Rockies and the University of Calgary for funding and support throughout the project. We would also especially like to thank Charles Mamo and Shelley Alexander for their valuable input and participation in the study.

LITERATURE CITED

Abrams, P.A. 1994. The fallacies of "ratio-dependent" predation. Ecology **75**:1842-1850.

Abrams, P.A. and L.R. Ginzburg. 2000. The nature of predation: prey dependent, ratio-dependent, or neither? Trends in Ecology & Evolution **15**:337-341.

Adams, J., L. P. Waits, and A. Beyer. 2001. Faecal sampling to detect the presence of coyotes and hybrids in the red wolf recovery zone. Canid Biology and Conservation Conference. Oxford, United Kingdom.

Adams, J., L. Waits, and B. Kelly. 2003a. Using faecal DNA sampling and GIS to monitor hybridization between red wolves (Canis rufus) and coyotes (Canis latrans). Molecular Ecology **12**:2175-2186.

Adams, J., J. Leonard, and L. P. Waits. 2003b. Genetic evidence for introgression of domestic dog mitochondrial DNA into the wild coyote population. Molecular Ecology **12**:541-546.

Aggarwal, R. K., J. Ramadevi, and L. Singh. 2003. Ancient origin and evolution of the Indian wolf: evidence from mitochondrial DNA typing of wolves from Trans-Himalayan region and peninsular India. Genome Biology **4**:6.

Aguilar, A., G. Roemer, S. Debenham, M. Binns, D. Garcelon, and R. K. Wayne. 2004. High MHC diversity maintained by balancing selection in an otherwise genetically monomorphic mammal. Proceedings of the National Academy of Sciences **101**:3490-3494.

Akcakaya, H. R., R. Arditi, and L. R. Ginzburg. 1995. Ratio-dependent predation: an abstraction that works. Ecology **76**:995-1004.

Alberta Conservation Association (ACA). 2002. 2001/02 annual report. ACA, Edmonton, Alberta.

Alberta Fish and Wildlife Division. 1991. Management plan for wolves in Alberta. Wildlife Management Planning Series Number 4, Publication No. T/237. Alberta Fish and Wildlife Division, Edmonton, Alberta.

Alberta Sustainable Resource Development. 2002. Wolves in Alberta. Alberta Sustainable Resource Development, Edmonton Alberta. Available from http://www.srd.gov.ab.ca/fishwildlife/wildlifeinalberta/wolvesalberta/default.aspx. (accessed August 2007).

Alberta Woodland Caribou Recovery Team. 2005. Alberta woodland caribou recovery plan, 2004/05 - 2013/14. Alberta species at risk recovery plan number 4. Alberta Sustainable Resource Development, Fish and Wildlife Division, Edmonton, Alberta.

Allen, D. and L. D. Mech. 1963. Wolves versus moose on Isle Royale. National Geographic **23**:200-219.

Allendorf, F. W., R. F. Leary; P. Spruell, and J. K. Wenburg. 2001. The problems with hybrids: setting conservation guidelines. Trends in Ecology and Evolution **16**:613-622.

American Society of Mammoligists (ASM). 1999. Mammalian predator control in the United States (resolution passed June 20-24, 1999). University of Washington, Seattle, Washington.

Andersen, R., J. D. C. Linnell, H. Hustad, and S. M. Brainerd, editors. 2003. Large predators and human communities in Norway: a guide to coexistence for the 21st century. Temahefte 25. Norwegian Institute for Nature Research, Trondheim, Norway.

Andersen, D. H., E. Fabbri, A. Santini, S. Paget, E. Cadieu, F. Galibert, C. Andre, and E. Randi. 2006. Characterization of 59 canine single nucleotide polymorphisms in the Italian wolf (Canis lupus) population. Molecular Ecology Notes **6**:1184-1187.

Anderson, D. R. and K. P. Burnham. 2002. Avoiding pitfalls when using information-theoretic methods. Journal of Wildlife Management **66**:912-918.

Andersone, Ž. 1998. Summer nutrition of the wolf (*Canis lupus*) in the Slītere Nature Reserve, Latvia. Proceedings of the Latvian Academy of Sciences, Section B **52**:79-80.

Andersone, Ž. 1999. Beaver: A new prey of wolves in Latvia? Comparison of winter and summer diet of, *Canis lupus*, Linnaeus, 1758. Pages 103-108 in P. Busher, and R. Dzięciołowski, editors. Beaver protection, management, and utilization in Europe and North America. Kluwer Academic and Plenum Publishers, New York, New York.

Andersone, Ž. 2003. Wolves in Latvia: past and present. WolfPrint **16**:13-14.

Andersone Ž. and J. Ozoliņš. 2004. Food habits of wolves, *Canis lupus*, in Latvia. Acta Theriologica **49**:357-367.

Andersone, Ž., L. Balčiauskas, and H. Valdmann. 2001. Human-wolf conflicts in the East Baltic – past, present and future. Pages 196-199 in R. Field, R. J. Warren, H. Okarma, and P. Sievert, editors. Wildlife, land and people: priorities for the 21st century: proceedings of the 2nd International Wildlife Management Congress. The Wildlife Society, Bethesda, Maryland.

Andersone, Ž., V. Lucchini, E. Randi, and J. Ozoliņš. 2002. Hybridisation between wolves and dogs in Latvia as documented using mitochondrial and microsatellite DNA markers. Mammalian Biology 67:79-90.

Andersone-Lilley, Ž. and J. Ozoliņš. 2005. Game mammals in Latvia: present status and future prospects. Scottish Forestry 59:13-18.

Andersson, T., A. Bjärvall, M. and Blomberg. 1977. Inställningen till varg i Sverige - en intervjuundersökning. SNV PM 850. Swedish Environmental Protection Agency, Stockholm, Sweden.

Andrén, H., T. Ebenhard, H. Ellegren, N. Ryman, and B.-E, Sæther. 1999. Vad är en livskraftig population? Rapport från arbetsgruppen för rovdjursutredningen. Pages 65–97 in S. Ekström, editor. Sammanhållen rovdjurspolitik: bilagor, Statens Offentliga Utredningar, vol. 146.

Anthony, R. G., Estes, J. A., Ricca, M. A., Miles, A. K., and E. D. Forsman. 2008. Bald eagles and sea otters in the Aleutian Archipelago: indirect effects of trophic cascades. Ecology 89: 2725-35.

Arcese, P., and A. R. E. Sinclair. 1997. The role of protected areas as ecological baselines. Journal of Wildlife Management 61:587-602.

Arino, A. and S. L. Pimm. 1995. On the nature of population extremes. Evolutionary Ecology 9:429-443.

Arnold, M. L. 1997. Natural hybridization and evolution. Oxford University Press, New York, New York.

Arons, C. D., and W. J. Shoemaker. 1992. The distribution of catecholamines and B-endorphins in the brains of three behaviorally distinct breeds of dogs and their F1 hybrids. Brain Research 594:31-39.

Aronson, Å., P. Wabakken, H. Sand, O. K. Steinset, and I. Kojola. 1999. Varg i Skandinavien: statusrapport för vintern 1998-99. Høgskolen i Hedmark, Rapport nr. 18.

Aspi, J., E. Roininen, M. Ruokonen, I. Kojola, and C. Vilà. 2006. Genetic diversity, population structure, effective population size and demographic history of the Finnish wolf population. Molecular Ecology 15:1561–1576.

Avise, J. C. 1994. Molecular markers, natural history and evolution. Chapman and Hall, New York.

Avise, J. C. 2000. Phylogeography: the history and formation of species. Harvard University Press, Cambridge, Massachusetts.

Baker, B.W., and E. F. Hill. 2003. Beaver: Castor canadensis. Pages 288-310 in G. A. Feldhamer, B. C. Thompson, and J. A. Chapman, editors. Wild mammals of North America: biology, management, and conservation. Johns Hopkins University Press, Baltimore, Maryland.

Balčiauskas, L. 2002. Possibilities of the development of the wolf population management plan for Lithuania. Acta Zoologica Lituanica 12:410-418.

Balčiauskas, L., L. Balčiauskienė, and H. Volodka. 2002. Preliminary assessment of damage caused by the wolf in Lithuania. Acta Zoologica Lituanica 12:419–427.

Ballard, W. B., and V. Van Ballenberghe. 1998. Moose-predator relationships: research and management needs. Alces 34:91-105.

Ballard, W. B., J. S. Whitman, and C. L. Gardner. 1987. Ecology of an exploited wolf population in south-central Alaska. Wildlife Monographs 98:1-54.

Ballard, W. B., L.A. Ayres, P. R. Krausman, D. J. Reed, and S. G. Fancy. 1997. Ecology of wolves in relation to a migratory caribou herd in northwest Alaska. Wildlife Monographs 135:1-47.

Ballard, W. B., L. N. Carbyn, and D. W. Smith. 2003. Wolf interactions with non-prey. Pages 259-271 in L. D. Mech and L. Boitani, editors. Wolves: behavior, ecology and conservation. University of Chicago Press, Chicago, Illinois.

Banerjee, I. and B. C. McDonald. 1975. Nature of esker sedimentation. Glaciofluvial and glaciolacustrine sedimentation. Pages 132-154 in A. V. Jopling and B. C. McDonald, editors. Tulsa, Society of Economic Paleontologists and Mineralogists, Special Publication No. 23.

Bangs, E. E., and S. H. Fritts. 1996. Reintroducing the gray wolf to central Idaho and Yellowstone National Park. Wildlife Society Bulletin 24:402-412.

Bangs, E. E. and J. Shivik. 2001. Managing wolf conflict with livestock in the northwestern United States. Carnivore Damage prevention News 3:2-5.

Bangs, E. E., S. H. Fritts, J. A. Fontaine, D. W. Smith, K. M. Murphy, C. M. Mack and C. C. Niemeyer. 1998. Status of the gray wolf restoration in Montana, Idaho and Wyoming. Wildlife Society Bulletin 26:785-798.

Barber-Meyer, S.M. 2006. Elk calf mortality following wolf restoration to Yellowstone National Park. Dissertation. University of Minnesota.

Barnes, I., P. Matheus, B. Shapiro, D. Jensen, and A. Cooper. 2002. Dynamics of pleistocene population extinctions in Beringian brown bears. Science 295:2267–2270.

Bascompte, J., C. J. Melian, and E. Sala. 2005. Interaction strength combinations and the overfishing of a marine food web. Proceedings of the National Academy of Sciences of the United States of America 102:5443-5447.

Basey, J.M. 1999. Foraging of beaver (Castor canadensis), plant secondary compounds, and management concerns. Pages 129-146 in P. E. Busher, and R. M. Dzieciolowski, editors. Beaver protection, management, and utilization in Europe and North America. Kluwer Academic, New York, New York.

Beaumont, M. A. and B. Rannala. 2004. The Bayesian revolution in genetics. Nature Reviews Genetics 5:251-261.

Bennett, P. 1999. Understanding responses to risk: some basic findings. Pages 3-19 in P. Bennett and K. Calman, editors. Risk communication and public health. Oxford University Press, New York, New York.

Bensch, S., H. Andrén, B. Hansson, H. C. Pedersen, H. Sand, D. Sejberg, P. Wabakken, M. Åkesson, and O. Liberg. 2006. Selection for heterozygosity gives hope to a wild population of inbred wolves. PLoS One 1:e72.

Berger J., and D. W. Smith. 2005. Restoring functionality in Yellowstone with recovering carnivores: gains and uncertainties. Pages 100-108 in J. C. Ray, K. H. Redford, R. S. Steneck, and J. Berger, editors. Large carnivores and the conservation of biodiversity. Island Press, Washington, D.C.

Bergerud, A. T. 1985. Antipredator strategies of caribou: dispersion along shorelines. Canadian Journal of Zoology 63:1324–1329.

Bergerud, A. T. 1992. Rareness as an antipredator strategy to reduce predation risk for moose and caribou. Pages 1009–1021 in D. R. McCullough and R. H. Barrett, editors. Wildlife 2001: populations. Elsevier Science Publishers, London, United Kingdom.

Bergerud, A. T., and R. E. Page. 1987. Displacement and dispersion of parturient caribou at calving as antipredator tactics. Canadian Journal of Zoology 65:1597–1606.

Bergerud, A. T., and J. P. Elliott. 1998. Wolf predation in a multiple-ungulate system in northern British Columbia. Canadian Journal of Zoology 64:1515-1529.

Bergerud, A. T., H. E. Butler, and D. R. Miller. 1984. Antipredator tactics of calving caribou: dispersion in mountains. Canadian Journal of Zoology 62:1566–1575.

Berggren K. T., and J. M. Seddon 2005. MHC promoter polymorphism in grey wolves and domestic dogs. Immunogenetics 57:267-272.

Bergman, E .J., R. A. Garrott, S. Creel, J. J. Borkowski, and R. M. Jaffe. 2006. Assessment of prey vulnerability through analysis of wolf movements and kill sites. Ecological Applications 16:273-284.

Bergström, R., H. Jernelid, S. Lavsund, K. Lundberg, and K. Wallin. 1995. Älgtäthet – betestryck – fodertillgång – skogstillstånd – skadenivåer – skaderisker. Slutrapport från projektet Balanserad älgstam ("Moose densities – browsing and damage". Final report from the research project "Balanced moose populations"). (In Swedish).

Berlocher, S. H. and J. L. Feder. 2002. Sympatric speciation in phytophagous insects: moving beyond controversy. Annual Review of Entomology 47:773-815.

Beschta, R. L. 2003. Cottonwoods, elk, and wolves in the Lamar valley of Yellowstone National Park. Ecological Applications 13:1295-1309.

Beverly Qamanirjuaq Management Board. 1999. Protecting Beverly and Qamanirjuaq caribou and caribou range. Beverly Qamanirjuaq Management Board, Northwest Territories. Available from http://www.arctic-caribou.com/bevreport.html (accessed October 2007).

Beyer, H. 2006. Wolves, elk, and willow on Yellowstone's northern range. University of Alberta. Msc. Thesis.

Bibikov, D. I. 1985. The wolf: history, systematics, morphology, ecology. Nauka Publishers, Moscow, Russia.

Bienen, L., and G. Tabor. 2006. Applying an ecosystem approach to brucellosis control: can an old conflict between wildlife and agriculture be successfully managed? Frontiers in Ecology and the Environment 4:319-327.

Bilyeu, D. 2006. Effects of elk browsing and water table on willow growth and physiology: implications for willow restoration in Yellowstone National Park. Colorado State University. Dissertation.

Bjarvell, A., and E. Isakson. 1982. Winter ecology of a pack of three wolves in Northern Sweden. Paqes 146-157 in F. H. Harrington and P. C. Paquet, editors. Wolves of the world, perspectives of behavior, ecology, and conservation. Noyes Publications, Park Ridge, New Jersey, USA.

Bjerke, T., O. Reitan, and S. R. Kellert. 1998. Attitudes towards wolves in SE Norway. Society and Natural Resources 11:169-178.

Bjorge, R. R. 1983. Mortality of cattle on two types of grazing areas in northwestern Alberta. Journal of Range Management 36:20-21.

Bjorge, R .R. and J. R. Gunson. 1985. Evaluation of wolf control to reduce cattle predation in Alberta. Journal of Range Management 38:483-487

Bobek B., K. Perzanowski, and W. Ijmietana. 1992. The influence of snow cover on the patterns of selection within red deer population by wolves in Bieszczady Mountains, Poland. Pages 341-348 in B. Bobek, K. Perzanowski and W. Regelin, editors. Global trends in wildlife management: transactions of the 18th IUGB congress, Kraków 1987. Ijwiat Press, Kraków-Warszawa, Poland.

Boertje, R. D., P. Valkenburg, and M. E. McNay. 1996. Increases in moose, caribou, and wolves following wolf control in Alaska. Journal of Wildlife Management 60:474-489.

Boitani, L. 1982. Wolf management in intensively used areas of Italy. Pages 158-172 in F. H. Harrington & P. C. Paquet, editors. Wolves of the world: Perspectives of behaviour, ecology, and conservation. Noyes Publications, Park Ridge, New York.

Boitani, L. 2003. Wolf conservation and recovery. Pages 317-340 in L. D. Mech & L. Boitani, editors, Wolves: behavior, ecology and conservation. The University of Chicago Press, Chicago, Illinois.

Boitani, L., F. Francisci, P. Ciucci, and G. Andreoli. 1995. Population biology and ecology of feral dogs in central Italy. Pages 217-244 in J. Serpell, editor. The domestic dog: its evolution, behavior, and interactions with people. Cambridge University Press. Cambridge, United Kingdom.

Borer, E. T., B. S. Halpern, and E. W. Seablooma, E.W. 2006. Asymmetry in community regulation: effects of predators and productivity. Ecology **87**: 2813–2820.

Botkin, D. B. 1992. Discordant harmonies: a new ecology for the twenty-first century. Oxford University Press, Oxford, United Kingdom.

Bourn, D. 1978. Cattle, rainfall and tsetse in Africa. Journal of Arid Environments **1**:49-61.

Boutin, S. 1992. Predation and moose population dynamics: a critique. Journal of Wildlife Management **56**:116-127.

Box, G. E. P., G. M. Jenkins, and G. C. Reinsel. 1994. Time series analysis, forecasting and control. Prentice Hall, Englewood Cliffs, New Jersey.

Boyce, M. S. 1998. Ecological-process management and ungulates: Yellowstone's conservation paradigm. Wildlife Society Bulletin **26**:391-398.

Boyce, M. S. 2000. Modeling predator-prey dynamics. Pages 253-287 in L. Boitani and T. Fuller, editors. Research techniques in animal ecology. Columbia University Press, New York, New York.

Boyce, M. S. 2005. Wolves are Consummate Predators. The Quarterly Review of Biology **80**:87–92.

Boyce, M. S, and E. M. Anderson. 1999. Evaluating the role of carnivores in the Greater Yellowstone Ecosystem. Pages 265-284 in T. K. Clark, A. P. Curlee, S. C. Minta, and P. M. Kareiva, editors. Carnivores in Ecosystems: The Yellowstone Experience. Yale University Press, New Haven, Connecticut.

Boyce, M. S. and L. L. McDonald. 1999. Relating populations to habitats using resource selection functions. Trends in Ecology and Evolution **17**:268-272.

Boyce, M. S., P. R. Vernier, S. E. Nielsen, and F. K. A. Schmiegelow. 2002. Evaluating resource selection functions. Ecological Modeling **157**:281-300.

Bradley, E. H. and D. H. Pletscher. 2005. Assessing factors related to wolf depredation of cattle in fenced pastures in Montana and Idaho. Wildlife Society Bulletin **33**:1256–1265.

Brainerd, S.C., Andren, H., Bangs, E.E., Bradley, E.H., Fontaine, J.A., Hall, W., Iliopoulos, Y., Jimenez, M.D., Jozwiak, E.A., Liberg, O., Mack, C.M., Meier, T.J., Niemeyer, C.C., Pedersen, H.C., Sand, H., Schultz, R.N., Smith, D.W., Wabakken, P. and Wydeven, A.P. 2008. The effects of breeder loss on wolves. The Journal of Wildlife Management **72**: 89-98.

Breitenmoser, U. 1998. Large predators in the Alps: the fall and rise of man's competitor. Biological Conservation **83**:279-289.

Brewster, W. G., and S. H. Fritts. 1995. Taxonomy and genetics of the gray wolf in western North America: a review. Pages 353-373 in L. N. Carbyn, S. H. Fritts, and D. R. Seip, editors. Ecology and conservation of wolves in a changing world. Canadian Circumpolar Institute, Edmonton, Alberta.

Brown, J. S. 1988. Patch use of an indicator of habitat preference, predation risk, and competition. Behavioral Ecology and Sociobiology **22**:37–47.

Brown, J. S. 1999. Vigilance, patch use and habitat selection: foraging under predation risk. Evolutionary Ecology Research **1**:49–71.

Bruford, M. W. and R. K. Wayne. 1993. Microsatellites and their application to population genetic studies. Current Biology **3**:939-943.

Bruskotter, J. T., R. H. Schmidt, and T. L. Teel. 2007. Are attitudes toward wolves changing? A case study in Utah. Biological Conservation **139**:211-218.

Burnham, K. P., and D. R. Anderson. 1998. Model selection and inference. Springer, New York, New York.

Byrd, D. M., and C. R. Cothern. 2000. Introduction to Risk Analysis: A Systematic Approach to Science-Based Decision Making. Government Institutes, Lanham, Maryland.

Calef, G. W. 1978. Population status of caribou in the Northwest Territories. Pages 9-16 in D. R. Klein and R. G. White, editors. Parameters of caribou population ecology in Alaska. Proceedings of the Symposiums and

Workshop, Biological Papers of the University of Alaska, Special Report No. 3. University of Alaska, Fairbanks, Alaska.

Callaghan, C. 2002. The ecology of gray wolf (*Canis lupus*) habitat use, survival, and persistence in the Central Rocky Mountains, Canada. Department of Zoology, University of Guelph. Dissertation.

Callicott, J. B. 1999. Beyond the land ethic: more essays in environmental philosophy. SUNY Press, Albany, New York.

Carbyn, L. N. 1982. Coyote population fluctuations and spatial distribution in relation to wolf territories in Riding Mountain National Park, Manitoba. Canadian Field-Naturalist **96**:176-183.

Carbyn, L. N. 1983. Wolf predation on elk in Riding Mountain National Park, Manitoba. Journal of Wildlife Management **47**:963-976.

Carmichael, L. E., J. A. Nagy, N. C. Larter, and C. Strobeck. 2001. Prey specialization may influence patterns of gene flow of wolves of the Canadian Northwest. Molecular Ecology **10**:2787–2798.

Carmichael, L. E., J. Krizan, J. A. Nagy, E. Fuglei, M. Dumond, D. Johnson, A. Veitch, D. Berteaux, and C. Strobeck. 2007. Historical and ecological determinants of genetic structure in arctic canids. Molecular Ecology **16**:3466-3483.

Caro, T., and C. Stoner. 2003. The potential for interspecific competition among African carnivores. Biological Conservation **110**:67-75.

Carpenter, S. R., J. M. Kitchell, and J. R. Hodgson. 1985. Cascading trophic interactions and lake productivity. Bioscience **35**:634-639.

Cartwright, N. 1989. Nature's capacities and their measurement. Clarendon, Oxford, United Kingdom.

Cederlund, G., and G. Markgren. 1987. The development of the Swedish moose population 1970-1983. Swedish Wildlife Research Supplement **1**:55-62.

Cederlund, G. N., and H. K.G. Sand. 1991. Population dynamics and yield of a moose population without predators. Alces **27**:31–40.

Chartier, J. and S. Gabler. 2001. Theory and application for the Canadian Food Inspection Agency: risk communication and government. Canadian Food Inspection Agency, Ottawa, Ontario. Available from http://www.

inspection.gc.ca/english /corpaffr/publications/riscomm/riscomme.shtml (accessed October 2007).

Chavez, A. S. and E. M. Gese. 2006. Landscape use and movements of wolves in relation to livestock in a wildland–agriculture matrix. Journal of Wildlife Management **70**:1079–1086.

Chess, C. 2001. Organizational theory and the stages of risk communication. Risk Analysis **21**:179-188.

Chiarelli, A. B. 1975. The chromosomes of the Canidae. Pages 40-53 in M. W. Fox, editor. The wild canids. Van Nostrand Reinhold, New York, New York.

Ciucci, P. and L. Boitani. 1998. Wolf and dog depredation on livestock in central Italy. Wildlife Society Bulletin **26**:504-514.

Ciucci, P., L. Boitani, F. Francisci, and G. Andreoli. 1997. Home range, activity and movements of a wolf pack in central Italy. Journal of Zoology, London **243**:803-819.

Ciucci, P., M. Masi, and L. Boitani. 2003. Winter habitat and travel route selection by wolves in the northern Apennines, Italy. Ecography **26**:223-235.

Clark, J. 2002. Southern foothill-mountain elk survey (March 2002): wildlife management unit's 303, 304, 305, 306, 308 and 402. Government of Alberta, Sustainable Resource Development, Fish and Wildlife Division, Blairmore, Alberta.

Cluff, H. D. and D. L. Murray. 1995. Review of wolf control methods in North America. Pages 491-504 in L. N. Carbyn, S. H. Fritts, and D. R. Seip, editors. Ecology and conservation of wolves in a changing world. Canadian Circumpolar Institute, Occasional Publication No. 35, Edmonton, Alberta, Canada.

Cluff, H. D., L. R. Walton, and P. C. Paquet. 2002. Movements and habitat use of wolves denning in the central Arctic, Northwest Territories and Nunavut, Canada. Final report to the West Kitikmeot Slave Study Society, Yellowknife, Northwest Territories, Canada.

Cole, G. F. 1971. An ecological rationale for the natural or artificial regulation of ungulates in Parks. Transaction of the North American Wildlife Conference **36**:417-425.

Conko, G. 2003. Safety, risk and the precautionary principle: rethinking precautionary approaches to the regulation of transgenic plants. Transgenic Research **12**: 639-647.

Conner, M. M., M. M. Jaeger, J. T. Weller, and D. R. McCullough. 1998. Effect of coyote removal on sheep depredation in northern California. Journal of Wildlife Management **62**:690-699.

Cook, C. W. 1966. Factors affecting utilization of mountain slopes by cattle. Journal of Range Management **19**:200-204.

Coppinger, R., and L. Coppinger. 1995. Interactions between livestock guarding dogs and wolves. Pages 523-526 in L. N. Carbyn, S. H. Fritts, and D. R Seip, editors. Ecology and conservation of wolves in a changing world. Occasional Publication No. 35. Canadian Circumpolar Institute, Edmonton, Alberta.

Coppinger, R., and R. Schneider. 1995. Evolution of the working dog. Pages 21-47 in J. Serpell, editor. The domestic dog: its evolution, behavior, and interactions with people. Cambridge University Press, Cambridge, United Kingdom.

Coppinger, R., and L. Coppinger. 2001. Dogs: a new understanding of canine origin, behavior and evolution. Scribner, New York, New York.

Coulon A., J. F. Cosson, J. M. Angibault, B. Cargnelutti, M. Galan, N. Morellet, E. Petit, S. Aulagnier, A. J. M. Hewison. 2004. Landscape connectivity influences gene flow in a roe deer population inhabiting a fragmented landscape: an individual-based approach. Molecular Ecology **13**:2841-2850.

Cowan, S. T. 1971. Sense and nonsense in bacterial taxonomy. Journal of General Microbiology **67**:1-8.

Cozza, K., R. Fico, M. L. Battistini, and E. Rogers. 1996. The damage-conservation interface illustrated by predation on domestic livestock in central Italy. Biological Conservation **78**:329-336.

Crabtree, R. L., and J. Sheldon. 1999. The ecological role of coyotes on Yellowstone's northern range. Yellowstone Science **7**:15-23.

Crandall, K. A., O. R. Bininda-Emonds, G. M. Mace, and R. K. Wayne. 2000. Considering evolutionary processes in conservation biology. Trends in Ecology and Evolution **15**:290-295.

Creel, S. and D.Christianson. 2008. Relationships between direct predation and risk effects. Trends in Ecology and Evolution **23**:194-201.

Creel, S., and J. A. Winnie. 2005. Responses of elk herd size to fine-scale spatial and temporal variation in the risk of predation by wolves. Animal Behavior **69**:1181-1189.

Creel, S., G. Spong, and N. Creel. 2001. Interspecific competition and the population biology of extinction-prone carnivores. Pages 35-60 in J. L. Gittleman, S. M. Funk, D. MacDonald, and R. K. Wayne, editors. Carnivore Conservation. Cambridge University Press, Cambridge, United Kingdom.

Creel S., G. Spong, J. L. Sands, J. Rotella, J. Ziegle, L. Joe, K. M. Murphy, and D. Smith. 2003. Population size estimation in Yellowstone wolves with error-prone noninvasive microsatellite genotypes. Molecular Ecology **12**:2003-2009.

Creel, S., D. Christianson, S. Liley, and J. A. Winnie, Jr. 2007. Predation risk affects reproductive physiology and demography of elk. Science **315**:960.

Cushman, S. A. 2006. Effects of habitat loss and fragmentation on amphibians: a review and prospectus. Biological Conservation **128**:231–240.

Czaplewski, R. L., D. M. Crowe, and L. L. McDonald. 1983. Sample sizes and confidence intervals for wildlife population ratios. Wildlife Society Bulletin **11**:121-128.

Dale, B. W., L. G. Adams, R. T. Bowyer. 1995. Winter wolf predation in a multiple ungulate prey system, Gates of the Arctic National Park, Alaska. Pages 223-230 in L. N. Carbyn, S. H. Fritts, and D. R. Seip, editors. Ecology and conservation of wolves in a changing world. Canadian Circumpolar Institute, Edmonton, Alberta.

Darimont, C. T., P. C. Paquet, and T. E. Reimchen. 2007. Stable isotopic niche predicts fitness in a wolf-deer system. Biological Journal of the Linnaean Society **90**:125-137.

Darwin, C. 1859. Letter to Asa Gray reprinted. Journal of the Proceedings of the Linnean Society (Zoology) **3**:50-53.

Darwin, C. 1903. The origin of species. Facsimile of first edition (1859-1860). Watts, London, United Kingdom.

Decker, D. J., C. C. Krueger, R. A. Baer Jr., B. A. Knuth, and M. E. Richmond. 1996. From clients to stakeholders: a philosophical shift for fish and wildlife management. Human Dimensions of Wildlife 1:70-82.

deFur, P. L., and M. Kaszuba. 2002. Implementing the precautionary principle. Science of the Total Environment 288:155-165.

Dennis, C. 2006. Conservation at a distance: A gentle way to age. Nature 442:507-508.

Despain, D. 1990. Yellowstone vegetation: consequences of environment and history in a natural setting. Roberts Rinehart Inc., Boulder, Colorado.

Despain, D. 2005. Alternative hypothesis for willow growth. Proceedings of the 8th biennial scientific conference on the greater Yellowstone ecosystem. Yellowstone National Park, Wyoming.

Doolittle, W. F. 2005. Some thoughts on the tree of life. The Harvey Lectures, Series 99:111-128. John Wiley, New York, New York.

Dorrance, M. J. 1982. Predation losses of cattle in Alberta. Journal of Range Management 35:690-692.

Drummond, A. J., A. Rambaut, B. Shapiro, and O. G. Pybus. 2005. Bayesian Coalescent Inference of Past Population Dynamics from Molecular Sequences. Molecular Biology and Evolution 22:1185-1192.

Duke, D. L., M. Hebblewhite, P. C. Paquet, C. Callaghan, and M. Percy. 2001. Restoration of a large carnivore corridor in Banff National Park, Alberta. Pages 261-276 in D. S. Maeher, R. F. Noss, and J. L. Larkin, editors. Large mammal restoration, Island Press, Washington, D.C.

Dyer, S. J., J. P. O'Neil, S. M. Wasel, and S. Boutin. 2001. Avoidance of industrial development by woodland caribou. Journal of Wildlife Management 65:531-542.

Ebenhard, T. 2000. Population viability analysis in endangered species management: the wolf, otter and peregrine falcon in Sweden. Ecological Bulletin 48:143-163.

Edwards, S. V., and P. W. Hedrick. 1998. Evolution and ecology of MHC molecules: from genomics to sexual selection. Trends in Ecology and Evolution 13:305-311.

Ekman, H., N. Hermansson, J. O. Pettersson, J. Rülker, M. Steen, and F. Stålfält. 1992 Älgen — djuret, skötseln och jakten. Svenska Jägareförbundet, Stockholm, Sweden.

Environmental Systems Research Institute (ESRI). 1999. ArcView 3.2. Environmental Systems Research Institute, Redlands, California.

Ericsson, G. and T. A. Heberlein. 2003. Attitudes of hunters, locals and the general public in Sweden now that the wolves are back. Biological Conservation 111:149–159.

Espuno, N., B. Lequette, M.-L. Poulle, P. Migot, and J-D. Lebreton. 2004. Heterogeneous response to preventive sheep husbandry during wolf recolonization of the French Alps. Wildlife Society Bulletin 32:1195-1208.

Estes, J. A., and D. O. Duggins. 1995. Sea otters and kelp forests in Alaska: generality and variation in a community ecological paradigm. Ecological Monographs 65:75-100.

Estes, J. A., E. M. Danner, D. F. Doak, B. Konar, A. M. Springer, P. D. Steinberg, M. T. Tinker, and T. M. Williams. 2004. Complex trophic interactions in kelp forest ecosystems. Bulletin of Marine Science 74:621-638.

Excoffier, L., and G. Heckel. 2006. Computer programs for population genetics data analysis: a survival guide. Nature Reviews Genetics 7: 745–758.

Fabbri, E., V. Lucchini, A. Santini, R. Caniglia, P. Taberlet, L. Fumagalli, J.M. Weber, F. Marucco, L. Boitani, and E. Randi. 2007. From the Apennines to the Alps: Colonization genetics of the naturally expanding Italian wolf (*Canis lupus*) population. Molecular Ecology 16:1661-1671.

Falush, D., M. Stephens and J. K. Pritchard. 2003. Inference of population structure using multilocus genotype data: Linked loci and correlated allele frequencies. Genetics 164:1567-1587.

Farnes, P., C. Heydon, and K. Hansen. 1999. Snowpack distribution across Yellowstone National Park. Final Project Report to Yellowstone National Park, Cooperative Agreement Number CA 1268-1-9017. Bozeman, Montana.

Favre, L., F. Balloux, J. Goudet, and N. Perrin. 1997. Female-biased dispersal in the monogamous mammal *Crocidura russula*: evidence from field data and microsatellite patterns. Proceedings of the Royal Society of London B **264**:127-132.

Federal Environmental Agency, German Remote Sensing Data Center of the German Aerospace Center. 2004. CORINE Land Cover Data. Available from: http://www.corine.dfd.dlr.de/intro_en.html (accessed January 2008).

Fedosenko, A. K., V .A. Zhiryakov, and Y. A. Grachev. 1978. Some data on the ecology and behaviour of wolves in the northern Tien-shan and Dzhungara Alatau. Byulleten Moskovskogo Obshchestva Ispytatelei Prirody, Otdel Biologicheski 83:5-18. (In Russian with English summary)

Felsenstein, J. 1971. The rate of loss of multiple alleles in finite haploid populations. Theoretical Population Biology 2:391-403.

Ferrell, R. E., D. C. Morizot, J. Horn, and C. J. Carley. 1978. Biochemical markers in species endangered by introgression: the red wolf. Biochemical Genetics **18**:39-49.

Ferrier, S., M. Drielsma, G. Manion, and G. Watson. 2002. Extended statistical approaches to modelling spatial pattern in biodiversity: the north-east New South Wales experience: I, species-level modelling. Biodiversity and Conservation **11**:2275-2307.

Filonov, K. P. 1989. Ungulates and large predators in wildlife reserves. Izdatelstvo Nauka, Moskva, Russia. [In Russian]

Flagstad, C., W. O. Walker, C. Vilà , A. K. Sundqvist, B. Fernholm, A. K. Hufthammer, O. Wiig, I. Koyola, and H. Ellegren. 2003. Two centuries of the Scandinavian wolf population: patterns of genetic variability and migration during an era of dramatic decline. Molecular Ecology **12**:869–880.

Flather, C. H., S. J. Brady, and M. S. Knowles. 1999. Wildlife resource trends in the United States: a technical document supporting the 2000 RPA Assessment. General Technical Report RMRSGTR-33. U.S. Department of Agriculture, Forest Service, Fort Collins, Colorado.

Foley, P. 1994. Predicting extinction times from environmental stochasticity and carrying capacity. Conservation Biology **8**:124-137.

Fonseca, F. P. 1990. O lobo (*Canis lupus signatus* Cabrera, 1907) em Portugal: Problemática da sua conservação. Ph.D. dissertation, University of Lisboa, Portugal.

Food and Agriculture Organisation of the United Nations (FAO). 2000. Global Forest Resources Assessment 2000. FAO, Rome, Italy. Available from http://www.fao.org/DOCREP/004/Y1997E/y1997e00.htm#Contents (accessed October 2007).

Forbes, S. H., and D. K. Boyd. 1997. Genetic structure and migration in native and reintroduced Rocky Mountain wolf populations. Conservation Biology 11:1226-1234.

Formozov, A. N. 1946. Snow cover as an integral factor of the environment and its importance in the ecology of mammals and birds. Materials for fauna and flora of the USSR, Zoological Section, New Series No. 5. Moscow Society of Naturalists, Moscow, Russia. (Translated by Prychodko, W. and W. O. Pruitt. 1963. University of Alberta Boreal Institue Occasional Paper No. 1.)

Fortin, D., H. Beyer, M. S. Boyce, D. W. Smith, T. Duchesne, and J. S. Mao. 2005. Wolves influence elk movements: behavior shapes a trophic cascade in Yellowstone National Park. Ecology 86:1320-1330.

Fowler, N. L., R. D. Overath, and C. M. Pease. 2006. Detection of density dependence requires density manipulations and calculation of lambda. Ecology 87:655-664.

Frank, D. A. 1998. Ungulate regulation of ecosystem processes in Yellowstone national park: direct and feedback effects. Wildlife Society Bulletin 26:410-418.

Franzmann, A. W., and C.C. Schwartz. 1998. Ecology and management of the North American moose. Smithsonian Institutional Press, London, United Kingdom.

Fredrickson, R. J., and P. W. Hedrick. 2006. Dynamics of hybridization and introgression in red wolves and coyotes. Conservation Biology 20:1272-1283.

Freeman, M. M. R. 1976. Inuit land use and occupancy project: volume 1, land use and occupancy. Indian and Northern Affairs Publication No. QS8054-001-EE-A1. Department of Indian and Northern Affairs, Government of Canada, Ottawa, Ontario.

Fretwell, S. D. 1987. Food chain dynamics: the central theory of ecology? Oikos **50**:291-301.

Fritts, S. H., W. J. Paul, L. D. Mech, and D. P. Scott. 1992. Trends and management of wolf-livestock conflicts in Minnesota. United States Fish and Wildlife Service Resource Publication No. 181. United States Fish and Wildlife Service, Washington, D.C.

Fritts, S. H., R. O. Stephenson, R. D. Hayes, and L. Boitani. 2003. Wolves and Humans. Pages 289-316 in L. D. Mech & L. Boitani, editors. Wolves: behavior, ecology and conservation. University of Chicago Press, Chicago, Illinois.

Fryxell, J. M., and P. Lundberg. 1997. Individual behavior and community dynamics. Chapman and Hall, New York, New York.

Fuller, T. K. 1983. Characteristics of gray wolf, *Canis lupus*, den and rendezvous sites in southcentral Alaska. Canadian Field-Naturalist **97**:299-302.

Fuller, T. K. 1989a. Population dynamics of wolves in north-central Minnesota. Wildlife Monographs **105**:1-41.

Fuller, T. K. 1989b. Denning behaviour of wolves in north-central Minnesota. American Midland Naturalist **121**:184-188.

Fuller, T. K. 1991a. Effect of snow depth on wolf activity and prey selection in north central Minnesota. Canadian Journal of Zoology **69**:283-287.

Fuller, T. K. 1991b. Erratum: effect of snow depth on wolf activity and prey selection in north central Minnesota. Canadian Journal of Zoology **69**:821.

Fuller, T. K., and L. B. Keith. 1980. Wolf population dynamics and prey relationships in northeastern Alberta. Journal of Wildlife Management **44**:583–601.

Fuller, T. K., and D. L. Murray. 1998. Biological and logistical explanations of variation in wolf population density. Animal Conservation **1**:153-157.

Fuller, T. K., L. D. Mech, and J. F. Cochrane. 2003. Wolf population dynamics. Pages 161-191 in L. D. Mech and L. Boitani, editors. Wolves: behavior, ecology, and conservation. University of Chicago Press, Chicago, Illinois.

Garrott, R. A., J. A. Gude, E. J. Bergmann, C. Gower, P. J. White, and K. L. Hamlin. 2005. Generalizing wolf effects across the greater Yellowstone area: a cautionary note. Wildlife Society Bulletin **33**:1245-1255.

Gasaway, W. C., R. D. Boertje, D. V. Grangaard, D. G. Kellyhouse, R. O. Stephenson, and D. G. Larsen. 1992. The role of predation in limiting moose at low densities in Alaska and Yukon and implications for conservation. Wildlife Monographs 120:1-59.

Gates, C. C., B. Stelfox, T. Muhly, T. Chowns, and R. J. Hudson. 2005. The ecology of bison movement and distribution in and beyond Yellowstone National Park: a critical review with implications for winter use and transboundary population management. University of Calgary Press, Calgary, Alberta.

Gause, G. F. 1934. The struggle for existence. Williams and Wilkins, Baltimore, Maryland.

Geffen, E., M. J. Anderson, and R. K. Wayne. 2004. Climate and habitat barriers to dispersal in the highly mobile grey wolf. Molecular Ecology 13:2481-2490.

Geist, V. 1963. On the behaviour of North American moose (*Alces alces* Andersoni Peterson, 1950) in British Columbia. Behaviour 20:377–416.

Geist, V. 1992. Endangered species and the law. Nature 357:274-276.

Gese, E. M. and L. D. Mech. 1991. Dispersal of wolves (*Canis lupus*) in northeastern Minnesota, 1969-1989. Canadian Journal of Zoology 69:2946-2955.

Gese, E. M., R. L. Ruff, and R. L. Crabtree. 1996. Foraging ecology of coyotes (*Canis latrans*): the influence of extrinsic factors and a dominance hierarchy. Canadian Journal of Zoology 74:769-783.

Gibson, G., and S. V. Muse. 2004. A Primer of Genome Science. 2nd Edition. Sinauer Associates, New York.

Gill, R. 1990. Monitoring the status of European and North American Cervids: The global environment monitoring system. GEMS Information Series No. 8, Nairobi, Kenya.

Girman, D. J., M. G. L. Mills, E. Geffen, and R. K. Wayne. 1997. A molecular genetic analysis of social structure, dispersal, and interpack relationships of the African wild dog (Lycaon pictus). Behavioral Ecology and Sociobiology 40:187-198.

Glöde, D., R. Bergström and F. Pettersson. 2004. Intäktsförluster på grund av älgbetning av tall i Sverige ("Income losses due to moose browsing on

Scots pine in Sweden"). Arbetsrapport Nr 570, Skogforsk, Uppsala. (In Swedish).

Goldstein, B. D., and R. S. Carruth. 2005. Implications of the precautionary principle: Is it a threat to science? Human and Ecological Risk Assessment **11**:209-219.

Goleman, D. 2005. Emotional intelligence: 10th anniversary edition. Bantam, New York, New York.

Goossens, B., L. Chikhi, M. Ancrenaz, I. Lackman-Ancrenaz, P. Andau, and M. W. Bruford. 2006. Genetic Signature of Anthropogenic Population Collapse in Orangutans. PLoS Biol 4:e25

Gottlieb, G. 1992. Individual development and evolution. Oxford University Press, New York, New York.

Government of Northwest Territories (GNWT). 2006. Caribou Forever – Our Heritage, Our Responsibility: a Barren-ground Caribou Management Strategy for the Northwest Territories 2006 – 2010. Government of the Northwest Territories, Environment and Natural Resources, Yellowknife, Northwest Territories.

Graur, D., L. Duret, and M. Gouy. 1996. Phylogenetic position of the order Lagomorpha (rabbits, hares and allies). Nature 379:333-335.

Grewal, P., J. Wilson, T. K. Kung, K. Shami, M. T. Theberge, J. B. Theberge, and B. N. White. 2004. A genetic assessment of the eastern wolf (*Canis lycaon*) in Algonquin Provincial Park. Journal of Mammalogy **85**:625–632.

Gude, J. A., R. A. Garrott, J. J. Borkowski, and F. King. 2006. Prey risk allocation in a grazing ecosystem. Ecological Applications **16**:285-298.

Guillot, G., A. Estoup, F. Mortier, and J. F. Cosson. 2005a. A spatial statistical model for landscape genetics. Genetics **170**:1261-1280.

Guillot, G., F. Mortier, and A. Estoup. 2005b. Geneland: a computer package for landscape genetics. Molecular Ecology Notes **5**:712-715.

Gunn, A., and F. L. Miller. 1986. Traditional behaviour and fidelity to calving grounds by barren-ground caribou. Rangifer Special Issue **1**:151-158.

Gunn, A. and A. D'Hont. 2002. Extent of calving for the Bathurst and Ahiak caribou herds. Manuscript Report No. 149. Department of Resources,

Wildlife and Economic Development, Government of the Northwest Territories, Yellowknife, Northwest Territories.

Gunn, A., J. Dragon, and J. Nishi. 1997. Bathurst calving ground survey 1996. File Report No. 119. Department of Resources, Wildlife and Economic Development, Government of the Northwest Territories, Yellowknife, Northwest Territories.

Gunn, A., B. Fournier, and J. Nishi. 2000. Abundance and distribution of the Queen Maud Gulf caribou herd, 1986-98. File Report No. 126. Department of Resources, Wildlife and Economic Development, Government of the Northwest Territories, Yellowknife, Northwest Territories.

Gunn, A., J. Dragon, and J. Boulanger. 2001. Seasonal movements of satellite-collared caribou from the Bathurst herd. Final Report to the West Kitikmeot Slave Study Society, Yellowknife, Northwest Territories, Canada.

Gunson, J. R. 1992. Historical and present management of wolves in Alberta. Wildlife Society Bulletin 20:330-339.

Gunther, K. A., and D. W. Smith. 2004. Interactions between wolves and female grizzly bears with cubs in Yellowstone National Park. Ursus 15:232-238.

Gursky, I. G. 1978. The wolf in the northwestern Black Sea region (habitats, structure of populations, reproduction). Byulleten Moskovskogo Obshchestva Ispytatelei Prirody, Otdelenie Biologii 83:29-38. [In Russian with English summary]

Haber, G. C. 1977. Socio-ecological dynamics of wolves and prey in a subarctic ecosystem. Ph.D. dissertation. University of British Columbia.

Haber, G. C. 1996. Biological, conservation, and ethical implications of exploiting and controlling wolves. Conservation Biology 10:1068-1081.

Haberman, S. J. 1973. The analysis of residuals in cross-classified tables. Biometrics 29:205-220.

Hadly, E. A., M. H. Kohn, J. A. Leonard, and R. K. Wayne. 1998. A genetic record of population isolation in pocket gophers during Holocene climatic change. Proceedings of the National Academy of Sciences 95:6893-6896.

Haglund, B. 1968. Winter habits of the brown bear (*Ursus arctos* L.) and the wolf (*Canis lupus*) as revealed by tracking in the snow. Viltrevy 5:213-361.

Haight, R. G., L. E. Travis, K. Nimerfro, and L. D. Mech. 2002. Computer simulation of wolf removal strategies for animal damage control. Wildlife Society Bulletin **30**:1-9.

Hairston, N. G., F. E. Smith, and L. B. Slobodkin. 1960. Community structure, population control, and competition. American Naturalist **94**:421-425.

Haldane, J. B. S. 1932. The causes of evolution. Princeton University Press, Princeton New Jersey.

Haldane, J. B. S. 1956. Can a species concept be justified? Pages 95-96 in P. C. Sylvester-Bradley, editor. The species concept in paleontology: a symposium. Systematics Association, London, United Kingdom.

Hancock, J. M. 1999. Microsatellites and other simple sequences: genomic context and mutational mechanisms. Pages 1-9 in D. B. Goldstein, and C. Schlötterer, editors. Microsatellites. Evolution and Applications. Oxford University Press, Oxford.

Hansen, A., L. Baril, R. Renkin, T. McEneaney, and D. W. Smith. 2005. Report to the Yellowstone Centre for Resources. Yellowstone National Park, Wyoming.

Hatter, I. W., and W. A. Bergerud. 1991. Moose recruitment, adult mortality, and rate of change. Alces **27**:65-73.

Havens, K. E., and N. G. Aumen. 2000. Hypothesis-driven experimental research is necessary for natural resource management. Environmental Management **25**:1-7.

Hayes, R. D. and J. R. Gunson. 1995. Status and management of wolves in Canada. Pages 21-33 in L. N. Carbyn, S. H. Fritts, and D. R. Seip, editors. Ecology and conservation of wolves in a changing world. Canadian Circumpolar Institute, Occasional Publication No. 35, Edmonton, Alberta, Canada.

Hayes, R. D. and A. S. Harestad. 2000. Demography of a recovering wolf population in the Yukon. Canadian Journal of Zoology **78**:36-48.

Hayes, R. D., A. M. Baer, and D. G. Larsen. 1991. Population dynamics and prey relationships of an exploited and recovering wolf population in the southern Yukon. Final report TR-91-1. Yukon Fish and Wildlife Branch, Whitehorse, Yukon.

Hayes, R. D., A. M. Baer, U. Wotschikowsky, and A. S. Harestad. 2000. Kill rate by wolves on moose in the Yukon. Canadian Journal of Zoology **78**:49-59.

Hayes, R. D., R. Farnell, R. M. P. Ward, J. Carey, M. Dehn, G. W. Kuzyk, A. M. Baer, C. L. Gardner, and M O'Donoghue. 2003. Experimental reduction of wolves in the Yukon: ungulate responses and management implications. Wildlife Monographs **152**:1-35.

Heard, D. C. 1983. Historical and present status of wolves in the Northwest Territories. Pages 44-47 in L. N. Carbyn, editor. Wolves in Canada and Alaska: their status, biology, and management. Canadian Wildlife Service report series, number 45. Canadian Wildlife Service, Ottawa, Ontario.

Heard, D. C., and T. M. Williams. 1992. Distribution of wolf dens on migratory caribou ranges in the Northwest Territories, Canada. Canadian Journal of Zoology **70**:1504-1510.

Hebblewhite, M. 2005. Predation interacts with the North Pacific Oscillation (NPO) to influence western North American elk population dynamics. Journal of Animal Ecology **74**:226-233.

Hebblewhite, M. 2006. Linking predation risk and forage to ungulate population dynamics. University of Alberta. Dissertation.

Hebblewhite, M. and E. H. Merrill. 2007. Multiscale wolf predation risk for elk: does migration reduce risk? Oecologia **152**:377-387.

Hebblewhite, M., D. H. Pletscher, and P. C. Paquet. 2002. Elk population dynamics in areas with and without predation by recolonizing wolves in Banff National Park, Alberta. Canadian Journal of Zoology **80**:789–799.

Hebblewhite, M. D., P. C. Paquet, and D. H. Pletscher. 2003. Development and application of a ratio-estimator to estimate wolf killing rates and variance in a multiple prey system. Wildlife Society Bulletin **31**:933–946.

Hebblewhite, M., P. C. Paquet, D. H. Pletscher, R. B. Lessard, C. J. Callaghan. 2004. Development and application of a ratio-estimator to estimate wolf killing rates and variance in a multiple prey system. Wildlife Society Bulletin **31**:933–946.

Hebblewhite, M., C. A. White, C. Nietvelt, J. M. McKenzie, T. E. Hurd, J. M. Fryxell, S. Bayley, and P. C. Paquet. 2005. Human activity mediates a trophic cascade caused by wolves. Ecology **86**:2135-2144.

Hebblewhite, M., E. H. Merrill, L. E. Morgantini, C. A. White, J. R. Allen, E. Bruns, L. Thurston, and T. E. Hurd. 2006. Is the migratory behaviour of montane elk herds in peril? The case of Alberta's Ya Ha Tinda elk herd. Wildlife Society Bulletin **34**:1280-1295.

Hebblewhite, M., J. Whittington, M. Bradley, G. Skinner, A. Dibb, and C. A. White. 2007. Conditions for caribou persistence in the wolf-elk-caribou systems of the Canadian Rockies. Rangifer **17**:79-90.

Hedrick, P. W., R. N. Lee, and D. Garrigan. 2002. Major histocompatibility complex variation in red wolves: evidence for common ancestry with coyotes and balancing selection. Molecular Ecology **11**:1905–1913.

Hedges, L. V., J. Gurevitch, and P. S. Curtis. 1999. The meta-analysis of response ratio's in experimental ecology. Ecology **80**:1150-1156.

Heisey, D. M., and T. K. Fuller 1985. Evaluation of survival and cause-specific mortality rates using telemetry data. Journal of Wildlife Management **49**:668-693.

Hendrickson, J., W. L. Robinson, and L. D. Mech. 1975. Status of the wolf in Michigan, 1973. American Midland Naturalist **94**:226-232.

Herrero, S. 2005. Biology, demography, ecology and management of grizzly bears in and around Banff National Park and Kananaskis country: the final report of the Eastern slopes grizzly bear project. Faculty of Environmental Design, University of Calgary, Calgary, Alberta.

Heyer, E., E. Zietkiewicz, A. Rochowski, V. Yotova, J. Puymirat, and D. Labuda. 2001. Phylogenetic and familial estimates of mitochondrial substitution rates: study of control region mutations in deep-rooting pedigrees. American Journal of Human Genetics 69:1113-1126.

Hickie, P. F. 1936. Isle Royale moose studies. Transactions of the North American Wildlife Conference **1**:396-399.

Hill, E. L. 1979. The ecology of the timber wolf (Canis lupus Linn.) in southern Manitoba - wilderness, recreational and agricultural aspects. University of Manitoba. Masters Thesis.

Hiraiwa-Hasegawa M. 1993. Skewed birth sex ratios in Primates: should high-ranking mothers have daughters or sons? Trends in Ecology & Evolution 8:395400.

Hobbs, N. T. 1996. Modification of ecosystems by ungulates. Journal of Wildlife Management **60**:695-713.

Holland, P. W. 1986. Statistics and causal inference. Journal of the American Statistical Association **81**:945-60.

Holland, W. D., and G. M. Coen. 1982. Ecological (biophysical) land classification of Banff and Jasper national parks, volume II: soil and vegetation resources. Alberta Institute of Pedology Publication SS-82-44. Alberta Institute of Pedology, Edmonton, Alberta.

Holland, W. D., and G. M. Coen. 1983. Ecological (biophysical) land classification of Banff and Jasper national parks, volume I: summary. Alberta Institute of Pedology Publication M-83-2. Alberta Institute of Pedology, Edmonton, Alberta.

Holroyd, G. L., and K. J. Van Tighem. 1983. Ecological (biophysical) land classification of Banff and Jasper National Parks, Volume 3: the wildlife inventory. Canadian Wildlife Service, Edmonton, Alberta.

Holt, R. D. 1977. Predation, apparent competition, and structure of prey communities. Theoretical Population Biology **12**:197-229.

Holt, R. D., and M. Roy. 2007. Predation can increase the prevalence of infectious disease. American Naturalist **169**:690-699.

Hosmer, D. W. and S. Lemeshow. 1989. Applied logistic regression. John Wiley and Sons, New York, New York.

Höss, M., M. Kohn, S. Pääbo, F. Knauer and W. Schröder. 1992. Excrement analysis by PCR. Nature **359**:199.

Houston, D. B. 1982. The Northern Yellowstone elk: Ecology and management. Macmillan, New York, New York.

Hubbell, S. P. 1997. A unified theory of biogeography and relative species abundance and its application to tropical rain forests and coral reefs. Coral Reefs 16:S9-S21.

Huber, N. K. 1983. The geologic story of Isle Royale National Park. United States Geological Survey Bulletin 1309. Washington, D. C.

Huggard, D. J. 1993a. Prey selectivity of wolves in Banff National Park. I. Prey species. Canadian Journal of Zoology **71**:130-139.

Huggard, D. J. 1993b. Prey selectivity of wolves in Banff National Park. II. Age, sex, and condition of elk. Canadian Journal of Zoology **71**:140-147.

Huggard, D. J. 1993c. Effect of snow depth on predation and scavenging by gray wolves. Journal of Wildlife Management **57**:382-388.

Hurford, A., M. Hebblewhite, and M. A. Lewis. 2006. A spatially explicit model for an Allee effect: Why wolves recolonize so slowly in Greater Yellowstone. Theoretical Population Biology **70**:244–254.

Hunter, M. D., and P. W. Price. 1992. Playing chutes and ladders: heterogeneity and the relative roles of bottom-up and top-down forces in natural communities. Ecology **73**:724-732.

Hurd, T. E. 1999. Factors limiting moose numbers and their interactions with elk and wolves in the Central Rocky Mountains, Canada. University of British Columbia. Master of Science.

Ingman, M., H. P. Kaessmann, S. Paabo, and U. Gyllensten. 2000. Mitochondrial genome variation and the origin of modern humans. Nature 408:708-713.

International Road Federation. 2006. World Road Statistics 2006. International Road Federation, Brussels, Belgium.

Irwin, T. 1995. Plato's ethics. Oxford University Press, Oxford, United Kingdom.

James, A. R. C., and A. K. Stuart-Smith. 2000. Distribution of caribou and wolves in relation to linear corridors. Journal of Wildlife Management **64**:154-159.

Jędrzejewska, B., and W. Jędrzejewski. 1998. Predation in vertebrate communities: the Białowieża primeval forest as a case of study. Springer Verlag, Berlin, Germany.

Jędrzejewska, B., W. Jędrzejewski, A. N. Bunevich, L. Miłkowski, and H. Okarma. 1996. Population dynamics of wolves, *Canis lupus*, in Białowieża Primeval Forest (Poland and Belarus) in relation to hunting by humans, 1847-1993. Mammal Review **26**:103-126.

Jędrzejewska, B., W. Jędrzejewski, A. N. Bunevich, L. Miłkowski, and Z. Krasiński. 1997. Factors shaping population densities and increase rates of ungulates in Białowieża Primeval Forest (Poland and Belarus) in the 19th and 20th centuries. Acta Theriologica **42**:399-451.

Jędrzejewski, W., B. Jędrzejewska, H. Okarma, and A. L. Ruprecht. 1992. Wolf predation and snow cover as mortality factors in the ungulate community of the Białowieża National Park, Poland. Oecologia **90**:27-36.

Jędrzejewski, W., B. Jędrzejewska, H. Okarma, K. Schmidt, K. Zub, and M. Musiani. 2000. Prey selection and predation by wolves in Białowieża Primeval Forest, Poland. Journal of Mammology **81**:197-212.

Jędrzejewski, W., K. Schmidt, J. Theurkauf, B. Jędrzejewska, and H. Okarma. 2001. Daily movements and territory use by radio-collared wolves (*Canis lupus*) in Białowieża Primeval Forest in Poland. Canadian Journal of Zoology **79**:1993-2004.

Jędrzejewski, W., S. Nowak, K. Schmidt, and B. Jędrzejewska. 2002a. The wolf and the lynx in Poland – results of a census conducted in 2001. Kosmos **51**:491-499. [In Polish with English summary]

Jędrzejewski, W., K. Schmidt, J. Theurkauf, B. Jędrzejewska, N. Selva, K. Zub, and L. Szymura. 2002b. Kill rates and predation by wolves on ungulate populations in Białowieża Primeval Forest (Poland). Ecology **83**: 1341-1356.

Jędrzejewski, W., M. Niedziałkowska, S. Nowak, and B. Jędrzejewska. 2004a. Habitat variables associated with wolf (*Canis lupus*) distribution and abundance in northern Poland. Diversity and Distributions **10**:225-233.

Jędrzejewski, W., K. Schmidt, B. Jędrzejewska, J. Theuerkauf, R. Kowalczyk, and K. Zub. 2004b. The process of a wolf pack splitting in Białowieża Primeval Forest, Poland. Acta Theriologica **49**:275-280.

Jędrzejewski, W., M. Niedziałkowska, R. W. Mysłajek, S. Nowak, and B. Jędrzejewska. 2005a. Habitat selection by wolves, *Canis lupus*, in the uplands and mountains of southern Poland. Acta Theriologica **50**:417-428.

Jędrzejewski, W., W. Branicki, C. Veit, I. Međugorac, M. Pilot, A. N. Bunevich, B. Jędrzejewska, K. Schmidt, J. Theuerkauf, H. Okarma, R. Gula, L. Szymura, and M. Forster. 2005b. Genetic diversity and relatedness within packs in an intensely hunted population of wolves, *Canis lupus*. Acta Theriologica **50**:3-22.

Jędrzejewski, W., K. Schmidt, J. Theuerkauf, B. Jędrzejewska, and R. Kowalczyk. 2007. Territory size of wolves (*Canis lupus*): linking local (Białowieża Primeval Forest, Poland) and Holarctic-scale patterns. Ecography **30**:66-76.

Jenks, S. M., and R. K. Wayne. 1992. Problems and policy for species threatened by hybridization: the red wolf as a case study. Pages 237-251 in D. R. McCullough and R. H. Barrett, editors. Wildlife 2001: Populations. Elsevier Science Publishers, London.

Jenness, J. 2003. Random point generator for ArcView 3.x. Version 1.27. Jenness Enterprises. Available from http://www.jennessent.com/arcview/random_points.htm (accessed August 2007).

Johnson, C. J., S. E. Nielsen, E. H. Merrill, T. L. McDonald, and M. S. Boyce. 2006. Resource selection functions based on use–availability data: theoretical motivation and evaluation methods. Journal of Wildlife Management **70**:347-357.

Jokinen, M. and J. T. Jorgenson. 2002. Calgary and Canmore areas aerial winter elk survey. Government of Alberta, Sustainable Resource Development, Fish and Wildlife Division. Canmore, Alberta.

Jorde, L. B., W. S. Watkins, M. J. Bamshad, M. E. Dixon, C. E. Ricker, M. T. Seielstad, and M. A. Batzer. 2000. The distribution of human genetic diversity: A comparison of mitochondrial, autosomal, and Y-chromosome data. The American Journal of Human Genetics **66**:979–988.

Kaleckaya, M. L. 1973. The wolf and its role as a predator in Darvinskii Reserve. Trudy Darvinskogo Gusudarstvennogo Zapovednika **11**:41-59. [In Russian]

Kaleckaya, M. L., and K. P. Filonov. 1987. Pack characteristics of wolf (*Canis lupus*) in Darwin Reserve. Zoologicheskii Zhurnal **68**:1230-1238. [In Russian with English summary]

Kaltenborn, B. P., T. Bjerke, and J. Vittersö, 1999. Attitudes towards large carnivores among sheep farmers, wildlife managers and research biologists in Norway. Human Dimensions of Wildlife **4**:57-73.

Kareiva, P. 1994. Special feature: higher order interactions as a foil to reductionist ecology. Ecology **75**:1527-1559.

Karlsson, J., and S. Thoresson, 2000. Jakthundar i vargrevir. En ja¨mfo¨ r-else av jakthundanva¨ndningen i fem olika vargrevir och statistiken o¨ ver vargangrepp pa° hundar 1999/2000. Available from http://www.viltskadecenter. com (accessed October 2007).

Karlsson, J. and Sjöström, M. 2007. Human attitudes towards wolf conservation, a matter of distance. Biological Conservation **137**:610–616.

Karns, P. D. 1997. Population distribution, density and trends. Pages 125-140 in A. W. Franzmann and C. C. Schwartz, editors. Ecology and management of the North American moose. Smithsonian Press, Washington, D. C.

Kauffman, M. J., N. Varley, D. W. Smith, D. R. Stahler, D. R. MacNulty and M. S. Boyce. 2007. Landscape heterogeneity shapes predation in a newly restored predator–prey system. Ecology Letters **10**:690–700.

Kay, C. E. 1990. Yellowstone's northern elk herd: A critical evaluation of the "Natural Regulation" paradigm. Utah State University. Dissertation.

Kay, C. E. 1994. Aboriginal overkill: the role of native Americans in structuring western ecosystems. Human Nature **5**:359-398.

Kay, C. E. 1998. Are ecosystems structured from the top-down or bottom up: a new look at an old debate. Wildlife Society Bulletin **26**:484-498.

Keating, K. A. and S. Cherry. 2004. Use and interpretation of logistic regression in habitat selection studies. Journal of Wildlife Management **68**:774-789.

Keiter, R. B., and M. S. Boyce. 1991. The Greater Yellowstone Ecosystem: redefining America's wilderness heritage. Yale University Press, New Haven, Connecticut.

Keith, L. B. 1983. Population dynamics of wolves. Pages 66-77 in L. N. Carbyn, editor. Wolves in Canada and Alaska: their status, biology, and management. Canadian Wildlife Service Report Series No. 45, Edmonton, Alberta.

Keller, E. F. 2002. Making sense of life. Harvard University Press, Cambridge, Massachusetts.

Kelsall, J. P. 1960. Co-operative studies of barren-ground caribou 1957-58. Canadian Wildlife Service, Wildlife Management Bulletin Series 1, No. 15. Canadian Wildlife Service, Ottawa, Ontario.

Kelsall, J. P. 1968. The migratory barren-ground caribou of Canada. Canadian Wildlife Service, Ottawa, Ontario, Canada.

Kelsall, J. P. 1969. Structural adaptations of moose and deer for snow. Journal of Mammalogy **50**:302-310.

Kennedy, P. K., M. L. Kennedy, P. L. Clarkson, and I. S. Liepins. 1991. Genetic variability in natural populations of the gray wolf, *Canis lupus*. Canadian Journal of Zoology **69**:1183-1188.

Kimura, M. 1968. Evolutionary rate at the molecular level. Nature **217**: 624-626.

Kirkness, E. F., V. Bafna, A. L. Halpern, S. Levy, K. Remington, D. B. Rusch, A. L. Delcher, M. Pop, W. Wang, C. M. Fraser, and J. C. Venter. 2003. The dog genome: survey sequencing and comparative analysis. Science **301**:1898–1903.

Kloppers, E. L., C. C. St Clair, and T. E. Hurd. 2005. Predator-resembling aversive conditioning for managing habituated wildlife. Ecology and Society **10**:31.

Kohn, M. H., and R. K. Wayne. 1997. Facts from feces revisited. Trends in Ecology and Evolution **12**:223-227.

Kohn M, E. C. York, D. A. Kamradt, G. Haught, R. M. Sauvajot, and R. K. Wayne. 1999a. Estimating population size by genotyping feces. Proceedings of the Royal Society of London, Series B **266**:657–663.

Kohn, B., J. Frair, D. Unger, T. Gehring, D. Shelley, E. Anderson, and P. Keenlance. 1999b. Impacts of a highway expansion project on wolves in Northwestern Wisconsin. Pages 53-65 in G. Evink, D. Zeigler, and P. Garret, editors. Proceedings of the Third International Conference on Wildlife Ecology and Transportation. Florida Department of Transportation, Tallahassee, Florida.

Kohn, M. H., W. J. Murphy, E. A. Ostrander, and R. K. Wayne. 2006. Genomics and conservation genetics. Trends in Ecology and Evolution **21**:629-637.

Kojola, I. 2000. Wolf-moose interrelationship and implications for the moose harvest. Suomen Riista **46**:76-81.

Kojola, I., S. Ronkainen, A. Hakala, S. Heikkinen, and S. Kokko. 2004. Interactions between wolves, *Canis lupus*, and dogs, *C. familiaris*, in Finland. Wildlife Biology **10**:101-105.

Kojola, I., J. Aspi, A. Hakala, S. Heikkinen, C. Ilmoni, and S. Ronkainen. 2006. Dispersal in an expanding wolf population in Finland. Journal of Mammalogy **87**:281-286.

Kolenosky, G. B. 1972. Wolf predation on wintering deer in eastcentral Ontario. Journal of Wildlife Management **36**:357-369.

Kortello, A. D. 2005. Interactions between cougars (*Puma concolor*) and wolves (*Canis lupus*) in the Bow Valley of Banff National Park, Alberta. University of Idaho. Masters Thesis.

Kortello, A. D., T. E. Hurd, and D. L. Murray. 2007. Interactions between wolves and cougars in Banff National Park, Alberta. Ecoscience **14**:214-222.

Krebs, J. R. and N. B. Davies. 1993. An introduction to behavioural ecology. Blackwell Science Limited, London, United Kingdom.

Kreeger, T. J. 2003. The internal wolf: Physiology, pathology and pharmacology. Pages 192-217 in L. D. Mech and L. Boitani, editors. Wolves: Behavior, ecology and conservation. University of Chicago Press, Chicago, Illinois.

Kübarsepp, M., and H. Valdmann. 2003. Winter diet and movements of wolf (*Canis lupus*) in Alam-Pedja Nature Reserve, Estonia. Acta Zooloogica Lituanica **13**:28-33.

Kudaktin, A. N. 1979. Territorial distribution and structure of the wolf population of the Caucasian Nature Reserve. Byulleten Moskovskogo Obshchestva Ispytatelei Prirody, Otdelenie Biologii **84**:56-65. [In Russian with English summary]

Kunkel, K. E. and D. H. Pletscher. 2001. Winter hunting patterns of wolves in and near Glacier National Park, Montana. Journal of Wildlife Management **65**:520-530.

Kuyt, E. 1972. Food habits and ecology of wolves on barren-ground caribou range in the Northwest Territories. Canadian Wildlife Service Report Series No. 21. Canadian Wildlife Service, Ottawa, Ontario.

Kuzyk, G. W. and K. M. Kuzyk. 2001. Wolf, *Canis lupus*, response to domestic sled dog, *Canis familiaris*, activities in central Yukon. Canadian Field-Naturalist **116**:125-126.

Kyle, C. J., A. R. Johnson, B. R. Patterson, P. J. Wilson, K. Shami, S. K. Grewal, and B. N. White. 2006. Genetic nature of eastern wolves: Past, present and future. Conservation Genetics **7**:273-287.

Laikre, L., and N. Ryman. 1991. Inbreeding depression in a captive wolf (*Canis lupus*) population. Conservation Biology **5**:33-40.

Lande, R., and S. J. Arnold. 1983. The measurement of selection on correlated characters. Evolution **37**:1210–1226.

Larivière, S., H. Jolicoeur, and M. Crête. 2000. Status and conservation of the gray wolf (*Canis lupus*) in wildlife reserves in Québec. Biological Conservation **94**:143-151.

Larsen, E. J., and W. J. Ripple. 2003. Aspen age structure in the northern Yellowstone ecosystem. Forest Ecology and Management **179**:469-482.

Laurenson, K., F. Shiferaw, and C. Sillero-Zubiri. 1997. Disease, domestic dogs, and the Ethiopian wolf: current situation. Pages 32-42 in C. Sillero-Zubiri and D. Macdonald, editors. The Ethiopian Wolf Status Survey and Conservation Action Plan. IUCN, Gland, Switzerland.

Lavsund, S. and F. Sandegren. 1989. Swedish moose management and harvest during the period 1964-1989. Alces **25**:58-62.

Lavsund S., T. Nygren, and E. J. Solberg. 2003. Status of moose populations and challenges to moose management in Fennoscandia. Alces **39**:109-130.

Lawrence, B., and W. H. Bossert. 1967. Multiple character analysis of Canis lupus, latrans, and familiaris, with a discussion of the relationships of Canis niger. American Zoologist **7**:223-232.

Lawrence, B., and W. H. Bossert. 1969. The cranial evidence for hybridization in New England. Canis Breviora **330**:1-13.

Leberg, P. 2005. Genetic approaches for estimating the effective size of populations. Journal of Wildlife Management **69**:1385–1399.

Lehman, N., A. Eisenhawer, K. Hansen, L. D. Mech, R. O. Peterson, P. J. P. Gogan, and R. K. Wayne. 1991. Introgression of coyote mitochondrial DNA into sympatric North American gray wolf populations. Evolution **45**:104-119.

Lehner, P. N. 1979. Handbook of ethological methods. Garland STPM Press, New York, New York.

Lemke, T. O. 2004. Origin, expansion, and status of mountain goats in Yellowstone National Park. Wildlife Society Bulletin **32**:532-541.

Lemke, T. O., J. A. Mack, and D. B. Houston. 1998. Winter range expansion by the northern range Yellowstone elk herd. Intermountain Journal of Sciences **4**:1-9.

Lemon, M. C. 2003. Philosophy of history. Routledge, New York, New York.

Leonard, J. A. and R. K. Wayne. 2007. Native Great Lakes wolves were not restored. Biology Letters 4: 95-98.

Leonard, J. A., R. K. Wayne, and A. Cooper. 2000. Population genetics of ice age brown bears. Proceedings of the National Academy of Sciences USA 97:1651-1654.

Leonard, J. A., R. K. Wayne, J. Wheeler, R. Valadez, E. Guillén, and C. Vilà. 2002. Ancient DNA evidence for old world origin of new world dogs. Science 298:1613-1616.

Leonard, J. A., C. Vilà , and R. K. Wayne. 2005. Legacy lost: genetic variability and population size of extirpated US grey wolves (*Canis lupus*). Molecular Ecology 14:9-17.

Lessard, R. B. 2005. Conservation of woodland caribou (*Rangifer tarandus caribou*) in west-central Alberta: a simulation analysis of multi-species predator-prey systems. University of Alberta. Dissertation.

Lewontin, R. C. 1974. The genetic basis of evolutionary change. Columbia University Press, New York, New York.

Lewontin, R. C. and L. C. Birch. 1966. Hybridization as a source of variation for adaptation to new environments. Evolution 20:315-336.

Liberg, O. 2005. Genetic aspects of viability in small wolf populations with special emphasis on the Scandinavian wolf population. Swedish Environmental Protection Agency, Report No. 5436. Swedish Environmental Protection Agency, Stockholm, Sweden.

Liberg, O. 2006. Genetic aspects of viability in small wolf populations with special emphasis on the Scandinavian wolf population. Report from an international expert workshop at Färna Herrgård, Rapport 5436. Swedish Environmental Protection Agency, Stockholm, Sweden.

Liberg, O., H. Andrén, H.-C. Pedersen, H. Sand, D. Sejberg, P. Wabakken, M. Åkesson, and S. Bensch. 2005. Severe inbreeding depression in a wild wolf, *Canis lupus*, population. Biology Letters 1:17-20.

Lima, S. L. 2002. Putting predators back into behavioral predator–prey interactions. Trends in Ecology and Evolution 17:70–75.

Lima, S. L., and L. M. Dill. 1990. Behavioral decisions made under the risk of predation: a review and prospectus. Canadian Journal of Zoology **68**:619-640.

Lima, S. L., and P. A. Bednekoff. 1999. Temporal variation in danger drives antipredator behavior: the predation risk allocation hypothesis. American Naturalist **153**:649-659.

Lima, M., Stenseth, N. C., and F. M. Jaksic. 2002. Population dynamics of a South American rodent: seasonal structure interacting with climate, density dependence, and predator effects. Proceedings of the Royal Society of London, B **269**:2579-2586.

Lindblad-Toh, K., C. M. Wade, T. S. Mikkelsen, E. K. Karlsson, D. B. Jaffe, M. Kamal, M. Clamp, J. L. Chang, E. J. Kulbokas, M. C. Zody, E. Mauceli, X. H. Xie, M. Breen, R. K. Wayne, E. A. Ostrander, C. P. Ponting, F. Galibert, D. R. Smith, P. J. deJong, E. Kirkness, P. Alvarez, T. Biagi, W. Brockman, J. Butler, C. W. Chin, A. Cook, J. Cuff, M. J. Daly, D. DeCaprio, S. Gnerre, M. Grabherr, M. Kellis, M. Kleber, C. Bardeleben, L. Goodstadt, A. Heger, C. Hitte, L. Kim, K. P. Koepfli, H. G. Parker, J. P. Pollinger, S. M. J. Searle, N. B. Sutter, R. Thomas, C. Webber, and E. S. Lander. 2005. Genome sequence, comparative analysis and haplotype structure of the domestic dog. Nature **438**:803-819.

Linnell, J. D. C., J. Odden, M. E. Smith, R. Aanes, and J. E. Swenson. 1999. Large carnivores that kill livestock: do "problem individuals" really exist? Wildlife Society Bulletin **27**:698-705.

Linnell, J. D. C., J. E. Swenson, and R. Andersen. 2001. Predators and people: conservation of large carnivores is possible at high human densities if management policy is favourable. Animal Conservation **4**:345-350.

Linnell, J. D. C., R. Andersen, Z. Andersone, L. Balciauskas, J. C. Blanco, L. Boitani, S. Brainerd, U. Breitenmoser, I. Kojola, O. Liberg, J. Løe, H. Okarma, H-C. Pedersen, C. Promberg, H. Sand, E. J. Solberg, H. Valdmann, and P. Wabakken. 2002. The fear of wolves: a review of wolf attacks on humans. NINA Oppdragsmelding **731**:1-65.

Linnell, J. D. C., E. J. Solberg, S. Brainerd, O. Liberg, H. Sand, P. Wabakken, and I. Kojola. 2003. Is the fear of wolves justified? A Fennoscandian perspective. Acta Zoologica Lituanica **13**:34-40.

Linnell, J. D. C., H. Broseth, E. J. Solberg, and S. M. Brainerd. 2005. The origins of the southern Scandinavian wolf *Canis lupus* population: potential for natural immigration in relation to dispersal distances, geography and Baltic ice. Wildlife Biology **11**: 383-391.

Lorenzini, R. and R. Fico. 1995. A genetic investigation of enzyme polymorphisms shared by wolf and dog: suggestions for conservation of the wolf in Italy. Acta Theriologica Supplement **3**:101-110.

Lucchini, V., E. Fabbri, F. Marucco, S. Ricci, L. Boitani, and E. Randi. 2002. Noninvasive molecular tracking of colonizing wolf (*Canis lupus*) packs in the western Italian Alps. Molecular Ecology **11**:857–868.

Lucchini, V., A. Galov, and E. Randi. 2004. Evidence of genetic distinction and long-term population decline in wolves (*Canis lupus*) in the Italian Apennines. Molecular Ecology **13**:523–535.

Luikart, G., and J. M. Cornuet. 1998. Empirical evaluation of a test for identifying recently bottlenecked populations from allele frequency data. Molecular Ecology **12**:228-237.

Lyengar, A., V. N. Babu, S. Hedges, A. Venkataraman, N. MacLean, and P. A. Morin. 2005. Phylogeography, genetic structure, and diversity in the dhole (*Cuon alpinus*). Molecular Ecology **14**:2281-2297.

MacNulty, D. R. 2002. The predatory sequence and the influence of injury risk on hunting behaviour in the wolf. University of Minnesota. Masters Thesis.

Majone, G. 2002. What price safety? The precautionary principle and its policy implications. Journal of Common Market Studies **40**:89-109.

Mallet, J. 2001. Subspecies, semispecies. Pages 523-526 in S. Levin, editor. Encyclopedia of biodiversity, Volume 5. Academic Press.

Mallet, J. 2007. Hybrid speciation. Nature **446**:279-283.

Manel, S., M. K. Schwartz, G. Luikart, and P. Taberlet. 2003. Landscape genetics: combining landscape ecology and population genetics. Trends in Ecology and Evolution **18**:189-197.

Manel, S., O. E. Gaggiotti, and R. S. Waples. 2005. Assignment methods: matching biological questions with appropriate techniques. Trends in Ecology & Evolution **20**:136–142.

Manly, B. F. J., L. L. McDonald, D. L. Thomas, T. L. McDonald, and W. P. Erickson. 2002. Resource selection by animals: statistical design for field studies. Kluwer Academic Publishers, Dordrecht, the Netherlands.

Männil, P., and M. Kübarsepp. 2006. Changes in the state of Estonian populations of wolf, lynx and bear in 2002-2006. Year-Book of the Estonian Naturalist's Society **84**:227-253. [In Estonian with English summary]

Mao, J. S., M. S. Boyce, D. W. Smith, F. J. Singer, D. J. Vales, J. M. Vore, and E. H. Merrill. 2005. Habitat selection by elk before and after wolf reintroduction in Yellowstone National Park, Wyoming. Journal of Wildlife Management **69**:1691–1707.

Margulies, M., M. Egholm, W. E. Altman, S. Attiya, J. S. Bader, L. A. Bemben, J. Berka, M. S. Braverman, Y. J. Chen Z. Chen, S. B. Dewell, L. Du, J. M. Fierro, X. V. Gomes, B. C. Godwin, W. He, S. Helgesen, C. H. Ho, G. P. Irzyk, S. C. Jando, M. L. Alenquer, T. P. Jarvie, K. B. Jirage, J. B. Kim, J. R. Knight, J. R. Lanza, J. H. Leamon, S. M. Lefkowitz, M. Lei, J. Li, K. L. Lohman, H. Lu, V. B. Makhijani, K. E. McDade, M. P. McKenna, E. W. Myers, E. Nickerson, J. R. Nobile, R. Plant, B. P. Puc, M. T. Ronan, G. T. Roth, G. J. Sarkis, J. F. Simons, J. W. Simpson, M. Srinivasan, K. R. Tartaro, A. Tomasz, K. A. Vogt, G. A. Volkmer, S. H. Wang, Y. Wang, M. P. Weiner, P. Yu, R. F. Begley, and J. M. Rothberg. 2005. Genome sequencing in microfabricated high-density picolitre reactors. Nature **437**:376–380.

Mayr, E. 1982. The growth of biological thought. Diversity, evolution, and inheritance. Belknap, Cambridge, Massachusetts.

McGregor, C. A. 1984. Ecological land classification and evaluation: Kananaskis Country, volume I: natural resource summary. Alberta Energy and Natural Resources, Resource Evaluation and Planning Division, Edmonton, Alberta.

McKenzie, J. A. 2001. The selective advantage of urban habitat use by elk in Banff National Park. University of Guelph. Master of Science Thesis.

McLaren, B. E., and R. O. Peterson. 1994. Wolves, moose, and tree rings on Isle Royale. Science **266**:1555-1558.

McLoughlin, P. D., L. R. Walton, H. D. Cluff, P. C. Paquet, and M. A. Ramsey. 2004. Hierarchical habitat selection by tundra wolves. Journal of Mammalogy 85:576-580.

Mech, L. D. 1966. The wolves of Isle Royale. Fauna of the National Parks of the United States, Fauna Series 7. United States National Park Service, Washington, D.C.

Mech, L. D. 1970. The Wolf: ecology and behaviour of an endangered species. Natural History Press, Garden City, New York.

Mech, L. D. 1995. The challenge and opportunity of recovering wolf populations. Conservation Biology 9:270-278.

Mech, L. D. and J. M. Packard. 1990. Possible use of wolf, *Canis lupus*, den over several centuries. Canadian Field-Naturalist 104:484-485.

Mech, L. D., and L. Boitani. 2003a. Conclusion. Pages 341-344 in L. D. Mech and L. Boitani, editors. Wolves: behavior, ecology, and conservation. Chicago University Press, Chicago, Illinois.

Mech, L. D., and L. Boitani. 2003b. Wolf social ecology. Pages 1-34 in L. D. Mech and L. Boitani, editors. Wolves: behavior, ecology, and conservation. Chicago University Press, Chicago, Illinois.

Mech, L. D. and R. O. Peterson. 2003. Wolf-prey relations. Pages 131-160 in Mech, L. D. and L. Boitani. Wolves: behavior, ecology, and conservation. The University of Chicago Press, Chicago, Illinois.

Mech, L. D., L. D. Frenzel, Jr., and P. D. Karns. 1971. The effect of snow conditions on the vulnerability of white-tailed deer to wolf predation. Pages in L. D. Mech and L. D. Frenzel, editors. Ecological studies of the timber wolf in Northeastern Minnesota. United States Department of Agriculture Forest Service Research Paper, NC-52. St. Paul, Minnesota.

Mech, L. D., S. H. Fritts, G. L. Radde, and W. J. Paul. 1988. Wolf distribution and road density in Minnesota. Wildlife Society Bulletin 16:85-87.

Mech, L.D., T.J. Meier, J.W. Burch, and L.G. Adams. 1995. Patterns of prey selection by wolves in Denali National Park Alaska. Pages 231-244 in L.N. Carbyn, S.H. Fritts, and D.R. Seip, editors. Ecology and conservation of wolves in a changing world. Canadian Circumpolar Institute, Edmonton, Alberta.

Mech, L. D., L. G. Adams, T. J. Meier, J. W. Burch, and B. W. Dale. 1998. The wolves of Denali. University of Minnesota Press, Minneapolis, Minnesota.

Mech, L. D., E. K. Harper, T. J. Meier, and W. J. Paul. 2000. Assessing factors that may predispose Minnesota farms to wolf depredations on cattle. Wildlife Society Bulletin 28:623-629.

Mech, L. D., D. W. Smith, K. M. Murphy, and D. R. MacNulty. 2001. Winter severity and wolf predation on a formerly wolf-free elk herd. Journal of Wildlife Management 65:998-1003.

Meffe, G. K. and R. C. Carroll. 1997. Principles of conservation biology. Sinauer Associates, Sunderland, Massachusetts.

Melis, C., P. Szafrańska, B. Jędrzejewska, and K. Bartoń. 2006. Biogeographical variation in the population density of wild boar (*Sus scrofa*) in western Eurasia. Journal of Biogeography 33:803-811.

Meriggi, A. and S. Lovari. 1996. A review of wolf predation in southern Europe: does the wolf prefer wild prey to livestock? Journal of Applied Ecology 33:1561-1571.

Messier, F. 1991. The significance of limiting and regulating factors on the demography of moose and white-tailed deer. Journal of Animal Ecology 60:377-393.

Messier, F. 1994. Unuglate population models with predation: a case study with the North American Moose. Ecology 75:478-488.

Messier, F. 1995a. On the functional and numeric responses of wolves to changing prey density. Pages 187-198 in L. N. Carbyn, S. H. Fritts, and D. R. Seip, editors. Ecology and conservation of wolves in a changing world. Canadian Circumpolar Institute, Edmonton, Alberta.

Messier, F. 1995b. Trophic interactions in two northern wolf-ungulate systems. Wildlife Research 22:131-146.

Messier, F., and M. Crête. 1985. Moose–wolf dynamics and the natural regulation of moose populations. Oecologia 65:503–512.

Messier, F. and D. O. Joly. 2000. Comment: regulation of moose populations by wolf predation. Canadian Journal of Zoology 78:506-510.

Miller, F. L. 1982. Caribou (*Rangifer tarandus*). Pages 923-959 in J. A. Chapman and G. A. Feldhamer, editors. Wild mammals of North America: biology, management, and economics. Johns Hopkins University Press, Baltimore, Maryland.

Miller, C. R., J. R. Adams, and L. P. Waits. 2003. Pedigree-based assignment tests for reversing coyote (*Canis latrans*) introgression into the wild red wolf (*Canis rufus*) population. Molecular Ecology **12**:3287–3301.

Mills, L. S., M .E. Soulé, and D. F. Doak. 1993. The keystone-species concept in ecology and conservation. Bioscience **43**:219-224.

Milner, J. M., E. B. Nilsen, and H. P. Andreassen. 2007. Demographic side effects of selective hunting in ungulates and carnivores. Conservation Biology **21**:36–47.

Minta, S. C., P. M. Kareiva, and A. P. Curlee. 1999. Carnivore research and conservation: learning from history and theory. Pages 323-404 in T. K. Clark, A. P. Curlee, S. C. Minta, and P. M. Kareiva, editors. Carnivores in ecosystems: The Yellowstone experience. Yale University Press, New Haven, Connecticut.

Miquelle, D. G., P. A. Stephens, E. N. Smirnov, J. M. Goodrich, O. J. Zaumyslova, and A. E. Myslenkov. 2005. Tigers and wolves in the Russian far east: competitive exclusion, functional redundancy, and conservation implications. Pages 177-207 in J. C. Ray, K. H. Redford, R. S. Steneck, and J. Berger, editors. Large carnivores and the conservation of biodiversity. Island Press, Washintgon, D.C.

Mitchell, A. 1998. Snowmobile hunt claims hundreds of wolves. Globe and Mail. February 26.

Mitchell-Jones, A. J., G. Amori, W. Bogdanowicz, B. Kryštufek, P. J. H. Reijnders, F. Spitzenberger, M. Stubbe, J. B. M. Thissen, V. Vohralík, and J.Zima. 1999. The atlas of European mammals. T & AD Poyser and Academic Press, London, United Kingdom.

Mivart, St. G. 1871. On the genesis of species. Macmillan, London, United Kingdom.

Mladenoff, D. J. and T. A. Sickley. 1998. Assessing potential gray wolf restoration in the northeastern United States: a spatial prediction of favorable habitat and potential population levels. Journal of Wildlife Management **62**:1-10.

Mladenoff, D. J., T. A. Sickley, R. G. Haight, and A. P. Wydeven. 1995. A regional landscape analysis and prediction of favorable gray wolf habitat in the northern great lakes region. Conservation Biology 9:279-294.

Mladenoff, D. J., T. A. Sickley, and A. P. Wydeven. 1999. Predicting gray wolf landscape recolonization: logistic regression models vs. new field data. Ecological Applications 9:37-44.

Mohr, C. O. 1947. Table of equivalent populations of North America small mammals. American Midland Naturalist 37:223-249.

Moore, K. D. 2005. The truth about barnacles: Rachel Carson and the moral significance of wonder. Environmental Ethics 27:265-277.

Moore, G. C., and G. R. Parker. 1992. Colonization by the eastern coyote (*Canis latrans*). Pages 23-27 in A. H. Boer, editor. Ecology and management of the eastern coyote ecology and management of the eastern coyote. University of New Brunswick, Fredericton.

Morin, P. A., G. Luikart, and R. K. Wayne. 2004. SNPs in ecology, evolution and conservation. Trends in Ecology & Evolution 19:208-216.

Morell, V. 2008. Wolves at the door of a more dangerous world. Science 319:890-892.

Müller-Schwartze, D. 1972. Responses of young black-tailed deer to predators odours. Journal of Mammalogy 53:393-394.

Müller-Wille, L. 1974. Caribou Never Die! Modern Caribou Hunting Economy of the Dene (Chipewyan) of Fond du Lac, Saskatchewan and N.W.T. The Musk Ox 14: 7-19.

Murdoch, W. M., C. J. Briggs, and R. M. Nisbet. 2003. Consumer-Resource Dynamics. Princeton University Press, Princeton, New Jersey.

Murie, A. 1934. The moose of Isle Royale. Miscellaneous Publications Museum of Zoology University of Michigan No. 25. University of Michigan, Ann Arbor, Michigan.

Murie, A. 1935. Preservation of wilderness on Isle Royale. Pages 14-15 in Summer 1991 issue of Horizons. Sigurd Olson Environmental Institute, Ashland, Wisconsin.

Murie, A. 1944. The wolves of Mount McKinley. Fauna of the National Parks of the United States, Fauna Series No. 5. United States Government Printing Office, Washington, D.C.

Murphy, K. M. 1998. The ecology of the cougar (*Puma concolor*) in the northern Yellowstone Ecosystem: interactions with prey, bears and humans. University of Idaho. Dissertation.

Murray, D. L. and L. P. Waits. 2006. Taxonomic status and conservation strategy of the endangered red wolf: a response to Kyle et al. Conservation Genetics **8**:1483–1485.

Musiani, M. 2003. Conservation biology and management of wolves and wolf-human conflicts in western North America. University of Calgary, Ph.D. Dissertation.

Musiani, M., and P. C. Paquet. 2004. The practices of wolf persecution, protection, and restoration in Canada and the United States. BioScience **54**:50-60.

Musiani, M., H. Okarma, and W. Jedrzejewski. 1998. Speed and actual distance travelled by wolves in the Bialowieza Forest (Poland). Acta Theriologica **43**:409-416.

Musiani, M., C. C. Gates, P. C. Paquet, H. D. Cluff, L. R Walton, P. J. Wilson, and B. N. White. 2001. Hunting, migration and sinks/sources among Northern Canadian wolf populations. Canid Biology and Conservation International Conference, Oxford, United Kingdom.

Musiani, M., C. Mamo, L. Boitani, C. Callaghan, C. C. Gates, L. Mattei, E. Visalberghi, S. Breck, and G. Volpi. 2003. Wolf depredation trends and the use of fladry barriers to protect livestock in western North America. Conservation Biology **17**:1538-1547.

Musiani, M., T. Muhly, C. Callaghan, C. C. Gates, M. Smith, S. Stone, and E. Tosoni. 2004. Recovery, conservation, conflicts and legal status of wolves in western North America. Pages 51-75 in N. Fascione, A. Delach and M. Smith, editors. Predators and people: from conflict to conservation. Island Press, Washington, D.C.

Musiani, M., T. Muhly, C. C. Gates, C. Callaghan, M. E. Smith, and E. Tosoni. 2005. Seasonality and reoccurrence of depredation and wolf control in western North America. Wildlife Society of Bulletin **33**:876-887.

Musiani, M., J. A. Leonard, H. D. Cluff, C. C. Gates, S. Mariani, P. C. Paquet, C. Vila, and R. K. Wayne. 2007. Differentiation of tundra/taiga and boreal coniferous forest wolves: genetics, coat colour and association with migratory caribou. Molecular Ecology 16:4149–4170.

Naess, A. 1989. Ecology, community, and lifestyle. Cambridge University Press, Cambridge, United Kingdom.

Naiman, R. J., J. M. Melillo, and J. E. Hobbie. 1986. Ecosystem alteration of boreal forest streams by beaver (*Castor canadensis*). Ecology 67:1254-1269.

Nasimovich, A. A. 1955. The role of the regime of snow cover in the life of ungulates in the USSR. Moskva: Akademiya Nauk SSR. Translated from Russian by Canadian Wildlife Service, Ottawa, Canada.

National Agriculture Statistical Services (NASS). 2002. 2002 census of agriculture. United States Department of Agriculture, Washington, D.C. Available from http://www.agcensus.usda.gov/Publications/2002/index.asp (accessed October 2007).

National Agricultural Statistics Service (NASS). 2006. Cattle death losses 2005. Agricultural Statistics Board, U.S. Department of Agriculture, Washington, D.C.

National Geographic Society. 1990. Atlas of the world. 6th edition. National Geographic Society. Washington, D.C.

Naughton-Treves, L., R. Grossberg, and A. Treves. 2003. Paying for tolerance: rural citizens' attitudes toward wolf depredation and compensation. Conservation Biology 17:1500–1511.

Nelson, M. E. and L. D. Mech. 1986. Relationship between snow depth and gray wolf predation on white-tailed deer. Journal of Wildlife Management 50:471-474.

Neter, J., M. H. Kutner, C. J. Nachtsheim, and W. Wasserman. 1989. Applied linear regression models. 3rd edition. Irwin, Chicago, Illinois.

Nietvelt, C. N. 2001. Herbivory interactions between beaver (*Castor canadensis*) and elk (*Cervus elaphus*) on willow (*Salix* spp.) in Banff National Park, Alberta. University of Alberta. Masters Thesis.

Nivet, C., and S. Frazie. 2004. A review of European wetland inventory information: report prepared in the framework of a pilot study towards a Pan-

European wetland inventory. Wetlands International, The Netherlands. Available from http://www.wetlands.org/RSIS/WKBASE/ (accessed October 2007).

Norwegian Directorate for Nature Management. 2005. Rovbase. Erstatningsoppgjøret (1999-2005). (Carnivore data base. Statistics for depredation and compensation for sheep [1999-2005]). Available from http://dnweb3.dirnat.no/rovbase/WEBErstVis.asp ?Fylke=Hele+landet&Aarstall=ALLE &valg1=on&valg2=on&B1=Vis (accessed November 2007).

Norwegian Ministry of the Environment. 2003. St.meld nr. 15 (2003–2004) "Rovvilt i norsk natur". (Government proposition on the management of large predators in Norway). Available from http://www.regjeringen.no/ nb/dep/md/dok/regpubl/ stmeld/20032004/Stmeld-nr-15-2003-2004-. html?id=403693 (accessed November 2007).

Norwegian Ministry of the Environment 2007. St. pr. nr. 1 (2007-2008) for budsjettåret 2008. (Parliamentary proposal for the national budget for 2008). Available from http://www.regjeringen.no/pages/2013904/PDFS/ STP200720080001_MDDDDPDFS.pdf (accessed November 2007).

Noss, R. F., H. B. Quigley, M. G. Hornocker, T. Merrill and P. C. Paquet. 1996. Conservation biology and carnivore conservation in the Rocky Mountains. Conservation Biology **10**:949-963.

Novembre, J., Johnson, T., Bryc, K., Kutalik, Z., Boyko, A. R., Auton, A., Indap, A., King, K. S., Bergmann, S., Nelson, M. R., Stephens, M. and C. D. Bustamante. 2008. Genes mirror geography within Europe. Nature **456**: 98-101.

Nowak, R. M., and J. L. Paradiso. 1983. Walker's mammals of the world. 4th edition. Johns Hopkins University Press, Baltimore, Maryland.

Nowak, S., R. W. Mysłajek, and B. Jędrzejewska. 2005. Patterns of wolf, *Canis lupus*, predation on wild and domestic ungulates in the Western Carpathian Mountains (S. Poland). Acta Theriologica **50**:263-276.

Nowak S., R. W. Mysłajek, and B. Jędrzejewska. (in press) Density and demography of wolf, *Canis lupus*, population in the Western Carpathian Mountains, 1996-2003. Folia Zoologica.

Oakleaf, J. K., C. Mack, and D. L. Murray. 2003. Effects of wolves on livestock calf survival and movements in Central Idaho. Journal of Wildlife Management **67**:299-306.

Oakleaf, J. K., D. L. Murray, J. R. Oakleaf, E. E. Bangs, C. M. Mack, D. W. Smith, J. A. Fontaine, M. D. Jimenez, T. J. Meier, and C. C. Niemeyer. 2006. Habitat selection by recolonizing wolves in the northern Rocky Mountains of the United States. Journal of Wildlife Management **70**:554–563.

O'Brien, S. J., and E. Mayr. 1991. Bureaucratic mischief: recognizing endangered species and subspecies. Science **251**:1187-1188.

Okarma, H. 1989. Distribution and numbers of wolves in Poland. Acta Theriologica **34**:497- 503.

Okarma, H. 1993. Status and management of the wolf in Poland. Biological Conservation **66**:153-158.

Okarma, H., B. Jedrzejewska, W. Jedrzejewski, L. Milkowski, and Krasinski, Z. 1995. The trophic ecology of wolves and their predatory role in ungulate communities of forest ecosystems in Europe. Acta Theriologica **40**: 335-386.

Okarma, H., W. Jędrzejewski, K. Schmidt, R. Kowalczyk, and B. Jędrzejewska. 1997. Predation by Eurasian lynx on roe deer and red deer in Białowieża Primeval Forest, Poland. Acta Theriologica **42**: 203-224.

Okarma, H., W. Jędrzejewski, K. Schmidt, S. Śnieżko, A. N. Bunevich, and B. Jędrzejewska. 1998. Home ranges of wolves in Białowieża Primeval Forest, Poland, compared with other Eurasian populations. Journal of Mammalogy **79**:842-852.

Oksanen, L., S. D. Fretwell, J. Arruda, and P. Niemela. 1981. Exploitation ecosystems in gradients of primary productivity. American Naturalist **118**:240-261.

Olsson, O., J. Wirtberg, M. Andersson, and I. Wirtberg. 1997. Wolf, *Canis lupus*, predation on moose, *Alces alces*, and roe deer, *Capreolus capreolus*, in south-central Sweden. Wildlife Biology **3**:13-25.

Orians, G. H., P. A. Cochran, J. W. Duffield, T. K. Fuller, R. J. Gutierrez, W. M. Haneman, F. C. James, P. Kareiva, S. R. Kellert, D. Klein, B. N. McLellan, P. D. Olson, and G. Yaska. 1997. Wolves, bears, and their prey in

Alaska: biological and social challenges in wildlife management. National Research Council, Washington, D.C.

Osenberg, C. W., O. Sarnelle, and S. D. Cooper. 1997. Effect size in ecolocial experiments: the application of biological models in meta-analysis. American Naturalist **150**:798-812.

Østgård, J. 1987. Status of moose in Norway in the 1970s and early 1980s. Pages 63-68 in G. Görasson and S. Lavsund, editors. Proceedings of the Second International Moose Symposium, Swedish Wildlife Research Supplement 1. Uppsala, Sweden.

Ozoliņš, J., Ž. Andersone, and A. Pupila. 2001. Status and management prospects of the wolf, *Canis lupus*, L. in Latvia. Baltic Forestry **2**:63-69.

Packer, C., R. D. Holt, P. J. Hudson, K. D. Lafferty, and A. P. Dobson. 2003. Keeping the herds healthy and alert: implications of predator control for infectious disease. Ecology Letters **6**:797-802.

Paine, R. T. 1969. A note on trophic complexity and community stability. American Naturalist **103**:91-93.

Palumbi, S. R. 2001. Human's as the world"s greatest evolutionary force. Science **293**:1786 -1790.

Paquet, P. C. 1989. Behavioural ecology of sympatric wolves (*Canis lupus*) and coyotes (*C. latrans*) in Riding Mountain National Park, Manitoba. Ph.D. Dissertation, University of Alberta, Edmonton, Canada.

Paquet, P. C. 1992. Prey use strategies of sympatric wolves and coyotes in Riding Mountain National Park, Manitoba. Journal of Mammalogy **73**:337-343.

Paquet, P. C. 1993. Summary reference document - ecological studies of recolonizing wolves in the central Canadian rocky mountains. Parks Canada, Banff National Park Warden Service, Banff, Alberta.

Paquet, P. C., and L. N. Carbyn. 2003. Wolf, *Canis lupus*. Pages 482-510 in G. A. Feldhamer, B. C. Thompson, and J. A. Chapman, editors. Wild mammals of North America: biology, management, and conservation. 2nd edition. Johns Hopkins University Press, Baltimore, Maryland.

Paquet, P. C., J. Wierzchowski, and C. Callaghan. 1996. Summary report on the effects of human activity on gray wolves in the Bow River Valley, Banff National Park. Pages 1-74 in J. C. Green, C. Pacas, L. Cornwell, and

S. Bayley, editors. Ecological outlooks project: a cumulative effects assessment and futures outlook of the Banff Bow Valley. Department of Canadian Heritage, Ottawa, Ontario.

Parker, G. R. 1973. Distribution and densities of wolves within barren-ground caribou range in northern mainland Canada. Journal of Mammalogy **54**:341-348.

Parker, J. 1998. Wolves killed in the NWT. The Saskatoon Star Phoenix. March 5.

Parsons, T. J., D. S. Muniec, K. Sullivan, N. Woodyatt, R. Alliston-Greiner, M. R. Wilson, D. L. Berry, K. A. Holland, V. W. Weedn, P. Gill, and M. M. Holland. 1997. A high observed substitution rate in the human mitochondrial DNA control region. Nature Genetics **15**:363-367.

Pascual, M., and S. P. Ellner. 2000. Linking ecological patterns to environmental forcing via nonlinear time series models. Ecology **81**:2767-2780.

Pastor, J., B. Dewey, R. Moen, D. J. Mladenoff, M. White, and Yosef Cohen. 1998. Spatial patterns in the moose-forest-soil ecosystem on Isle Royale, Michigan, USA. Ecological Applications **8**:411-424.

Pavlov, M. P. 1990. The wolf. Agropromizdat, Moskva, Russia.

Pearce, J. L. and M. S. Boyce. 2006. Modelling distribution and abundance with presence-only data. Journal of Applied Ecology **43**:405–412.

Pearl, J. 2000. Causality. Cambridge University Press, Cambridge, United Kingdom.

Pearse, D. E. and K. A. Crandall. 2004. Beyond FST: Analysis of population genetic data for conservation. Conservation Genetics **5**:585-602.

Pedersen, H. C., P. Wabakken, J. M. Arnemo, S. M. Brainerd, H. Brøseth, O. Hjeljord, O. Liberg, H. Sand, E. Solberg, B. Zimmermann, and H. K. Wam. 2005. Rovvilt og Samfunn (RoSa). Det skandinaviske ulveprosjektet SKANDULV. Oversikt over gjennomførte aktiviteter i 2000-2004. NINA Rapport 117.

Peterson, R. O. 1977. Wolf ecology and prey relationships on Isle Royale. United States National Park Service Science Monograph Series 11. United States National Park Service, Washington, D.C.

Peterson, R. O., and D. L. Allen. 1974. Snow conditions as a parameter in moose-wolf relationships. Naturaliste Canadien **101**:481-492.

Peterson, R. O., and R. E. Page. 1988. The rise and fall of Isle Royale wolves, 1975-1986. Journal of Mammalogy **69**:89-99.

Peterson, R. O., and R. E. Page. 1993. Detection of moose in midwinter from fixed-wing aircraft over dense forest cover. Wildlife Society Bulletin **21**:80-86.

Peterson, R. O., and J. A. Vucetich. 2002. Ecological studies of wolves on Isle Royale. 2001-2002 Annual Report. Michigan Technological University, Houghton, Michigan.

Peterson, R. O., and J. A. Vucetich. 2006. Ecological studies of wolves on Isle Royale, 2005-2006 Annual Report. Michigan Technological University, Houghton, Michigan.

Peterson, R. O., J. D. Woolington, and T. N. Bailey. 1984. Wolves of the Kenai Peninsula, Alaska. Wildlife Monograph **88**:1-52.

Peterson, R. O., J. D. Woolington, and T. N. Bailey. 1984. Wolves of the Kenai Peninsula Alaska. Wildlife Monographs **88**:1–52.

Peterson, R. O., N. J. Thomas, J. M. Thurber, J. A. Vucetich, and T. A. Waite. 1998. Population limitation and the wolves of Isle Royale. Journal of Mammalogy **79**:487-841.

Phillipi, T. E. 1993. Multiple regression: herbivory. Pages 183-210 in S. M. Scheiner and J. Gurevitch, editors. Design and analysis of ecological experiments. Chapman & Hall, New York, New York.

Pilot, M. 2005. Genetic variability and population structure of wolf, *Canis lupus*, in Central and Eastern Europe. Polish Academy of Sciences. Ph.D. Dissertation.

Pilot, M., W. Jędrzejewski, W. Branicki, V. E. Sidorovich, B. Jędrzejewska, K. Stachura, and S. M. Funk. 2006. Ecological factors influence population genetic structure of European grey wolves. Molecular Ecology **15**:4533-4553.

Plutynski, A. 2005. Parsimony and the Fisher–Wright debate. Biology and Philosophy **20**:697–713.

Polis, G. A. and D. R. Strong. 1996. Food web complexity and community dynamics. American Naturalist **147**:813-846.

Polis, G. A., A. L. W. Sears, G. R. Huxel, D. R. Strong, and J. Maron. 2000. When is a trophic cascade a trophic cascade? Trends in Ecology and Evolution **15**:473-475.

Potts, W. K., and E. K. Wakeland. 1993. Evolution of MHC genetic diversity: a tale of incest, pestilence and sexual preference. Trends in Genetics **9**:408-412.

Poulle, M. L., L. Carles, and B. Lequette. 1997. Significance of ungulates in the diet of recently settled wolves in the Mercantour mountains (southeastern France). Revue d'Ecologie – La Terre et la Vie **52**:357-368.

Power, M. E., D. Tilman, J. A. Estes, B. A. Menge, W. J. Bond, L. S. Mills, G. Daily, J. C. Castilla, J. Lubchenco, and R. T. Paine. 1996. Challenges in the quest for keystones. Bioscience **46**:609-620.

Pritchard, J. A. 1999. Preserving Yellowstones natural conditions: science and the perception of nature. University of Nebraska Press, Lincoln, Nebraska.

Pritchard, J. K., M. Stephens, and P. Donnelly. 2000. Inference of population structure using multilocus genotype data. Genetics **155**:945-959.

Promberger, C. and W. Schröeder. 1993. Wolves in Europe: Status and perspectives. Munich Wildlife Society, Ettal, Germany.

Prugh, L. R., C. E. Ritland, S. M. Arthur, and C. J. Krebs. 2005. Monitoring coyote population dynamics by genotyping faeces. Molecular Ecology **14**:1585-1596.

Prugnolle, F., and T. de Meeus. 2002. Inferring sex-biased dispersal from population genetic tools: a review. Heredity **88**:161–165.

Pruitt, W. O., Jr. 1959. Snow as a factor in the winter ecology of the barren ground caribou. Arctic **12**:159-179.

Pruitt, W. O., Jr. 1960. Animals in the snow. Scientific American **202**:60-68.

Pulliainen, E. 1982. Behavior and structure of an expanding wolf population in Karelia, Northern Europe. Pages 134-145 in F. H. Harrington and P. C. Paquet, editors. Wolves of the world, perspectives of behavior, ecology, and conservation. Noyes Publications, Park Ridge, New Jersey, USA.

Radinsky, L. B. 1981. Evolution of skull shape in carnivores, 1: representative modern carnivores. Biological Journal of the Linnaean Society **15**:369-388.

Räikkönen, J., A. Bignert, P. Mortensen, and B. Fernholm. 2006. Congenital defects in a highly inbred wild wolf population (*Canis lupus*). Mammalian Biology **71**:65-73.

Randall, D. A., J. P. Pollinger, R. K. Wayne, L. A. Tallents, P. J. Johnson, and D. W. Macdonald. 2007. Inbreeding is reduced by female-biased dispersal and mating behavior in Ethiopian wolves. Behavioral Ecology **18**:579-589.

Randi, E. and V. Lucchini. 2002. Detecting rare introgression of domestic dog genes into wild wolf (*Canis lupus*) populations by Bayesian admixture analyses of microsatellite variation. Conservation Genetics **3**:31–45.

Randi, E., V. Lucchini, F. Francisci. 1993. Allozyme variability in the Italian wolf (Canis lupus) population. Heredity **71**:516-522.

Randi, E., V. Lucchini, M. F. Christensen, N. Mucci, S. M. Funk, G. Dolf, and V. Loeschke. 2000. Mithocondrial DNA variability in Italian and east European wolves: detecting the consequences of small population size and hybridization. Conservation Biology **14**:464–473.

Ray, N. 2005. Pathmatrix: a geographical information system tool to compute effective distances among samples. Molecular Ecology Notes **5**:177-180.

Reyer, H. U. 2008. Mating with the wrong species can be right. Trends in Ecology and Evolution **23**: 289-292.

Riley, S. P. D., J.P. Pollinger, R. M. Sauvajot, E. C. York, C. Bromley, T. K. Fuller, and R. K. Wayne. 2006. A southern California freeway is a physical and social barrier to gene flow in carnivores. Molecular Ecology **15**:1733–1741.

Ripple, W. J. and R. L. Bechsta. 2003. Wolf reintroduction, predation risk and cottonwood recovery in Yellowstone National Park. Forest Ecology and Management **184**:299–313.

Ripple, W. J., and R. L. Beschta. 2005. Linking Wolves and Plants: Aldo Leopold on Trophic Cascades. Bioscience **55**:613-621.

Ripple, W. J., and R. L. Beschta. 2006. Linking wolves to willows via risk-sensitive foraging by ungulates in the northern Yellowstone ecosystem. Forest Ecology and Management **230**:96-106.

Ripple, W. J., E. J., Larsen, R. A., Renkin, and D. W. Smith. 2001. Trophic cascades among wolves, elk, and aspen on Yellowstone National Park's northern range. Conservation Biology 102:227–234.

Roath, L. R. and W. C. Krueger. 1982. Cattle grazing behaviour on a forested range. Journal of Range Management 35:332-338.

Robel, R. J., A. D. Dayton, F. R. Henderson, R. L. Meduna, and C. W. Spaeth. 1981. Relationships between husbandry methods and sheep losses to canine predators. Journal of Wildlife Management 45:894-911.

Rootsi, I. 2003. Rabid wolves and the man in Estonia of the 18th-19th centuries. Acta Zoologica Lituanica 13:72-77.

Rosenberg, A. 2005. Philosophy of science: a contemporary introduction. Routledge, New York, New York.

Rosenberg, N. A., and M. Nordborg. 2002. Genealogical trees, coalescent theory and the analysis of genetic polymorphisms. Nature Reviews Genetics 3:380-390.

Roy, M. S., E. Geffen, D. Smith, E. Ostrander, and R. K. Wayne. 1994. Patterns of differentiation and hybridization in North American wolf-like canids revealed by analysis of microsatellite loci. Molecular Biology and Evolution 11:553-570.

Roy, M. S., E. Geffen, D. Smith, and R. K. Wayne. 1996. Molecular genetics of pre-1940 red wolves. Conservation Biology 10:1413-1424.

Royama, T. 1992. Analytical population dynamics. Chapman and Hall, London, United Kingdom.

Russell, B. 1913. On the notion of cause. *Proceedings of the Aristotelian Society* 13:1-26.

Ruth, T. K. 2004. Ghost of the Rockies: the Yellowstone cougar project. Yellowstone Science 12:13-24.

Ryabov, L. S. 1988. Characteristics of wolves' (*Canis lupus* L.) reproduction in the Central Black Earth Region. Ekologiya 6:42-48. [In Russian]

Sacks, B. N., S. K. Brown, and H. B. Ernest. 2004. Population structure of California coyotes corresponds to habitat-specific breaks and illuminates species history. Molecular Ecology 13:1265-1275.

Sacks, B. N., B. R. Mitchell, C. L. Williams, and H. B. Ernest. 2005. Coyote movements and social structure along a cryptic population genetic subdivision. Molecular Ecology **14**:1241-1249.

Sand, H., B. Zimmerman, P. Wabakken, H. Andrén, and H. C. Pedersen. 2005. Using GPS technology and GIS cluster analyses to estimate kill rates in wolf-ungulate ecosystems. Wildlife Society Bulletin **33**:914-925.

Sand, H., C. Wikenros, P. Wabakken, and O. Liberg. 2006a. Cross-continental differences in patterns of predation: will naïve moose in Scandinavia ever learn? Proceedings of the Royal Society of London, Series B **273**:1421-1427.

Sand, H., C. Wikenros, P. Wabakken, and O. Liberg. 2006b. Wolf (*Canis lupus*) hunting success on moose (*Alces alces*): effects of hunting group size, snow depth, and age of breeding wolves. Animal Behaviour **72**:781-789.

SAS Institute. 1995. SAS software. Cary, North Carolina.

Savolainen, P., Y. Zhang, J. Luo, J. Lundeberg, and T. Leitner. 2002. Genetic evidence for an East Asian origin of domestic dogs. Science **298**:1610-1613.

Scandura, M., C. Claudia, I. Laura, and M. Apollonio. 2006. An empirical approach for reliable microsatellite genotyping of wolf DNA from multiple noninvasive sources. Conservation Genetics **7**:813-823.

Schmidt, K., W. Jędrzejewski, J. Theurkauf, R. Kowalczyk, H. Okarma, and B. Jędrzejewska. 2008. Reproductive behaviour of wild-living wolves in Białowieża Primeval Forest (Poland). Journal of Ethology 26:69-78.

Schmitz, O. J. 2005. Scaling from plot experiments to landscapes: studying grasshoppers to inform forest ecosystem management. Oecologia **145**:225-234.

Schmitz, O. J. 2006. Predators have large effects on ecosystem properties by changing plant diversity, not plant biomass. Ecology **87**:1432-1437.

Schmitz, O. J., A. P. Beckerman, and K. M. O'Brien. 1997. Behaviorally mediated trophic cascades: effects of predation risk on food web interactions. Ecology **78**:1388-1399.

Schmitz, O. J., P. A. Hämback, and A. P. Beckerman. 2000. Trophic cascades in terrestrial systems: a review of the effects of carnivore removals on plants. The American Naturalist **155**:141-153.

Schwartz, C. C., S. D. Miller, and M. A. Haroldson. 2003. Grizzly bear. Pages 556-586 in G. A. Feldhammer, B. C. Thompson, and J. A. Chapman, editors. Wild mammals of North America: biology, management, and conservation. Johns Hopkins University Press, Baltimore, Maryland.

Schwartz, C. C., M. A. Haroldson, G. C. White, R. B. Harris, S. Cherry, K. A. Keating, D. Moody, and C. Servheen. 2006. Temporal, spatial, and environmental influences on the demographics of grizzly bears in the greater Yellowstone ecosystem. Wildlife Monographs 161:1-68.

Seddon, J. M., and H. Ellegren. 2002. MHC class II genes in European wolves: a comparison with dogs. Immunogenetics 54:490–500.

Seddon J. M., and H. Ellegren. 2004. A temporal analysis shows major histocompatibility complex loci in the Scandinavian wolf population are consistent with neutral evolution. Proceedings of the Royal Society of London: B-Biological Sciences 271:2283–2291.

Seddon, J. M., H. G. Parker, E. A. Ostrander, and H. Ellegren. 2005. SNPs in ecological and conservation studies: a test in the Scandinavian wolf population. Molecular Ecology 14:503–511.

Seddon, J. M., A. K. Sundqvist, S. Bjornerfeldt, and H. Ellegren. 2006. Genetic identification of immigrants to the Scandinavian wolf population. Conservation Genetics 7:225-230.

Seielstad, M.T., E. Minch, and L.L. Cavalli-Sforza. 1998. Genetic evidence for a higher female migration rate in humans. Nature Genetics 20:278-280.

Seip, D. R. 1992. Factors limiting woodland caribou populations and their interrelationships with wolves and moose in southeastern British Columbia. Canadian Journal of Zoology 70:1494-1503.

Selva, N., B. Jędrzejewska, W. Jędrzejewski, and A. Wajrak. 2003. Scavenging on European bison carcasses in Bialowieza Primeval Forest (eastern Poland). Ecoscience 10:303-311.

Selva, N., B. Jędrzejewska, W. Jędrzejewski, and A. Wajrak. 2005. Factors affecting carcass use by a guild of scavengers in European temperate woodland. Canadian Journal of Zoology 83:1590-1601.

Shaffer, M. L. 1981. Minimum viable populations sizes for species conservation. BioScience 31:131-134.

Shapiro, B., A. Drummond, A. Rambaut, M. C. Wilson, P. E. Matheus, A. V. Sher, O. G. Pybus, M. T. Gilbert, I. Barnes, J. Binladen, E. Willerslev,

A. J. Hansen, G. F. Baryshnikov, J. A. Burns, S. Davydov, J. C. Driver, D. G. Froese, C. R. Harington, G. Keddie, P. Kosintsev, M. L. Kunz, L. D. Martin, R. O. Stephenson, J. Storer, R. Tedford, S. Zimov, and A. Cooper. 2004. Rise and fall of the Beringian steppe bison. Science **306**:1561-1565.

Shipley, B. 2002. Cause and correlation in biology: a users guide to path analysis, structural equations and causal inference. Cambridge University Press, Cambridge, UK.

Shivik, J. A. 2006. Tools for the edge: what's new for conserving carnivores? BioScience **56**:253-259.

Shivik, J. A., A. Treves, and P. Callahan. 2003. Nonlethal techniques for managing predation: primary and secondary repellents. Conservation Biology **17**:1531-1537.

Shurin, J. B., E. T. Borer, E. W. Seabloom, K. Anderson, C. A. Blanchette, B. Broitman, D. Cooper, and S. Halpern. 2002. A cross-system comparison of the strength of trophic cascades. Ecology Letters **5**:785-791.

Sidorovich, V. E., L. L. Tikhomirova, and B. Jędrzejewska. 2003. Wolf, Canis lupus numbers, diet and damage to livestock in relation to hunting and ungulate abundance in northeastern Belarus during 1990-2000. Wildlife Biology 9:103-111.

Sidorovich, V. E. and M. E. Nikiforov. 2007. Kaznit nelzya, pomilovat [Don't sentence to death, do pardon]. Lesnoe i okhotniche khozaistvo **2**:33-38. [In Russian]

Sidorovich, V. E., V. P. Stolyarov, N. N. Vorobei, N. V. Ivanova, and B. Jędrzejewska. 2007. Litter size, sex ratio, and age structure of gray wolves, *Canis lupus*, in relation to population fluctuations in northern Belarus. Canadian Journal of Zoology **85**:295-300.

Sikes, D. S. 1994. Influence of ungulate carcasses on coleopteran communities in Yellowstone National Park. Montana State University. Master of Science thesis.

Sillero-Zubiri, C., D. Gottelli, and D. W. Macdonald. 1996. Male philopatry, extra-pack copulations and inbreeding avoidance in Ethiopian wolves *Canis simensis*. Behavioural Ecology and Sociobiology **38**:331-340.

Silver, H. and W. Silver. 1969. Growth and behavior of the coyote-like canid of northern New England with observations of canid hybrids. Wildlife Monographs 17:1-44.

Simmons, G. 1992. Calculus gems. McGraw Hill, New York, New York.

Sinclair, A. R. E. 1989. Population regulation in animals. Pages 197-241 in J. M. Cherret, editor. Ecological concepts. Blackwell Scientific, Oxford, United Kingdom.

Sinclair, A. R. E. 1991. Science and the practice of wildlife management. Journal of Wildlife Management 55:767-773.

Singer, F. J., L. C. Mark, and R. C. Cates. 1994. Ungulate herbivory of willows on Yellowstone's northern winter range. Journal of Wildlife Management 47:435-443.

Sjölander-Lindqvist, A. 2006. Den är ju inte i fårhagen på studiebesök. Report 2006:1, CEFOS. Gothenburg University, Göteborg, Sweden.

Skogen, K. and H. Haaland. 2001. En ulvehistorie fra Östfold. Samarbeid og konflikter mellom forvaltning, forskning og lokalbefolkning. NINA fagrapport 52. Lillehammer, Norway.

Skogen, K., and O. Krange. 2003. A wolf at the gate: the anti-carnivore alliance and the symbolic construction of community. Sociologia Ruralis 43:309-325.

Skyrms, B. 1980. Causal necessity. Yale University Press, New Haven, Connecticut.

Slatkin, M. 1993. Isolation by distance in equilibrium and non-equilibrium populations. Evolution 47:264-279.

Slovic, P. 1986. Informing and educating the public about risk. Risk Analysis 6:403-415.

Śmietana, W., and A. Klimek. 1993. Diet of wolves in Bieszczady Mountains, Poland. Acta Theriologica 38:245-251.

Śmietana, W., and J. Wajda. 1997. Wolf number changes in Bieszczady National Park, Poland. Acta Theriologica 42:241-253.

Smith, D. W. 2005. Ten years of Yellowstone wolves 1995-2005. Yellowstone Science 13:7-33.

Smith, D., T. Meier, E. Geffen, L. D. Mech, J. W. Burch, L. G. Adams, and R. K. Wayne. 1997. Is incest common in gray wolf packs? Behavahioral Ecology 8:384-391.

Smith, D. W., R. O. Peterson, and D. B. Houston. 2003. Yellowstone after wolves. Bioscience 53:330-340.

Smith, D. W., T. D. Drummer, K. M. Murphy, D. S. Guernsey and S. B. Evans. 2004. Winter prey selection and estimation of wolf kill rates in Yellowstone National Park, 1995–2000. Journal of Wildlife Management 68:153–166.

Smith, D. W., D. R. Stahler, D. S. Guernsey, and E. E. Bangs. 2006. Wolf restoration in Yellowstone National Park. Pages 242-253 in D. R. McCullough, K. Kaji and. M.Yamanaka, editors. Wildlife in Shiretoko and Yellowstone National Park: Lessons in wildlife conservation from two world heritage sites. Shiretoko Nature Foundation, Japan.

Smith, M. E., J. D. C. Linnell, J. Odden, and J. E. Swenson. 2000a. Review of methods to reduce livestock depredation II: aversive conditioning, deterrents, and repellents. Acta Agriculturae Scandinavica: Section A, Animal Science 50:291-303.

Smith, M. E., J. D. C. Linnell, J. Odden, and J. E. Swenson. 2000b. Review of methods to reduce livestock depredation: guardian animals. Acta Agriculturae Scandinavica: Section A, Animal Science 50:279-290.

Snyder, W. E., G. B. Snyder, D. L. Finke, and C. S. Straub. 2006. Predator biodiversity strengthens herbivore suppression. Ecology Letters 9:789-796.

Sokal, R. R. and F. J. Rohlf. 1995. Biometry: the principles and practice of statistics in biological research. W H Freeman, New York, New York.

Solberg, E. J., B. E. Saether, O. Strand, and A. Loison. 1999. Dynamics of a harvested moose population in a variable environment. Journal of Animal Ecology 68:186–204.

Solberg, E. J., H. Sand, J. D. C. Linnell, S. M. Brainerd, R. Andersen, J. Odden, H. Brøseth, J. E. Swenson, O. Strand, and P. Wabakken, 2003. Utredninger i forbindelse med ny rovviltmelding: Store rovdyrs innvirkning på hjorteviltet i Norge: Økologiske prosesser og konsekvenser for jaktuttak og jaktutøvelse. NINA Fagrapport 63.

Soper, J. D. 1928. A faunal investigation of southern Baffin Island. National Museum of Canada, Biological Series No. 15, Bulletin No. 53. National Museum of Canada, Ottawa, Ontario.

SPSS 14.0. 2006. SPSS Inc. Chicago, Illinois.

Stahler, D., B. Heinrich, and D. Smith. 2002. Common ravens, *Corvus corax*, preferentially associate with grey wolves, *Canis lupus*, as a foraging strategy in winter. Animal Behaviour **64**:283-290.

Staloff, D. 1998. The Search for a meaningful past: philosophies, theories, and interpretations of human history. The Teaching Company, Chantilly, Virginia.

Statistics Canada. 2003. Aboriginal peoples of Canada: a demographic profile. 2001 Statistics Canada, Ottawa, Ontario. Available from http://www12. statcan.ca/english/ census01/products/analytic/companion/abor/contents. cfm (Accessed October 2007).

Statistics Sweden. 2006. Jordbruksstatistisk årsbok. Available from http://www. scb.se (accessed November 2007).

Stephens, P. W., and R. O. Peterson. 1984. Wolf-avoidance strategies of moose. Holarctic Ecology **7**:239–244.

Stephens, D. W. and J. R. Krebs. 1986. Foraging theory. Princeton University Press, Princeton, New Jersey.

Stiller, M., R. E.Green, M. Ronan, J. F. Simons, L. Du, W. He, M. Egholm, J. Rothberg, S. G. Keats, N. D. Ovodov, E. E. Antipina, G. F. Baryshnikov, Y. V. Kuzmin, A. A. Vasilevski, G. E. Wuenschell, J. Termini, M. Hofreiter, V. Jaenicke-Després, and S. Pääbo. 2006. Patterns of nucleotide misincorporations during enzymatic amplification and direct large-scale sequencing of ancient DNA. Proceedings of the National Academy of Sciences **103**:13578-13584.

Stockwell, D. and D. Peters. 1999. The GARP modeling system: problems and solutions to automated spatial prediction. International Journal of Geographic Information Science **13**:143-158.

Storfer, A., M. A. Murphy, J. S. Evans, C. S. Goldberg, S. Robinson, S. F. Spear, R. Dezzani, E. Delmelle, L. Vierling, and L. P. Waits. 2007. Putting the "'landscape" in landscape genetics. Heredity **98**:128–142.

Stoskopf, M. K., K. Beck, B. Fazio, T. K. Fuller, E. M. Gese, B. T. Kelly, F. F. Knowlton, D. L. Murray, W. Waddell, and L. Waits. 2005. Implementing recovery of the red wolf – Integrating research scientists and managers. Wildlife Society Bulletin 33:1145-1152.

Strickland, M. D. and L. L. McDonald. 2006. Introduction to the special section on resource selection. Journal of Wildlife Management 70:321–323.

Strimmer, K., and O. G. Pybus. 2001. Exploring the demographic history of DNA sequences using the generalized skyline plot. Molecular Biology and Evolution 18:2298–2305.

Sundqvist, A. K., H. Ellegren, M. Olivier, and C. Vilà. 2001. Y chromosome haplotyping in Scandinavian wolves (*Canis lupus*) based on microsatellite markers. Molecular Ecology 10:1959-1966.

Sundqvist, A. K., S. Bjornerfeldt, J. Leonard, F. Hailer, A. Hedhammar, H. Ellegren, and C. Vilà. 2006. Unequal contribution of sexes in the origin of dog breeds. Genetics 172:1121-1128.

Sutter, N.B., Bustamante, C.D., Chase, K., Gray, M. M., Zhao, K., Zhu, L., Padhukasahasram, B., Karins, E., Davis, S., Jones, P.G., Quignon, P., Johnson, G. S., Parker, H. G., Fretwell, N., Mosher, D. S., Lawler, D. F., Satyaraj, E., Nordborg, M., Lark, K. G., Wayne, R. K. and E. A. Ostrander. 2007. A Single IGF1 Allele Is a Major Determinant of Small Size in Dogs. Science 316: 112-115.

Swedish Ministry of Environment. 2000. Government proposition 2000/01:57. "En sammanhållen Rovdjurspolitik".

Swenson, J. E. and H. Andrén. 2005. A tale of two countries: large carnivore depredations and compensation schemes in Sweden and Norway. Pages 323-339 in R. Woodroffe, S. Thirgood, and A. Rabinowitz, editors. People and wildlife: conflict or co-existence? Cambridge University Press, Cambridge, United Kingdom.

Swenson, J. E., Sandergren, F., Soderberg, A., Bjarvall, V., Franzen, R. and P. Wabakken. 1997. Infanticide caused by hunting of male bears. Nature 368: 450-451.

Systat. 2002. Systat software. San Jose, California, USA.

Taylor, P. W. 1986. Respect for nature: a theory of environmental ethics. Princeton University Press, Princeton, New Jersey.

Telfer, E. S, and J. P. Kelsall. 1979. Studies of morphological parameters affecting ungulate locomotion in snow. Canadian Journal of Zoology 57:2153-2159.

Telfer, E. S., and J. P. Kelsall. 1984. Adaptation of some large North American mammals for survival in snow. Ecology 65:1828-1834.

Templeton, A. R. 1999. Human races: a genetic and evolutionary perspective. American Anthropologist 100:632-650.

Terborgh, J. 2005. The green world hypothesis revisited. Pages 82-97 in J. C. Ray, K. H. Redford, R. S. Steneck and J. Berger, editors. Large Carnivores and the Conservation of Biodiversity. Island Press, Washington, D.C.

Terborgh, J., J. A. Estes, P. C. Paquet, K. Ralls, D. Boyd-Heger, B. Miller, and R. Noss. 1999. The role of top carnivores in regulating terrestrial ecosystems. Pages 60-103 in M. E. Soulé and J. Terborgh, editors. Continental Conservation: Scientific foundations of regional reserve networks. Island Press, Washington, D.C.

Tessier, A. J. and P. Woodruff. 2002. Cryptic trophic cascade along a gradient of lake size. Ecology 83:1263-1270.

Theuerkauf, J. W. Jedrzedjewski, K. Schmidt, and R. Gula. 2001. Impact of human activity on daily movement patterns of wolves, *Canis lupus*, in the Białowieża forest, Poland. Pages 206-208 in R. Field, R. J. Warren, H. Okarma and P. R. Sievert, editors. Wildlife, land, and people: priorities for the 21st century. Proceedings of the Second International Wildlife Management Congress. The Wildlife Society, Bethesda, Maryland.

Theuerkauf, J., W. Jędrzejewski, K. Schmidt, and R. Gula. 2003. Spatiotemporal segregation of wolves from humans in the Białowieża Forest (Poland). Journal of Wildlife Management 67:706-716.

Thiel, R. P. 1985. Relationship between road densities and wolf habitat suitability in Wisconsin. American Midland Naturalist 113:404-407.

Thompson, D. W. 1942. On growth and form. 2nd ed. Cambridge University Press, Cambridge, United Kingdom.

Thompson, D. Q. 1952. Travel, range, and food habits of timber wolves in Wisconsin. Journal of Mammalogy 33:429-442.Thurber, J. M., and R. O. Peterson. 1993. Effects of population-density and pack size on the foraging ecology of gray wolves. Journal of Mammalogy 74:879-889.

Thurber, J. M., and R. O. Peterson. 1993. Effects of population density and pack size on the foraging ecology of gray wolves. Journal of Mammalogy 74:879–889.

Thurber, J. M., R. O. Peterson, T. D. Drummer, and S. A. Thomasma. 1994. Gray wolf response to refuge boundaries and roads in Alaska. Wildlife Society Bulletin 22:61-68.

Tilman, D., P. B. Reich, J. M. H. Knops, D. Wedin, T. Mielke, and C. K. Lehman. 2001. Diversity and productivity in a long-term grassland experiment. Science 294:843-845.

Todd, N. B. 1970. Karyotypic fissioning and canid phylogeny. Journal of Theoretical Biology 26:445-480.

Tompa, F. S. 1983. Problem wolf management in British Columbia: conflict and program evaluation. Canadian Wildlife Service Report Series 45:112-119.

Treves, A., R. R. Jurewicz, L. Naughton-Treves, R. A. Rose, R. C. Willging, and A. P. Wydeven. 2002. Wolf depredation on domestic animals in Wisconsin, 1976-2000. Wildlife Society Bulletin 30:231-241.

Treves, A., L. Naughton-Treves, E. K. Harper, D. J. Mladenoff, R. A. Rose, T. A. Sickley, and A. P. Wydeven. 2004. Predicting human-carnivore conflict: a spatial model derived from 25 years of data on wolf predation on livestock. Conservation Biology 18:114-125.

Tsuda, K., Y. Kikkawa, H. Yonekawa, and Y. Tanabe. 1997. Extensive interbreeding occurred among multiple matriarchal ancestors during the domestication of dogs: evidence from inter- and intraspecies polymorphisms in the D-loop region of mitochondrial DNA between dogs and wolves. Genes and Genetic Systems 72:229-238.

Turchin, P. 2003. Complex population dynamics: a theoretical/empirical synthesis. Princeton University Press, Princeton, New Jersey.

Tyers, D. B. 2003. Winter ecology of moose on the northern Yellowstone winter range. Montana State University. PhD Dissertation.

Tyshkevich, V. E., and E. K. Vostokov. 2007. Kaznit, nelzya pomilovat [Do sentence to death, don't pardon]. Lesnoe i okhotniche khozaistvo **2/2007**:39-42. [In Russian]

Usher, P. 1971. The Banks islanders: economy and ecology of a frontier trapping community: volume 2, economy and ecology. Department of Indian Affairs and Northern Development, Northern Science Research Group Publication No. NSRG 71-4. Department of Indian Affairs and Northern Development, Government of Canada, Ottawa, Ontario.

Valdmann, H., Z. Andersone-Lilley, O. Koppa, J. Ozoliņš, and G. Bagrade. 2005. Winter diets of wolf, *Canis lupus*, and lynx, *Lynx lynx*, in Estonia and Latvia. Acta Theriologica **50**:521-527.

Varis, O., and S. Kuikka. 1999. Learning Bayesian decision analysis by doing: lessons from environmental and natural resources management. Ecological Modelling **119**:177-195.

Varley, N., and M. S. Boyce. 2006. Adaptive management for reintroductions: updating a wolf recovery model for Yellowstone national park. Ecological Modeling **193**:315-339.

Verardi, A., V. Lucchini, and E. Randi. 2006. Detecting introgressive hybridization between free-ranging domestic dogs and wild wolves (*Canis lupus*) by admixture linkage disequilibrium analysis. Molecular Ecology **15**:2845–2855.

Vilà, C., and R. K. Wayne. 1999. Hybridization between dogs and wolves. Conservation Biology **13**:195-198.

Vilà, C., P. Savolainen, J. E. Malconado, I. R. Amorim, J. E. Rice, R. L. Honeycutt, K. A. Crandell, J. Lundeberg, and R. K. Wayne. 1997. Multiple and ancient origins of the domestic dog. Science **276**:687-89.

Vilà, C., I. R. Amorim, J. A. Leonard, D. Posada, J. Castroviejo, F. Petrucci-Fonseca, K. A. Crandall, H. Ellegren, and R. K. Wayne. 1999. Mitochondrial DNA phylogeography and population history of the grey wolf Canis lupus. Molecular Ecology 8:2089-2103.

Vilà, C., A-K. Sundqvist, Ø. Flagstad, J. Seddon, S. Björnerfeldt, I. Kojola, A. Casulli, H. Sand, P. Wabakken, and H. Ellegren. 2003a. Rescue of a serverely bottlenecked wolf (*Canis lupus*) population by a single immigrant. Proceedings of the Royal Society of London, Series B **270**:91-97.

Vilà, C., C. Walker, A-K. Sundqvist, Ø. Flagstad, Ž. Andersone, A. Casulli, I. Kojola, H. Valdmann, J. Halverson, and H. Ellegren. 2003b. Combined use of maternal, paternal and bi–parental genetic markers for the identification of wolf–dog hybrids. Heredity **90**:17–24.

vonHoldt, B. M., D. R. Stahler, D. W. Smith, D. A. Earl, J. P. Pollinger, and R. K. Wayne. 2008. The genealogy and genetic viability of reintroduced Yellowstone grey wolves. Molecular Ecology **17**:252-74.

Vos, J. 2000. Food habits and livestock depredation of two Iberian wolf packs (*Canis lupus signatus*) in the north of Portugal. Journal of Zoology **251**:457-462.

Vucetich, J. A., and T. A. Waite. 1998. The number of censuses required for demographic estimation of the effective population size. Conservation Biology **12**:1023-1030.

Vucetich, J. A., and R. O. Peterson. 2004a. The influence of prey consumption and demographic stochasticity on population growth rate of Isle Royale wolves (Canis lupus). Oikos **107**:309-320.

Vucetich, J. A. and R. O. Peterson. 2004b. The influence of top-down, bottom-up, and abiotic factors on the moose (Alces alces) population of Isle Royale. Proceedings of the Royal Society of London, B **271**:183-189.

Vucetich, J. A., R. O. Peterson, and C. L. Schaefer. 2002. The effect of prey and predator densities on wolf predation. Ecology **83**: 3003-3013.

Vucetich, J. A., R. O. Peterson, and T. A. Waite. 2004. Raven scavenging favors group foraging in wolves. Animal Behaviour **67**:1117-1126.

Vucetich, J. A., D. W. Smith, and D. R. Stahler. 2005. Influence of harvest, climate, and wolf predation on Yellowstone elk, 1961-2004. Oikos **111**:259-270.

Wabakken, P., H. Sand, O. Liberg, and A. Bjärvall. 2001. The recovery, distribution, and population dynamics of wolves on the Scandinavian peninsula, 1978-1998. Canadian Journal of Zoology **79**:710-725.

Wabakken, P., Å. Aronson, T. H. Strømseth, H. Sand, and I. Kojola, 2006. Ulv i Skandinavia : statusrapport for vinteren 2005-2006. Høgskolen i Hedmark, Oppdragsrapport 2.

Wagner, F. H. 2006. Yellowstone's destabilized ecosystem: elk effects, science, and policy conflict. Oxford University Press, Oxford, United Kingdom.

Waits, L., and D. Paetkau. 2005. New noninvasive genetic sampling tools for wildlife biologists: a review of applications and recommendations for accurate data collection. Journal of Wildlife Management **69**:1419–1433.

Wallace, L. L., M. G. Turner, W. H. Romme, R. V. O'Neill, and Y. G. Wu. 1995. Scale of Heterogeneity of Forage Production and Winter Foraging by Elk and Bison. Landscape Ecology **10**:75-83.

Walters, C. J. 1986. Adaptive management of renewable resources. Blackburn Press, New York, New York.

Walters, C. J., and R. Hilbron. 1978. Ecological optimization and adaptive management. Annual Review of Ecology and Systematics **9**:157-188.

Walton, L. R. 2000. Investigation into the movements of migratory wolves in the central Canadian arctic. University of Saskatchewan. Master's Thesis.

Walton, L. R., H. D. Cluff, P. C. Paquet, and M. A. Ramsay. 2001a. Movement patterns of barren-ground wolves in the central Canadian arctic. Journal of Mammalogy **82**:867-876.

Walton, L. R., H. D. Cluff, P. C. Paquet, and M. A. Ramsay. 2001b. Performance of 2 models of satellite collars for wolves. Wildlife Society Bulletin **29**:180-186.

Waples, R. S. 1989. A generalized approach for estimating effective population size from temporal changes in allele frequency. Genetics **121**:379–391.

Waples, R. S. 2005. Genetic estimates of contemporary effective population size: to what time periods do the estimates apply? Molecular Ecology **14**:3335-3352.

Wayne, R. K., and S. J. O'Brien. 1987. Allozyme divergence within the Canidae. Systematic Zoology **36**:339-355.

Wayne, R. K., and S. M. Jenks. 1991. Mitochondrial DNA analysis supports extensive hybridization of the Endangered Red Wolf (*Canis rufus*). Nature **351**:565-568.

Wayne, R. K. and K. P. Koepfli. 1996. Demographic and historical effects on genetic variation of carnivores. Pages 453-484 in J. L. Gittleman, editor, Carnivore behavior, ecology, and evolution, Volume 2. Cornell University Press. Ithaca, New York.

Wayne, R. K. and D. Gottelli. 1997. Systematics, population genetics and genetic management of the Ethiopian wolf. Pages 43-50 in C. Sillero-Zubiri and D. Macdonald, editors. The Ethiopian wolf: status survey and conservation action plan. IUCN/SSC Canid Specialist Group, Oxford, United Kingdom.

Wayne, R. K., and D. M. Brown. 2001. Hybridization and conservation of carnivores. Pages 145-162 in J. L. Gittleman, S. M. Funk, D. Macdonald, and R. K. Wayne, editors. Carnivore conservation. Cambridge University Press, Cambridge.

Wayne, R. K., and C. Vilà. 2003. Molecular genetic studies of wolves. Pages 218-238 in L. D. Mech, and L. Boitani, editors. The Ecology and Behavior of the Gray Wolf. University of Chicago Press, Chicago.

Wayne, R. K., and P. A. Morin. 2004. Conservation genetics age in the new molecular. Frontiers in Ecology and the Environment 2:89-97.

Wayne, R. K., W. G. Nash, and S. J. O'Brien. 1987. Chromosomal evolution of the Canidae. Cytogenetics and Cell Genetics 44:123-133.

Wayne, R. K., N. Lehman, D. Girman, P. J. P. Gogan, D. A. Gilbert, K. Hansen, R. O. Peterson, U. S. Seal, A. Eisenhawer, L. D. Mech, and R. J. Krumenaker. 1991. Conservation genetics of the endangered Isle Royale gray wolf. Conservation Biology. 5:41-51.

Wayne, R. K., N. Lehman, M. W. Allard, and R. L. Honeycutt. 1992. Mitochondrial DNA variability of the gray wolf - genetic consequences of population decline and habitat fragmentation. Conservation Biology 6:559-569.

Wayne, R. K., J. A. Leonard, and A. Cooper. 1999. Full of sound and fury: The recent history of ancient DNA. Annual Review of Ecology and Systematics 30:457-477.

Weaver, J. 1978. The wolves of Yellowstone. Natural Resources report No. 14. United States National Parks Service, Washington, D.C.

Weaver, J. L. 1994. Ecology of wolf predation amidst high ungulate diversity in Jasper National Park, Alberta. University of Montana. Dissertation.

Weaver, J. L., P. C. Paquet, and L. F. Ruggiero. 1996. Resilience and conservation of large carnivores in the Rocky Mountains. Conservation Biology 10:964-976.

Weckworth, B. V., S. Talbot, G. K. Sage, D. K. Person, and J. Cooks. 2005. A signal for independent coastal and continental histories among North American wolves. Molecular Ecology **14**:917–930.

West Kitikmeot Slave Study (WKSS) 2007. West Kitikmeot Slave Study (WKSS) state of knowledge report – 2006 update. WKSS Study, Yellowknife, NWT, Canada.

Wheeldon, T., and B. N. White. 2009. Genetic analysis of historic western Great Lakes region wolf samples reveals early Canis lupus/lycaon hybridization. Biology Letters **5**:101-4.

White, C. A. 2001. Aspen, Elk, and Fire in the Canadian Rocky Mountains. Department of Forest Sciences, University of British Columbia. Dissertation.

White, P. J., and R. A. Garrott. 2005. Yellowstone's ungulates after wolves - expectations, realizations, and predictions. Biological Conservation **125**:141-152.

White, C. A., C. E. Olmstred, and C. E. Kay. 1998. Aspen, elk, and fire in the Rocky Mountain national parks of North America. Wildlife Society Bulletin **26**:449-462.

White, C. A., M. C. Feller, and S. Bayley. 2003. Predation risk and the functional response of elk-aspen herbivory. Forest Ecology and Management **181**:77-97.

Whittington, J., C. C. St. Clair, and G. Mercer. 2004. Path tortuosity and the permeability of roads and trails to wolf movement. Ecology and Society **9**:4. [online] URL: http://www.ecologyandsociety.org/vol9/iss1/art4/

Williams, T. M. 1995. Beverly calving ground surveys June 5-16 1993 and June 2-13 1994. File Report No. 114. Department of Resources, Wildlife and Economic Development, Government of the Northwest Territories, Yellowknife, Northwest Territories.

Williams, C. K., G. Ericsson, and T. A. Heberlein. 2002. A quantitative summary of attitudes toward wolves and their reintroduction (1972-2000). Wildlife Society Bulletin **30**:575-584.

Wilmers, C.C., and W. M. Getz. 2005. Gray wolves as climate change buffers. PLoS Biology 3:e92.

Wilmers, C. C., R. L. Crabtree, D. W. Smith, K. M. Murphy, and W. M. Getz. 2003. Trophic facilitation by introduced top predators: grey wolf subsidies to scavengers in Yellowstone National Park. Journal of Animal Ecology 72:909-916.

Wilmers, C.C., E. S. Post, R. O. Peterson, and J. A. Vucetich. 2006. Disease mediated switch from top-down to bottom-up control exacerbates climatic effects on moose population dynamics. Ecology Letters 9:383-389.

Wilson, E. O. 1999. Diversity of life. W.W. Norton & Company, New York, New York.

Wilson, G. A. and B. Rannala. 2003. Bayesian inference of recent migration rates using multilocus genotypes. Genetics 163:1177-1191.

Wilson, P. J., S. Grewal, I. D. Lawford, J. N. M. Heal, A. G. Granacki, D. Pennock, J. B. Theberge, M. T. Theberge, D. R. Voigt, W. Waddell, R. E. Chambers, P. C. Paquet, G. Goulet, D. Cluff, and B. N. White. 2000. DNA profiles of the eastern Canadian wolf and the red wolf provide evidence for a common evolutionary history independent of the gray wolf. Canadian Journal of Zoology 78:2156-2166.

Wilson, P. J., S. Grewal, T. McFadden, R. C. Chambers and B. N. White. 2003. Mitochondrial DNA extracted from eastern North American wolves killed in the 1800s is not of gray wolf origin. Canadian Journal of Zoology 81:936-940.

Wittmer, H. U., A. R. E. Sinclair, and B. N. Mclellan. 2005. The role of predation in the decline and extirpation of woodland caribou. Oecologia 144:257-267.

Wolff, J. O., and T. Van Horn. 2003. Vigilance and foraging patterns of American elk during the rut in habitats with and without predators. Canadian Journal of Zoology 81:266–271.

Wolsan, M., M. Bieniek, and T. Buchalczyk. 1992. The history of distributional and numerical changes of the wolf (*Canis lupus*) in Poland. Pages 375-380 in B. Bobek, K. Perzanowski, and W. Regelin, editors. Global trends in wildlife management. Świat Press, Kraków-Warszawa, Poland.

Wood, A. E. 1957. What, if anything, is a rabbit? Evolution 11:417-425.

Woodroffe, R., and J. R. Ginsberg. 2005. King of the beasts? Evidence for guild redundancy among large mammalian carnivores. Pages 154-176 in J. C. Ray, K. H. Redford, R. S. Steneck, and J. Berger, editors. Large carnivores and the conservation of biodiversity. Island Press, Washintgon, D.C.

Woods, J. G. 1991. Ecology of a partially migratory elk population. University of British Columbia. Ph.D. Dissertation.

Wooldridge, J. M. 2001. Econometric analysis of cross section and panel data. MIT Press, Massachusetts.

Wydeven, A. P., R. N. Schultz, and R. P. Thiel. 1995. Gray wolf *(Canis lupus)* population monitoring in Wisconsin 1979-1991. Pages 147-156 in L. N. Carbyn, S. H. Fritts, and D. P. Seip, editors. Ecology and conservation of wolves in a changing world. Canadian Circumpolar Institute, Occasional Publication No. 35, Edmonton, Alberta, Canada.

Yankelovich, D. 1991. Coming to public judgement: making democracy work in a complex world. Syracuse University Press, Syracuse, New York.

Zalozny, D. V. 1980. Some peculiarities of wolf ecology in Gurievskoi oblasti. Pages 77-89 in D. I. Bibikov, editor. Behaviour of the wolf. AN USSR, Moskva. (English translation provided by D. Bibikov)

Zaniewski, A. E., A. Lehmann, and J. M. Overton. 2002. Predicting species distribution using presence-only data: a case study of native New Zealand ferns. Ecological Modelling **157**:261-280.

Zar, J. H. 1984. Biostatistical analysis. 2nd edition. Prentice Hall, Englewood Cliffs, New Jersey.

Zimmermann, B., P. Wabakken, and M. Dötterer. 2001. Human-carnivore interactions in Norway: how does the re-appearance of large carnivores affect people's attitude and fear? Forest Snow and Landscape Research **76**:137-153.

Zimmermann, B., P. Wabakken, H. Sand, H-C. Pedersen, and O. Liberg. 2007. Wolf movement patterns – a key to estimation of kill rate? Journal of Wildlife Management **71**:1177–1182.

Zub, K., J. Theuerkauf, W. Jędrzejewski, B. Jędrzejewska, K. Schmidt, R. Kowalczyk. 2003. Wolf pack territory marking in the Białowieża Primeval Forest (Poland). Behaviour **140**:635-648.

Colour Photos

In this photo from Wyoming, U.S.A., some wolves start consuming a big male elk, which can feed a whole pack and provide energy for a week or so. In this volume, Jędrzejewski et al., as well as Hebblewhite and Smith, explain wolf feeding habits and impact on prey populations in Europe and North America and conclude that wolves really prefer elk (or red deer in Europe) and can influence densities of this and other ungulate prey species. ©Olson

355

Even pups coming from the northern-most regions of wolf's distribution range are born brownish- grey. Probably, this is the best coloration for camouflage in the immediate surroundings of dens, which are generally on sandy soil. Pups like these from the Northwest Territories of Canada will very often acquire white or pale coloration when adults. As described by Cluff at al. (this volume), wolf pelts are sometimes taken by hunters and sold on international markets. ©Frame

As they grow, pups like these in Yellowstone explore the environment together. To have five pups born and surviving until the autumn is absolutely normal for a pack. This allows for substantial population growth rates and sudden increases, like those documented from just a few recolonizing wolves in Scandinavia (Liberg et al., this volume). ©Weselmann

This is a very rare photo of one of the five or so wolves that have recently recolonized Switzerland. These wolves came from Italy, sometimes through France. It is possible that Italy's historic lack of a centralized government, and consequent lack of coordinated wildlife management, has contributed to wolves surviving there for centuries, whereas in more organized European countries wolves were extirpated as pests. Currently, wolves are protected in Europe (see chapters by Jędrzejewski et al. and Liberg et al., this volume). ©Dettling

Recent analyses suggest multiple wolf ecotypes exist in the Arctic, each corresponding to a distinct habitat type and varying in migratory behaviour. In this volume, Wayne explains the genetic evidence that wolves that prey on and follow migratory caribou in the Arctic, like the one in this photo from northern Canada, might be genetically distinct from those which hunt resident prey, as is the case for most temperate regions in North America or Europe (opposite page). ©Cluff

Ironically, findings about wolves seem to be revisited in five-year cycles. Seminal ecological hypotheses about the wolves (Lower Panel) and moose ecosystem of Isle Royale have been generated, with broader implications for predator-prey dynamics, and later rejected by continuing to observe the same system (see Vucetich et al., this volume). Note how wolf coloration is camouflaged in the forested environments of the island (Lower Panel (©Vucetich)) and of Yellowstone National Park (Upper Panel (©Olson)).

THE WORLD OF WOLVES

Using genetic analysis of grey wolf populations from North America and Europe, researchers traced the source of the dominant gene responsible for dark coat colour in wolves to domesticated dogs and concluded the trait was passed to the grey wolf population, as well as to coyotes, by mating between the closely related wild and domestic canid species. Other aspects and some paradoxes of wolf domestication and of dog evolution are detailed in this volume by Coppinger et al. ©Dettling

In this photo from Jasper National Park, Canada, three wolves belonging to the same pack exemplify much of the colour variation of wolf furs, which range from white to grey and black. In these environments, the colours of grasses, bushes, and trees during the summer and autumn seasons seem to blend better with grey-coloured wolves. Thus, grey wolves can approach prey undetected better than wolves of other colours, and these individuals might therefore disproportionately contribute to the pack's hunting success. ©Olson

This photo taken from Yellowstone National Park, U.S.A., demonstrates how during the winter season both white and grey wolves may be well camouflaged, as the environment is predominantly composed of white snow and grey, dormant vegetation (compare to photo in opposite page). It is still unknown why black wolves are not selected against by evolutionary forces, as they might not be camouflaged in the environment as shown in both this photo and the photo in the opposite page. ©Weselmann

All four photos in these two pages are of interactions and communication among individual wolves and other pack members. In the National Parks of Banff, Canada (Upper Panel (©Dettling)) and Yellowstone, U.S.A. (Lower Panel (©Weselmann)) field observations confirmed that wolves frequently seek contact. A wolf may expose its neck to another wolf's muzzle, a sign of extreme confidence and likely of social dominance (right of Upper Panel). Interactions can also get aggressive – although very rarely are these deadly (Lower Panel) – and may also serve to establish hierarchies in the pack.

The World of Wolves

A number of studies correlated pack sizes to sizes of wolf prey present in different areas, as bigger prey would provide enough food for larger packs. However, packs are typically composed of fewer than six individuals also in areas like Isle Royale, U.S.A. (photos) where wolf specialize on moose, a very large prey item. In these photos, some wolves communicate with another pack member by howling to each other, a means of communication particularly useful at great distance and where vegetation precludes visual contact. ©Vucetich

One of the most exciting and also fortuitous experiences for a field biologist is that of observing (typically from a distance, with spotting scope) a real wolf hunt, like the one documented in these photos from Yellowstone National Park, U.S.A. Anecdotally, one of the editors of this book was once bumped away from a spotting scope by another researcher, also a book co-author, just out of excitement for a wolf hunt. Wolves may surprise prey and suddenly 'show up' in the middle of an elk herd (note wolves on top of hill; Upper Panel). Elk might also detect wolf presence and flee together; a real chase then takes place (Lower Panel). ©Dettling

THE WORLD OF WOLVES

Wolves may stalk their prey and attempt to remain undetected until they are very close and it is too late for a prey individual to flee and escape. However, more often wolves chase their prey, and all that counts under these circumstances is speed and endurance, as in this photo of a single wolf chasing an elk in Yellowstone National Park, U.S.A. (note the wolf is panting). ©Weselmann

A wolf from Yellowstone National Park starts consuming an elk by eating its insides, a readily available source of protein and fat. Better eat fast, before something unexpected happens, like a bear who wants your prey! In this volume, a number of chapters describe wolf's dependence for food upon different ungulate prey species in a number of areas in Europe (Liberg et al., Jędrzejewski et al.) and in North America (Hebblewhite and Smith, Vucetich et al., Cluff et al.). Muhly et al. also explain how wolves could target domestic ungulates, for example cattle and sheep. ©Weselmann

THE WORLD OF WOLVES

A prey item does not provide food only for a wolf (like in the opposite page), but also for other wolves of the pack and for some scavengers, like the magpies in this photo, also from Yellowstone. Also note how the colour of one wolf perfectly blends with vegetation and the colour of the other wolf resembles that of the snow in the background. ©Weselmann

After a prey has been killed with much difficulty and effort by one (photo) or by more wolves, the carcass may be consumed on the spot, an activity that may require hours of work. Wolf prey species are massive mammals with thick skin that must be cut open to access the softer parts. ©Weselmann

Sometimes wolves choose to consume some parts of their prey elsewhere. They might bring flesh (photos) to other pack members, for example to pups who may be waiting at rendezvous sites used during the summer. Alternatively, they might bring some parts to other spots to be eaten or buried under the soil and frozen by the winter temperatures, thus serving as food-caches. Regardless, scavengers such as ravens are always around to profit from the kill. ©Weselmann

Most chases end with prey escaping and surviving. Water is a good escape route, because although wolves are good swimmers, it is not easy to actually chase and kill in deep water. The elk in the photo survived. ©Weselmann

Wolf prey may not reach deep water soon enough to swim and escape. In shallow water, wolves might prevail. Then, the typical sequence of consumption takes place (as explained in the previous pages), with a number of pack members and some scavengers eating as well. (Upper Panel ©Weselmann) (Lower Panel ©Dettling)

Wolves often kill a prey item only to have the carcass then taken by a stronger competitor, like the black bear in this photo from Yellowstone National Park. Despite their attempts, wolves may not get back to the carcass until much of it has been consumed. As a result, in areas where bears are present wolves should kill more prey, resulting in stronger influences on prey numbers, like those described and compared by Hebblewhite and Smith in this volume. ©Smith

Bears, whether grizzly bears (like the one in this photo from Yellowstone) or black bears, are tremendous opponents for even an entire pack of wolves when both species meet at a kill, like the partially visible bison carcass in the photo. Bears can consume a significant amount of the carcass and prevent wolves from accessing food, while the ravens merely have to wait. Five different scavengers visit virtually every wolf kill: coyotes, ravens, magpies, and golden and bald eagles (see Hebblewhite and Smith, this volume). ©Weselmann

The photos on this and the following page were taken in Banff National Park, Canada. Field biologists and the photographer both say that this bear had two strange behavioural characteristics. First of all, he had learned to stay close to these wolves, perhaps to profit from the pack's kills. Second, he very often kept sitting (see explanation, opposite page). ©Dettling

Frequently, there were interactions and confrontations between the grizzly bear and the wolves. In general, bears have very powerful front legs and sharp claws. Wolves may be quicker and capable of avoiding bear charges. However, every now and then the wolves could reach the bear from the back and bite him there, which explains why the bear often kept sitting. This grizzly bear was hit by a train and died last year; as far as we know, this wolf pack is still alive and its behaviour is documented also by Paquet et al. in this volume. ©Dettling

Biologists and ecologists need to gather information on wolf behaviour and for this reason may capture wolves to deploy radio- or satellite-collars, which allow monitoring of movements. In this photo, Doug Smith (a co-author of this book) approaches a wolf with a helicopter. Wolves may be captured by anesthetizing dart or by casting nets to immobilize them. It is very difficult to get close to wolves in these operations, as they run and veer to elude the researchers' efforts. Often, when intimidated (as is the case with a helicopter over their head), wolves will bark, much like dogs. ©Smith

The World of Wolves

These wolves were captured with nets (red piles in the back, Upper Panel) that were cast from a helicopter. They were then anaesthetized and fitted with satellite collars. Collars transmitting locations to satellites are ideal for use in remote areas such as the Canadian tundra, where roads are not present, ruling out monitoring wolves from the ground with radio-equipment. Wolf anaesthetization allows for weighing them (Lowe Panel) and conducting measurement of other important health parameters. ©Cluff

Wolves were reintroduced by people into Yellowstone National Park, U.S.A., and little by little learned to prey on bison too, a species that they were not exposed to in the Canadian regions of origin. As explained by Hebblewhite and Smith in this volume, Yellowstone wolves very rarely prey on bison, as there are more accessible prey species available there. Regardless, wolves often get close to bison and 'test' their reaction – nervous individuals that run away are chased more frequently than those that stand their ground. ©Weselmann

It is critical for wolves to move around their home ranges, meet the prey species available (their potential food source, like bison in Yellowstone National Park, U.S.A.) and sometimes try to chase them down. During their wanderings, wolves may get close to roads, more due to curiosity about prey than with any intention to encounter people. ©Dettling

Wolves may use roads because these are placed in proximity to areas with good grass and herbivore abundance (wolf food). In addition, roads are free of obstacles like thick vegetation and provide good opportunity for fast movement between areas of wolf home ranges. Paquet et al. (this volume) explain how wolves in areas such as Banff National Park, Canada (photo) may use roads to travel faster and therefore meet more prey, and how these effects are more pronounced during winter when roads are ploughed and the surroundings have deep snow. ©Dettling

For all the good reasons explained in the opposite page, wolves may use roads, which are also frequented by people for reasons of transportation. Often, people are moving in cars and distracted; therefore, wolves are not detected. In areas such as Yellowstone National Park, U.S.A. (photos) eco-tourists seek wolf encounters, and these are more frequent on roads than in other environments. Wolf reintroduction to Yellowstone and the subsequent influx of wolf fanatics has meant a substantial increase every year in tourism-related revenue. ©Dettling

Some human-wolf encounters are deadly for wolves. In Canada, wolf hunting and trapping are both allowed, and hunters may consider this a positive experience or an opportunity to generate income, which can also be significant if a number of pelts are sold on International markets (see Cluff et al., this volume). In addition, ranchers and their delegates (often trappers) can kill wolves that are considered a threat to their livestock year-round (see Muhly et al., this volume). Finally, some provincial and territorial governments may kill wolves to diminish the predators' pressure on prey populations. ©Paquet

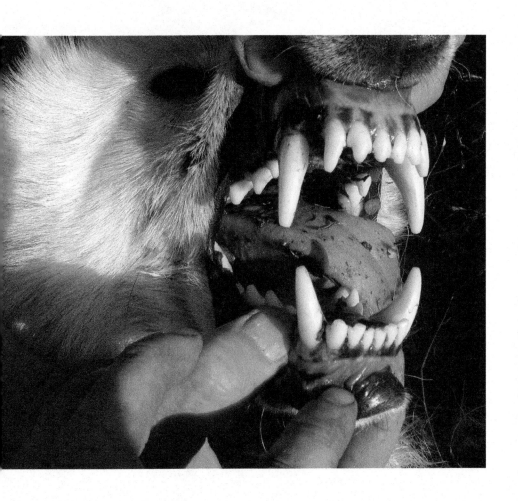

A teeth inspection exemplifies a number of wolf characteristics that scare people. Yes, wolves may be very versatile carnivores, also capable of feeding on carrion or on leftovers provided by error by humans, for example at garbage dumps. Yes, this volume may provide plenty of accounts of wolf attacks on wild and domestic ungulates, but very little or no mention of wolf attacks on people of the Little-Red- Riding-Hood variety. However, wolf dentition is that of a powerful predator capable of killing big mammalian prey, as exemplified by the canine, which can reach critical arteries and veins. ©Cluff

Wolves may dislike ravens because they can steal important parts of a wolf kill. However, this wolf from Yellowstone National Park, U.S.A., spent a significant amount of time and effort chasing ravens away, more than any energy cost and benefit analysis might warrant. This volume only focuses on rational and logical explanations of the key roles played by wolves in ecology and for wildlife management planning. This photo perhaps highlights that wolves and humans may not always be rational, while books such as this are always partial to rational behaviours. ©Weselmann

INDEX

hybridization with coyotes, 1
largely eliminated from western states, 33
great gray owl, 91
Great Lakes Region, 31–32, 215
pack sizes, 217
ungulate species, 219
Great Slave Lake, 249–50, 253
green-world hypothesis, 70–71
grizzly bears, 77, 91, 267
Banff National Park (BNP), 76, 78
Yellowstone National Park (YNP), 92, 95,
99–100, 106–7, 112

H

Hansen, A., 104
hare, 227
Hebblewhite, Mark, xxvii, 4, 6
Hedmark county, 196
Hedmark University College, 181
herbivore densities, 71
affected by wolf predation and by anti-
predator behaviour, 5
herbivores, 5, 71. See also ungulates
effect on plant densities and other animal
species, 6
heterozygosity, 23, 48, 222
high Arctic wolves, 29
high genetic polymorphism, 222
historical demography, 38
historical diversity, 32–33
historical perspective, 20, 24
through low copy or degraded DNA, 19
historical reconstructions, 23–24
hogs, 267
Holmes, Oliver Wendell, 144
horses, 211
human attitude toward wolves. See also wolf-
human conflicts
rural vs. urban, 175, 177–78, 200
human-caused alterations of snow conditions.
See anthropogenically modified
snow conditions
human-caused decline in wild ungulates
caused wolves to kill domestic animals,
226–27, 231
human density, 7, 91
human ecological impact, 177. See also long-
term exploitation by humans
evolutionary consequences, 173, 226
human hunting. See wolves killed by humans

human infrastructure, 26, 91, 110. See also
anthropogenic barriers to dispersal;
roads
increase in wolf predation efficiency, 7, 90
wolf density and, 263
human modified trails, 163, 170. See also
anthropogenically modified snow
conditions; roads
alters predator-prey dynamics, 157, 170,
175
benefits to wolves, 169–70
chase lengths, 169
rates of wolf kills, 167
use of cover and, 166–67
use of prey, 167
wolves traverse otherwise inaccessible
areas, 166, 169–72
human relationship with nature, 144
hunters, 7, 177, 202, 243
Aboriginal (See Aboriginal hunters)
hunting rights (Scandinavia), 177
hunting sustainability
northern Canada (Northwest Territories
and Nunavut), 254–57
husbandry model, 272, 275–76
predicting spatial occurrence of livestock
depredation, 275
valid in predicting attacks, 280
husbandry practices, 10, 265, 273
and depredation probability, 264
free range grazing of livestock, 264, 267
livestock depredation and, 261–62, 264,
281
livestock depredation probability models,
270–71
supervision of livestock, 264, 266, 271,
273, 276, 283
hybrid assignment, 32, 42
hybridization, 16–17, 58, 61, 65
agricultural sense, 62–63
with coyotes, 3, 31–32, 63
gray wolves and other canids of Great
Lakes Region, 31
human influence, 3
long genetic legacy, 32
natural, 45
novel adaptation to new habitat, 65
prevention to preserve species, 31, 62–63
seen as threat to wolf population, 63, 67
source of genetic variation, 64
sub-specific, 64
hybridization between wolves and dogs, 17,
31, 63–64, 221
hybridization in nature, 45, 62–66

I

Ice Age isolation, 26, 33
illegal killing. *See* poaching
immigrants, identifying, 26, 31. *See also* dispersal
inbreeding, 22, 126
inbreeding avoidance behaviour, 23
inbreeding depression, 8, 22–23, 184–86, 200–201
indirect competition, 75
indirect effects of wolves, 70, 73, 75, 87–91, 100–107, 113
    Brucellosis and other diseases, 114
    on songbirds, 88
    on willow and aspen growth, 79, 87, 107
indirect trophic cascade effects, 84–88, 97–98, 100–107, 116
inductive reasoning in ecological science, 134, 152
inheritance, conditions of, 58
Interagency Grizzly Bear Study Team, 106
interference competition, 73–74, 86, 99
    coyotes and wolves, 98
    wolves and grizzly bears, 99
interspecific competition, 71, 98–100
    wolves and cougars, 85–86, 111
    wolves and other carnivores, 4, 112
intra-guild competition, 107, 111
Isle Royale, 22, 70, 123–54
    extreme events, 145
    forest habitat, 124
    moose (*See* Isle Royale moose)
    natural history, 124–27
Isle Royale moose, 5, 124, 126
    diet, 127
    malnutrition, 127
Isle Royale wolf kill rate
    poorly predicted by moose abundance, 150
Isle Royale wolf-moose system, 5, 152
    moose collapse (1990s), 142, 145
    numerical analysis, 129–32
    qualitative analysis and discussion, 132–33
    research history, 127–28
Isle Royale wolves
    diet, 127
    genetically isolated and inbred, 126
    wolf decline (1980s), 132, 145
Italian wolf population, 25
    genetically distinct, 25–26
    hybridization with dogs, 31, 63
    Ice Age isolation, 64
    population bottleneck, 25
    recent loss of habitat, 26

J

Jasper National Park, 89–90, 160, 162, 165
Jędrzejewski, Włodzimierz, xxvii, 8, 221
Journal of Wildlife Management, 265

K

karyoptic change, 62
keystone species, 10–11, 69, 102, 117
kinship, 35
    effects on inbreeding depression, 23
    influence on behaviour and dispersal, 22
Kootenay National Park, 161–62
Kruskal-Wallis test, 165, 272

L

land use practices in Sweden and Norway, 195. *See also* husbandry practices
landscape effect on wolf predation, 98
landscape genetic approaches, 15, 29
landscape obstacles to individual dispersal, 20
landscape use by wolves, 169
large carnivores
    protective legislation for, 178 (*See also* wolf conservation; wolf protection)
Latvia, 208–10
    legal harvest of wolves, 214
    wolf depredation on domestic animals, 230
    wolf population, 211, 214
lethal control of wolves, 184, 201, 261–62, 266, 269, 283
Liberg, Olof, xxviii, 7–8, 16, 22–23
lichens, 251
Lithuania, 208–10
    legal harvest of wolves, 214
    wolf depredation on domestic animals, 230
    wolf population, 211
litter size, 185–86, 219
livestock damage compensation programs, 8, 196, 267, 285
    compensation for dog owners, 198
    livestock and reindeer depredation, 196
    Poland, 230
    Sweden, 196
livestock depredation, 8, 189, 265–66, 273
    biophysical factors, 262–64
    husbandry practices and, 262–64
    predicting spatial attacks, 261–62
livestock depredation probability map, 276
livestock depredation probability models, 270

livestock depredation risk
  on flat terrain, 281
  higher closer to forest cover, 283
  higher closer to quarter sections with
    buildings, 281
  lower closer to roads, 273, 281
  positive correlation with elk density, 281
livestock husbandry practices. *See* husbandry
  practices
lone wolves, 216
long-and short-tailed and least weasel, 91
long-term exploitation by humans, 3. *See also*
    human ecological impact
  evolutionary adaptation from, 220
  important factor in wolf life-history, 219
low copy or degraded DNA samples, 19
  non-invasive population monitoring, 16
lynx, 76, 91, 196–97, 228

M

Mackenzie River, 29
Madison-Firehole herd, 92, 96
magpies, 90–91, 105
managing wolves. *See* wolf management
Mann-Whitney U test, 272
marten, 91
masked shrew, 91
maternal-foetal interactions, 18
Mexican gray wolf, 33
migrants, 23, 26–27, 32. *See also* dispersal
migratory wolves (following caribou), 239,
    250–54, 256
mink, 91
molecular biology, 44
Montana, 93
moose, 5, 70, 76, 78–79, 113, 161–62, 170,
    210, 228, 267
  Banff National Park (BNP), 77
  declines, 88
  Isle Royale, 124, 126–27 (*See also* Isle
    Royale wolf-moose system)
  traffic mortality, 193
  willow growth and, 101
  Yellowstone National Park (YNP), 92,
    101
moose (Scandinavia), 177, 189–93
  wolf predation, 127, 134, 192–93
moose and elk
  apparent competition, 88–89
moose diet, 128, 135
moose genetics, 128

moose ticks, 128, 142, 145, 150
mouflon, 210
mountain goat, 76–77, 92, 162
mountain hare, 189, 210
mountain sheep, 162, 170
mule deer, 76–77, 85, 92, 161–62, 267
multi-use areas (livestock, hunting, and
    recreation), 7–8, 200
museum collections
  DNA repository, 32
  genetic analysis, 32
  historical perspective from, 19–20
Musiani, Marco, xxv
mutation, 58
mutualism, 74

N

National Parks Service goal, 119
National Topographic Survey base maps, 162
natural hybridization, 45, 62–65
natural selection, 41, 64
natural trails, 163, 166–67
nature's intrinsic value, 144
neutral mutation heterozygosity, 49
neutral mutation theory, 55, 63
new genetic markers, 17–18, 38
non-invasive monitoring, 16, 19, 35, 38, 180
North American wolf, 3, 31. *See also*
    Algonquin or New World wolf
  maybe separate species with formerly large
    geographic range, 33
  not a sexually isolated population, 55
northern Yellowstone herd, 92, 96–97
Northwest Territories, 29, 235, 237
  bounty on wolves, 241
  historical wolf management, 241–42
  hunting season, 240
  migratory caribou territories (*See* caribou
    migration routes and winter
    ranges)
  monitoring the wolf hunt, 242–43
  NWT Wildlife Act, 238, 240
  regulations governing wolf hunts, 240
  trappers from Scandinavia and southern
    Canada, 241
  tundra-taiga ecosystem, 239
  use of snowmobiles, 239–40
  wolf fur, 240–43
  wolf poisoning campaigns, 241
  wolf populations, 254–55
  wolves' travel distances, 247

Norway, 7, 177
  anti-poaching activities, 200
  compensation for dog owners, 198
  compensation for livestock and reindeer
      depredation, 196–97
  measures aimed at reducing conflict, 196
  monitoring efforts, 181
  moose harvest, 177
  rural communities, 178
  sheep grazing on open range, 177, 195–96
  wolf policy influenced by rural interests,
      178
  wolf zoning policy in, 178, 200
Norwegian Institute for Natural Research,
    181
Norwegian Nature Inspectorate, 181
Nunavut, 239, 242, 254, 257

O

Olson, David C., xxx
On Growth and Form (Thomson), 150
overdominance, 18

P

pack sizes, 185, 216–17, 219
  adoption of non-related adult males, 216
  human hunting and, 216, 221
Paquet, Paul C., xxvi, 7
Parks Canada mandate, 119
partial Mantel's tests, 29
pedigree construction, 22, 35
Peter Lougheed Provincial Park, 160, 162,
    165
Pialowieza Primeval Forest, 221
pine marten, 90
pine nuts, 106–7
ploughed roads. *See* human modified trails
poaching, 184–87, 200–201, 208, 216
Poland, 159, 208–10
  compensation for animals killed by
      wolves, 230, 232
  legal harvest of wolves, 214
  pack size, 216–17
  potential for development of wolf range,
      215
  wolf densities, 224
  wolf population, 29, 211, 214
  wolf prey, 228
  wolf protection, 211, 232
  wolf scavenging on ungulate carcasses,
      227

polymorphism, 18
population connectivity, 16, 20–21
population genetics
  human influences on, 3
  recent advances, 15–38
population genetics studies, 20, 208, 220
population modelling, 180
population pedigree, 22, 35
population structure, 25–27
Precautionary Principle, 143–44
predation on livestock. *See* depredation on
      livestock and dogs
predation refugia, 90, 110
predator control campaigns, 208. *See also* wolf
      control; wolves killed by humans
predator exclusion
  dramatic effects, 69
predator-prey-dependent model, 136
predicting future ecological phenomena, 130,
      135, 139–40, 142–44, 150, 152
predictive wolf attack model based on
      husbandry, 283–84
prey densities, 2. *See also* names of prey
      animals
prey-dependent model, 136–37
prey skills (learned as adolescents), 29
prey species as habitat components, 30
pronghorn antelope, 92, 95
protective legislation for large carnivores, 178.
      See also wolf protection
Pukaskwka National Park, 161
pup survival, 208, 211, 219

Q

Qamanirjuraq caribou herd, 238, 251, 253

R

'rabbit debate,' 44
rabid wolves, 231–32
raccoon dog, 227
raven, 91, 105, 153
red deer, 189, 210, 227
  human harvest, 228
  preferred prey of wolves, 217, 228
red fox, 76, 227
red wolf recovery program, 42
red wolves, 55, 63
  considered a species, 41–42, 56–57, 59, 63
  endangered species list, 3
  hybridization with coyotes, 3, 31–32, 35,
      63–64

hybrids of gray wolves and/or coyotes, 41, 63
project designed to keep pure, 32, 63–64
reindeer, 177, 189, 195–98
reindeer summer grazing range, 178
    barrier to interchange between populations, 184
Rennie Lake area, 237–38, 247, 250
    Beverly caribou herd, 251, 253
    boreal forest-tundra transition, 238, 253
    poisoning campaign, 241
    sink area for wolves, 9
    wolf kill statistics, 244–46
Rennie Lake area (1997/98)
    unusual congregation of caribou, 252–55
    unusual number of wolves, 253–55
Rennie Lake wolf hunt, 235–39, 257
    media coverage, 235–36, 256
    monitoring needs, 258
    public reaction and perceptions, 238–39
    sustainability, 239, 255–57
    variability in annual wolf kill, 236, 257
reproductive skew, 22
resource management
    ethical considerations, 144
    fear-based, 144
    Precautionary Principle, 143–44
    wonder and respect based, 144
Resource Selection Functions (RSFs) approach, 265–66, 270, 272
Riding Mountain National Park, 160–61
riparian songbirds, 5, 88, 95, 104, 108, 110
risk analysis, 143
road kill, 208
roads, 6, 191, 210, 266, 270, 273, 281
Rocky Mountain Parks, 167. *See also* names of individual parks
    movements of wolves, 166
    rates of kill on modified *vs.* natural trails, 167, 169
    snow conditions, 162
    ungulate prey, 162
    wolf trails, 165
Rocky Mountains, 75, 92, 167, 267
roe deer, 189, 210, 227–28
"Rovbasen" (data base), 181
"Rovdjursforum" (data base), 181
rural communities, 178
    attitudes toward wolves, 175, 177–78, 200
rural ranching communities. *See also* Alberta ranchlands study
    managing for persistence of wolves, 6

S

Sámi people
    compensation for verified presence of wolves, 198
    reindeer grazing, 177
Scandinavia
    human population density, 177, 191
    moose population, 192–94, 201
    SKASNDULV project, 179–82, 202–3
Scandinavian wolf management
    different political and economic situations, 178–79
Scandinavian Wolf Research Project. *See* SKANDULV project
Scandinavian wolves, 16, 175–204
    breeding history and pedigree, 181–83
    conflicts with humans, 177, 185, 200
    depredation on domestic stock and dogs, 195–200
    dispersal, 187
    extended absence, 176
    favourable resource environment, 185
    founders from Finnish/Russian population, 181–83
    handling time, 191
    hunting success, 194
    inbreeding depression, 184
    incomplete consumption of carcasses, 191
    kill rates, 190–92
    kinship relations, 181
    legal killing, 184, 186
    multi-use landscape, 200
    need for further immigration, 184, 201
    poaching, 184
    population growth, 186
    prey, 177, 189
    reproduction and pack sizes, 185
    resting far from killed prey, 191
    small and isolated population, 181
    survival, 185–86, 200
scat. *See* fecal DNA
scavenging, 74–75, 85
    beetles, 107
    by black bears, 106
    causing sociality in wolves, 105, 153
    by grizzly bears, 106
    human hunting and, 105
    on wolf kills, 90–91, 105–7
    by wolves, 227
scientific research
    important to coexistence, 175
    integrating with wolf management, 200–204

CPSIA information can be obtained
at www.ICGtesting.com
Printed in the USA
BVOW07s1603081117
499763BV00012BA/610/P